THE FIN DE SIÈCLE

A READER IN CULTURAL HISTORY, *c.*1880–1900

EDITED BY

Sally Ledger and Roger Luckhurst

OXFORD

UNIVERSITY PRESS

OXFORD

UNIVERSITY PRESS

Great Clarendon Street, Oxford OX2 6DP

Oxford University Press is a department of the University of Oxford.
It furthers the University's objective of excellence in research, scholarship,
and education by publishing worldwide in

Oxford New York

Athens Auckland Bangkok Bogotá Buenos Aires Calcutta
Cape Town Chennai Dar es Salaam Delhi Florence Hong Kong Istanbul
Karachi Kuala Lumpur Madrid Melbourne Mexico City Mumbai
Nairobi Paris São Paulo Shanghai Singapore Taipei Tokyo Toronto Warsaw

and associated companies in Berlin Ibadan

Oxford is a registered trade mark of Oxford University Press
in the UK and certain other countries

Published in the United States
by Oxford University Press Inc., New York

British Library Cataloguing in Publication Data

Data available

Library of Congress Cataloging in Publication Data

Data available

ISBN 0–19–874278–9
ISBN 0–19–874279–7 (Pbk.)

1 3 5 7 9 10 8 6 4 2

Typeset by Best-set Typesetter Ltd., Hong Kong
Printed in Great Britain
on acid-free paper by
T. J. International Ltd,
Padstow, Cornwall

Acknowledgements

We would like to thank Jason Freeman, formerly editor at Oxford University Press, for encouraging us to submit this proposal, and Sophie Goldsworthy and Matthew Hollis for seeing the project through to completion with such good grace. Thanks also to Janet Moth for the excellent copyediting work. This project could not have been completed without funding from research grants awarded by the Research Steering Committee of the School of English and Humanities, Birkbeck College, and from a generous award from the Faculty of Arts research fund at Birkbeck in the final stages of the book. Professor David Wells was particularly supportive of our research when Dean, and we record our appreciation here. The last research grant allowed us to employ the lightning fingers of Julie Crofts, whose speedy transcriptions and good humour helped considerably.

We thank the librarians at Birkbeck College, University of London Library, the British Library at St Pancras and Colindale, the Wellcome Institute, and the University of Bristol for their assistance. For discussions about contents of specific chapters, and assistance with tracing some elusive references, we would like to thank the following for their advice: Laurel Brake, Carolyn Burdett, Peter Mudford, Elaine Showalter, Michael Slater, Herbert Tucker, Lynnette Turner, Chris Willis (who also did some transcription for us), Mark Willis, and the anonymous readers at Oxford University Press. Thanks are also due to Joseph Bristow, Regenia Gagnier, Bill Greenslade, Scott McCracken, Josephine McDonagh, and John Stokes, whose friendship and expertise have been a continuing source of inspiration.

In the few instances where material is still in copyright, every effort has been made to secure permissions for reproduction. If we have failed in any case to trace a copyright holder, we apologize for any apparent negligence. We thank the Society of Authors for their assistance in the tracing of copyright holders. We would also like to thank the following: John Johnson (Authors' Agent) Ltd, on behalf of R. B. Cunninghame Graham's Estate, for permission to quote from 'Bloody Niggers'; A. P. Watt Ltd, on behalf of the Literary Executors of the Estate of H. G. Wells, for permission to quote from 'Zoological Retrogression'; The Society of Authors, on behalf of the Bernard Shaw Estate, for permission to quote from 'The Economic Basis of Socialism' and 'The Sanity of Art'; Sigmund Freud Copyrights, The Institute of Psycho-Analysis and The Hogarth Press, for permission to quote from *The Standard Edition of the Complete Psychological Works of Sigmund Freud*, translated and edited by James Strachey; Phyllis Grosskurth, for permission to quote from *The Memoirs of John Addington Symonds* (published by Hutchinson); Brian Read, for permission to quote from 'At the Alhambra', 'The Decadent Movement in Literature' and 'Henrik Ibsen', by Arthur Symons; Betty Ballantine (Rufus Publications), for permission to quote from 'Anarchism', by Emma Goldman; and Greenwood Publishing Group, Inc., Westport, Conn., for permission to quote from *The Voice of Terror: A Biography of Johann Most*, by Frederic Trautmann.

Contents

Introduction

READING THE 'FIN DE SIÈCLE'

Sally Ledger and Roger Luckhurst

The Victorian fin de siècle was an epoch of endings and beginnings. The collision between the old and the new that characterized the turn of the century marks it as an excitingly volatile and transitional period; a time when British cultural politics were caught between two ages, the Victorian and the Modern; a time fraught with anxiety and with an exhilarating sense of possibility. At the very moment that Max Nordau famously lamented the encroaching 'Dusk of nations, in which all suns and all stars are gradually waning, and mankind with all its institutions and creations is persisting in the midst of a dying world',[1] Britain's cultural and political landscape was being lit up by a constellation of new formations: the new woman, the new imperialism, the new realism, the new drama, and the new journalism, all arriving alongside 'new' human sciences like psychology, psychical research, sexology, and eugenics. This was an era of extraordinary technological advance (duplex telegraphy, the gramophone, the telephone, wireless telegraphy, X-rays, cinematography), of educational and democratic reform, of transformations in political representation, and yet it was also an age of very real decline, in which Britain's primacy as global economic power was rivalled by Germany and America.[2] This contradiction, the way in which assertions of the limitless generative power of the British nation were haunted by fantasies of decay and degeneration, is a highly specific moment, we might say, of experiencing the *ambivalence of modernity*.[3]

Perhaps this is why we remain fascinated by the fin de siècle. The allure of the 1890s might have less to do with its alleged 'naughtiness', or with seeking parallels to our own late twentieth-century millennial fantasies, than with the sense that the period has provided both enduring cultural icons of ambivalence, as well

---

[1] Max Nordau, *Degeneration* [1892] (Lincoln: University of Nebraska Press, 1993), 1.

[2] 'Britain, we may say, was becoming a parasitic rather than competitive world economy, living off the remains of world monopoly, the undeveloped world, her past accumulations of wealth, and the advance of her rivals': Eric Hobsbawm, *Industry and Empire* (Harmondsworth: Penguin, 1969), 192.

[3] Zygmunt Bauman, *Modernity and Ambivalence* (Cambridge: Polity Press, 1991).

as a difficult historical legacy to which we are still, in many ways, indebted, and are still working through. Certainly, this might explain the intense interest that has come to be focused on the era by a number of disciplines and disciplinary approaches over the last fifteen years or so. This is one very timely reason for a reader in the fin de siècle: cultural and social historians, urban theorists, historians of science, psychologists, literary critics, post-colonial critics, feminist writers, and gay and lesbian theorists have, in diverse ways, come to regard the late nineteenth century as a crucial moment in the formation or transformation of their object of study. We can provide a portrait of how the Victorian fin de siècle has been reconstructed by traversing some of these disciplinary engagements.

One of the most important developments in the humanities has been a shift to a more broadly conceived 'cultural studies'. One important aim of this disciplinary reframing has been to extend and redefine 'culture' in its broadest sense, and question assertions of immanent value in high art against the more immediate 'gratifications' of popular culture. The fin de siècle has become historically important to both of these aims. A number of critics have observed that conceptions of 'culture'—in both its narrow, Arnoldian meaning and its more general sense—owe much to ethnological and anthropological writings of the late nineteenth century.[4] Equally, the fin de siècle has come to be identified as the moment of emergence, in their modern configuration, of the forms and definitions of 'high' and 'low' culture.[5] The *Daily Mail* begins, but so does the *Times Literary Supplement*; Henry James defines the art of the novel and begins to find uses for obscurity,[6] but this is also the moment at which mass generic forms—detective fiction, the spy novel, science fiction—take on the shapes that remain recognizable today. The hegemonic vehicle of Realism, the three-volume novel, died in 1894; the romance is propagandistically revived and the newly named 'short story' fills the vast acreage of columns in the new magazines. Terms like the 'bestseller' are coined. It is these cheap, mass forms which produce, in a period of amazing intensity, the Time Traveller and the Invisible Man, Sherlock Holmes and Watson, Svengali and his damsel Trilby, Dracula and his many damsels, Jekyll and Hyde. W. T. Stead begins the New Journalism at the *Pall Mall Gazette* in the 1880s; Northcliffe and others finance the rise of the tabloid in the 1890s. New printing techniques and photographic technologies transform print culture; the 'celebrity interview' takes off; the resituation of the royal family from

---

[4] See especially Robert J. C. Young, *Colonial Desire: Hybridity, in Theory, Culture, and Race* (London: Routledge, 1996).

[5] See Patrick Brantlinger, *Rule of Darkness: British Literature and Imperialism, 1830–1914* (Ithaca, NY: Cornell University Press, 1988) and *In Crusoe's Footsteps: Cultural Studies in Britain and America* (London: Routledge, 1990).

[6] A reference to Allon White, *The Uses of Obscurity: The Fiction of Early Modernism* (London: Routledge, 1981).

bourgeois seclusion to public figureheads of empire renews popular expressions of patriotic fervour.[7]

The audience for such popular literatures was perhaps the first generation to benefit from the 1870 Education Act. Ambivalence marks 'informed' opinion. What good was literacy if it was only to foster such literatures?[8] Massification became a crucial problem in a number of aspects, perhaps most visibly reflected in the intensification of concern over the problem of the large population of the London poor in the late nineteenth century. This has left a complex legacy. There is a discourse of degenerative urban blight and a set of representations of the poor, in which the 'residuum' are more feared than pitied.[9] James Cantlie wrote in 1885: 'the close confines and foul air of our cities are shortening the life of the individual, and raising up a puny and ill-developed race . . . It is beyond prophecy to guess even what the rising generation will grow into, what this Empire will become after they have got charge of it.'[10] Much of the political language concerning 'immigrant' populations and the aims of 'urban regeneration' derives from this moment. There is the remorseless statistical regulation of the city, mapped by Charles Booth in twenty-four volumes between 1889 and 1903, which replaces the anecdotalism of Henry Mayhew or Dickens, London's East End moving from a mythical 'Darkest England' to object of positive knowledge. Booth's transformative project, in which a conservative businessman setting out to challenge socialist statistics on poverty ends up advocating limited forms of state support for the 'deserving' poor, marks a shift from somewhat *ad hoc* philanthropy to the beginnings of the systematic interventions of a Welfare State. And there is, entangled in the origins of welfarist ideals, in the model housing, in the public parks and baths, an element of wishing for eugenic control over the breeding habits of a new mass population, an artificial intervention into a natural evolution 'gone wrong' in its proliferation of the 'weakest'. It is difficult not to want to read the discourse of this sort of social Darwinism teleologically—as if its trajectory towards Nazism was inevitable. There is a certain cosy hindsight, however, in the recent 'outing' of H. G. Wells as holding eugenic views.[11] The pervasiveness of such racialized thought across the political and cultural spectrum reflects the authority of science and the power of the evolutionary analogy in the late Victorian era.

---

[7] For the best surveys of these changes in high and low cultural forms, see David Trotter, *The English Novel in History 1895–1920* (London: Routledge, 1993), and Peter Keating, *The Haunted Study: A Social History of the English Novel 1875–1914* (London: Fontana, 1991).

[8] This is discussed in Joseph Bristow, *Empire Boys: Adventures in a Man's World* (London: Harper-Collins, 1991).

[9] See Gareth Stedman Jones, *Outcast London* (Harmondsworth: Penguin, 1971).

[10] James Cantlie, *Degeneration Amongst Londoners* (London: Field & Tuer, 1885), 35 and 52.

[11] See the recent biography by Michael Coren, *The Invisible Man: The Life and Liberties of H. G. Wells* (London: Bloomsbury, 1993). Such teleological views are eloquently warned against in Daniel Pick, *Faces of Degeneration: Anatomy of a European Disorder c.1848–1918* (Cambridge: Cambridge University Press, 1989).

The New Science, too, was the impetus for the development of literary natural-ism at the fin de siècle. Simultaneously influenced by the literature of urban exploration and by theories of heredity, literary naturalism—represented in Britain by George Gissing, Arthur Morrison, and George Moore—mimicked the developing technology of photography in its 'objective' scrutiny of city life. The often unsympathetic accounts of working-class city dwellers fuelled existing fears of degeneration.

Famously, it was the difficulty in raising sufficiently healthy recruits amongst the population of London for the Boer War of 1899–1902 that intensified the fan-tasies of racial decline and degeneration. The advancing front of the empire was threatened from the very centre. The fin de siècle again provides remarkably enduring icons and residues—whether from 'heroes' like General Gordon, Cecil Rhodes, and Lord Kitchener, resonating events like the battle of Rorke's Drift or the Relief of Mafeking, institutions like the Boy Scouts, or popular characters like Gunga Din, immortal Ayesha, or the diamonds of King Solomon's mines. Popu-lar culture of the time was fascinated by exotic, imperial terrors—fantasies of reverse invasion by the French or Germans, the stirring of mummies in the British Museum as Egypt and the Sudan were annexed, the evil genius of Fu Manchu and the 'yellow peril' as trade routes in the Far East were contested.[12] This welter of images undoubtedly reflects the paradox of empire in the last quarter of the nine-teenth century: a massive expansion, particularly into Africa following the Berlin Conference of imperial powers in 1885, but an expansion which was motored by anxieties over decay and decline.[13] The model of Gibbon's 'rise and fall' of the Roman empire haunted many articulations in the period. If the 'sun never set' on the British empire, puzzled readers of a fractured two-part story, *Heart of Dark-ness*, could probably have discerned that the opening description of magnificent sunset over the Thames was a jaundiced rebuke to such pretensions. Neverthe-less, the death of Gordon, or defeat at the hands of disciplined Zulus or handfuls of Boers, almost propelled the hardening ideology of empire. Newly 'jingoistic' defences of empire were also responding to the loosening of the consensus over the validity of imperialism, whether from socialist or anarchist voices, or within the ranks of the liberal intelligentsia, which fractured over the prosecution of the Boer War. Apologists for empire could seek justification in the scientific dis-

[12] For invasion fantasies, see I. F. Clarke, *The Tale of the Next Great War: 1871–1914* (Liverpool: Liver-pool University Press, 1995). For Gothic exoticisms, see Stephen Arata, 'The Occidental Tourist: *Drac-ula* and the Anxiety of Reverse Colonisation', *Victorian Studies*, 33/4 (1990), 621–45; David Glover, *Vampires, Mummies and Liberals: Bram Stoker and the Politics of Popular Fiction* (Durham, NC: Duke University Press, 1996); and Kelly Hurley, *The Gothic Body: Sexuality, Materialism and Degeneration at the Fin de Siècle* (Cambridge: Cambridge University Press, 1996).

[13] For histories, see Eric Hobsbawm, *The Age of Empire: 1875–1914* (London: Weidenfeld & Nicolson, 1987), and, for Africa, Ronald Robinson, John Gallagher, and Alice Denny, *Africa and the Victorians: The Official Mind of Imperialism*, 2nd edn. (London: Macmillan, 1981).

courses of racialized Darwinism, which placed the spatial diffusion of different peoples along a single temporal axis, moving from the 'primitive' to the 'civilized'. By the 1890s, however, such 'armchair anthropology' was beginning to be undermined by the complex findings of workers 'in the field'. When Haddon, Rivers, and others set out on the Torres Straits expedition in 1898, a more relativistic, modern anthropology was in the process of developing.[14]

In many ways, Edward Said's book *Orientalism*, first published in 1978, and its important contribution to the subsequent academic founding of 'post-colonial studies' has had a major impact on recovering much of this material.[15] In a largely decolonized world, liberal guilt or simple bad faith did much to suppress aspects of British and European imperial history. Said's emphasis on Orientalism as a 'textual attitude,' however, has meant that populist imperial texts, whether speeches, travel narratives, *Boy's Own* papers or fictions, have been resituated as significant textual constructions of colonial discourse. Said's trenchant insistence that such racial paradigms still operated in the geopolitics of the late twentieth century is an injunction to confront the persistent residues of the past.

The same is true for questions of contemporary identity, whether concerning gender politics, sexual identity, or conceptions of subjectivity itself. The feminist project of 'recovering' gendered occlusions has had notable successes in reconceiving social and literary histories, and as part of the process of tracking the origins of modern feminism the cultural representations of the New Woman in the 1890s have emerged as a vital adjunct to concurrent suffrage campaigns.[16] The icon of the New Woman was double-coded: it could mark an image of sexual freedom and assertions of female independence, promising a bright democratic future; it could also mark an apocalyptic warning of the dangers of sexual degeneracy, the abandonment of motherhood, and consequent risk to the racial future of England. Such political codings are not always easy to distribute, and indeed self-nominated New Women could themselves be advocates of conservative causes. One of the most famous New Woman novelists, Sarah Grand, was an enthusiastic exponent of social purity. Her novels *The Heavenly Twins* (1893) and *The Beth Book* (1897) were outspoken attacks on male sexuality in a way which

[14] For standard history, see George Stocking, *Victorian Anthropology* (London: Free Press, 1987). For shifting conceptions and modes of anthroplogical professionalism see also George Stocking (ed.), *Observers Observed: Essays on Ethnographic Fieldwork* (Madison, Wis.: University of Wisconsin Press, 1983).

[15] Edward Said, *Orientalism: Western Conceptions of the Orient* (Harmondsworth: Penguin, 1985).

[16] See Elaine Showalter, *Sexual Anarchy: Gender and Culture at the Fin de Siècle* (London: Bloomsbury, 1991); Lyn Pykett, *The Improper Feminine: The Women's Sensation Novel and New Women Writing* (London: Routledge, 1992); Sally Ledger, *The New Woman: Fiction and Feminism at the Fin de Siècle* (Manchester: Manchester University Press, 1997); and Ann Ardis, *New Women, New Novels: Feminism and Early Modernism* (Brunswick, NJ: Rutgers University Press, 1990).

abutted onto social purity campaigns to suppress all forms of sexual expression. Such problematic complicities and ambivalences at the beginnings of modern feminist thought have proved productive sites for thinking through the articulation of gender with other significant markers of identity.

The historicization of 'sexuality' as a thoroughly social rather than natural category has resulted in further excavations of the fin de siècle. Feminist social purity campaigns of the time and William Stead's formative attempt at sensationalist investigative journalism in 'The Maiden Tribute of Modern Babylon' in 1885 led to a raising of the age of consent to the current age of 16 in the Criminal Law Amendment Act, and, as a late addition, the criminalizing of 'acts of gross indecency' between men. The martyrdom of Oscar Wilde to the full punishment provided by the Act, two years of hard labour, has always provided the main focus for the Decadent 1890s. The image of Wilde, dressed in a T-shirt emblazoned with the legend 'Queer as Fuck' hints at shifting conceptions of the 'Wilde icon', however.[17] The ambivalent legacy of Wilde to gay men in the present day has been brilliantly investigated in books like Neil Bartlett's *Who Was That Man?*, a biography of Wilde and an autobiography of Bartlett, in which the link between the reversible dates 1891 and 1981 is seen as essential to the possible construction of something like a continuous gay history, a history which Wilde at once severely jeopardizes and yet also makes possible.[18] The industry around Oscar Wilde[19] has not obscured other valuable work on the 'invention' of homosexuality, as Michel Foucault polemically phrased it in *An Introduction to the History of Sexuality*, or analyses of the excited tabulation of perversions by the new science of sexology.[20] We owe terms like 'nymphomania' to the period, but also the sexual meanings of concepts such as 'fetishism' or 'perversion'. Many literary histories have (somewhat contentiously) begun to seek hidden lines between contemporary 'queer' identities, and those of the late Victorian period, learning to read the silences and ambivalences of a Henry James or Robert Louis Stevenson text as markers of emerging modern sexualities.[21]

[17]   See illustrations in Alan Sinfield, *The Wilde Century: Effeminacy, Oscar Wilde and the Queer Moment* (London: Cassell, 1994).

[18]   Neil Bartlett, *Who Was That Man? A Present for Mr Oscar Wilde* (London: Serpent's Tail, 1988).

[19]   See also Jonathan Dollimore, *Sexual Dissidence: From Augustine to Wilde, Freud to Foucault* (Oxford: Oxford University Press, 1991); Ed Cohen, *Talk on the Wilde Side* (London: Routledge, 1993); John Stokes, *Oscar Wilde* (London: Macmillan, 1996); and Sos Eltis, *Revising Wilde* (Oxford: Oxford University Press, 1995).

[20]   See, most influentially, Sander Gilman, *Difference and Pathology: Stereotypes of Sexuality, Race and Madness* (Ithaca, NY: Cornell University Press, 1985).

[21]   For a fairly queer Henry James, see Eve Kosofsky Sedgwick, *Epistemology of the Closet* (Brighton: Harvester, 1991). For a discussion of Jamesian ambivalence, see Kelly Cannon, *Henry James and Masculinity: The Man at the Margins* (London: Macmillan, 1997). For Robert Louis Stevenson, see Wayne Koestenbaum, *Double Talk: The Erotics of Male Literary Collaboration* (London: Routledge, 1989) and Showalter, *Sexual Anarchy*.

We might, finally, identify one last contemporary question which owes much to the fin de siècle. The current dispute over the psychiatric technique of retrieving lost memories—'recovered memory' if you believe it is possible, 'false memory syndrome' if you consider it isn't—has been discussed from the academic conference and technical monograph to the popular book and sensational chat show. The forgetting and recovery of traumatic memories, 'locked up' or 'encrypted' in the psyche, is held to explain a host of contemporary psychological disorders. Whether these memories, centrally concerning familial sexual abuse, are actual or phantasmal has often reverted to the minute examination of the letters and texts of Sigmund Freud in the 1890s. It was Jeffrey Masson's explosive book, *The Assault on Truth: Freud and Child Sexual Abuse*, which alleged that Freud had uncovered massive, systematic abuse in his early female patients, but then turned away from the facts, to found the phantasmal science of psychoanalysis.[22] Freud has become a token in what have been termed, by another critic, *The Memory Wars*.[23] Other work since Masson, however, has begun to excavate the way in which current psychiatric illnesses, like Multiple Personality Disorder, owe much to long-forgotten late Victorian conceptions of 'double consciousness'. The sudden flowering and then equally sudden disappearance of Multiple Personality Disorder as an illness in the 1980s could learn much from the diagnostic 'fashions' of the late nineteenth century—neurasthenia, hysteria, and the 'alternating personalities' that so fascinated people of the time. This is what historians of psychology like Janet Oppenheim and Adam Crabtree have done.[24] Indeed, Ian Hacking has shown that the model of traumatic forgetting on which advocates of recovered memory depend relies more on Freud's contemporaries and rivals—Pierre Janet's work, most obviously—than on Freud's own work.[25] This has necessitated a return to recovering those psychologies competing with the psychoanalysis that arrived in

[22] Jeffrey Masson, *The Assault on Truth: Freud and Child Sexual Abuse* (Harmondsworth: Penguin, 1985).

[23] Frederick Crews *et al.*, *The Memory Wars: Freud's Legacy in Dispute* (London: Granta, 1997). Crews is crusadingly anti-Freudian. For other views on the same material, see Ann Scott, *Revisiting Real Events: Fantasy, Memory and Psychoanalysis* (London: Virago, 1996) and Mikkel Borch-Jacobsen, 'Neurotica: Freud and the Seduction Theory', *October*, 76 (Spring 1996), 15–43. For a summary of disputes, see Roger Luckhurst, 'Memory Recovered/Recovered Memory', in Roger Luckhurst and Peter Marks (eds.), *Literature and the Contemporary* (London: Longman, 1999), 80–93.

[24] Janet Oppenheim, *'Shattered Nerves': Doctors, Patients and Depression in Victorian England* (Oxford: Oxford University Press, 1991); Adam Crabtree, *From Mesmer to Freud* (New Haven: Yale University Press, 1993).

[25] Ian Hacking, *Rewriting the Soul: Multiple Personality and the Sciences of Memory* (Princeton, NJ: Princeton University Press, 1995). All historians of psychiatry rely, of course, on Henri Ellenberger's monumental *The Discovery of the Unconscious: The History and Evolution of Dynamic Psychiatry* [1970] (London: Fontana, 1994), despite its rather overwhelming teleology towards Freud.

1896, and a clearer sense of how our models of subjective self, the 'unconscious', or memory, are products of a specific conjuncture.[26]

On all of these issues, then—on formations of 'culture', on mass urban populations and the future of the English 'race', on the legacies of imperialism, on the constructions of gender, sexuality, and self—the fin de siècle has come to be regarded as a critical historical matrix. This brief account reflects only a fraction of the available material on the period. Amidst this multidisciplinary convergence, certain sources, texts, and concepts have come to be regarded as vital to an understanding of the period. Until now, though, many of these documents have been relatively inaccessible to students and teachers, except as ceaselessly cited references or scattered across single-discipline anthologies.

This reader tries to respond to the current climate of interdisciplinary work, and to provide a wide range of primary sources from the period, offering complete texts where possible and sensitively edited extracts where not. Our thirteen sections move from the cultural politics of metropolitan life, the New Woman and the literary manifestos of the Decadents and the Romancers, through the new politics of socialism and anarchism, to the newly emerging 'human' sciences, trying to provide original sources and documents for the issues that have made the fin de siècle so important.

This is an avowedly interdisciplinary reader, although, given that both editors work and were trained in literary studies, one with an inevitably culturalist bias. Political historians may well wonder at the exclusion of the split of the Liberal Party over Irish Home Rule; historians of science might lament the absence of any documents from the revolution in physics in the 1890s or the rescue of Mendel's genetic researches that rapidly transformed understandings of animal and human heredity right at the turn of the century. If there are inevitable limits on interdisciplinarity, we nevertheless want to assert that this reader can offer some of the primary material that might begin to recover the echoes, interconnections, and different orders of knowledge that operated in the fin de siècle. To cite Michel Foucault:

Different *œuvres*, dispersed books, that whole mass of texts that belong to a single discursive formation—and so many authors who know or do not know one another, criticise one another, invalidate one another, pillage one another, meet without knowing it, and obstinately intersect their unique discourses in a web of which they are not the masters, of which they cannot see the whole, and of whose breadth they have a very inadequate idea—all communicate by . . . a

---

[26] See Sally Shuttleworth and Jenny Bourne Taylor (eds.), *Embodied Selves: An Anthology of Psychological Texts 1830–90* (Oxford: Oxford University Press, 1997). For further indications of seeking other psychologies, see the reprint of Théodore Flournoy's 1899 bestselling book on the 'subliminal consciousness' and 'multiple personality' of an alleged spirit medium, *From India To Planet Mars* (Princeton, NJ: Princeton University Press, 1993), with an excellent introduction by Sonu Shamdasani.

field in which formal identities, thematic continuities, translations of concepts, and polemical interchanges may be deployed.[27]

Foucault's *Archaeology of Knowledge* sketches out a method which necessitates situating each discourse 'in relation to those that are contemporary with it or related to it. One must therefore study the *economy of the discursive constellation* to which it belongs.'[28] This process ends by outlining a 'territory' which 'may extend to "literary" or "philosophical" texts, as well as scientific ones. Knowledge is to be found not only in demonstrations, it can also be found in fiction, reflexion, narrative accounts, institutional regulations, and political decisions.'[29] In a scaled-down but hopefully productive way, we want the reader to act as a means of negotiating the *constellated* discourses of the fin de siècle. So, for instance, to examine a question of 'race' might mean moving between the pseudo-scientific assertions of 'racial science', discourses of degeneration, imperial history, and the representations of popular culture. Similarly, to situate a question of sex might mean tracing a passage between Mrs Ormiston's purity campaign against *The Empire*, Krafft-Ebing's sexological taxonomy of perversions, concerns over moral decline, and the portrait of artists as moral degenerates provided by Max Nordau or Hugh Stutfield. Different routes and patternings of information should therefore be activated by this reader.

This is not proposed in the service of any particular species of historicism, however (neither editor would wish to be considered *homo calvus* Foucauldians). We have selected this range of discourses in order to reflect the extra-ordinary sense of cross-fertilization between forms of knowledge that marks one of the identifying features of the fin de siècle. Such frantic interconnections might be signalled by tracking, for instance, W. T. Stead's appearance across the anthology. A journalist moving to London in 1880, his editorship of the *Pall Mall Gazette* from 1883 inaugurates, in Matthew Arnold's phrase, 'the new journalism'. So influential were Stead's campaigns that his 'The Truth About the Navy' resulted in a supplementary £3 million of government spending, and his 'Maiden Tribute', as we have seen, altered the age of consent. 'Government by Journalism' looked like a real prospect for a few years—startling to a London Establishment dictated to by a northern radical dissenter. Stead's career gets stranger. He reappeared as apologist for the arch-imperialist Cecil Rhodes, yet was one of the most outspoken critics of the Boer War, diminishing his influence on public opinion. This had mostly already dispersed on his discovery of a talent for 'automatic writing' messages from the dead, and his turn to spiritualism and psychical research in his journal *Borderland* between 1893 and 1897. In an almost impossible

---

[27] Michel Foucault, *The Archaeology of Knowledge*, trans. Alan Sheridan (London: Tavistock Press, 1972), 126–7.
[28] Ibid. 66.   [29] Ibid. 183.

synchronicity with his times, Stead even met his death on the *Titanic*, with all the loaded symbolism that event possesses for the passing of a certain era. Are Stead's interests idiosyncratic or in some way representative of the period? Similar cross-disciplinary figures like Andrew Lang suggest the latter. Lang was a prolific reviewer (championing the unknown Rudyard Kipling in 1889), classicist, historian of Scotland, popular novelist (co-writing *The World's Desire* with Rider Haggard in 1890), advocate of the vigorous romance against the sapping miseries of the naturalist novel, psychical researcher, and also armchair anthropologist, writing books on magic and totemism and the origins of religion. This might seem a frankly bizarre collocation of interests in isolation; in the late Victorian period, however, different pathways and networks existed, and showing some of the key elements of this discursive constellation can open up the interconnection of these structures again.

This is the logic behind our principles of selection; it remains to say a few brief words on the principles of organization. One of the advantages of hypertext for anthologies is the liberation from linearity, the way in which a reader can construct different priorities and routes through a mass of material. Inevitably, our ordering of selections will be taken to imply hierarchies or manipulative interpretations of the historical record. However, one function of this introduction has been to provide mini-narratives for how to move about the material—whether following disciplinary, analogic parallel, or biographical routes, or whether seeking for continuites or discontinuities with the contemporary moment. This is a way of saying there is no prescription as to how or in what order to read the material.

On the other hand, the period can risk dissolving without some organizing framework, and we announce ours in the opening section of the book, 'Degeneration'. This, we feel, is one defining structure which can be tracked across many disciplines; indeed, since degeneration was rarely invoked without its twin concept of 'regeneration', these are the terms in which the period articulated to itself that experience of ambivalence with which we started. There is a burgeoning secondary literature explaining the ways in which the theory of degeneration moves from biology through to sociology, criminology, psychology and ethics, aesthetics, and eschatology.[30] The degenerate was the thief, the undeserving pauper, the madman, the Decadent artist, the sexually active woman, the gambler, the Jew, the sub-human residuum that threatened the race—anything deviating from a middle-class-defined 'normalcy'. Nordau's diatribe caused a major sensation when published in translation in 1895, popularizing a notion that had been in scientific circles since the 1850s. Part of that sensation, however, was a host of

[30] See J. Edward Chamberlain and Sander Gilman (eds.), *Degeneration: The Dark Side of Progress* (New York: Columbia University Press, 1986); William Greenslade, *Degeneration, Culture and the Novel 1880–1940* (Cambridge: Cambridge University Press, 1994); Pick, *Faces of Degeneration*.

responses that rubbished or mocked Nordau's overheated rhetoric of decline and fall—William James considered it a 'pathological book on a pathological subject', Egmont Hake released an impressively weighty tome, *Regeneration: A Reply to Max Nordau*, within months, and Bernard Shaw's riposte became equally famous.[31] The current focus on the fin de siècle has risked becoming too fascinated with the 'gothic' science of degeneration, forgetting a host of other voices that contested visions of collapse with dreams of regeneration. These might be socialists looking forward to the promise of the new century, anarchists plotting a future of 'mutual aid', feminists figuring the New Woman as promising a new dawn, psychical researchers hinting that evidences of the spirit signalled a new phase of mental evolution, or eugenicists planning to reverse decline and regenerate the race. This dialectic between de- and re-generation was played out on a broad scale between different political stances and different philosophies, and often in factions within disciplines.

We have tried to suggest the energy of this debate both in the overall organization of the reader and in individual sections, in which competing voices, whether psychologists, literary commentators, metropolitan *flâneurs*, or factional politicos, uttered starkly different assessments of the age. There are of course other possible trajectories through the dense networks of the fin de siècle, and we offer this reader as one guide, but also, we hope, as a means for re-forming the period along other routes.

[31] See Ch. 1 below.

Editors' Note

Omissions from material as originally published are marked by ellipses within square brackets, thus: [. . .]. A number of footnotes in original texts have been silently excised. All footnotes, unless otherwise indicated, are by the editors; each section ends with biographical and contextual notes on entries. Original spelling and punctuation have been retained where possible.

1

DEGENERATION

From the beginning of the 1880s, the end-of-century experience generated an enormous amount of scientific and cultural debate concerning the future of civilization and of the human race itself. Would the turn of the century herald a new evolutionary dawn, allowing the upward curve of humanity's progress to continue unabated? Or would the fin-de-siècle years usher in what Max Nordau characterized as a 'Dusk of nations, in which all suns and all stars are gradually waning, and mankind with all its institutions and creations is persisting in the midst of a dying world'? Positing itself as a universally applicable scientific discourse, 'degeneration theory' was very much a product of the social and cultural climate of the late nineteenth century. Discourses on degeneration had been current from the mid-century in the work of Benedict Morel in France (who coined the term *dégénérescence* in 1857) and Cesare Lombroso in Italy; but they reached a highly developed stage in the 1880s and 1890s. The historians Edward Chamberlain and Sander Gilman have tracked the ways in which the precise biological meanings of degeneration were extended figuratively into many other fields, and make a strong case that it was one of the most influential concepts in late Victorian culture.

Darwinian theories of evolution provided the basis for notions of racial and cultural degeneration. The idea of progress, which went hand in hand with mid-Victorian social and economic confidence, was bolstered by Darwin's theory of evolution, the Victorians regarding themselves and their society as the acme of human development. But the economic recession of the 1880s, combined with a fear that the great 'Age of Empire' might be short-lived, meant that ideas of progress were increasingly countered by fears of cultural—nearly always expressed as racial—decline. Max Nordau, a German polymath, synthesized the work of scientists in his attack on late nineteenth-century culture. The extract we have included here, from what is a weighty tome, illustrates the 'scientific' drift of his argument; but the bulk of his book constitutes a diatribe against a long list of writers, poets, dramatists, artists, and composers of the second half of the nineteenth century—Ibsen, Wagner, Tolstoy, Ruskin, Burne-Jones, Rossetti, Zola, Nietzsche, Baudelaire, to name just a few. First translated into English in 1895, in the year that one of his 'degenerates' (Oscar Wilde) was sentenced to two years' hard labour for committing acts of 'gross indecency', Nordau's treatise received a lot of attention from cultural critics in the late twentieth century. Its contemporary significance should not, though, be overstated. It was often laughingly dismissed, and we have included the views of William James and Bernard Shaw. Shaw humorously identifies Nordau's tirade as 'nothing but the familiar delusion of the used-up man that the world is going to the dogs'; James sees it as the work of 'a victim of insane delusions about a conspiracy of hysterics and degenerates'.

Hysterical as Nordau's book undoubtedly is, the 'scientific' texts which inspired it wielded considerable cultural influence. This is represented here by essays by Edwin Lankester and H. G. Wells. Lankester's biological vocabulary signals degeneration theory's debt to Darwin. His essay none the less retains—as does all such work—a cultural dimension: in expressing the fear that modern European civilizations may be on the brink of a radical decline he makes an analogy with the fall of the Greek and Roman empires. H. G. Wells's 'zoological' exploration of the same issues equally slides between 'scientific' (zoological and physiological) discourse and social and cultural analysis. Wells's ostensibly tongue-in-cheek account of the 'life history' of the 'professional classes' who as young men pass through an energetic period of 'Sturm und Drang' but finally end up 'settling down' into social and cultural passivity, is part of a serious rhetorical strategy whereby the lives of the moribund members of British society's highest social groups are compared by analogy with the species-history of the 'Sea Squirts, or Ascidians, of our coasts', whose downward evolutionary spiral finally reduces them to 'a merely vegetative excrescence on a rock'—eloquently presaging the passivity and degenerative qualities of Wells's 'Eloi', in *The Time Machine* (1895), and displaying the political and cultural basis of much degeneration theory.

Secondary reading: Chamberlain and Gilman; Greenslade; Jones; Ledger, 'In Darkest England'; Mosse; Pick; Williams.

1   from Edwin Ray Lankester, *Degeneration:*
               A Chapter in Darwinism (1880)

It is clearly enough possible for a set of forces such as we sum up under the heading 'natural selection' to so act on the structure of an organism as to produce one of three results, namely these; to keep it *in statu quo*; to increase the complexity of its structure; or lastly, to diminish the complexity of its structure. We have as possibilities either BALANCE, or ELABORATION, or DEGENERATION.

Owing, as it seems, to the predisposing influence of the systems of classification in ascending series proceeding steadily upwards from the 'lower' or simplest forms to the 'higher' or more complex forms,—systems which were prevalent before the doctrine of transformism had taken firm root in the minds of naturalists, there has been up to the present day an endeavour to explain every existing form of life on the hypothesis that it has been maintained for long ages in a state of Balance; or else on the hypothesis that it has been Elaborated, and is an advance, an improvement, upon its ancestors. Only one naturalist—Dr. Dohrn, of Naples[1]—has put forward the hypothesis of Degeneration as capable of wide application to the explanation of existing forms of life; and his arguments in favour of a general application of this hypothesis have not, I think, met with the consideration they merit. [. . .]

Degeneration may be defined as a gradual change of the structure in which the organism becomes adapted to *less* varied and *less* complex conditions of life; whilst Elaboration is a gradual change of structure in which the organism becomes adapted to more and more varied and complex conditions of existence. In Elaboration there is a new *expression* of form, corresponding to new perfection of work in the animal machine. In Degeneration there is *suppression* of form, corresponding to the cessation of work. Elaboration of some one organ *may* be a necessary accompaniment of Degeneration in all the others; in fact, this is very generally the case; and it is only when the total result of the Elaboration of some organs, and the Degeneration of others, is such as to leave the whole animal in a *lower* condition, that is fitted to less complex action and reaction in regard to its surroundings, than was the ancestral form with which we are comparing it (either actually or in imagination) that we speak of that animal as an instance of Degeneration.

Any new set of conditions occurring to an animal which render its food and safety very easily attained, seem to lead as a rule to Degeneration; just as an active healthy man sometimes degenerates when he suddenly becomes possessed of a fortune; or as Rome degenerated when possessed of the riches of the ancient

---

[1] Anton Dohrn, zoologist and entomologist, writing in the 1860s and 1870s.

world. The habit of parasitism clearly acts upon animal organisation in this way. Let the parasitic life once be secured, and away go legs, jaws, eyes, and ears; the active, highly-gifted crab, insect or annelid may become a mere sac, absorbing nourishment and laying eggs. [. . .]

All that has been, thus far, here said on the subject of Degeneration is so much zoological specialism, and may appear but a narrow restriction of the discussion to those who are not zoologists. Though we may establish the hypothesis most satisfactorily by the study of animal organisation and development, it is abundantly clear that degenerative evolution is by no means limited in its application to the field of zoology. [. . .]

The traditional history of mankind furnishes us with notable examples of degeneration. High states of civilisation have decayed and given place to low and degenerate states. At one time it was a favourite doctrine that the savage races of mankind were degenerate descendants of the higher and civilised races. This general and sweeping application of the doctrine of degeneration has been proved to be erroneous by careful study of the habits, arts, and beliefs of savages; at the same time there is no doubt that many savage races as we at present see them are actually degenerate and are descended from ancestors possessed of a relatively elaborate civilisation. As such we may cite some of the Indians of Central America, the modern Egyptians, and even the heirs of the great oriental monarchies of pre-Christian times. Whilst the hypothesis of universal degeneration has a very large share in the explanation of the condition of the most barbarous races, such as the Fuegians, the Bushmen, and even the Australians. They exhibit evidence of being descended from ancestors more cultivated than themselves.

With regard to ourselves, the white races of Europe, the possibility of degeneration seems to be worth some consideration. In accordance with the tacit assumption of universal progress—an unreasoning optimism—we are accustomed to regard ourselves as necessarily progressing, as necessarily having arrived at a higher and more elaborated condition than that which our ancestors reached, and as destined to progress still further. On the other hand, it is well to remember that we are subject to the general laws of evolution, and are as likely to degenerate as progress. As compared with the immediate forefathers of our civilisation—the ancient Greeks—we do not appear to have improved so far as our bodily structure is concerned, nor assuredly so far as some of our mental capacities are concerned. Our powers of perceiving and expressing beauty of form have certainly *not* increased since the days of the Parthenon and Aphrodite of Melos. In matters of reason, in the development of the intellect, we may seriously inquire how the case stands. Does the reason of the average man of civilised Europe stand out clearly as an evidence of progress when compared with that of the men of bygone ages? Are all the inventions and figments of human superstition and folly, the self-inflicted torturing of mind, the reiterated substitution of wrong for right, and of falsehood for truth, which disfigure our modern civilisation—are these evidences of progress? In such respects we have at least reason to fear that we may be degenerate. Possibly we are all drifting, tending to the condition of intellectual Barnacles or Ascidians.[2] It is possible for us—just as the Ascidian throws away its tail and its eye and sinks into a quiescent state of inferiority—to reject the good gift of reason with which every child is born, and to degenerate into a contented life of material enjoyment accompanied by ignorance and superstition. The unprejudiced, all-questioning spirit of childhood may not inaptly be compared to the tadpole tail and eye of the young Ascidian: we have to fear lest the prejudices, preoccupations, and dogmatism of modern civilisation should in any way lead to the atrophy and loss of the valuable mental qualities inherited by our young forms from primaeval man.

There is only one means of estimating our position, only one means of so shaping our conduct that we may with certainty avoid degeneration and keep an onward course. We are as a race more fortunate than our ruined cousins—the degenerate Ascidians. For us it is possible to ascertain what will conduce to our higher development, what will favour our degeneration. To us has been given the power to *know the causes of things*, and by the use of this power it is possible for us to control our destinies. It is for us by ceaseless and ever hopeful labour to try to gain a knowledge of man's place in nature. When we have gained this fully and minutely, we shall be able by the light of the past to guide ourselves in the future. In proportion as the whole of the past evolution of civilised man, of which we at present perceive the outlines, is assigned to its causes, we and our successors on the globe may expect to be able duly to estimate that which makes for, and that which makes against, the progress of the race. The full and earnest cultivation of Science—the Knowledge of Causes—is that to which we have to look for the protection of our race—even of this English branch of it—from relapse and degeneration.

2   H. G. Wells, 'Zoological Retrogression' (1891)

Perhaps no scientific theories are more widely discussed or more generally misunderstood among cultivated people than the views held by biologists regarding the past history and future prospects of their province—life. Using their technical

[2] Sub-class of marine organisms—the most common being the sea squirt. This was the favourite zoological example of degeneration, as they begin their life cycle as free-swimming larvae before attaching to rocks and regressing in form. Discussed at length by H. G. Wells in the article below.

phrases and misquoting their authorities in an invincibly optimistic spirit, the educated public has arrived in its own way at a rendering of their results which it finds extremely satisfactory. It has decided that in the past the great scroll of nature has been steadily unfolding to reveal a constantly richer harmony of forms and successively higher grades of being, and it assumes that this 'evolution' will continue with increasing velocity under the supervision of its extreme expression—man. This belief, as effective, progressive, and pleasing as transformation scenes at a pantomime, receives neither in the geological record nor in the studies of the phylogenetic embryologist any entirely satisfactory confirmation.[3]

On the contrary, there is almost always associated with the suggestion of advance in biological phenomena an opposite idea, which is its essential complement. The technicality expressing this would, if it obtained sufficient currency in the world of culture, do much to reconcile the naturalist and his traducers. The toneless glare of optimistic evolution would then be softened by a shadow; the monotonous reiteration of 'Excelsior' by people who did not climb would cease;[4] the too sweet harmony of the spheres would be enhanced by a discord, this evolutionary antithesis—degradation.

Isolated cases of degeneration have long been known, and popular attention has been drawn to them in order to point well-meant moral lessons, the fallacious analogy of species to individual being employed. It is only recently, however, that the enormous importance of degeneration as a plastic process in nature has been suspected and its entire parity with evolution recognised.

It is no libel to say that three-quarters of the people who use the phrase 'organic evolution,' interpret it very much in this way:—Life began with the amoeba, and then came jelly-fish, shell-fish, and all those miscellaneous invertebrate things, and then *real* fishes and amphibia, reptiles, birds, mammals, and man, the last and first of creation. It has been pointed out that this is very like regarding a man as the offspring of his first cousins; these, of his second; these, of his relations at the next remove, and so forth—making the remotest living human being his primary ancestor. Or, to select another image, it is like elevating the modest poor relation at the family gathering to the unexpected altitude of fountain-head—a proceeding which would involve some cruel reflections on her age and character. The sounder view is, as scientific writers have frequently insisted, that living species

---

[3] Degeneration theory owes much to the notion that the individual's development rehearses the evolution of the species—that 'ontogeny recapitulates phylogeny'. The human embryo, for example, was held to progress through 'primitive' cellular stages then through lower animal forms, before arriving at the most complex mammalian form. Wells's argument relies extensively on the possibilities of reversing this development. Principally associated with the German physiologist Ernst von Baer (1792–1836) and Wells's contemporary Ernst Haeckel (1834–1919), the German Darwinian theorist.

[4] Excelsior means 'ever higher'.

have varied along divergent lines from intermediate forms, and, as it is the object of this paper to point out, not necessarily in an upward direction.

In fact, the path of life, so frequently compared to some steadily-rising mountain-slope, is far more like a footway worn by leisurely wanderers in an undulating country. Excelsior biology is a popular and poetic creation—the *real* form of a phylum, or line of descent, is far more like the course of a busy man moving about a great city. Sometimes it is underground, sometimes it doubles and twists in tortuous streets, now it rises far overhead along some viaduct, and, again, the river is taken advantage of in these varied journeyings to and fro. Upward and downward these threads of pedigree interweave, slowly working out a pattern of accomplished things with which the word 'evolution' is popularly associated.

The best known, and, perhaps, the most graphic and typical, illustration of the downward course is to be found in the division of the *Tunicata*. These creatures constitute a group which is, in several recent schemes of classification, raised to the high rank of a sub-phylum, and which includes, among a great variety of forms, the fairly common Sea Squirts, or *Ascidians*, of our coasts. By an untrained observer a specimen of these would at first very probably be placed in the mineral or vegetable kingdoms. Externally they are simply shapeless lumps of a stiff, semi-transparent, cartilaginous substance, in which pebbles, twigs, and dirt are imbedded, and only the most careful examination of this unpromising exterior would discover any evidence of the living thing within. A penknife, however, serves to lay bare the animal inside this house, or 'test,' and the fleshy texture of the semi-transparent body must then convince the unscientific investigator of his error.

He would forthwith almost certainly make a fresh mistake in his classification of this new animal. Like most zoologists until a comparatively recent date, he would think of such impassive and, from the human point of view, lowly beings as the oyster and mussel as its brethren, and a superficial study of its anatomy might even strengthen this opinion. As a matter of fact, however, these singular creatures are far more closely related to the vertebrata—they lay claim to the quarterings, not of molluscs, but of imperial man! and, like novelette heroes with a birth-mark, they carry their proofs about with them.

This startling and very significant fact is exhibited in the details of their development. It is a matter of common knowledge that living things repeat in a more or less blurred and abbreviated series their generalized pedigree in their embryological changes. For instance, as we shall presently remind the reader, the developing chick or rabbit passes through a fish-like stage, and the human foetus wears an undeniable tail. In the case of these ascidians, the fertilized egg-cell, destined to become a fresh individual, takes almost from the first an entirely different course from that pursued by the molluscs. Instead, the dividing and growing ovum exhibits phases resembling in the most remarkable way those of the low-liest among fishes, the Lancelet, or *Amphioxus*. The method of division, the for-mation of the primitive stomach and body-cavity, and the origin of the nervous system are identical, and a stage is attained in which the young organism dis-plays—or else simulates in an altogether inexplicable way—vertebrate character-istics. It has a *notochord*, or primary skeletal axis, the representative or forerunner in all vertebrata of the backbone; it displays gill-slits behind its mouth, as do all vertebrated animals in the earlier stages only or throughout life; and, finally, the origin and position of its nervous axis are essentially and characteristically verte-brate. In these three independent series of structures the young ascidian stands apart from all invertebrated animals and manifests its high descent. In fact, at this stage it differs far more widely from its own adult form than it does from *Amphioxus* or a simplified tadpole.

Like a tadpole, the animal has a well-developed tail which propels its owner vigorously through the water. There is a conspicuous single eye, reminding the zoologist at once of the Polyphemus eye that almost certainly existed in the cen-tral group of the vertebrata. There are also serviceable organs of taste and hear-ing, and the lively movements of the little creature justify the supposition that its being is fairly full of endurable sensations. But this flush of golden youth is sadly transient: it is barely attained before a remarkable and depressing change appears in the drift of development.

The ascidian begins to take things seriously—a deliberate sobriety gradually succeeds its tremulous vivacity. L' Allegro dies away; the tones of Il Penseroso become dominant.

On the head appear certain sucker-like structures, paralleled, one may note, in the embryos of certain ganoid fishes. The animal becomes dull, moves about more and more slowly, and finally fixes itself by these suckers to a rock. It has settled down in life. The tail that waggled so merrily undergoes a rapid process of absorption; eye and ear, no longer needed, atrophy completely, and the skin secretes the coarse, inorganic-looking 'test.' It is very remarkable that this 'test' should consist of a kind of cellulose—a compound otherwise almost exclusively confined to the vegetable kingdom. The transient glimpse of vivid animal life is forgotten, and the rest of this existence is a passive receptivity to what chance and the water bring along. The ascidian lives henceforth an idyll of contentment, glued, head downwards, to a stone,

The world forgetting, by the world forgot.[5]

Now here, to all who refer nature to one rigid state of precedence, is an altogether inexplicable thing. A creature on a level, at lowest, immediately next to verte-

---

[5] The opening line of R. L. Stevenson's poem, 'My wife and I, in our romantic cot'.

brated life, turns back from the upward path and becomes at last a merely vegetative excrescence on a rock.

It is lower even than the patriarchal amoeba of popular science if we take psychic life as the standard: for does not even the amoeba crawl after and choose its food and immediate environment? We have then, as I have read somewhere— I think it was in an ecclesiastical biography—a career not perhaps teemingly eventful, but full of the richest suggestion and edification.

And here one may note a curious comparison which can be made between this life-history and that of many a respectable pinnacle and gargoyle on the social fabric. Every respectable citizen of the professional classes passes through a period of activity and imagination, of 'liveliness and eccentricity,' of '*Sturm und Drang*.'[6] He shocks his aunts. Presently, however, he realizes the sober aspect of things. He beomes dull; he enters a profession; suckers appear on his head; and he studies. Finally, by virtue of these he settles down—he marries. All his wild ambitions and subtle aesthetic perceptions atrophy as needless in the presence of calm domesticity. He secretes a house, or 'establishment,' round himself, of inorganic and servile material. His Bohemian tail is discarded. Henceforth his life is a passive receptivity of what chance and the drift of his profession bring along; he lives an almost entirely vegetative excrescence on the side of the street, and in the tranquillity of his calling finds that colourless contentment that replaces happiness.

But this comparison is possibly fallacious, and is certainly a digression.

The ascidian, though a pronounced case of degradation, is only one of an endless multitude. Those shelly warts that cover every fragment of sea-side shingle are degraded crustaceans; at first they are active and sensitive creatures, similar essentially to the earlier phases of the life-history of a prawn. Other Cirripeds and many Copepods sink down still deeper, to almost entire shapelessness and loss of organization. The corals, sea-mats, the immobile oysters and mussels are undoubtedly descended from free-living ancestors with eye-spots and other sense-organs. Various sea-worms and holothurians have also taken to covering themselves over from danger, and so have deliberately foregone their dangerous birthright to a more varied and active career. The most fruitful and efficient cause of degradation, however, is not simply akin to it—an aptness for parasitism. There are whole orders and classes thus pitifully submerged. The *Acarina*, or Mites, include an immense array of genera profoundly sunken in this way, and the great majority of both the flat and round worms are parasitic degeneration forms. The vile tapeworm, at the nadir, seems to have lost even common sensation; it has become an insensible mechanism of evil—a multiplying disease spot, living to that extent, and otherwise utterly dead.

[6] Literally 'storm and stress', signifying the fervent idealism and emotionalism of youth, deriving from the German Romanticism of figures like Goethe and Schiller.

Such evident and indisputable present instances of degeneration alone would form a very large proportion of the catalogue of living animals. If we were to add to this list the names of all those genera the ancestors of which have at any time sunk to rise again, it is probable that we should have to write down *the entire roll of the animal kindgom!*

In some cases the degradation has been a strategic retrogression—the type has stooped to conquer. This is, perhaps, most manifest in the case of the higher vertebrate types.

It is one of the best-known embryological facts that a bird or mammal starts in its development as if a fish were in the making. The extremely ugly embryo of such types has gill-slits, sense-organs, facial parts, and limbs resembling far more closely those of a dog-fish than its own destined adult form. To use a cricketing expression, it is 'pulled' subsequently into its later line of advance.

The comparative anatomy of almost every set of organs in the adult body enforces the suggestion of this ovarian history. We find what are certainly modified placoid fish scales, pressed into the work of skull-covering, while others retain their typical enamel caps as teeth. The skull itself is a piscine cranium, ossified and altered, in the most patchy way, to meet the heavier blows that bodies falling through air, intead of water, deliver. The nasal organ is a fish's nasal organ, constructed to smell in water, and the roof of the mouth and front of the skull have been profoundly altered to meet a fresh set of needs in aerial life. The ear-drum, in a precisely similar way, is derived from a gill-slit twisted up to supplement the aquatic internal ear, which would otherwise fail to appreciate the weaker sound-waves in air. The bathymetric air-bladder becomes a lung; and so one might go on through all the entire organisation of a higher vertebrate. Everywhere we should find the anatomy of a fish twisted and patched to fit a life out of water; nowhere organs built specially for this very special condition. There is nothing like this in the case of a fish. There the organs are from the first recognizable sketches of their adult forms, and they develop straightforwardly. But the higher types go a considerable distance towards the fish, and then turn round and complete their development in an entirely opposite direction.

This turning is evidently precisely similar in nature, though not in effect, to the retrogression of the ascidian after its pisciform or larval stage.

If the reader can bear the painful spectacle of his ancestor's degradation, I would ask him to imagine the visit of some bodiless Linnaeus to this world during the upper Silurian period.[7] Such a spirit would, of course, immediately begin to classify animated nature, neatly and swiftly.

---

[7] Carl Linnaeus (1707–78) was the figure who organized a taxonomical system to classify all animals, plants, and minerals—thus, for Wells, the exemplary naturalist–observer.

It would be at once apparent that the most varied and vigorous life was to be found in the ocean. On the land a monotonous vegetation of cryptograms would shelter a sparse fauna of insects, gasteropods, and arachnids; but the highest life would certainly be the placoid fishes of the seas—the ancient representatives of the sharks and rays. On the diverse grounds of size, power, and activity, these would head any classification he planned. If our Linnaeus were a disembodied human spirit, he would immediately appoint these placoids his ancestors, and consent to a further analysis of the matter only very reluctantly, and possibly even with some severe remarks and protests about carrying science too far.

The true forefathers of the reader, however, had even at that early period very probably already left the seas, and were—with a certain absence of dignity—accommodating themselves to the necessities of air-breathing.

It is almost certain that the seasonal differences of that time were very much greater than they are now. Intensely dry weather followed stormy rainy seasons, and the rivers of that forgotten world—like some tropical rivers of to-day—were at one time tumultuous floods and at another baking expanses of mud. In such rivers it would be idle to expect self-respecting gill-breathing fish. Our imaginary zoological investigator would, however, have found that they were not altogether tenantless. Swimming in the pluvial waters, or inert and caked over by the torrid mud, he would have discovered what he would certainly have regarded as lowly, specially modified, and degenerate relations of the active denizens of the ocean—the *Dipnoi*, or mud-fish. He would have found in conjunction with the extremely primitive skull, axial skeleton, and fin possessed by these Silurain mud-fish, a remarkable adaptation of the swimming-bladder to the needs of the waterless season. It would have undergone the minimum amount of alteration to render it a lung, and blood-vessels and other points of the anatomy would show correlated changes.

Unless our zoological investigator were a prophet, he would certainly never have imagined that in these forms vested the inheritance of the earth, nor have awarded them a high place in the category of nature. Why were they living thus in inhospitable rivers and spending half their lives half baked in river-mud? The answer would be the old story of degeneration again; they had failed in the struggle, they were less active and powerful than their rivals of the sea, and they had taken the second great road of preservation—flight. Just as the ascidian has retired from an open sea too crowded and full of danger to make life worth the trouble, so in that older epoch did the mud-fish. They preferred dirt, discomfort, and survival to a gallant fight and death. Very properly, then, they would be classed in our zoologist's scheme as a degenerate group.

Some conservative descendants of these mud-fish live to-day in African and

Australian rivers, archaic forms that have kept right up to the present the structure of Palaeozoic days. Others of their children, however, have risen in the world again. The gill-breathing stage becomes less and less important, and the air-bladder was constantly elaborated under the slow, incessant moulding of circumstances to the fashion of a more and more efficient breathing-organ. Emigrants from the rivers swarmed over the yet uncrowded land. Aldermanic amphibia were the magnates of the great coal measure epoch, to give place presently to the central group of reptiles. From these sprang divergently the birds and mammals, and, finally, the last of the mud-fish family, man, the heir of ages. He it is who goes down to the sea in ships, and, with wide-sweeping nets and hooks cunningly baited, beguiles the children of those who drove his ancestors out of the water. Thus the whirligig of time brings round its revenges; still, in an age of excessive self-admiration, it would be well for man to remember that his family *was* driven from the waters by the fishes, who still—in spite of incidental fish-hooks, seines, and dredges—hold that empire triumphantly against him.

Witness especially the trout; I doubt whether *it* has ever been captured except by sheer misadventure.

These brief instances of degradation may perhaps suffice to show that there is a good deal to be found in the work of biologists quite inharmonious with such phrases as 'the progress of ages,' and the 'march of mind.' The zoologist demonstrates that advance has been fitful and uncertain; rapid progress has often been followed by rapid extinction or degeneration, while, on the other hand, a form lowly and degraded has in its degradation often happened upon some fortunate discovery or valuable discipline and risen again, like a more fortunate Antaeos, to victory. There is, therefore, no guarantee in scientific knowledge of man's permanence or permanent ascendancy. He has a remarkably variable organisation, and his own activities and increase cause the conditions of his existence to fluctuate far more widely than those of any animal have ever done. The presumption is that before him lies a long future of profound modification, but whether that will be, according to present ideals, upward or downward, no one can forecast. Still, so far as any scientist can tell us, it may be that, instead of this, Nature is, in unsuspected obscurity, equipping some now humble creature with wider possibilities of appetite, endurance, or destruction, to rise in the fulness of time and sweep *homo* away into the darkness from which his universe arose. The Coming Beast must certainly be reckoned in any anticipatory calculations regarding the Coming Man.

3   from Max Nordau, *Degeneration* (1895)

BOOK ONE: *FIN-DE-SIÈCLE*

THE DUSK OF NATIONS

[. . .] One epoch of history is unmistakably in its decline, and another is announcing its approach. There is a sound of rending in every tradition, and it is as though the morrow would not link itself with to-day. Things as they are totter and plunge, and they are suffered to reel and fall, because man is weary, and there is no faith that it is worth an effort to uphold them. Views that have hitherto governed minds are dead or driven hence like disenthroned kings, and for their inheritance they that hold the titles and they that would usurp are locked in struggle. Meanwhile interregnum in all its terrors prevails; there is confusion among the powers that be; the million, robbed of its leaders, knows not where to turn; the strong work their will; false prophets arise, and dominion is divided amongst those whose rod is the heavier because their time is short. Men look with longing for whatever new things are at hand, without presage whence they will come or what they will be. They have hope that in the chaos of thought, art may yield revelations of the order that is to follow on this tangled web. The poet, the musician, is to announce, or divine, or at least suggest in what forms civilization will further be evolved. What shall be considered good to-morrow—what shall be beautiful? What shall we know to-morrow—what believe in? What shall inspire us? How shall we enjoy? So rings the question from the thousand voices of the people, and where a market-vendor sets up his booth and claims to give an answer, where a fool or a knave suddenly begins to prophesy in verse or prose, in sound or colour, or professes to practise his art otherwise than his predecessors and competitors, there gathers a great concourse, crowding around him to seek in what he has wrought, as in oracles of the Pythia, some meaning to be divined and interpreted. And the more vague and insignificant they are, the more they seem to convey of the future to the poor gaping souls gasping for revelations, and the more greedily and passionately are they expounded.

Such is the spectacle presented by the doings of men in the reddened light of the Dusk of Nations. Massed in the sky the clouds are aflame in the weirdly beautiful glow which was observed for the space of years after the eruption of Krakatoa. Over the earth the shadows creep with deepening gloom, wrapping all objects in a mysterious dimness, in which all certainty is destroyed and any guess seems plausible. Forms lose their outlines, and are dissolved in floating mist. The day is over, the night draws on. The old anxiously watch its approach, fearing they will not live to see the end. A few amongst the young and strong are conscious of the vigour of life in all their veins and nerves, and rejoice in the coming sunrise. Dreams, which fill up the hours of darkness till the breaking of the new day bring to the former comfortless memories, to the latter high-souled hopes. And in the artistic products of the age we see the form in which these dreams become sensible.

Here is the place to forestall a possible misunderstanding. The great majority of the middle and lower classes is naturally not *fin-de-siècle*. It is true that the spirit of the times is stirring the nation down to their lowest depths, and awaking even in the most inchoate and rudimentary human being a wondrous feeling of stir and upheaval. But this more or less slight touch of moral sea-sickness does not excite in him the cravings of travailing women, nor express itself in new aesthetic needs. The Philistine or the Proletarian still finds undiluted satisfaction in the old and oldest forms of art and poetry, if he knows himself unwatched by the scornful eye of the votary of fashion, and is free to yield to his own inclinations. He prefers Ohnet's novels to all the symbolists, and Mascagni's *Cavalleria Rusticana* to all Wagnerians and to Wagner himself;[8] he enjoys himself royally over slap-dash farces and music-hall melodies, and yawns or is angered at Ibsen; he contemplates gladly chromos of paintings depicting Munich beer-houses and rustic taverns, and passes the open-air painters without a glance. It is only a very small minority who honestly find pleasure in the new tendencies, and announce them with genuine conviction as that which alone is sound, a sure guide for the future, a pledge of pleasure and of moral benefit. But this minority has the gift of covering the whole visible surface of society, as a little oil extends over a large area of the surface of the sea. It consists chiefly of rich educated people, or of fanatics. The former give the *ton* to all the snobs, the fools, and the blockheads; the latter make an impression upon the weak and dependent, and intimidate the nervous. All snobs affect to have the same taste as the select and exclusive minority, who pass by everything that once was considered beautiful with an air of the greatest contempt. And thus it appears as if the whole of civilized humanity were converted to the aesthetics of the Dusk of the Nations. [. . .]

DIAGNOSIS

The manifestations [. . .] must be patent enough to everyone, be he never so narrow a Philistine. The Philistine, however, regards them as a passing fashion and nothing more; for him the current terms, caprice, eccentricity, affectation of novelty, imitation, instinct, afford a sufficient explanation. The purely literary mind, whose merely aesthetic culture does not enable him to understand the connections of things, and to seize their real meaning, deceives himself and others as

---

[8] Georges Ohnet (1845–1918), was an extremely successful popular novelist, widely translated and dramatized in the 1890s, and widely despised by the literary establishment. Pietro Mascagni (1863–1945) composed the *Cavalleria* in 1889. The one-act opera, using popular melodies, was a Europe-wide success in the early 1890s. The operas of Richard Wagner (1813–83) remained a powerful influence over music and art in the 1890s.

to his ignorance by means of sounding phrases and loftily talks of a 'restless quest of a new ideal by the modern spirit,' 'the richer vibrations of the refined nervous system of the present day,' 'the unknown sensations of an elect mind.' But the physician, especially if he has devoted himself to the special study of nervous and mental maladies, recognises at a glance, in the *fin-de-siècle* disposition, in the tendencies of contemporary art and poetry, in the life and conduct of the men who write mystic, symbolic and 'decadent' works, and the attitude taken by their admirers in the tastes and aesthetic instincts of fashionable society, the confluence of two well-defined conditions of disease, with which he is quite familiar, viz. degeneration (degeneracy) and hysteria, of which the minor stages are designated as neurasthenia. These two conditions of the organism differ from each other, yet have many features in common, and frequently occur together; so that it is easier to observe them in their composite forms, than each in isolation.

The conception of degeneracy, which, at this time, obtains throughout the science of mental disease, was first clearly grasped and formulated by Morel.[9] In his principal work—often quoted, but, unfortunately, not sufficiently read—the following definition of what he wishes to be understood by 'degeneracy,' is given by this distinguished expert in mental pathology, who was, for a short time, famous in Germany, even outside professional circles.

'The clearest notion we can form of degeneracy is to regard it as *a morbid deviation from an original type*. This deviation, even if, at the outset, it was ever so slight, contained transmissible elements of such a nature that anyone bearing in him the germs becomes more and more incapable of fulfilling his functions in the world; and mental progress, already checked in his own person, finds itself menaced also in his descendants.'

When under any kind of noxious influences an organism becomes debilitated, its successors will not resemble the healthy, normal type of the species, with capacities for development, but will form a new sub-species, which, like all the others, possesses the capacity of transmitting to its offspring, in a continuously increasing degree, its peculiarities, these being morbid deviations from the normal form—gaps in development, malformations and infirmities. That which distinguishes degeneracy from the formation of new species (phylogeny) is, that the morbid variation does not continuously subsist and propagate itself, like one that is healthy, but, fortunately, is soon rendered sterile, and after a few generations often dies out before it reaches the lowest grade of organic degradation.

Degeneracy betrays itself among men in certain physical characteristics, which are denominated 'stigmata,' or brandmarks—an unfortunate term derived from a false idea, as if degeneracy were necessarily the consequence of a fault, and the

---

[9] Nordau quotes from B. A. Morel's *Traité des dégénérescences physiques, intellectuelles et morales* (1857).

indication of it as a punishment. Such stigmata consist of deformities, multiple and stunted growths in the first line of asymmetry, the unequal development of the two halves of the face and cranium; then imperfection in the development of the external ear, which is conspicuous for its enormous size, or protrudes from the head, like a handle, and the lobe of which is either lacking or adhering to the head, and the helix of which is not involuted; further, squint-eyes, hare lips, irregularities in the form and position of the teeth; pointed or flat palates, webbed or supernumerary fingers. [. . .] Lombroso has conspicuously broadened our knowledge of stigmata, but he apportions them merely to his 'born criminals'—a limitation which from the very scientific standpoint of Lombroso himself cannot be justified, his 'born criminals' being nothing but a subdivision of degenerates. Féré[10] expresses this very emphatically when he says, 'Vice, crime and madness are only distinguished from each other by social prejudices.'

There might be a sure means of proving that the application of the term 'degenerates' to the originators of all the *fin-de-siècle* movements in art and literature is not arbitrary, that it is no baseless conceit, but a fact; and that would be a careful physical examination of the persons concerned, and an inquiry into their pedigree. In almost all cases, relatives would be met with who were undoubtedly degenerate, and one or more stigmata discovered which would indisputably establish the diagnosis of 'Degeneration.' [. . .]

In the mental development of degenerates, we meet with the same irregularity that we have observed in their physical growth. The asymmetry of face and cranium finds, as it were, its counterpart in their mental faculties. Some of the latter are completely stunted, others morbidly exaggerated. That which nearly all degenerates lack is the sense of morality and of right and wrong. For them there exists no law, no decency, no modesty. [. . .]

Another mental stigma of degenerates is their emotionalism. [. . .] He laughs until he sheds tears, or weeps copiously without adequate occasion; a commonplace line of poetry or of prose sends a shudder down his back; he falls into raptures before indifferent pictures or statues; and music, especially, even the most insipid and least commendable, arouses in him the most vehement emotions. He is quite proud of being so vibrant a musical instrument, and boasts that where the Philistine remains completely cold, he feels his inner self confounded, the depths of his being broken up, and the bliss of the Beautiful possessing him to the tips of his fingers. [. . .]

Besides moral insanity and emotionalism, there is to be observed in the degenerate a condition of mental weakness and despondency, which, according to the circumstances of his life, assumes the form of pessimism, a vague fear of all men, and of the entire phenomenon of the universe, or self-abhorrence. [. . .] In this

---

[10]   Charles Féré published widely on psychology in the 1880s and 1890s, and worked alongside Jean-Martin Charcot at his famous asylum, the Salpêtrière hospital in Paris (see Ch. 10 below).

picture of the sufferer from melancholia; downcast, sombre, despairing of himself and the world, tortured by fear of the Unknown, menaced by undefined but dreadful dangers, we recognise in every detail the man of the Dusk of the Nations and the *fin-de-siècle* frame of mind, described in the first chapter. [. . .]

I have enumerated the most important features characterizing the mental condition of the degenerate. The reader can now judge for himself whether or not the diagnosis 'degeneration' is applicable to the originators of the new aesthetic tendencies.

4   from [Egmont Hake], *Regeneration:*
          A Reply to Max Nordau (1895)

WHO IS THE CRITIC?

Politicians, sociologists, economists, biologists, theologians and the aesthetes have had their say and each in their turn exercised a periodical spell over the public mind. It is now the turn of the alienists. Dr. Max Nordau has by his book entitled 'Degeneration' produced no small sensation throughout the world, not least in this country. Though his work may not have made the stir of a sensational novel read by the millions, there can be little doubt that it has imposed itself on every educated mind in the country. It is no exaggeration to say that, like a sharp trumpet-blast, it has awakened the educated classes from the lethargy consequent upon the din of clashing opinions and contradictory systems. This volume has once more roused us to the fact that we, as individuals, as a nation, as a race, are travelling at comet-speed towards a goal of which we have no inkling. It sternly suggests that we are on the wrong road and that a fate of a most horrible description is rapidly befalling us—an affliction in most people's view worse than annihilation. Madness is shown to be insidiously invading our minds. [. . .]

For characteristics revealed in his work, the observant reader will, no doubt, conclude that Max Nordau belongs to the Jewish race. [. . .] He is evidently a free-thinking Jew, a type which we meet with everywhere, and against which as few objections can be raised as against any other type of man. The free-thinking Jew is generally clever, well-instructed, moral, and cheerful. His good qualities however do not prevent him from having his peculiar characteristics, which naturally influence his perceptions and feelings. He has generally a cut-and-dried life-philosophy based on science and common-sense as well as on Jewish authorities. [. . .]

REGENERATION

We cannot believe, with Max Nordau, that such signs as we see of degeneration spring from moral and intellectual weakness. In the external circumstances, we find sufficient cause for far more demoralisation than actually exists; and the Germans, taken as individuals, show themselves to possess plenty of those mental and moral qualities which are the only possible foundations of a healthy State. They bear witness to the fact that, despite unfavourable outward circumstances, the race is not decaying; and that the present corruption and demoralisation may be decay only of one stage of human development, from which in obedience to some strong impulse a new regenerating era may arise. [. . .]

In every country there are numbers of people striving and hoping to bring about a better state of things, even at the cost and sacrifice of some of the leading features of our civilization. There is a mass of evidence, including those peculiar features of modern society, on which Max Nordau has dwelt so largely, showing that a deep unrest has taken hold of humanity. The feeling is not only that we are moving in a wrong position, but that we are moving in a wrong direction. The general fear is not that degeneration has set in, but that, moving on the road that we do, we cannot escape it.

The most striking characteristic of our time is that in no nation do we find, on either side of the Atlantic, any distinct indication of the road which can lead us past the Slough of Despond. The moral state of the civilized world is like a nation preparing for revolt against a tyrant: gloomy, discontented, and excited men are encouraging one another with secret signs and pass-words, mustering and drilling in secret places, to be ready for action, but without any trustworthy leaders, without any plans for the future, without even any tactics for the first struggle. In some countries the cry is for leaders; but the old faith that the situations will bring out the men seems to have been utterly falsified: for everywhere mediocrity, prejudice, and corruption, hold the helm. The cry in England and other countries is not for leaders, but for more light. We want a higher philosophy, nobler arts, a loftier literature, sounder principles of legislation, a purer religion.

No nation holds a higher responsibility than the English. Its vast possessions all over the globe, its financial and commercial supremacy, its ethical influence over all the English-speaking countries, marks it out as the standard-bearer of civilization. Nothing great can happen among us without re-echoing in the remotest corners of the earth, and any step onward taken by us will send a thrill throughout humanity. Degenerate Englishmen may still wish to meekly follow other nations, but our mission is to be the practical, energetic, daring pioneers heading the march of progress. By using its great power and influence, the British nation can render invaluable service to humanity in the present crisis. On

England must therefore rest our hopes for the practical solution of the grave questions on which progress and retrogression depend. From England alone can proceed that electrifying impulse of which the bewildered nations stand in need, that they may marshal the forces and focus the goal of progress.

In our political circles, in the ranks of literature, and throughout all the strata of society, there are already unmistakable signs that the period of scepticism, selfishness, and rant will end with the century; that scientific superstition and sickly Collectivist chimeras are doomed; and that the nation is sternly entering upon the mission of leading humanity towards good laws and intitutions based on liberty, and thus inaugurating a universal movement which by its glorious results shall demonstrate that the alarming symptoms of degeneration, revealed by the psychologists, are the first symptoms of regeneration.

5   from William James, review of *Degeneration* by Max Nordau (1895)

A pathological book on a pathological subject. If one were to apply Herr Nordau's method to the description of his own person, one could hardly help writing him down as a degenerate of the worst sort. He is a 'graphomaniac'; a misanthrope and a 'misoneoist' a 'coprolalic' ('idiot,' 'imbecile' are his mildest terms of endearment); an 'erotomaniac' of the prudish sort, haunted by horror of other people's sexuality; an *obsédé*, pursued without respite by images of odious works of art; a 'megalomaniac' of the arrogant and insulting type; and, finally, a victim of insane delusions about a conspiracy of hysterics and degenerates menacing the moral world with destruction unless the sound-minded speedily arm and organize in its defence. Add to this equipment the earnestness of the gloomily insane, and their complete inability to see a joke (pages of heavy invective against Oscar Wilde's epigrams!) and one gets a not altogether consoling diagnosis of Herr Nordau's case. On the other side, it must be admitted that he is really learned, not only in contemporary German, French and English *belles lettres*, but in the literature of neurological medicine as well, and that many of his objects by whose odiousness his imagination is afflicted, Parisian 'pornographic' novels are loathsome indeed. When, however, hardly a contemporary name, however great, escapes his abuse, and the course over which he runs-a-muck lies through Wagner, Tolstoi, Ruskin, Burne-Jones, Rossetti, Zola, Ibsen, and Nietzsche, as well as through Baudelaire and his descendants, it must be admitted that his volumes are little more than a pathological 'document' on an enormous scale, and an exhibition in minute detail of an individual's temperamental restrictions in the way of enjoying art.

---

6   from George Bernard Shaw, *The Sanity of Art: An Exposure of the Current Nonsense About Artists Being Degenerate* (1895/1908)

[. . .] After this long preamble, you will have no difficulty in understanding the sort of book Nordau has written. Imagine a huge volume, stuffed with the most slashing of the criticisms which were hurled at the Impressionists, the Tone Poets, and the philosophers and dramatists of the Schopenhauerian revival, before these movements had reached the point at which it began to require some real courage to attack them. Imagine a rehash not only of the newspaper criticisms of this period, but of all its little parasitic paragraphs of small-talk and scandal, from the long-forgotten jibes against Oscar Wilde's momentary attempt to bring knee-breeches into fashion years ago, to the latest scurrilities about 'the New Woman.' Imagine the general staleness and occasional putrescence of this mess disguised by a dressing of the terminology invented by Krafft-Ebing, Lombroso, and all the latest specialists in madness and crime, to describe the artistic faculties and propensities as they operate in the insane. Imagine all this done by a man who is a vigorous and capable journalist, shrewd enough to see that there is a good opening for a big reactionary book as a relief to the Wagner and Ibsen booms, bold enough to let himself go without respect to persons or reputations, lucky enough to be a stronger, clearer-headed man than ninety-nine out of a hundred of his critics, besides having a keener interest in science: a born theorist, reasoner, and busybody; therefore able, without insight, or even any remarkable intensive industry (he is, like most Germans, extensively industrious to an appalling degree), to produce a book which has made a very considerable impression on the artistic ignorance of Europe and America. For he says a thing as if he meant it; he holds superficial ideas obstinately, and sees them clearly; and his mind works so impetuously that it is a pleasure to watch it—for a while. All the same, he is the dupe of a theory which would hardly impose on one of those gamblers who have a system or martingale founded on a solid rock of algebra, by which they can infallibly break the bank at Monte Carlo. 'Psychiatry' takes the place of algebra in Nordau's martingale.

    This theory of his is, at bottom, nothing but the familiar delusion of the used-up man that the world is going to the dogs. But Nordau is too clever to be driven back on ready-made mistakes: he makes them for himself in his own way. He appeals to the prodigious extension of the quantity of business a single man can transact through the modern machinery of social intercourse: the railway, the telegraph and telephone, the post, and so forth. He gives appalling statistics of the increase of railway mileage and shipping, of the number of letters written per head of the population, of the newspapers which tell us things (mostly lies) of which we used to know nothing. 'In the last fifty years,' he says, 'the population of Europe has not doubled, whereas the sum of its labours has increased tenfold: in part, even fiftyfold. Every civilized man furnishes, at the present time, from five to twenty-five times as much work as was demanded of him half a century ago.' Then follow more statistics of 'the constant increase of crime, madness, and suicide,' of increases in mortality from diseases of the nerves and heart, of increased consumption of stimulants, of new nervous diseases like 'railway spine and railway brain,' with the general moral that we are all suffering from exhaustion, and that symptoms of degeneracy are visible in all directions, culminating at various points in such hysterical horrors as Wagner's music, Ibsen's dramas, Manet's pictures, Tolstoy's novels, Whitman's poetry, Dr Jaeger's woollen clothing, vegetarianism, scepticism as to vivisection and vaccination, and, in short, everything that Dr. Nordau does not happen to approve of. [. . .]

He is so utterly mad on the subject of degeneration that he finds the symptoms of it in the loftiest geniuses as plainly as in the lowliest jailbirds, the exceptions being himself, Lombroso, Krafft-Ebing, Dr. Maudsley,[11] Goethe, Shakespear, and Beethoven. Perhaps he would have dwelt on a case so convenient in many ways for his theory as Coleridge but that it would spoil the connection between degeneration and 'railway spine.' If a man's senses are acute, he is degenerate, hyperaesthesia having been observed in asylums. If they are dull, he is degenerate, anaesthesia being the stigma of the craziness which made old women confess to witchcraft. If he is particular as to what he wears, he is degenerate: silk dressing-gowns and knee-breeches are grave symptoms, and woollen shirts conclusive. If he is negligent in these matters, clearly he is inattentive and therefore degenerate. If he drinks, he is neurotic: if he is a vegetarian and teetotaller, let him be locked up at once. If he lives an evil life, that fact condemns him without further words: if on the other hand his conduct is irreproachable, he is a wretched 'mattoid,' incapable of the will and courage to realize his vicious propensities in action. If he writes verse, he is afflicted with echolalia; if he writes prose, he is a graphomaniac; if in his books he is tenacious of his ideas, he is obsessed; if not, he is 'amorphous' and 'inattentive.' Wagner, as we have seen, contrived to be both obsessed and inattentive, as might be expected from one who was 'himself alone charged with a greater abundance of degeneration than all the other degenerates put together.' And so on and so forth.

---

[11] Henry Maudsley (1835–1918) was one of the most prominent adherents of degeneration in the psychology profession, and an important figure in institutional psychiatry (there is still a Maudsley Hospital in south London). His books, which include *Body and Mind* (1873), *Body and Will* (1883), and *The Pathology of Mind* (1895), argue the inevitability of degenerative decline.

There is, however, one sort of mental weakness, common among men who take to science, as so many people take to art, without the necessary brain power, which Nordau, with amusing unconsciousness of himself, has omitted. I mean the weakness of the man who, when his theory works out into a flagrant contradiction of the facts, concludes 'So much the worse for the facts: let them be altered,' instead of 'So much the worse for my theory.' What in the name of common-sense is the value of a theory which identifies Ibsen, Wagner, Tolstoy, Ruskin, and Victor Hugo with the refuse of our prisons and lunatic asylums? What is to be said of the state of mind of an inveterate pamphleteer and journalist who, instead of accepting that identification as a *reductio ad absurdum* of the theory, desperately sets to work to prove it by pointing out that there are numerous resemblances; that they all have heads and bodies, appetites, aberrations, whims, weaknesses, asymmetrical features, erotic impulses, fallible judgments, and the like common properties, not merely of all human beings, but all vertebrate organisms. Take Nordau's own list: 'vague and incoherent thought, the tyranny of the association of ideas, the presence of obsessions, erotic excitability, religious enthusiasm, feebleness of perception, will, memory, and judgment, as well as inattention and instability.' Is there a single man capable of understanding these terms who will not plead guilty to some experience of all of them, especially when he is accused vaguely and unscientifically, without any statement of the subject, or the moment, or the circumstances to which the accusation refers, or any attempt to fix a standard of sanity? [. . .]

And now, my dear Tucker, I have told you as much about Nordau's book as it is worth. In a country where art was really known to the people, instead of being merely read about, it would not be necessary to spend three lines on such a work. But in England, where nothing but superstitious awe and self-mistrust prevents most men from thinking about art as Nordau boldly speaks about it; where to have a sense of art is to be one in a thousand, the other nine hundred and ninety-nine being either Philistine voluptuaries or Calvinistic anti-voluptuaries, it is useless to pretend that Nordau's errors will be self-evident. Already we have native writers, without half his cleverness or energy of expression, clumsily imitating his sham-scientific vivisection in their attacks on artists whose work they happen to dislike.

EDITORS' NOTES

1. Edwin Ray Lankester (1847–1929) was educated in Cambridge in Natural Sciences, and was Professor of Zoology at University College, London from 1874 to 1891. A Fellow of Royal Society (1875), and director of the Natural History section of the

British Museum (1898–1907, for which he was knighted), Lankester was a prominent proponent of scientific naturalism (see Chapter 9), and a committed follower of Darwin's theories of evolution. He wrote a sequence of popular science books, including *Science from an Easy Chair* (1908). A vigorous campaigner, he took up a private prosecution with Horatio Bryan Donkin (see Chapter 10) against a spiritualist in 1876, considering such beliefs an offence to common scientific sense. 'Degeneration' was first delivered as a lecture to the British Association for the Advancement of Science in 1879—it received only a lukewarm reaction in *Nature*.

2. H. G. Wells (1866–1946). Journalist, novelist, and political thinker, who exerted an enormous influence on British cultural life up to the Second World War. From an impoverished lower-middle-class family, he was an apprentice before attending the Normal School of Science in South Kensington. He studied briefly under T. H. Huxley (see Chapter 9). He did not complete his studies, but his thought was subsequently suffused with Darwinian biological notions. He was a journalist and reviewer from 1890, gaining fame for *The Time Machine* (1895), a text which plays out very precisely a futurological vision of racial degeneration as a product of the social divisions of the 1890s. This 'scientific romance' was rapidly followed by a series of fictions which help define the nascent genre of science fiction. From 1901 his work combined social-political essays with more realist, didactic fiction.

3. Max Nordau (1849–1923). From a Hungarian Jewish family (he changed his surname from Südfeldt—'southern field'—to Nordau—'northern meadow'), he trained as a doctor in Paris in the 1880s before becoming a journalist. *Degeneration*, when published in English in 1895, was a sensation for a short season, and ironically helped crystallize the 'decadent' and 'modernist' movements in European culture more than any other text of the period. The book also marked the end of the first phase of Nordau's career. In 1896 he covered the trial of the Jewish cavalry officer, Dreyfus, in France, a case which exposed the extensive institutional anti-Semitism of French life. Nordau became an important Zionist, campaigning for a Jewish homeland in Palestine.

4. *Regeneration* was published anonymously; the University of London Library catalogue ascribes it to Egmont Hake. Hake was probably best known for editing the last journals of the great imperialist hero General Gordon in 1885 (see Chapter 6). He also wrote on economics (*Free Trade in Capital*, 1890) and on poverty and hygiene in London (*Suffering London*, 1892). *Regeneration* was merely the most substantial of many ripostes to Nordau's work, commonly deemed to display the very manias it aimed to classify.

5. William James (1842–1910). Eldest brother of the novelist Henry James. Like Henry and their invalid sister Alice, William suffered from delicate health throughout his life. A peripatetic European education led to his first career choice as a painter in 1860; he abandoned this for science at Harvard University in 1861. He went to Harvard Medical School in 1864, although a sequence of illnesses meant his studies were not completed until 1869, after which he collapsed for three years. He lectured in physiology at Harvard from 1873, eventually becoming Professor of Philosophy in 1885. He went on to produce the enormously influential *Principles of Psychology* (1890), which

is still in print (see Chapter 10). He was at the centre of developing the distinctively American philosophy of pragmatism.

6. George Bernard Shaw (1856–1950). Playwright, novelist, socialist, and freethinker, whose career as a critic in the 1880s and 1890s exerted an enormous influence on the fin de siècle. Shaw had written *The Quintessence of Ibsenism* in 1891, and since Ibsen was a central degenerate in Max Nordau's book, Shaw's riposte was published quickly. It originally appeared in the anarchist paper *Liberty* in 1895, in the form of a letter to its editor, Benjamin Tucker. In the introduction to its revised form in 1908, Shaw commented that 'There was a brisk sale of copies [of *Liberty*] in London among the cognoscenti. And Degeneration was never heard of again.' The 1908 pamphlet version of the essay was prompted by Holbrook Jackson (author of *The Eighteen Nineties*), who, with A. R. Orage, had taken over the journal *The New Age*, and wished to launch their editorship with a suitably polemical bang. See also the Editors' Note on Shaw at the end of Chapter 7.

2

OUTCAST LONDON

The literature of social exploration flourished in the second half of the nineteenth century, led by Henry Mayhew's forays into areas of London unknown to all but their inhabitants. *London Labour and the London Poor* (1851), first published serially in the *Morning Chronicle*, presented Mayhew's excursions into London's more squalid recesses as a journey into an 'other' country, to districts populated by a mêlée of deprived, exotic, and sometimes savage peoples. Such a literature was given a new impetus from the 1880s for a number of interrelated reasons. First, the economic stability which is generally accepted as characterizing the 1850s to 1870s was perceived to have come to an abrupt end in 1880s Britain; a renewed onset of the economic crisis and incipient social collapse which distinguished the 'Hungry '30s and '40s' brought with it a sense of political urgency, a desire to confront poverty in all its horror. The second factor in the growth of social exploration writing was the rise of what became known in the twentieth century as the modern mass media, namely the tabloid press; the rapid growth in literacy in the second half of the nineteenth century, an indirect result of the Industrial Revolution, created an expanding pool of newspaper readers which eagerly lapped up sensationalist accounts of urban poverty and moral squalor. The third most significant influence on the literature of social exploration was the heightened awareness of Britain's imperialist project which was a phenomenon of the fin de siècle: the death of General Gordon in Khartoum, in 1885, widely publicized and lamented (see Chapter 6), instilled in the British cultural imagination a fear that imperialism's heyday might turn out to be short-lived; Henry Stanley's contemporaneous adventures in Africa provided a counterbalance to such fears, reassuring the imperial nation that British heroes could venture into unknown lands and return triumphant.

It was the appeal of the adventurer into unknown territories which underpinned the literature of social exploration, the author of such literature providing the reader with the vicarious thrill of plunging into the nation's hinterlands. There is a tension in this body of writing between a genuine desire to awaken Britain to the plight of its poor and a simultaneous impetus to write good journalistic matter. The former is uppermost in *The Bitter Cry of Outcast London* (1883), which pleaded with its readers to act to rescue the denizens of London's most sordid slumlands; none the less, having been published as a penny pamphlet, it caused an immediate sensation and was much publicized by W. T. Stead's *Pall Mall Gazette*. Such popularization had the benefit of influencing large numbers of readers: Mearns's pamphlet has been credited by some as a major influence on the setting up of the Royal Commission on the Housing of the Working Classes (1884–5). More sensational still was Stead's notorious 'Maiden Tribute of Modern Babylon' which provided his *Pall Mall Gazette* with the popular publishing coup of the year and, like Mearns's pamphlet, probably influenced the direction of legislation: the Criminal Law Amendment Act of 1885 raised the age of consent for girls from 13 to 16 and allowed for the police regulation of brothels. Stead, though, had to pay a price for the publicity that his lurid accounts of child prostitution brought him; he was arrested and imprisoned for three months for procuring a virgin, an act he claimed he undertook simply to prove that it could readily be done. Charles Booth's *Life and Labour of the People in London*, totalling seventeen volumes and produced between 1889 and 1903, was an altogether more sober and weighty project, providing a statistical methodology for modern social science. Firmly committed to the objectivity of scientific analysis, Booth's empiricism by no means excludes a sympathy for his subjects. He was aware, all the same, that the methodology he was developing was at least as important as the conclusions he came to about London's labourers. William Booth's moral mission is much more in evidence in *In Darkest England and the Way Out* (1890). Booth, the founder of the Salvation Army, realized that his religious campaign to convert moribund souls could not succeed unless combined with attempts to tackle poverty. Using the analogy of Stanley's 'Darkest Africa', and advocating the creation of work colonies both at home and abroad, Booth's crusading style is much influenced by Stead's journalistic technique (Stead in fact helped Booth to write his tract).

Secondary reading: Dyos and Wolff; Nord; Keating, *Into Unknown England*; Ledger, 'In Darkest England'; Roy Porter; G. S. Jones; Walkowitz, *City of Dreadful Delight* and *Prostitution and Victorian Society*.

1   from Andrew Mearns and others, *The Bitter*
Cry of Outcast London: An Inquiry into the Condition
of the Abject Poor (1883)

There is no more hopeful sign in the Christian Church of today than the increased attention which is being given by it to the poor and outcast classes of society. Of these it has never been wholly neglectful, if it had it would have ceased to be Christian. But it has, as yet, only imperfectly realized and fulfilled its mission to the poor. Until recently it has contented itself with sustaining some outside organizations, which have charged themselves with this special function, or what is worse, has left the matter to individuals or to little bands of Christians having no organization. For the rest it has been satisfied with a superficial and inadequate district visitation, with the more or less indiscriminate distribution of material charities, and with opening a few rooms here and there into which the poorer people have been gathered, and by which a few have been rescued. All this is good in its way and has done good; but by all only the merest edge of the great dark region of poverty, misery, squalor and immorality has been touched. We are not losing sight of the London City Mission, whose agents are everywhere, and whose noble work our investigations have led us to value more than ever, but after all has been done the churches are making the discovery that seething in the very centre of our great cities, concealed by the thinnest crust of civilization and decency, is a vast mass of moral corruption, of heart-breaking misery and absolute godlessness, and that scarcely anything has been done to take into this awful slough the only influences that can purify or remove it.

Whilst we have been building our churches and solacing ourselves with our religion and dreaming that the millennium was coming, the poor have been growing poorer, the wretched more miserable, and the immoral more corrupt; the gulf has been daily widening which separates the lowest classes of the community from our churches and chapels, and from all decency and civilization. [. . .] We must face the facts; and these compel the conviction that THIS TERRIBLE FLOOD OF SIN AND MISERY IS GAINING UPON US. It is rising every day. This statement is made as the result of a long, patient and sober inquiry, undertaken for the purpose of discovering the actual state of the case and the remedial action most likely to be effective. [. . .]

Two cautions it is important to bear in mind. First, the information given does not refer to selected cases. It simply reveals a state of things which is found in house after house, court after court, street after street. Secondly, there has been absolutely no exaggeration. It is a plain recital of plain facts. [. . .]

NON-ATTENDANCE AT WORSHIP

It is perhaps scarcely necessary to say of the hundreds of thousands who compose the class referred to, that very few attend any place of worship. It is a very tame thing to say, and a very little thing compared with what must follow, but it is needful to a proper statement of our case. Before going to the lower depths, where our investigations were principally carried on, we find in the neighbourhood of Old Ford,[1] in 147 consecutive houses, inhabited for the most part by the respectable working class, 212 families, 118 of which never, under any circumstances, attend a place of worship. Out of 2,290 persons living in consecutive houses at Bow Common,[2] only 88 adults and 47 children ever attend, and as 64 of these are connected with one Mission Hall, only 24 out of the entire number worship elsewhere [. . .] indeed, with the exception of a very small proportion, the idea of going has never dawned upon these people. And who can wonder? Think of

THE CONDITION IN WHICH THEY LIVE

We do not say the condition of their homes, for how can those places be called homes, compared with which the lair of a wild beast would be a comfortable and healthy spot? Few who will read these pages have any conception of what these pestilential human rookeries are, where tens of thousands are crowded together amidst horrors which call to mind what we have heard of the middle passage of the slave ship. To get into them you have to penetrate courts reeking with poisonous and malodorous gases arising from accumulations of sewage and refuse scattered in all directions and often flowing beneath your feet; courts, many of them which the sun never penetrates, which are never visited by a breath of fresh air, and which rarely know the virtues of a drop of cleansing water. You have to ascend rotten staircases, which threaten to give way beneath every step, and which, in some places, have already broken down, leaving gaps that imperil the limbs and lives of the unwary. You have to grope your way along dark and filthy passages swarming with vermin. Then, if you are not driven back by the intolerable stench, you may gain admittance to the dens in which these thousands of beings who belong, as much as you, to the race for whom Christ died, herd together. Have you pitied the poor creatures who sleep under railway arches, in carts or casks, or under any shelter which they can find in the open air? You will see that they are to be envied in comparison with those whose lot it is to seek refuge here. Eight feet square—that is about the average size of very many of these

---

[1] Old Ford is an area in the East End of London, with Hackney and Homerton to the north and Mile End to the south.

[2] Another district in London's East End, Bow Common is bounded by Bow to the north and Limehouse to the south.

rooms. Walls and ceiling are black with the accretions of filth which have gathered upon them through long years of neglect. It is exuding through cracks in the boards overhead; it is running down the walls; it is everywhere. What goes by the name of a window is half of it stuffed with rags or covered by boards to keep out wind and rain; the rest is so begrimed and obscured that scarcely can light enter or anything be seen outside. Should you have ascended to the attic, where at least some approach to fresh air might be expected to enter from open or broken window, you look out upon the roofs and ledges of lower tenements, and discover that the sickly air which finds its way into the room has to pass over the putrefying carcasses of dead cats or birds, or viler abominations still. The buildings are in such miserable repair as to suggest the thought that if the wind could only reach them they would soon be toppling about the heads of their occupants. As to furniture—you may perchance discover a broken chair, the tottering relics of an old bedstead, or the mere fragment of a table; but more commonly you will find rude substitutes for these things in the shape of rough boards resting upon bricks, an old hamper or box turned upside down, or more frequently still, nothing but rubbish and rags.

Every room in these rotten and reeking tenements houses a family, often two. In one cellar a sanitary inspector reports finding a father, mother, three children, and four pigs! In another room a missionary found a man ill with small-pox, his wife just recovering from her eighth confinement, and the children running about half naked and covered with dirt. Here are seven people living in one underground kitchen, and a little dead child lying in the same room. Elsewhere is a poor widow, her three children, and a child who had been dead thirteen days. Her husband, who was a cabman, had shortly before committed suicide. Here lives a widow and her six children, including one daughter of 29, another of 21, and a son of 27 [. . .]

Who can wonder that little children taken from these hovels to the hospital cry, when they are well, through dread of being sent back to their former misery? Who can wonder that young girls wander off into a life of immorality, which promises release from such conditions? Who can wonder that the public-house is 'the Elysian field of the tired toiler?'

IMMORALITY

is but the natural outcome of conditions like these. 'Marriage,' it has been said, 'as an institution, is not fashionable in these districts.' And this is only the bare truth. Ask if the men and women living together in these rookeries are married, and your simplicity will cause a smile. Nobody knows. Nobody cares. Nobody expects that they are. In exceptional cases only could your question be answered in the affirmative. Incest is common; and no form of vice and sensuality causes surprise or attracts attention. Those who appear to be married are often separated by a mere quarrel, and they do not hesitate to form similar companionships immediately. One man was pointed out who for some years had lived with a woman, the mother of his three children. She died and in less than a week he had taken another woman in her place [. . .] Entire courts are filled with thieves, prostitutes and liberated convicts. In one street are 35 houses, 32 of which are known to be brothels. In another district are 43 of these houses, and 428 fallen women and girls, many of them not more than 12 years of age. A neighbourhood whose population is returned at 10,100, contains 400 who follow this immoral traffic, their ages varying from 13 to 50; and of the moral degradation of the people, some idea may be formed from an incident which was brought to our notice. An East-end missionary rescued a young girl from an immoral life, and obtained for her a situation with people who were going abroad. He saw her to Southampton, and on his return was violently abused by the girl's grandmother, who had the sympathy of her neighbours, for having taken away from a poor old woman her means of subsistence.

The misery and sin caused by drink in these districts have often been told, but these horrors can never be set forth either by pen or artist's pencil. In the district of Euston Road[3] is one public-house to every 100 people, counting men, women and children. Immediately around our chapel in Orange Street, Leicester Square,[4] are 100 gin-palaces, most of them very large; and these districts are but samples of what exists in all the localities which we have investigated. [. . .]

Another difficulty with which we have to contend, and one in large measure the cause of what we have described, is the

POVERTY

of these miserable outcasts. The poverty, we mean, of those who try to live honestly; for notwithstanding the sickening revelations of immorality which have been disclosed to us, those who endeavour to earn their bread by honest work far outnumber the dishonest. And it is to their infinite credit that it should be so, considering that they are daily face to face with the contrast between their wretched earnings and those which are the produce of sin. A child seven years old is known easily to make 10s. 6d. a week by thieving, but what can he earn by such work as match-box making, for which 24d. a week gross is paid, the maker having to find his own fire for drying the boxes, and his own paste and string? Before he can gain

---

[3] Euston Road is a major thoroughfare running from west to east from Regent's Park to King's Cross station. Somers Town, to the north of Euston Road, was an increasingly impoverished area in the 19th century, due to the building and extension of Euston station (in 1837) and King's Cross station (in 1852).

[4] Leicester Square was (and remains) part of London's theatre land in the West End, where poverty and prostitution existed cheek by jowl with affluence. The area targeted by Mrs Ormiston Chant for social purity campaigns (see Ch. 3).

as much as the young thief he must make 56 gross of match-boxes a week, or 1,296 a day. It is needless to say that this is impossible, for even adults can rarely make more than an average of half that number. How long then must the little hands toil before they can earn the price of the scantiest meal! Women, for the work of trousers finishing (i.e., sewing in linings, making button-holes and stitching on the buttons) receive 2½ d. a pair, and have to find their own thread. We ask a woman who is making tweed trousers, how much she can earn in a day, and are told one shilling. But what does a day mean to this poor soul? Seventeen hours! From five in the morning to ten at night—no pause for meals. She eats her crust and drinks a little tea as she works, making in very truth, with her needle and thread, not her living only, but her shroud. [. . .]

Amidst such poverty and squalor it is inevitable that one should be constantly confronted with scenes of

HEART-BREAKING MISERY

misery so pitiful that men whose daily duty it has been for years to go in and out amongst these outcasts, and to be intimately acquainted with their sufferings, and who might, therefore, be supposed to regard with comparatively little feeling that which would overwhelm an unaccustomed spectator, sometimes come away from their visits so oppressed in spirit and absorbed in painful thought, that they know not whither they are going. [. . .] Who can even imagine the suffering which lies behind a case like the following? A poor woman in an advanced stage of consumption, reduced almost to a skeleton, lives in a single room with a drunken husband and five children. When visited she was eating a few green peas. The children were gone to gather some sticks wherewith a fire might be made to boil four potatoes which were lying on the table, and which would constitute the family dinner for the day. [. . .]

WHAT IT IS PROPOSED TO DO

That something needs to be done for this pitiable outcast population must be evident to all who have read these particulars as to their condition—at least, to all who believe them. We are quite prepared for incredulity. Even what we have indicated seems all too terrible to be true. But we have sketched only in faintest outline. Far more vivid must be our colours, deeper and darker far the shades, if we are to present a truthful picture of 'Outcast London' [. . .] Incredulity is not the only difficulty in the way of stirring up Christian people to help. Despair of success in any such undertaking may paralyse many. We shall be pointed to the fact that without State interference nothing effectual can be accomplished upon any large scale.

The State must make short work of this iniquitous traffic, and secure for the poorest the rights of citizenship; the right to live in something better than fever dens; the right to live as something better than the uncleanest of brute beasts. This must be done before the Christian missionary can have much chance with them. But because we cannot do all we wish, are we to do nothing? Even as things are something can be accomplished. Is no lifeboat to put out and no life-belt to be thrown because only half-a-dozen out of the perishing hundreds can be saved from the wreck? [. . .]

We shall not wonder if some, shuddering at the revolting spectacle, try to persuade themselves that such things cannot be in Christian England, and that what they have looked upon is some dark vision conjured by a morbid pity and a desponding faith. To such we can only say, Will you venture to come with us and see for yourselves the ghastly reality? Others, looking on, will believe, and pity, and despair. But another vision will be seen by many, and in this lies our hope—a vision of Him who had 'compassion upon the multitude because they were as sheep having no shepherd,' looking with Divine pity in His eyes, over this outcast London, and then turning to the consecrated host of His Church with the appeal, 'Whom shall we send and who will go for us?'

---

2   from W. T. Stead, 'The Maiden Tribute of
                  Modern Babylon' (1885)

'WE BID YOU BE OF HOPE'

The report of our Secret Commission will be read to-day with a shuddering horror that will thrill throughout the world. After this awful picture of the crimes at present committed as it were under the very aegis of the law has been fully unfolded before the eyes of the public, we do not doubt that the House of Commons will find time to raise the age during which English girls are protected from inexpiable wrong. The evidence which we shall publish this week leaves no room for doubt—first, as to the reality of the crimes against which the Amendment Bill[5] is directed, and secondly, as to the efficacy of the protection extended by raising

---

[5] The Criminal Law Amendment Act was eventually passed in August 1885, just over a month after Stead's articles had been published. 'Carnal knowledge' of girls under the age of 13 became a felony, with five years' imprisonment the maximum penalty. Sex with a girl between 13 and 16 became a misdemeanour, with two years in prison the maximum penalty. Brothel-owners were subject to the same penalties for assisting such crimes. Clause 11 of the bill, added at a late stage by the radical MP Henry Labouchère, read: 'Any male person who, in public or in private, commits, or is party to the commission of, procures or attempts to procure the commission by any male person of, any act of gross indecency with another male person, shall be guilty of a misdemeanour.' This anomalous clause, in an act 'for the Protection of Women and Girls', was the article under which Oscar Wilde was prosecuted in 1895.

the age of consent. When the report is published, the case for the bill will be complete, and we do not believe that members on the eve of a general election will refuse to consider the bill protecting the daughters of the poor, which even the House of Lords has in three consecutive years declared to be imperatively necessary.

This, however, is but one, and that one of the smallest, of the considerations which justify the publication of the Report. The good it will do is manifest. These revelations, which we begin to publish today, cannot fail to touch the heart and rouse the conscience of the English people. Terrible as is the exposure, the very horror of it is an inspiration. It speaks not of leaden despair, but with a joyful promise of better things to come. [. . .]

THE MAIDEN TRIBUTE OF MODERN BABYLON—I

In ancient times, if we may believe the myths of Hellas, Athens, after a disastrous campaign, was compelled by her conqueror to send once every nine years a tribute to Crete of seven youths and seven maidens. The doomed fourteen, who were selected by lot amid the lamentations of the citizens, returned no more. The vessel that bore them to Crete unfurled black sails as the symbol of despair, and on arrival her passengers were flung into the famous Labyrinth of Daedalus, there to wander about blindly until such time as they were devoured by the Minotaur, a frightful monster, half man, half bull, the foul product of unnatural lust. 'The labyrinth was as large as a town and had countless courts and galleries. Those who entered it could never find their way out again. If they hurried from one to another of the numberless rooms looking for the entrance door, it was all in vain. They only became more hopelessly lost in the bewildering labyrinth, until at last they were devoured by the Minotaur.' Twice at each ninth year the Athenians paid the maiden tribute to King Minos, lamenting sorely the dire necessity of bowing to his iron law. When the third tribute came to be exacted, the distress of the city of the Violet Crown was insupportable. From the King's palace to the peasant's hamlet, everywhere were heard cries and groans and the choking sob of despair, until the whole air seemed to vibrate with the sorrow of an unutterable anguish. Then it was that the hero Theseus volunteered to be among those who drew the black balls from the brazen urn of destiny, and the story of his self-sacrifice, his victory, and his triumphant return is among the most familiar of the tales which since the childhood of the world have kindled the imagination and fired the heart of the human race. [. . .]

The fact that the Athenians should have taken so bitterly to heart the paltry maiden tribute that once in nine years they had to pay to the Minotaur seems incredible, almost inconceivable. This very night in London, and every night, year in and year out, not seven maidens only, but many times seven, selected almost as much by chance as those who in the Athenian market-place drew lots as to which should be flung into the Cretan labyrinth, will be offered up as the Maiden Tribute of Modern Babylon. Maidens they were this morning dawned, but to-night their ruin will be accomplished, and to-morrow they will find themselves within the portals of the maze of London brotheldom. Within that labyrinth wander, like lost souls, the vast host of London prostitutes, whose numbers no man can compute, but who are probably not much below 50,000 strong. Many, no doubt, who venture but a little way within the maze make their escape. But multitudes are swept irresistibly on and on to be destroyed in due season, to give place to others, who will also share their doom. The maw of the London Minotaur is insatiable, and none that go into the secret recesses of his lair return again. After some years' dolorous wandering in this palace of despair [. . .] most of the ensnared to-night will perish, some of them in horrible torture. Yet, so far from this great city being convulsed with woe, London cares for none of these things, and the cultured man of the world, the heir of all the ages, the ultimate product of a long series of civilisations and religions, will shrug his shoulders in scorn at the folly of any one who ventures in public print to raise even the mildest protest against a horror a thousand times more horrific than that which, in the youth of the world, haunted like a nightmare the imagination of mankind. Nevertheless, I have not yet lost faith in the heart and conscience of the English folk, the sturdy innate chivalry and right thinking of our common people; and although I am no vain dreamer of Utopias peopled solely by Sir Galahads and vestal virgins, I am not without hope that there may be some check placed upon this vast tribute of maidens, unwitting or unwilling, which is nightly levied in London by the vices of the rich upon the necessities of the poor. [. . .]

LIBERTY FOR VICE, REPRESSION FOR CRIME

To avoid all misapprehension as to the object with which I propose to set forth all the ghastly and criminal features of this infernal traffic, I wish to say emphatically at the outset that however strongly I may feel as to the imperative importance of morality and chastity, I do not ask for any police interference with the liberty of vice. I ask only for the repression of crime. Sexual immorality, however evil it may be in itself or in its consequences, must be dealt with not by the policeman but by the teacher, so long as the persons contracting are of full age, are perfectly free agents, and in their sin are guilty of no outrage on public morals. Let us by all means apply the sacred principles of free trade to trade in vice, and regulate the relations of the sexes by the higgling of the market and the liberty of private contract. Whatever may be my belief as to the reality and the importance of a transcendental theory of purity in the relations between man and woman, that is an affair for the moralist, not the legislature. So far from demanding any increased power for the police, I would rather incline to say to the police, 'hands off,' when they interfere arbitrarily with the ordinary operations of the maker of vice. But the more freely we permit to adults absolute liberty to dispose of their persons in accordance with the principles of private contract and free trade, the more stringent must be our precautions against the innumerable crimes which spring from vice, as vice itself springs from the impure imaginings of the heart of man. These crimes flourish on every side, unnoticed and unchecked—if indeed they are not absolutely encouraged by the law, as they are certainly practised by some legislators and winked at by many administrators of the law. To extirpate vice by Act of Parliament is impossible; but because we must leave vice free that is no reason why we should acquiesce helplessly in the perpetration of crime. And that crime of the most ruthless and abominable description is constantly and systematically practised in London without let or hindrance, I am in a position to prove from my own personal knowledge—a knowledge purchased at a cost of which I prefer not to speak. Those crimes may be roughly classified as follows:—

I.   The sale and purchase and violation of children.

II. The procuration of virgins.

III. The entrapping and ruin of women.

IV. The international slave trade in girls.

V.   Atrocities, brutalities and unnatural crimes.

That is what I call sexual criminality, as opposed to sexual immorality. It flourishes in all its branches on every side to an extent of which even those specially engaged in rescue work have but little idea. Those who are constantly engaged in its practice naturally deny its existence. But I speak of that which I do know, not from hearsay or rumour but of my own personal knowledge.

HOW THE FACTS WERE VERIFIED

When the Criminal Law Amendment Bill was talked out just before the defeat of the Ministry it became necessary to rouse public attention to the necessity for legislation on this painful subject. I undertook an investigation into the facts. The evidence taken before the House of Lords' Committee in 1882 was useful, but the facts were not up to date, and that duty—albeit with some reluctance—I resolutely undertook. For four weeks, aided by two or three coadjutors of whose devotion and self-sacrifice, combined with a rare instinct for investigation and a singular personal fearlessness, I cannot speak too highly, I have been enjoying the London Inferno. It has been a strange and unexampled experience. For a month I have oscillated between the noblest and the meanest of mankind, the saviours and the destroyers of their race, spending hours alternately in brothels and hospitals, in the streets and in refuges in the company of procuresses and of bishops.

London beneath the gas glare of its innumerable lamps became, not like Paris in 1795—'a naphtha lighted city of Dis'—but a resurrected and magnified City of the Plain, with all the vices of Gomorrah, daring the vengeance of long-suffering Heaven. It seemed a strange, inverted world, that in which I lived in those terrible weeks—the world of the streets and of the brothel. [. . .]

THE CONFESSIONS OF A BROTHEL-KEEPER

Here, for instance, is a statement made to me by a brothel-keeper, who formerly kept a noted house in the Mile-End road,[6] but who is now endeavouring to start life afresh as an honest man. I saw both him and the wife, herself a notorious prostitute whom he had married off the streets, where she had earned her living since she was fourteen:—

'Maids as you call them—fresh girls as we know them to the trade—are constantly in request, and a keeper who knows his business has his eyes open in all directions. His stock of girls is constantly getting used up, and needs replenishing, and he has to be on the alert for likely "marks" to keep up the reputation of his house. I have been in my time a good deal about the country on these errands. The getting of fresh girls takes time, but it is simple and easy enough when once you are in it. I have gone and courted girls in the country under all kinds of disguises, occasionally assuming the disguise of a parson, and made them believe that I intended to marry them, and so got them in my power to please a good customer. How is it done? Why, after courting my girl for a time, I propose to bring her to London to see the sights. I bring her up, take her here and there, giving her plenty to eat and drink—especially drink. I take her to the theatre, and usually contrive it that she loses her last train. By this time she is very tired, a little dazed with the drink and excitement, and very frightened at being left in town with no friends. I offer her lodgings for the night: she goes to bed in my house, and then the affair is managed. My client gets his maid, I get my £10 or £20 commission, and in the morning the girl, who has lost her character, and dare not go home, in all probability will do as the others do, and become one of my "marks"—that is, she will make her living in the streets, to the advantage of my house. The brothel-keeper's profit is first the commission down for the price of a maid, and secondly, the continuous profits of the addition of a newly seduced, attractive girl to his establishment. That is a fair sample case of the way in which we recruit. Another very simple mode of supplying maids is by breeding them. Many women who are on the streets have female children. They are worth keeping. When they get to be twelve or thirteen

---

[6] One of the poorest districts of London's East End.

they become merchantable. For a very likely "mark" of this kind, you may get as much as £20 or £40. I sent my own daughter out on the street from my own brothel. I know a couple of very fine little girls now who will be sold before very long. They are bred and trained for the life. They must take the first step sometime, and it is bad business not to make as much out of that as possible. Drunken parents often sell their children to brothel keepers. In the East-End you can always pick up as many fresh girls as you want. In one street in Dalston[7] you might buy a dozen. Sometimes the supply is in excess of the demand, and you have to seduce your maid yourself, or to employ someone else to do it, which is bad business in a double sense. There is a man called S— who a famous house used to employ to seduce young girls and make them fit for active service when there was no demand for maids and there was a demand for girls who had been seduced. But as a rule the number seduced ready to hand is ample, especially among very young children. Did I ever do anything in the way of recruiting? Yes, I remember one case very well. The girl, a likely "mark", was a simple country lass living at Horsham.[8] I had heard of her, and I went down to Horsham to see what I could do. Her parents believed that I was in regular business in London, and they were very glad when I proposed to engage their daughter. I brought her to town and made her a servant in our house. We petted her and made a good deal of her, gradually initiated her into the kind of life it was; then I sold her to a young gentleman for £15. When I say that I sold her, I meant that he gave me the gold and I gave him the girl, to do what he liked with. He took her away and seduced her. I believe he treated her rather well afterwards, but that was not my affair. She was his after he paid for her and took her away. If her parents had inquired I would have said that she had been a bad girl and run away with a young man. How could I help that? I once sold a girl twelve years old for £20 to a clergyman, who used to come to my house professedly to distribute tracts. The East is the great market for the children who are imported into West-end houses, or taken abroad wholesale when trade is brisk. I know of no East-End houses, having always lived at Dalston or thereabouts, but agents pass to and fro on the course of business. They receive the goods, depart and no questions are asked.

Mrs S., a famous procuress, has a mansion at —— which is one of the worst centres of the trade, with four other houses in other districts, one at St John's Wood. This lady, when she discovers ability, cultivates it—that is, if a comely young girl of fifteen falls into her net, with some intelligence, she is taught to read and write, and to play the piano.'

[7] An area on the fringes of the East End, sandwiched between Hackney to the east and Islington to the west.

[8] A market town in West Sussex, one of the prosperous 'Home Counties' newly accessible by railway.

THE LONDON SLAVE-MARKET

The brothel-keeper was a smart fellow, and had been a commercial traveller once, but drink had brought him down. Anxious to test the truth of his statement, I asked him through a trusty agent, if he would undertake to supply me in three days with a couple of fresh girls, maids, whose virginity would be attested by a doctor's certificate. At first he said that it would require a longer time. But on being pressed, and assured that money was no object, he said that he would make inquiries and see what could be done. In two days I received from the same confidential source an intimation that for £10 commission he would undertake to deliver to my chambers, or to any other spot which I might choose to select, two young girls, each with a doctor's certificate of the fact that she was a *virgo intacta*.[9] Hesitating to close with this offer, my agent received the following telegram:—'I think all right. I am with parties. Will tell you all to-morrow about twelve o'clock'. On calling H— said:—

[']I will undertake to deliver at your rooms within two days two children at your chambers. Both are the daughters of brothel-keepers whom I have known and dealt with, and the parents are willing to sell in both cases. I represented that they were intended for a rich old gentleman who had led a life of debauchery for years. I was suspected of baby-farming—that is, peaching, at first, and it required all my knowledge of the tricks of the trade to effect my purpose. However, after champagne and liquors, my old friend G—, M— Lane, Hackney,[10] agreed to hand me over her own child, a pretty girl of eleven, for £5, if she could get no more. The child was *virgo intacta*, so far as her mother knew. I then went to Mrs. N— of B— Street, Dalston (B— Street is a street of brothels from end to end). Mrs N— required little persuasion, but her price was higher. She would not part with her daughter under £8 or £10, as she was pretty and attractive, and a virgin, aged thirteen or so, who would probably fetch more in the open market. These two children I could deliver up within two days if the money was right. I would, on the same conditions, undertake to deliver half-a-dozen girls, ages varying from ten to thirteen, within a week or ten days.'

I did not deem it wise to carry the negotiations any further. The purchase price was to be paid on delivery, but it was to be returned if the girls were found to have been tampered with. [. . .]

---

[9]   Doctors were paid to confirm that the hymen remained 'intact' and that the girl was therefore guaranteed a virgin.

[10]   A district bordering London's East End, actually rather prosperous in the late 19th century (see Charles Booth's comments on it in section 'H' of 'The Eight Classes' on p. 44 below).

3   from Charles Booth, *Life and Labour of the People of London* (1889)

EAST LONDON: THE EIGHT CLASSES

The area dealt with [. . .] contains in all about 900,000 inhabitants. [. . .] The eight classes into which I have divided these people are:

A. The lowest class of occasional labourers, loafers and semi-criminals
B. Casual earnings—'very poor'
C. Intermittent earnings ⎫
D. Small regular earnings ⎭ together 'the poor'
E. Regular standard earnings—above the line of poverty
F. Higher class labour
G. Lower middle class
H. Upper middle class

The divisions indicated here by 'poor' and 'very poor' are necessarily arbitrary. By the word 'poor' I mean to describe those who have a sufficiently regular though bare income, such as 18s to 21s per week for a moderate family, and by 'very poor' those who from any cause fall much below this standard. The 'poor' are those whose means may be sufficient, but are barely sufficient, for decent independent life; the 'very poor' those whose means are insufficient for this according to the usual standard of life in this country. My 'poor' may be described as living under a struggle to obtain the necessaries of life and make both ends meet; while the 'very poor' live in a state of chronic want. It may be their own fault that this is so: that is another question; my first business is simply with the numbers who, from whatever cause, so live under conditions of poverty of destitution. [. . .]

A. The lowest class, which consists of some occasional labourers, street-sellers, loafers, criminals and semi-criminals, I put at 11,000, or 1 and a ¼ per cent of the population, but this is no more than a very rough estimate, as these people are beyond enumeration, and only a small proportion of them are on the School Board visitors' books. If I had been content to build up the total of this class from those of them who are parents of children at school in the same proportions as has been done with the other classes, the number indicated would not have greatly exceeded 3,000, but there is little regular family life among them and the numbers given in my tables are obtained by adding in an estimated number from inmates of common lodging houses, and from the lowest class of streets. With these ought to be counted the homeless outcasts who on any given night take shelter where they can and so may be supposed to be in part outside of any census. Those I have attempted to count consist mostly of casual labourers of low character, and their families, together with those in a similar way of life who pick up a living without labour of any kind. Their life is the life of savages, with vicissitudes of extreme hardship and occasional excess. Their food is of the coarsest description, and their only luxury is drink. It is not easy to say how they live; the living is picked up, and what is got is frequently shared; when they cannot find 3d for their night's lodging, unless favourably known to the deputy, they are turned out at night into the street, to return to the common kitchen in the morning. From these come the battered figures who slouch through the streets and play the beggar or the bully, or help to foul the record of the unemployed; these are the worst class of corner men who hang round the doors of public houses, the young men who spring forward on any chance to earn a copper, the ready materials for disorder when occasion serves. They render no useful service, they create no wealth: more often they destroy it. They degrade whatever they touch, and as individuals are perhaps incapable of improvement; they may be to some extent a necessary evil in every large city, but their numbers will be affected by the economical condition of the classes above them and by the discretion of 'the charitable world'; their way of life by the pressure of police supervision.

It is much to be desired and hoped that this class may become less hereditary in its character. There appears to be no doubt that it is now hereditary to a very considerable extent.[11] The children are the street arabs, and are to be found separated from the parents in pauper or industrial schools, and in such homes as Dr Barnardo's.[12] Some are in the Board schools, and more in ragged schools, and the remainder, who cannot be counted, and may still be numerous, are every year confined within narrowing bounds by the persistent pressure of the School Board and other agencies. [. . .]

Class B—Casual earnings—very poor—add up almost exactly to 100,000, or 11 and a $\frac{1}{4}$ per cent of the whole population. This number is made up of men, women and children in about the following proportions:

Married men	17,000
Their wives	17,000
Unmarried men	7,000
Widows	6,500
Unmarried women	5,000
Young persons, 15–20	9,500
Children	38,000
	100,000

[11] The elimination of this 'residuum' of barely human class by controlling their breeding was central to the project of eugenics: see the contributions of Pearson and Galton in Ch. 13.

[12] Thomas John Barnardo (1845–1905) founded the East End Mission for destitute children in 1867, as well as a number of homes in Greater London which became known as the 'Barnardo Homes'.

Widows or deserted women and their families bring a large contingent to this class, but its men are mostly [casual labourers]. [. . .] This classification cannot be made exact. These sections not only melt into each other by insensible degrees, but the only divisions which can be made are rather divisions of sentiment than of positive fact: the line between loafers and casual labourers is of this character, difficult to test, and not otherwise to be established; and the boundaries [. . .] are constantly fluctuating; for the casual labourer, besides being pressed on from below, when times are hard is also flooded from above; every class, even artisans and clerks, furnishing those who, failing to find a living in their own trade, compete at the dock gates for work. [. . .]

The labourers of class B do not, on the average, get as much as three days' work a week, but it is doubtful if many of them could or would work full time for long together if they had the opportunity. From whatever section Class B is drawn, except the sections of poor women, there will be found many of them who from shiftlessness, helplessness, idleness, or drink, are inevitably poor. The ideal of such persons is to work when they like and play when they like; these it is who are rightly called the 'leisure class' amongst the poor—leisure bounded very closely by the pressure of want, but habitual to the extent of second nature. They cannot stand the regularity and dulness of civilised existence, and find the excitement they need in the life of the streets, or at home as spectators of or participators in some highly coloured domestic scene. There is drunkenness amongst them, especially amongst the women; but drink is not their special luxury, as with the lowest class, nor is it their passion, as with a portion of those with higher wages and irregular but severe work. [. . .]

Class C—Intermittent earnings—numbering more nearly 75,000 or about 8 per cent of the population, are more than any others the victims of competition, and on them falls with particular severity the weight of recurrent depressions of trade. [. . .] Here may perhaps be found the most proper field for systematic charitable assistance; provided always some evidence of thrift is made the pre-condition or consequence of assistance. [. . .] Class C consists of men who usually work by the job, or who are in or out of work according to the season or the nature of their employment. This irregularity of employment may show itself in the week or in the year: stevedores and waterside porters may secure only one or two days' work in a week, whereas labourers in the building trades may get only eight or nine months in the year. [. . .] The great body of the labouring class (as distinguished from the skilled workmen) have a regular steady income, such as it is.

Some of the irregularly employed men earn very high wages, fully as high as those of the artisan class. These are men of great physical strength, working on coal or grain, or combining aptitude and practice with strength, as in handling timber. It is amongst such men, especially those carrying grain and coal, that the passion for drink is most developed. [. . .]

Besides those whose living depends on the handling of merchandise, there are in this section all the builders' labourers, and some others whose work is regulated by the seasons. With regard to these employments the periods of good and bad work are various, one trade being on while another is off; more goods to be handled, for instance, on the whole, in winter than in summer, against the stoppage of building in cold weather. I do not think, however, that one employment is dovetailed with another to any great extent; it would not be easy to arrange it, and most of the men make no effort of the kind. They take things as they come; work when they can get work in their own line, and otherwise go without, or, if actually hard up, try, almost hopelessly, for casual work. The more enterprising ones who fill up their time in some way which ekes out their bare earnings are the exceptions. [. . .] The pressure is also very severe where there are many young children: a man and his wife by themselves can get along, improvident or not, doing on very little when work fails; the children who have left school, if they live at home, readily keep themselves, and sometimes do even more. It is in the years when the elder children have not yet left school, while the younger ones are still a care to the mother at home, that the pressure of family life is most felt. [. . .]

I fear that the bulk of those whose earnings are irregular are wanting in ordinary prudence. Provident thrift, which lays by for tomorrow, is not a very hardy plant in England, and needs the regular payment of weekly wages to take root freely.

Class D—Small regular earnings, poor—are about 129,000, or nearly 14 and a ½ per cent of the population. It must not be understood that the whole of these have quite regular work; but only that the earnings are constant enough to be treated as a regular income, which is not the case with the earnings of class C. Of D and C together we have 203,000, and if this number is equally divided to represent those whose earnings are regular and irregular, which would be to place the standard of regularity a little higher than has been done in this inquiry, the result would be equal numbers of each grade of poverty—100,000 of B or casual, 100,000 of C or intermittent, and 100,000 of D or regular earnings, out of a total population of 900,000, or one-ninth of each grade. [. . .]

The men [. . .] are the better end of the casual dock and water-side labour, those having directly or indirectly a preference for employment. It includes also a number of labourers in the gas works whose employment falls short in summer but never entirely ceases. The rest of this section are the men who are in regular work all the year round at a wage not exceeding 21s a week. These are drawn from various sources, including in their numbers factory, dock, and warehouse labourers, carmen, messengers, porters, etc.: a few of each class. Some of these are recently married men, who will, after a longer period of service, rise into the next class; some are old and superannuated, semi-pensioners; but others are heads of families, and instances are to be met with (particularly among carmen) in which men have remained fifteen or twenty years at a stationary wage of 21s or even less, being in a comparatively comfortable position at the start, but getting poorer and poorer as their family increased, and improving again as their children became able to add their quota to the family income. In such cases the loss of elder children by marriage is sometimes looked upon with jealous disfavour.

Of the whole section none can be said to rise above poverty, unless by the earnings of the children, nor are many to be classed as very poor. What they have comes in regularly, and except in times of sickness in the family, actual want rarely presses, unless the wife drinks. As a general rule these men have a hard struggle to make ends meet, but they are, as a body, decent steady men, paying their way and bringing up their children respectably. The work they do demands little intelligence. [. . .]

E. Regular Standard Earnings. [. . .] A large proportion of the artisans and most other regular wage earners. I also include here, as having equal means, the best class of street sellers and general dealers, a large proportion of the small shopkeepers, the best off amongst the home manufacturers, and some of the small employers. This is by far the largest class of the population under review, adding up to 377,000, or over 42 per cent.

[It] contains all, not artisans or otherwise scheduled, who earn from 22s to 30s a week for regular work. There are some of them who, when wages are near the lower figure, or the families are large, are not lifted above the line of poverty; but few of them are very poor, and the bulk of this large section can, and do, lead independent lives, and possess fairly comfortable homes. As a rule the wives do not work, but the children all do: the boys commonly following the father (as is everywhere the case above the lowest classes), the girls taking to local trades, or going out to service. The men in this section are connected with almost every form of industry, and include in particular carmen, porters and messengers, warehousemen, permanent dock labourers, stevedores, and many others. Of these some, such as the market porters and stevedores, do not earn regular wages, but both classes usually make a fair average result for the week's work. [. . .]

It may be noted that Classes D and E together form the actual middle class in this district, the numbers above and below them being fairly balanced. [. . .]

Class F consists of higher class labour [. . .] and the best paid of the artisans, together with others of equal means and position from other sections, and amounts to 121,000, or about 13 and a ½ per cent of the population. [. . .] Besides foremen are included City warehousemen of the better class, and first-hand lightermen; they are usually paid for responsibility, and are men of very good character and much intelligence.

This [. . .] is not a large section of the people, but it is a distinct and very honourable one. These men are the noncommissioned officers of the industrial army. No doubt there are others as good in the ranks, and vacant places are readily filled with men no less honest and trustworthy; all the men so employed have been selected out of many. The part they play in industry is peculiar. They have nothing to do with the planning or direction (properly so called) of business operations; their work is confined to superintendence. They supply no initiative, and having no responsibility of this kind they do not share in profits; but their services are very valuable, and their pay enables them to live reasonably comfortable lives, and provide adequately for old age. No large business could be conducted without such men as its pillars of support, and their loyalty and devotion to those whom they serve is very noteworthy. Most employers would admit this as to their own foremen, but the relation is so peculiar and personal in its character that most employers also believe no other foremen to be equal to their own.

Their sons take places as clerks, and their daughters get employment in first-class shops or places of business; if the wives work at all, they either keep a shop, or employ girls at laundry work or at dressmaking. There is a great difference between these men and the artisans who are counted with them as part of Class F: the foreman of ordinary labour generally sees things from the employer's point of view, while the skilled artisan sees them from the point of view of the employed. Connected with this fact it is to be observed that the foremen are a more contented set of men than the most prosperous artisans. [. . .]

G—Lower Middle Class—Shopkeepers and small employers, clerks, etc., and subordinate professional men. A hard-working, sober, energetic class, which I will not more fully describe here, as they no doubt will be comparatively more numerous in other districts of London. Here they number 34,000, or nearly 4 per cent. It is to be noted that Class G, which in the whole district compares with the class above it as 34 to 45, for East London proper compares as 32 to 12. The exaggeration of Class H, as compared to Class G, is entirely due to Hackney.

H. Upper Middle Class—All above G are here lumped together, and may be shortly defined as the servant-keeping class. They count up to about 45,000, or 5 per cent of the population. Of these more than two-thirds are to be found in Hackney, where one-fifth of the population live in houses which, owing to their high rental, are not scheduled by the School Board visitors. In the other districts scattered houses are to be found above the value at which the School Board usually draws the line; but the visitors generally know something of the inmates. In Hackney, however, there are many streets as to which the visitors have not even the names in their books. The estimated number of residents in these unscheduled houses I have placed in Class H, to which they undoubtedly belong, excepting that the servants (also an estimated number) appear under class E, from which they are mostly drawn.

It is to be remembered that the dividing lines between all these classes are indistinct; each has, so to speak, a fringe of those who might be placed with the next division above or below; nor are the classes, as given, homogeneous by any means. Room may be found in each for many grades of social rank. [. . .]

---

4   from William Booth, *In Darkest England and the Way Out* (1890)

WHY 'DARKEST ENGLAND'?

This summer the attention of the civilised world has been arrested by the story which Mr. Stanley has told of Darkest Africa[13] and his journeyings across the heart of the Lost Continent. In all that spirited narrative of heroic endeavour, nothing has so much impressed the imagination, as his description of the immense forest, which offered an almost impenetrable barrier to his advance. The intrepid explorer, in his own phrase, 'marched, tore, ploughed, and cut his way for one hundred and sixty days through this inner womb of the true tropical forest.' The mind of man with difficulty endeavours to realise this immensity of wooded wilderness, covering a territory half as large again as the whole of France, where the rays of the sun never penetrate, where in the dark, dank air, filled with the steam of the heated morass, human beings dwarfed into pygmies and brutalised into cannibals lurk and live and die. Mr Stanley vainly endeavours to bring home to us the full horror of that awful gloom. [. . .]

The denizens of this region are filled with a conviction that the forest is endless—interminable. In vain did Mr. Stanley and his companions endeavour to convince them that outside the dreary wood were to be found sunlight, pasturage and peaceful meadows. [. . .]

[The denizens of the forest] are comparatively few; only some hundreds of thousands living in small tribes from ten to thirty miles apart, scattered over an area on which ten thousand million trees put out the sun from a region four times as wide as Great Britain. Of these pygmies there are two kinds; one a very degraded specimen with ferretlike eyes, close-set nose, more nearly approaching the baboon than was supposed to be possible, but very human; the other very handsome, with frank open innocent features, very prepossessing. They are quick and intelligent, capable of deep affection and gratitude, showing remarkable industry and patience. A pygmy boy of eighteen worked with consuming zeal; time with him was too precious to waste in talk. His mind seemed ever concentrated on work. Mr. Stanley said:—

---

[13]   H. M. Stanley's *In Darkest Africa* was published in 1890.

'When I once stopped him to ask him his name, his face seemed to say, "Please don't stop me. I must finish my task."'

'All alike, the baboon variety and the handsome innocents, are cannibals. They are possessed with a perfect mania for meat. We were obliged to bury our dead in the river, lest the bodies should be exhumed and eaten, even when they had died from smallpox.'

Upon the pygmies and all the dwellers of the forest has descended a devastating visitation in the shape of the ivory raiders of civilisation. The race that wrote the Arabian Nights, built Bagdad and Granada, and invented Algebra, sends forth men with the hunger for gold in their hearts, and Enfield muskets in their hands, to plunder and to slay.[14] They exploit the domestic affections of the forest dwellers in order to strip them of all they possess in the world. That has been going on for years. It is going on to-day. It has come to be regarded as the natural and normal law of existence. Of the religion of these hunted pygmies Mr. Stanley tells us nothing, perhaps because there is nothing to tell. But an earlier traveller, Dr. Kraff, says that one of these tribes, by name Doko, had some notion of a Supreme Being, to whom, under the name of Yer, they sometimes addressed prayers in moments of sadness or terror. In these prayers they say; 'Oh Yer, if Thou dost really exist why dost Thou let us be slaves? We ask not for food or clothing, for we live on snakes, ants, and mice. Thou hast made us, wherefore dost Thou let us be trodden down?'

It is a terrible picture, and one that has engraved itself deep on the heart of civilisation. But while brooding over the awful presentation of life as it exists in the vast African forest, it seemed to me only too vivid a picture of many parts of our own land. As there is a darkest Africa is there not also a darkest England? Civilisation, which can breed its own barbarians, does it not also breed its own pygmies? May we not find a parallel at our own doors, and discover within a stone's throw of our cathedrals and palaces similar horrors to those which Stanley has found existing in the great Equatorial forest?

The more the mind dwells upon the subject, the closer the analogy appears. The ivory raiders who brutally traffic in the unfortunate denizens of the forest glades, what are they but the publicans who flourish on the weakness of our poor? The two tribes of savages the human baboon and the handsome dwarf, who will not speak lest it impede him in his task, may be accepted as the two varieties who are continually present with us—the vicious, lazy lout, and the toiling slave. They, too, have lost all faith of life being other than it is and has been. As in Africa, it is all trees, trees, trees with no other world conceivable; so is it here—it

---

[14] Africa was economically plundered by brutal Arab colonizers in advance of the incursions made by European empire-builders. Stanley's own controversial methods of exploration were often legitimated by a humanitarian appeal to the prevention of Arab slave-trading in Africa.

is all vice and poverty and crime. To many the world is all slum, with the Work-house as an intermediate purgatory before the grave. And just as Mr. Stanley's Zanzibaris lost faith, and could only be induced to plod on in brooding sullen-ness of dull despair, so the most of our social reformers, no matter how cheerily they may have started off, with forty pioneers swinging blithely their axes as they force their way in to the wood, soon become depressed and despairing. Who can battle against the ten thousand million trees? Who can hope to make headway against the innumerable adverse conditions which doom the dweller in Darkest England to eternal and immutable misery? [. . .]

An analogy is as good as a suggestion; it becomes wearisome when it is pressed too far. But before leaving it, think for a moment how close the parallel is, and how strange it is that so much interest should be excited by a narrative of human squalor and human heroism in a distant continent, while greater squalor and heroism not less magnificent may be observed at our very doors. [. . .]

The lot of a negress in the Equatorial Forest is not, perhaps, a very happy one, but is it so very much worse than that of many a pretty orphan girl in our Christ-ian capital? We talk about the brutalities of the dark ages, and we profess to shud-der as we read in books of the shameful exaction of the rights of feudal superior. And yet here, beneath our very eyes, in our theatres, in our restaurants, and in many other places, unspeakable though it be but to name it, the same hideous abuse flourishes unchecked. A young penniless girl, if she be pretty, is often hunted from pillar to post by her employers, confronted always by the alterna-tive—Starve or Sin. And when once the poor girl has consented to buy the right to earn her living by the sacrifice of her virtue, then she is treated as a slave and an outcast by the very men who have ruined her. Her word becomes unbelievable, her life an ignominy, and she is swept downward ever downward, into the bot-tomless perdition of prostitution. But there, even in the lowest depths, excom-municated by Humanity and outcast from God, she is far nearer the pitying heart of the One true Saviour than all the men who forced her down, aye, and than all the Pharisees and Scribes who stand silently by while these Fiendish wrongs are perpetrated before their very eyes.

The blood boils with impotent rage at the sight of these enormities, callously inflicted, and silently borne by these miserable victims. Nor is it only women who are the victims, although their fate is the most tragic. Those firms which reduce sweating to a fine art, who systematically and deliberately defraud the workman of his pay, who grind the faces of the poor, and who rob the widow and the orphan, and who for a pretence make great professions of public spirit and philanthropy, these men nowadays are sent to Parliament to make laws for the people. The old prophets sent them to Hell—but we have changed all that. They send their victims to Hell, and are rewarded by all that wealth can do to make their lives comfortable. Read the House of Lords' Report on the

Sweating System,[15] and ask if any African slave system, making due allowance for the superior civilisation, and therefore sensitiveness, of the victims, reveals more misery.

Darkest England, like Darkest Africa, reeks with malaria. The foul and fetid breath of our slums is almost as poisonous as that of the African swamp.[16] Fever is almost as chronic there as on the Equator. Every year thousands of children are killed off by what is called defects of our sanitary system. They are in reality starved and poisoned, and all that can be said is that, in many cases, it is better for them that they were taken away from the trouble to come.

Just as in Darkest Africa it is only a part of the evil and misery that comes from the superior race who invade the forest to enslave and massacre its miserable inhabitants, so with us, much of the misery of those whose lot we are considering arises from their own habits. Drunkenness and all manner of uncleanness, moral and physical, abound. Have you ever watched by the bedside of a man in delirium tremens? Multiply the sufferings of that one drunkard by the hundred thousand, and you have some idea of what scenes are being witnessed in all our great cities at this moment.[17] As in Africa streams intersect the forest in every direction, so the gin-shop stands at every corner with its River of the Water of Death flowing seventeen hours out of the twenty-four for the destruction of the people. A population sodden with drink, steeped in vice, eaten up by every social and physical malady, these are the denizens of Darkest England amidst whom my life has been spent, and to whose rescue I would now summon all that is best in the manhood and womanhood of our land.

But this book is no mere lamentation of despair. For Darkest England, as for Darkest Africa, there is a light beyond. I think I see my way out, a way by which these wretched ones may escape from the gloom of their miserable existence into a higher and happier life. Long wandering in the Forest of the Shadow of Death at our doors, has familiarised me with its horrors; but while the realisation is a vigorous spur to action it has never been so oppressive as to extinguish hope. Mr. Stanley never succumbed to the terrors which oppressed his followers. He had lived in a larger life, and knew that the forest, though long, was not interminable. Every step forward brought him nearer his destined goal, nearer to the light of the

---

[15]   The sweated system of labour—much in evidence in the East End in the 19th century—was, broadly, that in which employees were paid for piece work, often working in their own homes as out-workers. Seamstresses, for example, were often paid according to the number of shirts or pairs of trousers they made up, being paid very small amounts for each item. They generally worked either from home or in a 'sweatshop', frequently having to provide their own thread and candles (to give light to work from). The 'sweating' system persists today in the East End, with the Bangladeshi community its most recent victim.

[16]   In *Degeneration Amongst Londoners* (London; Field & Tuer, 1885), James Cantlie railed against 'urbomorus'—a specific city disease—arguing that 'the close confinement and the foul air of our cities are shortening the life of the individual, and raising up a puny and ill-developed race' (p.33).

[17]   Temperance is one of the moral tenets which continues to underpin Salvation Army doctrine.

sun, the clear sky, and the rolling uplands of the grazing land. Therefore he did not despair. The Equatorial Forest was, after all, a mere corner of one quarter of the world. In the knowledge of the light outside, in the confidence begotten by past experience of successful endeavour, he pressed forward; and when the 160 days' struggle was over, he and his men came out into a pleasant place where the land smiled with peace and plenty, and their hardships and hunger were forgotten in the joy of a great deliverance.[18]

So I venture to believe it will be with us. But the end is not yet. We are still in the depths of the depressing gloom. It is in no spirit of light-heartedness that this book is sent forth into the world as if it was written some ten years ago. [. . .]

What a satire it is upon our Christianity and our civilisation that the existence of these colonies of heathens and savages in the heart of our capital should attract so little attention! It is no better than a ghastly mockery—theologians might use a stronger word—to call by the name of One who came to seek and to save that which was lost those Churches which in the midst of lost multitudes either sleep in apathy or display a fitful interest in a chasuble. Why all this apparatus of temples and meeting-houses to save men from perdition in a world which is to come, while never a helping hand is stretched out to save them from the inferno of their present life? Is it not time that, forgetting for a moment their wranglings about the infinitely little or infinitely obscure, they should concentrate all their energies on a united effort to break this terrible perpetuity of perdition, and to rescue some at least of those for whom they profess to believe their Founder came to die?

Before venturing to define the remedy, I begin by describing the malady. But even when presenting the dreary picture of our social ills, and describing the difficulties which confront us, I speak not in despondency but in hope. 'I know in whom I have believed.' I know, therefore do I speak. Darker England is but a fractional part of 'Greater England.' There is wealth enough abundantly to minister to its social regeneration so far as wealth can, if there be but heart enough to set about the work in earnest. And I hope and believe that the heart will not be lacking when once the problem is manfully faced, and the method of its solution plainly pointed out. [. . .]

---

[18] William Booth was writing before the scandal broke over what proved to be Stanley's last expedition. In December 1890 the Christian humanitarians of the Aborgines' Protection Society revealed that Stanley had flogged his native carriers, burnt villages, and killed natives, and that he had employed Tippoo Tib, one of the most notorious Arab slave-traders, to drive the acquisition of territory. This was not quite the model enlightener Booth had had in mind.

EDITORS' NOTES

1. *The Bitter Cry of Outcast London, An Inquiry into the Condition of the Abject Poor* was published anonymously as a penny pamphlet in 1883 and, taken up and publicised by W. T. Stead in the *Pall Mall Gazette*, caused something of a furore. As well as almost certainly contributing to the setting up of the Royal Commission on the Housing of the Working Classes (1884–5), the pamphlet also initiated a series of comparable articles and tracts concerning poverty and deprivation in Britain. *The Bitter Cry* was authored by the Reverend Andrew Mearns, who was Secretary to the London Congregational Union (a nonconformist sect). Mearns acknowledged the help of James Munro in surveying housing conditions, and of W. C. Preston in the writing of the pamphlet itself.

2. W. T. Stead (1849–1912) was a radical campaigning journalist, who edited the *Northern Echo* for ten years before moving to the *Pall Mall Gazette* in 1880 as assistant editor to John Morley. Once Morley had been elected as Liberal MP, Stead was editor from 1883 to 1889, after which he launched his own *Review of Reviews* as well as the occult journal *Borderland* (see Chapter 11). Under his leadership the *Pall Mall Gazette*, one aim of which was to combine newspaper journalism with more literary articles, gained a sensationalist cachet. Stead, a leading proponent of the so-called 'New Journalism' of the fin de siècle (the term was coined by Matthew Arnold in 1887 with Stead in mind), anticipated twentieth-century tabloid reportage in his infamous 'Maiden Tribute' series. His editorship was socially and politically influential: his interview with General Gordon was widely held to have pushed the government to send him to Egypt; his exposé of the state of naval defences forced a major increase in the defence budget. His evangelical low-church radicalism dictated the social agenda of the *Pall Mall Gazette*: not only did he draw attention to the plight of London's poor (see editorial notes 1 above and 4 below), he also exposed the extent of criminal vice in the city. The 'Maiden Tribute' series contributed substantially to the passing of the Criminal Law Amendment Act of 1885, which raised the age of consent for girls from 13 to 16 and allowed for the police regulation of brothels. Stead's motivation was, though, called into question, partly by those in the Establishment who felt his journalistic power and low-church politics were beginning to dictate government policy: he was himself arrested for procuring a virgin, even though he claimed to have undertaken this in order to expose the ease with which it could be achieved. He famously edited the *Gazette* from his prison cell for three months, turning a disaster into another journalistic triumph. Stead's influence declined somewhat after the 1880s, particularly when opposing the prosecution of the Boer War, a stance totally out of sympathy with the mass readerships he had helped create. Reports of the sinking of the *Titanic* in 1912, however, often concentrated on Stead's death as the most famous man aboard.

3. Charles Booth (1840–1916), born in Liverpool into a merchant Unitarian family, started up a steamship company with his brother at the age of 22. After a breakdown, and retirement from business, he settled in London in 1873 dedicating himself to the study of poverty in the city. The first volume of *Life and Labour of the People of London*, from which the present extract is taken, was published in 1889 and deals

solely with the East End. The second volume (1891) concerns itself with poverty across the whole of London. A further seven volumes appeared in 1897, and another eight in 1902–3, bringing the total to seventeen. Booth did much to develop methodologies which have influenced modern social science.

4. William Booth (1829–1919), the founder of the Salvation Army, had humble beginnings. When his father's Nottingham building trade collapsed when he was 13, Booth was apprenticed to a pawnbroker. Moving to London and becoming a Methodist in 1844, he continued in the pawnbroking trade, but in 1861 he and his wife Catherine began the revivalist movement which would become known as the Salvation Army. The Army's emphasis was initially on the saving of souls through personal conversion, but Booth later came to believe that without an alleviation of poverty his religious campaign could not succeed: *In Darkest England* suggests how this could be accomplished. Booth was assisted in the writing of his book by W. T. Stead (see note 2 above) to whom the sometimes lurid, rhetorical style owes a debt. *In Darkest England* promotes the eradication of poverty through work colonies; the current extract is taken from the introductory chapters.

3

THE METROPOLIS

'Outcast London' represents only one, albeit highly significant, dimension of metropolitan life at the end of the nineteenth century. The rapid expansion of the late Victorian city also led to a flourishing of new forms of urban entertainment; it acted as a catalyst for new fields of employment; and it facilitated the development of new ways of conceptualizing human experience in the metropolitan 'crowd'. The intellectual mediocrity and propensity for extreme behaviour of Gustave Le Bon's urban 'crowd' identifies his 'The Mind of Crowds' as a reaction to a perceived 'massification' of cultural life in the metropolis. His study lays the foundations for all subsequent accounts of group psychology, importantly anticipating Freud's account of the crowd in *Group Psychology and an Analysis of the Ego*. Le Bon's central insight is that once part of a crowd, 'the intellectual aptitudes of the individuals, and in consequence their individuality, are weakened'. Georg Simmel takes the opposite view of the effects of metropolitan life on the individual. It is the very crowdedness of the city which leads, in Simmel's view, to the intense desire of city dwellers to differentiate themselves from the crowd. The sheer volume of experiences and sensations produced in the metropolitan environment is the starting-point for Simmel's essay, in which he argues that what he characterizes as the 'intellectualistic' and 'rationalistic' qualities of the metropolitan mind are a product of the constant need to sift and process a swiftly changing kaleidoscope of events.

Fleeting visions of the cultural world of the theatre effectively convey the sheer pace and bustle of the late Victorian metropolitan experience in Arthur Symons's *jeu d'esprit*, 'At the Alhambra'. Gazing upon the rouge-wearing ballet dancers at the Alhambra Theatre, Symons presents himself here as a city archetype: he is the *flâneur* of Baudelaire's Paris of the Second Empire. The *flâneur*, as formulated by Charles Baudelaire, was characterized by his freedom to roam through the streets of the nineteenth-century metropolis, observing without being observed, strolling and watchful, without ever interacting with the other social actors in the city. Symons is at liberty to stroll and to gaze at the metropolitan pageant.

Women, though, occupied the public spaces of the city on rather different terms: whilst men had always had a legitimate, authorized role in the urban public sphere, any woman wandering the streets could all too easily be mistaken as a street-walker. It was as part of a wider campaign to make the public spaces of the city safe and wholesome for 'respectable' women that Laura Ormiston Chant, as recorded here in *Why We Attacked the Empire*, attempted to purge London's theatres of prostitutes. Concerned that the city's street-walkers were increasingly infesting places of public entertainment, Chant was one of the many New Women of the late nineteenth-century metropolis who campaigned against prostitution. Condemned as prudes and puritans, the members of London's National Vigilance Association, of which Chant was a leading light, none the less provided support for victims of sexual assault, rape, and 'seduction', including the services of a solicitor. They also campaigned for the introduction of women magistrates and police. The feminist campaigns against vice in the late nineteenth-century metropolis gave women access to the public world of politics and more generally to a public sphere which was rapidly being transformed along gender lines. For the 'separate spheres' ideology which had attempted to establish itself at the mid-century was increasingly challenged at the fin de siècle as women in their thousands poured into the streets of the city as shop workers, as lady shoppers in the new department stores, as music-hall stars and dancers, as philanthropists, as platform speakers, and as part of a new army of clerical workers who exploited the new technology of typewriting to find themselves a place in the metropolitan landscape. The late nineteenth-century metropolis was, then, a contested social and cultural terrain, with New Women, *flâneurs*, shop girls, typists, theatre-goers, music-hall 'stars', and prostitutes jostling for position on the variegated city streets.

Secondary reading: Beckson, *London in the 1890s*; Bland *Banishing the Beast*; Dyos and Wolff; Feldman and Jones; Nord; Roy Porter; Schneer; Walkowitz, *City of Dreadful Delight* and *Prostitution and Victorian Society*.

1   from Gustave Le Bon, 'The Mind of Crowds' (1895)

In its ordinary sense the word 'crowd' means a gathering of individuals of whatever nationality, profession, or sex, and whatever be the chances that have brought them together. From the psychological point of view the expression 'crowd' assumes quite a different signification. Under certain given circumstances, and only under those circumstances, an agglomeration of men presents new characteristics very different from those of the individuals composing it. The sentiments and ideas of all the persons in the gathering take one and the same direction, and their conscious personality vanishes. A collective mind is formed, doubtless transitory, but presenting very clearly defined characteristics. The gathering has thus become what, in the absence of a better expression, I will call an organised crowd, or, if the term is considered preferable, a psychological crowd. It forms a single being, and is subjected to the *law* of the mental unity of *crowds.*

It is evident that it is not by the mere fact of a number of individuals finding themselves accidentally side by side that they acquire the character of an organised crowd. A thousand individuals accidentally gathered in a public place without any determined object in no way constitute a crowd from the psychological point of view. To acquire the special characteristics of such a crowd, the influence is necessary of certain predisposing causes of which we shall have to determine the nature.

The disappearance of conscious personality and the turning of feelings and thoughts in a different direction, which are the primary characteristics of a crowd about to become organised, do not always involve the simultaneous presence of a number of individuals on one spot. Thousands of isolated individuals may acquire at certain moments and under the influence of certain violent emotions—such, for example, as a great national event—the characteristics of a psychological crowd. It will be sufficient in that case that a mere chance should bring them together for their acts to at once assume the characteristics peculiar to the acts of a crowd. At certain moments half a dozen men might constitute a psychological crowd, which may not happen in the case of hundreds of men gathered together by accident. On the other hand, an entire nation, though there may be no visible agglomeration, may become a crowd under the action of certain influences.

A psychological crowd once constituted, it acquires certain provisional but determinable general characteristics. To these general characteristics there are adjoined particular characteristics which vary according to the elements of which the crowd is composed, and may modify its mental constitution. Psychological crowds, then, are susceptible of classification; and when we come to occupy ourselves with this matter, we shall see that a heterogeneous crowd—that is, a crowd composed of dissimilar elements—presents certain characteristics in common with homogeneous crowds—that is, with crowds composed of elements more or less akin (sects, castes, and classes)—and side by side with these common characteristics particularities which permit of the two kinds of crowds being differentiated.

But before occupying ourselves with the different categories of crowds, we must first of all examine the characteristics common to them all. We shall set to work like the naturalist, who begins by describing the general characteristics common to all the members of a family before concerning himself with the particular characteristics which allow the differentiation of the genera and species that the family includes.

It is not easy to describe the mind of crowds with exactness, because its organisation varies not only according to race and composition, but also according to the nature and intensity of the exciting causes to which crowds are subjected. The same difficulty, however, presents itself in the psychological study of an individual. It is only in novels that individuals are found to traverse their whole life with an unvarying character. It is only the uniformity of the environment that creates the apparent uniformity of characters. I have shown elsewhere that all mental constitutions contain possibilities of character which may be manifested in consequence of a sudden change of environment. This explains how it was that among the most savage members of the French Convention were to be found inoffensive citizens who, under ordinary circumstances, would have been peaceable notaries or virtuous magistrates. The storm past, they resumed their normal character of quiet, law-abiding citizens. Napoleon found amongst them his most docile servants.

It being impossible to study here all the successive degrees of organisation of crowds, we shall concern ourselves more especially with such crowds as have attained to the phase of complete organisation. In this way we shall see what crowds may become, but not what they invariably are. It is only in this advanced phase of organisation that certain new and special characteristics are superposed on the unvarying and dominant character of the race; then takes place that turning already alluded to of all the feelings and thoughts of the collectivity in an identical direction. It is only under such circumstances, too, that what I have called above the *psychological* law of the mental unity of *crowds* comes into play.

Among the psychological characteristics of crowds there are some that they may present in common with isolated individuals, and others, on the contrary, which are absolutely peculiar to them and are only to be met with in collectivities. It is these special characteristics that we shall study, first of all, in order to show their importance.

The most striking peculiarity presented by a psychological crowd is the following. Whoever be the individuals that compose it, however like or unlike be their mode of life, their occupations, their character, or their intelligence, the fact that they have been transformed into a crowd puts them in possession of a sort of collective mind which makes them feel, think, and act in a manner quite different from that in which each individual of them would feel, think, and act were he in a state of isolation. There are certain ideas and feelings which do not come into being, or do not transform themselves into acts except in the case of individuals forming a crowd. The psychological crowd is a provisional being formed of heterogeneous elements, which for a moment are combined, exactly as the cells which constitute a living body form by their reunion a new being which displays characteristics very different from those possessed by each of the cells singly.

Contrary to an opinion which one is astonished to find coming from the pen of so acute a philosopher as Herbert Spencer, in the aggregate which constitutes a crowd there is in no sort a summing-up of or an average struck between its elements.[1] What really takes place is a combination followed by the creation of new characteristics, just as in chemistry certain elements, when brought into contact-bases and acids, for example—combine to form a new body possessing properties quite different from those of the bodies that have served to form it.

It is easy to prove how much the individual forming part of a crowd differs from the isolated individual, but it is less easy to discover the causes of this difference.

To obtain at any rate a glimpse of them it is necessary in the first place to call to mind the truth established by modern psychology, that unconscious phenomena play an altogether preponderating part not only in organic life, but also in the operations of the intelligence. The conscious life of the mind is of small importance in comparison with its unconscious life. The most subtle analyst, the most acute observer, is scarcely successful in discovering more than a very small number of the unconscious motives that determine his conduct. Our conscious acts are the outcome of an unconscious substratum created in the mind in the main by hereditary influences. This substratum consists of the innumerable common characteristics handed down from generation to generation, which constitute the genius of a race. Behind the avowed causes of our acts there undoubtedly lie secret causes that we do not avow, but behind these secret causes there are many others more secret still which we ourselves ignore. The greater part of our daily actions are the result of hidden motives which escape our observation.

It is more especially with respect to those unconscious elements which constitute the genius of a race that all the individuals belonging to it resemble each other, while it is principally in respect to the conscious elements of their character—the fruit of education, and yet more of exceptional hereditary

---

[1] Herbert Spencer (1820–1903), an evolutionary philosopher who applied evolutionary theory to sociology (see Ch. 13 below for a selection from his *Principles of Sociology*).

conditions—that they differ from each other. Men the most unlike in the matter of their intelligence possess instincts, passions, and feelings that are very similar. In the case of everything that belongs to the realm of sentiment—religion, politics, morality, the affections and antipathies, etc.—the most eminent men seldom surpass the standard of the most ordinary individuals. From the intellectual point of view an abyss may exist between a great mathematician and his bootmaker, but from the point of view of character the difference is most often slight or non-existent.

It is precisely these general qualities of character, governed by forces of which we are unconscious, and possessed by the majority of the normal individuals of a race in much the same degree—it is precisely these qualities, I say, that in crowds become common property. In the collective mind the intellectual aptitudes of the individuals, and in consequence their individuality, are weakened. The heterogeneous is swamped by the homogeneous, and the unconscious qualities obtain the upper hand.

This very fact that crowds possess in common ordinary qualities explains why they can never accomplish acts demanding a high degree of intelligence. The decisions affecting matters of general interest come to by an assembly of men of distinction, but specialists in different walks of life, are not sensibly superior to the decisions that would be adopted by a gathering of imbeciles. The truth is, they can only bring to bear in common on the work in hand those mediocre qualities which are the birthright of every average individual. In crowds it is stupidity and not mother-wit that is accumulated. It is not all the world, as is so often repeated, that has more wit than Voltaire, but assuredly Voltaire that has more wit than all the world, if by 'all the world' crowds are to be understood.[2]

If the individuals of a crowd confined themselves to putting in common the ordinary qualities of which each of them has his share, there would merely result that striking of an average, and not, as we have said is actually the case, the creation of new characteristics. How is it that these new characteristics are created? This is what we are now to investigate.

Different causes determine the appearance of these characteristics peculiar to crowds, and not possessed by isolated individuals. The first is that the individual forming part of a crowd acquires, solely from numerical considerations, a sentiment of invincible power which allows him to yield to instincts which, had he been alone, he would perforce have kept under restraint. He will be the less disposed to check himself from the consideration that, a crowd being

---

[2] Voltaire was the pseudonym of François-Marie Arouet (1694–1778), French satirist, novelist, historian, poet, dramatist, polemicist, moralist, and critic. Regarded as the universal genius of the Enlightenment and lauded by freethinking circles in Paris, Voltaire was committed to the Bastille for his satires in 1717–18 and exiled to Britain in 1726–9.

anonymous, and in consequence irresponsible, the sentiment of responsibility which always controls individuals disappears entirely.

The second cause, which is contagion, also intervenes to determine the manifestation in crowds of their special characteristics, and at the same time the trend they are to take. Contagion is a phenomenon of which it is easy to establish the presence, but that it is not easy to explain. It must be classed among those phenomena of a hypnotic order, which we shall shortly study. In a crowd every sentiment and act is contagious, and contagious to such a degree that an individual readily sacrifices his personal interest to the collective interest. This is an attitude very contrary to his nature, and of which a man is scarcely capable, except when he makes part of a crowd.

A third cause, and by far the most important, determines in the individuals of a crowd special characteristics which are quite contrary at times to those presented by the isolated individual. I allude to that suggestibility of which, moreover, the contagion mentioned above is neither more nor less than an effect.

To understand this phenomenon it is necessary to bear in mind certain recent physiological discoveries. We know to-day that by various processes an individual may be brought into such a condition that, having entirely lost his conscious personality, he obeys all the suggestions of the operator who has deprived him of it, and commits acts in utter contradiction with his character and habits. The most careful observations seem to prove that an individual immersed for some length of time in a crowd in action soon finds himself—either in consequence of the magnetic influence given out by the crowd, or from some other cause of which we are ignorant—in a special state, which much resembles the state of fascination in which the hypnotised individual finds himself in the hands of the hypnotiser.[3] The activity of the brain being paralysed in the case of the hypnotised subject, the latter becomes the slave of all the unconscious activities of his spinal cord, which the hypnotiser directs at will. The conscious personality has entirely vanished; will and discernment are lost. All feelings and thoughts are bent in the direction determined by the hypnotiser.

Such also is approximately the state of the individual forming part of a psychological crowd. He is no longer conscious of his acts. In his case, as in the case of the hypnotised subject, at the same time that certain faculties are destroyed, others may be brought to a high degree of exaltation. Under the influence of a suggestion, he will undertake the accomplishment of certain acts with irresistible impetuosity. This impetuosity is the more irresistible in the case of crowds than in that of the hypnotised subject, from the fact that, the suggestion

---

[3] Le Bon is here deploying a relatively new discourse on *suggestibility* under hypnosis. Throughout the 1890s in France, the so-called 'Nancy School' of hypnosis proposed that criminal acts could be induced by an expert hypnotist, against the will of the victim. Le Bon transposes this discourse to the crowd and its 'mesmeric' leader.

being the same for all the individuals of the crowd, it gains in strength by reciprocity. The individualities in the crowd who might possess a personality sufficiently strong to resist the suggestion are too few in number to struggle against the current. At the utmost, they may be able to attempt a diversion by means of different suggestions. It is in this way, for instance, that a happy expression, an image opportunely evoked, have occasionally deterred crowds from the most bloodthirsty acts.

We see, then, that the disappearance of the conscious personality, the predominance of the unconscious personality, the turning by means of suggestion and contagion of feelings and ideas in an identical direction, the tendency to immediately transform the suggested ideas into acts; these we see, are the principal characteristics of the individual forming part of a crowd. He is no longer himself, but has become an automaton who has ceased to be guided by his will.

Moreover, by the mere fact that he forms part of an organised crowd, a man descends several rungs in the ladder of civilisation. Isolated, he may be a cultivated individual; in a crowd, he is a barbarian—that is, a creature acting by instinct. He possesses the spontaneity, the violence, the ferocity, and also the enthusiasm and heroism of primitive beings, whom he further tends to resemble by the facility with which he allows himself to be impressed by words and images—which would be entirely without action on each of the isolated individuals composing the crowd—and to be induced to commit acts contrary to his most obvious interests and his best-known habits. An individual in a crowd is a grain of sand amid other grains of sand, which the wind stirs up at will.

It is for these reasons that juries are seen to deliver verdicts of which each individual juror would disapprove, that parliamentary assemblies adopt laws and measures of which each of their members would disapprove in his own person. Taken separately, the men of the Convention were enlightened citizens of peaceful habits.[4] United in a crowd, they did not hesitate to give their adhesion to the most savage proposals, to guillotine individuals most clearly innocent, and, contrary to their interests to renounce their inviolability and to decimate themselves.

It is not only by his acts that the individual in a crowd differs essentially from himself. Even before he has entirely lost his independence, his ideas and feelings have undergone a transformation, and the transformation is so profound as to change the miser into a spendthrift, the sceptic into a believer, the honest man into a criminal, and the coward into a hero. The renunciation of all its privileges which the nobility voted in a moment of enthusiasm during the celebrated night

---

[4] The National Convention was the name of the sovereign assembly which governed France from 21 Sept. 1792 to 26 Oct. 1795. The middle part of this reign (1793–4) has become known as 'The Terror', due to the large number of summary executions carried out.

of August 4, 1789, would certainly never have been consented to by any of its members taken singly.[5]

The conclusion to be drawn from what precedes is, that the crowd is always intellectually inferior to the isolated individual, but that, from the point of view of feelings and of the acts these feelings provoke, the crowd may, according to circumstances, be better or worse than the individual. All depends on the nature of the suggestion to which the crowd is exposed. This is the point that has been completely misunderstood by writers who have only studied crowds from the criminal point of view. Doubtless a crowd is often criminal, but also it is often heroic. It is crowds rather than isolated individuals that may be induced to run the risk of death to secure the triumph of a creed or an idea, that may be fired with enthusiasm for glory and honour, that are led on—almost without bread and without arms, as in the age of the Crusades—to deliver the tomb of Christ from the infidel, or, as in '93, to defend the fatherland.[6] Such heroism is without doubt somewhat unconscious, but it is of such heroism that history is made. Were peoples only to be credited with the great actions performed in cold blood, the annals of the world would register but few of them.

---

2   from Georg Simmel, 'The Metropolis and Mental Life' (1903)

The deepest problems of modern life flow from the attempt of the individual to maintain the independence and individuality of his existence against the sovereign powers of society, against the weight of the historical heritage and the external culture and technique of life. This antagonism represents the most modern form of the conflict which primitive man must carry on with nature for his own bodily existence. The eighteenth century may have called for liberation from all the ties which grew up historically in politics, in religion, in morality and in economics in order to permit the original natural virtue of man, which is equal in everyone, to develop without inhibition; the nineteenth century may have sought to promote, in addition to man's freedom, his individuality (which is connected with the division of labour) and his achievements which make him unique and indispensable but which at the same time make him so much the more dependent on the complementary activity of others; Nietzsche[7] may have seen the relentless

[5]   Another reference to a key moment of the French Revolution.

[6]   The Crusades were a series of military expeditions undertaken by the Christians of Europe in 11th, 12th, and 13th centuries, professedly to recover the Holy Land from the Muslims. ''93' is a reference to resistance to 'The Terror' of 1793 in France.

[7]   Friedrich Nietzsche (1844–1900), a German philosopher who expressed contempt for the 'masses'. His philosophy is underpinned by the 'will to power' of the individual.

struggle of the individual as the prerequisite for his full development, while Socialism found the same thing in the suppression of all competition; but in each of these the same fundamental motive was at work, namely the resistance of the individual to being levelled, swallowed up in the social-technological mechanism. [. . .]

The psychological foundation, upon which the metropolitan individuality is erected, is the intensification of emotional life due to the swift and continuous shift of external and internal stimuli. Man is a creature whose existence is dependent on differences, i.e., his mind is stimulated by the difference between present impressions and those which have preceded. Lasting impressions, the slightness in their differences, the habituated regularity of their course and contrasts between them, consume, so to speak, less mental energy than the rapid telescoping of changing images, pronounced differences within what is grasped at a single glance, and the unexpectedness of violent stimuli. To the extent that the metropolis creates these psychological conditions; with every crossing of the street, with the tempo and multiplicity of economic, occupational and social life; it creates in the sensory foundations of mental life, and in the degree of awareness necessitated by our organization as creatures dependent on differences, a deep contrast with the slower, more habitual, more smoothly flowing rhythm of the sensory-mental phase of small town and rural existence. Thereby the essentially intellectualistic character of the mental life of the metropolis becomes intelligible as over against that of the small town which rests more on feelings and emotional relationships. [. . .]

Instead of reacting emotionally, the metropolitan type reacts primarily in a rational manner, thus creating a mental predominance through the intensification of consciousness, which in turn is caused by it. Thus the reaction of the metropolitan person to those events is moved to a sphere of mental activity which is least sensitive and which is furthest removed from the depths of the personality. This intellectualistic quality which is thus recognized as a protection of the inner life against the domination of the metropolis, becomes ramified into numerous specific phenomena. The metropolis has always been the seat of money economy because the many-sidedness and concentration of commercial activity have given the medium of exchange an importance which it could not have acquired in the commercial aspects of rural life. But money economy and the domination of the intellect stand in the closest relationship to one another. They have in common a purely matter-of-fact attitude in the treatment of persons and things in which a formal justice is often combined with an unrelenting hardness. [. . .]

What is essential here as regards the economic-psychological aspect of the problem is that in less advanced cultures production was for the customer who ordered the product so that the producer and the purchaser knew one another. The modern city, however, is supplied almost exclusively by production for the market, that is, for entirely unknown purchasers who never appear in the actual field of vision of the producers themselves. Thereby, the interests of each party acquire a relentless matter-of-factness, and its rationally calculated economic egoism need not fear any divergence from its set path because of the imponderability of personal relationships. [. . .] The modern mind has become more and more a calculating one. The calculating exactness of practical life which has resulted from a money economy corresponds to the ideal of natural science, namely that of transforming the world into an arithmetical problem and of fixing every one of its parts in a mathematical formula. [. . .]

It is, however, the conditions of the metropolis which are cause as well as effect for this essential characteristic. The relationships and concerns of the typical metropolitan resident are so manifold and complex that, especially as a result of the agglomeration of so many persons with such differentiated interests, their relationships and activities intertwine with one another into a many-membered organism. In view of this fact, the lack of the most exact punctuality in promises and performances would cause the whole to break down into an inextricable chaos. [. . .] For this reason the technique of metropolitan life in general is not conceivable without all of its activities and reciprocal relationships being organized and coordinated in the most punctual way into a firmly fixed framework of time which transcends all subjective elements. But here too there emerge those conclusions which are in general the whole task of this discussion, namely, that every event, however restricted to this superficial level it may appear, comes immediately into contact with the depths of the soul, and that the most banal externalities are, in the last analysis, bound up with the final decisions concerning the meaning and the style of life. Punctuality, calculability, and exactness, which are required by the complications and extensiveness of metropolitan life are not only most intimately connected with its capitalistic and intellectualistic character but also colour the content of life and are conducive to the exclusion of those irrational, instinctive, sovereign human traits and impulses which originally seek to determine the form of life from within instead of receiving it from the outside in a general, schematically precise form. Even though those lives which are autonomous and characterized by these vital impulses are not entirely impossible in the city, they are, none the less, opposed to it in *abstracto*. It is in the light of this that we can explain the passionate hatred of personalities like Ruskin and Nietzsche for the metropolis; personalities who found the value of life only in unschematized individual expressions which cannot be reduced to exact equivalents and in whom, on that account, there flowed from the same source as did that hatred, the hatred of the money economy and of the intellectualism of existence.[8]

The same factors which, in the exactness and the minute precision of the form of life, have coalesced into a structure of the highest impersonality, have, on the other hand, an influence in a highly personal direction. There is perhaps no psychic phenomenon which is so unconditionally reserved to the city as the blasé outlook. It is at first the consequence of those rapidly shifting stimulations of the nerves which are thrown together in all their contrasts and from which it seems to us the intensification of metropolitan intellectuality seems to be derived. On that account it is not likely that stupid persons who have been hitherto intellectually dead will be blasé because it stimulates the nerves to their utmost reactivity until they finally can no longer produce any reaction at all, so, less harmful stimuli, through the rapidity and the contradictoriness of their shifts, force the nerves to make such violent responses, tear them about so brutally that they exhaust their last reserve of strength and, remaining in the same milieu, do not have time for new reserves of strength to form. This incapacity to react to new stimulations with the required amount of energy constitutes in fact that blasé attitude which every child of a large city evinces when compared with the products of the more peaceful and more stable milieu. [. . .]

Whereas the subject of this form of existence must come to terms with it for himself, his self-preservation in the face of the great city requires of him a no less negative type of social conduct. The mental attitude of the people of the metropolis to one another may be designated formally as one of reserve. If the unceasing external contact of numbers of persons in the city should be met by the same number of inner reactions as in the small town, in which one knows almost every person he meets and to each of whom he has a positive relationship, one would be completely atomized internally and would fall into an unthinkable mental condition. Partly this psychological circumstance and partly the privilege of suspicion which we have in the face of the elements of metropolitan life (which are constantly touching one another in fleeting contact) necessitates in us that reserve, in consequence of which we do not know by sight neighbors of years standing and which permits us to appear to small-town folk so often as cold and uncongenial. Indeed, if I am not mistaken, the inner side of this external reserve is not only indifference but more frequently than we believe, it is a slight aversion, a mutual strangeness and repulsion which, in a

---

[8] John Ruskin (1819–1900), English author, art critic, and social commentator. In his 'On the Nature of the Gothic' in *The Stones of Venice* (1851–3), Ruskin championed Gothic architecture of the Middle Ages on the grounds that it expresses the personality and craft skills of individual stonemasons, a far cry from the alienated labour of industrial capitalism against which Ruskin vehemently protested. For Nietzsche see n. 1 above.

close contact which has arisen any way whatever, can break out into hatred and conflict. [. . .]

Cities are above all the seat of the most advanced economic division of labour. [. . .] Exactly in the measure of its extension the city offers to an increasing degree the determining conditions for the division of labour. It is a unit which, because of its large size, is receptive to a highly diversified plurality of achievements while at the same time the agglomeration of individuals and their struggle for the customer forces the individual to a type of specialized accomplishment in which he cannot be so easily exterminated by the other. The decisive fact here is that in the life of a city, struggle with nature for the means of life is transformed into a conflict with human beings and the gain which is fought for is granted, not by nature, but by man. For here we find not only the previously mentioned source of specialization but rather the deeper one in which the seller must seek to produce in the person to whom he wishes to sell ever new and unique needs. The necessity to specialize one's product in order to find a source of income which is not yet exhausted and also to specialize a function which cannot be easily supplanted is conductive to differentiation, refinement and enrichment of the needs of the public which obviously must lead to increasing personal variation within this public.

All this leads to the narrower type of intellectual individuation of mental qualities to which the city gives rise in proportion to its size. There is a whole series of causes for this. First of all there is the difficulty of giving one's own personality a certain status within the framework of metropolitan life. Where quantitative increase of value and energy has reached its limits, one seizes on qualitative distinctions, so that, through taking advantage of the existing sensitivity to differences, the attention of the social world can, in some way, be won for oneself. This leads ultimately to the strangest eccentricities, to specifically metropolitan extravagances of self-distanciation, of caprice, of fastidiousness, the meaning of which is no longer to be found in the content of such activity itself but rather in its being a form of being different; of making oneself noticeable. For many types of persons these are still the only means of saving for oneself, through the attention gained from others, some sort of self-esteem and the sense of filling a position. In the same sense there operates an apparently insignificant factor which in its effects, however, is perceptibly cumulative, namely, the brevity and rarity of meetings which are allotted to each individual as compared with the social intercourse in a small city. For here we find the attempt to appear to-the-point, clear-cut and individual with extraordinarily greater frequency than where frequent and long association assures to each person an unambiguous conception of the other's personality.

This appears to me to be the most profound cause of the fact that the metropolis places emphasis on striving for the most individual forms of personal existence; regardless of whether it is always correct or always successful. [. . .]

The eighteenth century found the individual in the grip of powerful bonds which had become meaningless; bonds of a political, agrarian, guild and religious nature; delimitations which imposed upon the human being at the same time an unnatural form and for a long time an unjust inequality. In this situation arose the cry for freedom and equality; the belief in the full freedom of movement of the individual in all his social and intellectual relationships which would then permit the same noble essence to emerge equally from all individuals as Nature had placed it in them and as it had been distorted by social life and historical development. Alongside of this liberalistic ideal there grew up in the nineteenth century from Goethe and the Romantics, on the one hand, and from the economic division of labour on the other, the further tendency, namely, that individuals who had been liberated from their historical bonds sought now to distinguish themselves from one another.[9] No longer was it the general human quality in every individual but rather his qualitative uniqueness and irreplaceability that now became the criteria of his value. In the conflict and shifting interpretations of these two ways of defining the position of the individual within the totality is to be found the external as well as the internal history of our time. It is the function of the metropolis to make a place for the conflict and for the attempts at unification of both of these in the sense that its own peculiar conditions have been revealed to us as the occasion and the stimulus for the development of both. Thereby they attain a quite unique place, fruitful with an inexhaustible richness of meaning in the development of the mental life. They reveal themselves as one of those great historical structures in which conflicting life-embracing currents find themselves with equal legitimacy. Because of this, however, regardless of whether we are sympathetic or antipathetic with their individual expressions, they transcend the sphere in which a judge-like attitude on our part is appropriate. To the extent that such forces have been integrated, with the fleeting existence of a single-cell, into the root as well as the crown of the totality of historical life to which we belong—it is our task not to complain or to condone but only to understand.

---

[9]   Johann Wolfgang von Goethe (1749–1832), German Romantic whose most influential literary works were *The Sorrows of Young Werthe* (1774) and his two *Wilhelm Meister* novels (1795–6). The latter initiated the form of the *Bildungsroman*, the novel of 'education', which focuses intensely on one individual's self-development.

3   from Arthur Symons, 'At the Alhambra:
         Impressions and Sensations' (1896)

At the Alhambra I can never sit anywhere but in the front row of the stalls.[10] As a point of view considered in the abstract, I admit that the position has its disadvantages. Certainly, the most magical glimpse I ever caught of an Alhambra ballet was from the road in front, from the other side of the road, one night when two doors were suddenly flung open just as I was passing. In the moment's interval before the doors closed again, I saw, in that odd, unexpected way, over the heads of the audience, far off in a sort of blue mist, the whole stage, its brilliant crowd drawn up in the last pose, just as the curtain was beginning to descend. It stamped itself in my brain, an impression caught just at the perfect moment by some rare felicity of chance. But that is not an impression that can be respected. In the general way I prefer to see my illusions very clearly, recognising them as illusions and yet, to my own perverse and decadent way of thinking, losing none of their charm. I have been reproved, before now, for singing 'the charms of rouge on fragile cheeks,' but it is a charm that I fully appreciate. Maquillage, to be attractive, must of course be unnecessary. As a disguise for age or misfortune, it has no interest for me. But, of all places, on the stage, and of all people, on the cheeks of young people: there, it seems to me that make-up is intensely fascinating and its recognition is of the essence of my delight in a stage performance. I do not for a moment want really to believe in what I see before me; to believe that those wigs are hair, that grease-paint a blush; any more than I want really to believe that the actor whom I have just been shaking hands with has turned into a real live emperor since I left him. I know that a delightful imposition is being practised upon me; that I am to see fairyland for a while; and to me all that glitters shall be gold. But I would have no pretence of reality: I do not, for my part, find that the discovery of a stage-trick lessens my appreciation of what that trick effects. There is this charming person, for instance, at the Alhambra: in the street she is handsome rather than pretty; on the stage she is pretty rather than handsome. I know exactly how she will look in her different wigs, exactly what her make-up will bring out in her and conceal; I can allow, when I see her on the stage, for every hair's breadth of change; yet does my knowledge of all this interfere with my sensation of pleasure as I see her dancing on the other side of the footlights? Quite the contrary; and I will go further, and admit that there is a special charm to me in a yet nearer view of these beautiful illusions. That is why I like to alternate the point of view of the front row of the stalls with the point of view of behind the scenes. [. . .]

[10] The Alhambra was a theatre on Charing Cross Road in London's West End.

It is ten minutes before the ballet is to commence. [. . .] All around me are the young faces that I know so well, both as they are and as the footlights show them. Now I see them in all the undisguise of make-up: the exact lure of red paint along the lips, every shading of black under the eyes, the pink of the ears and cheeks, and just where it ends under the chin and along the rim of throat. In a plain girl make-up only seems to intensify her plainness: for make-up does but give colour and piquancy to what is already in a face, it adds nothing new. But in a pretty girl how exquisitely becoming all this is, what a new kind of exciting savour it gives to her real charm! It has, to the remnant of Puritan conscience or consciousness that is the heritage of us all, a certain sense of dangerous wickedness, the delight of forbidden fruit. The very phrase, painted woman, has come to have an association of sin; and to have put paint on her cheeks, though for the innocent necessities of her profession, gives to a woman a sort of symbolic corruption. At once she seems to typify the sorceries and entanglements of what is most deliberately enticing in her sex—

Femina dulce malum, pariter favus atque venenum[11]—

with all that is most subtle, and least like nature, in her power to charm. Then there is the indiscretion of long use; these girls travestied as boys, so boyish sometimes, in their slim youth; the feminine contours now escaping, now accentuated. All are jumbled together in a brilliant confusion; the hot faces, the shirt-sleeves of scene-shifters, striking rapidly through a group of princes, peasants, and fairies. In a corner some of the children are doing a dance; now and again an older girl, in a sudden access of gaiety, will try a few whimsical steps; there is a chatter of conversation, a coming and going; some one is hunting everywhere for a missing 'property'; some one else has lost a shoe, or a glove, or is calling for a pin to repair the loss of a button. And now three girls, from opposite directions, will make a simultaneous rush at the stage-manager. 'Mr Forde, I can't get on my wig!' 'Please, Mr Forde, may I have a sheet of notepaper?' 'Oh, Mr Forde, may Miss — stay off? She has such a bad headache she can hardly stand.' Meanwhile, the overture has commenced; and now a warning clap is heard, and all but those who appear in the first scene retreat hurriedly to the wings.

To watch a ballet from the wings is to lose all sense of proportion, all knowledge of the piece as a whole; but, in return, it is fruitful in happy accidents, in momentary points of view, in chance felicities of light and shade and movement. It is almost to be in the performance oneself, and yet passive, as spectator, with the leisure to look about one. You see the reverse of the picture; the girls at the back lounging against the set scenes, turning to talk with someone at the side; you see how lazily the lazy girls are moving, and how mechanical and irregular are the motions that flow into rhythm when seen from the front. Now one is in the centre

---

[11] 'A woman, sweet misfortune, equally honey and poison.'

of a jostling crowd hurrying past one on to the stage, now the same crowd returns, charging at full speed between the scenery, everyone trying to reach the dressing room stairs first. And there is the constant shifting of scenery, from which one has a series of escapes, as it bears down unexpectedly, in some new direction. The ballet, half seen in the centre of the stage, seen in sections, has, in the glimpses that can be caught of it, a contradictory appearance of mere nature and of absolute unreality. And beyond the footlights, on the other side of the orchestra, one can see the boxes near the stalls, the men standing by the bar, an angle cut sharply off from the stalls, with the light full on the faces, the intent eyes, the gray smoke curling up from the cigarettes. It is all a bewilderment; but to me, certainly, a bewilderment that is always delightful. [. . .]

---

4   from Mrs Ormiston Chant, *Why We Attacked the Empire*[12] (1895)

The following pages have been written in response to a very wide demand. The feeling that was aroused last autumn in consequence of the action of the London County Council with regard to the licensing of certain places of amusement was very deep, and this, not because people really believed that London's amusements were in danger, but because evils lying at the back of some of those amusements were touched—evils which the many would gladly hush up—ignore—or if this is impossible, arrange for as ordinary occurrences.[13] But the conscience of London spoke out unmistakably in endorsing the action of the L.C.C. It said, 'We don't want to lessen the amusements of the people, but we will have them decent. They shall not be as highways to ruin to the young, licensed opportunities for the vicious, stimulants to the traffic in human lives.' [. . .]

What had the Empire Theatre done, or not done, that on October 10th, 1894, its licence was opposed, and the Licensing Committee of the London County Council made certain stipulations that must be complied with before the licence could be renewed?

Why was it that not London only, but the whole of England, and many people in other countries, such as France, Germany, India, South Africa, and the United States, were roused to keenest interest over what is of annual occurrence when licences have to be granted or refused?

---

[12] The Empire Theatre was in Leicester Square, at the heart of London's theatreland in the West End.

[13] On 10 Oct. 1894 the London County Council (LCC) Licensing Committee met to consider applications for the renewal of music-hall and theatre licences. Licensing of approximately 400 such venues in London had passed from magistrates to the LCC when it took over the administration of London under the Local Government Act of 1888.

Why did a certain section of the press behave in such a ridiculous fashion, as though they imagined that the amusements of the people were in danger, and that the monopolist, the money-lender, and the libertine were those to whom the nation must turn for help and sympathy in the hour of need?

In answer to the first question, [. . .] the Temple of Amusement and Recreation has [. . .] to be periodically purged of the tables of the money changers, and those that sell and buy the doves of ignorance, innocence, poverty and helplessness. The 'Empire' Theatre [. . .] was [. . .] a haunt of vice [. . .] and that too on the showing of its most powerful press ally who plaintively demanded what would be the state of the streets already so disgraceful, if the denizens of the 'promenade' were turned onto them?

That the managers of the 'Empire' recognized the habits of their promenaders was clearly proved from their evidence given before the Licensing Committee. One official testifying that he knows the face of every street-walker in London, and that *street-walkers* are not allowed admission to the Empire. Another, that if a woman is seen 'markedly soliciting' she is touched on the shoulder *by an official appointed for the purpose*, and cautioned, and if need be, turned out. From which testimony we gather that gilded vice draws the line of the promenade at the street-walker; and that solicitation must be 'markedly' such before it is considered objectionable. [. . .]

But the most eloquent testimony of all as to the nature of the promenade, was given when the County Council granted a renewal of the Empire licence on condition that several rows of seats should be placed in the promenade, so as to leave only a good-sized gangway, and that no intoxicating drink should be sold in the auditorium. The management declared itself.

> 'Close the promenade,' it said—'compel us to pull down the partitions so that the entertainment from the stage can be seen from the promenade,— forbid the sale of drink in the auditorium?—why the Empire will be ruined, and we shall have to shut the place up!'

Moreover, to prove the reality of the impending ruin, its employees were solemnly gathered together after the evening performance to receive notice of dismissal. All the great gaudy show, and the talent of innumerable 'stars,' counting as nothing beside the use of the promenade, and the temptations to drink, in piling up the huge dividend that so astonished the public.

Of course it was necessary in acting out the unsuccessful farce, to cast as much obloquy as possible on those who had dared to demand that a place of amusement shall not be a trapdoor to ruin.

Accordingly the champions of a dividend of 75 percent[14] pointed to the seven

---

[14]   This was the level of profits paid to shareholders at the time when the licence was refused.

hundred employees as about to be turned out into the streets to join the ranks of the 'unemployed' at the bidding of heartless Puritans. [. . .]

In answer to the second question as to why there was such a world-wide stir of excitement over what is of annual occurrence when licences are dealt with, it is necessary to point out that there were four classes of people who felt their supposed interests to be in danger, and who railed in various degrees of indignation against the upsetters of those interests.

1st. There were those to whom money is the be-all and end-all of life, and to whom a dividend, no matter how earned, nor by what sin or misery to others, is a sacred thing. [. . .]

2nd. There were those to whom amusement and pleasure are the chief ends to be pursued, no matter by what sacrifice of happiness and character their quest is gained. [. . .]

3rd. There were those who belong to the centres of Art, Literature and Science or who dwell in the suburbs thereof, who fondly imagine that man shall gather the grapes of Beauty, Life, and Wisdom from the thorns of impurity, cruelty, and greed in the end of the nineteenth century, though he has not done so in any previous one; [. . .]

4th. There was the sad mournful army who minister entirely to the demands of lust, and who love darkness and secrecy because their lives and deeds are evil. No wonder these cried out in papers that were not ashamed to be their mouthpiece, and their language was vented in much slanderous and vulgar abuse. Then there were also a large number of people who do not think much for themselves, and who catch up any cry and repeat it parrot-like with great noise; they called out loudly against bigots and fanatics who they declared were trying to shut up theatres and music-halls, and were interfering with 'liberty of the subject'; they asked in passionate tones if London was to be governed by women, and yet clamoured about an irresponsible body of men like the L.C.C. having the power to grant licences, forgetting that there is not one woman on the County Council. [. . .]

But against all these rose the calm steady voice of righteous public opinion, the Non-Conformist conscience, as some call it, in congratulation for the triumph of right over might, and in deep and earnest sympathy.

There was no need to assure these that the crusaders were aiming not at amusement, but vice. [. . .]

Lastly, in answer to the question as to the attitude of a certain section of the Press, it is not surprising that so low a tone was taken by these when it is remembered that they exist but as the mouthpieces of England's three great enemies—viz., Drink, Vice, and Gambling. Most of them are in direct opposition at all times to any movement that threatens the prosperity of the Drink Traffic, or interference with the 'liberty' of the profligate, or to stop the lucrative operations of the betting fraternity. They did but as they always do in scurrilizing and ridiculing the efforts of those who desire a purer, happier England. Only, and there was the difference, they suddenly assumed a wonderful anxiety on behalf of the unemployed, and the friendless outcast on the streets, also a deep concern for the amusement of the poor. Hitherto it had been the upholders of Social Purity, Temperance, and justice, whose names have been identified with arduous endeavour in the cause of labour, shorter hours, fair wages, and constant employment; but when the Empire licence was attacked, lo, the capitalist and moneylender, the libertine and the sweater, all lifted pious hands of horror, and cried through the pages of their various organs in tones of unaccustomed and sudden sympathy with the down-trodden! What a farce it was! A still greater sham was the hypocritical outcry on behalf of the outcast. Lofty sentiments were uttered about mercy and pity for the fallen sister on the streets, and denunciation of the puritanical harshness of those who it was said were trying to thrust her out of the haven-like promenade of the great music-hall, on to the cold misery of the pavement.

To be sure, these utterances came from those who have never been known to do anything to relieve or lessen the piteous numbers of the knocked-down victims of lust; and they were hurled especially at men and women to whom the storm-beaten outcast has never appealed in vain, and whose names are household words in philanthropic circles as the friends and unfailing succourers of the waif, the destitute, and the fallen. [. . .]

EDITORS' NOTES

1. Gustave Le Bon (1841–1930) was a French social psychologist who significantly influenced Sigmund Freud's work. Freud devoted a chapter of his 1920s study *Group Psychology and the Analysis of the Ego* to Le Bon's work, describing it as 'his brilliantly executed picture of the group mind'. Le Bon frequently refers to the events of the French Revolution to corroborate his social psychology of crowd behaviour (writing a book entitled *The Psychology of Revolution*), but was clearly also addressing the development of democratic politics and metropolitan life in late nineteenth-century France.

2. Georg Simmel (1858–1918), born into a wealthy manufacturing family in Berlin, became a university professor of philosophy. He predominantly wrote on sociology, history, ethics, and art. It is for his sociological thought that he is now best remembered.

3. Arthur Symons (1865–1945) was a leading spirit in the Decadent literary movement in England. His *The Symbolist Movement in Literature* (1899) introduced French Symbolism to England; as editor of the *Savoy* he published Aubrey Beardsley, Ernest

Dowson, and L. P. Johnson amongst other fin-de-siècle writers. As a poet, his *Days and Nights* (1889) and *London Nights* (1895) celebrate Decadence and the *demi-monde* of the theatre, the streets, and the Café Royal. His poem 'Stella Maris' (using the iconography of the Virgin Mary to describe a street prostitute) caused outrage when first published in *The Yellow Book* in 1895.

4. Laura Ormiston Chant (1848–?) was a well-known speaker in the 1890s for women's suffrage, sexual purity, and temperance. She was also a member of the executive committee of the Women's Liberal Federation, and wrote poems and songs. Henrietta Müller, the feminist editor of the *Woman's Penny Paper* referred to Chant in 1888 as 'the most popular of our lady speakers' (1 December 1888), whilst the *Adult*, the journal of the anarchist Legitimation League, accused her of having a 'limited range of intellect, and a plentiful lack of imagination, humour and perspective' ('Two Purity Societies', August 1898). An influential representative of the 'social purity' wing of the late Victorian women's movement, Chant could as easily have been included in Chapter 4 on the 'New Woman': she had considerable affinities, in her attacks on male sexuality, with, for example, the New Woman novelist, Sarah Grand.

4

THE NEW WOMAN

'New Woman' entered the vocabulary as a popular term in 1894, in a pair of articles by Sarah Grand and 'Ouida' in the *North American Review*. It quickly became a familiar phrase in the journalistic vernacular of the day, and made regular appearances in periodical articles throughout the last decade of the nineteenth century. The New Woman was a cultural phenomenon made possible by the burgeoning women's movement of the late Victorian years. She became, in the 1890s in particular, a ubiquitous fictional archetype, appearing in novels by overtly feminist writers such as Sarah Grand, Mona Caird, Menie Muriel Dowie, and Ella Hepworth Dixon, as well as infiltrating fiction by male writers who weren't necessarily wholeheartedly committed to women's emancipation (Thomas Hardy, George Gissing, Grant Allen, Henry James, Bram Stoker). The New Woman also frequently took centre stage in short stories of the period, with George Egerton most memorably articulating a definitively 'feminine' consciousness using the short-story form. Plays from the period by Arthur Pinero, George Bernard Shaw, Sidney Grundy, and Elizabeth Robins also feature New Woman characters; New Woman poets include Amy Levy, 'Michael Field', Constance Naden, and Mathilde Blind.

The identity of the fictional New Woman was by no means homogeneous. Her opponents represented her as, variously, a 'mannish', overeducated bore (frequently a 'Girton Girl'), a bad mother (if not an embittered spinster), and as lacking in all the attributes usually associated with ideal Victorian womanhood (a penchant for self-sacrifice, a talent for home-making, a willingness to defer to men). She was also sometimes configured as an oversexed vamp (Bram Stoker's Lucy Westenra in *Dracula*, 1897, and Marie Corelli's Sybil Elton in *The Sorrows of Satan*, 1895). The New Woman was frequently lampooned in *Punch*, which printed a plethora of articles and cartoons ridiculing and condemning her throughout the mid-1890s. The 'Character Note' printed in this chapter is typical of anti-feminist responses to the New Woman in the 1890s.

Those writers who were keen to promote the New Woman and her cause represented her as an intelligent, sensitive, and sexually healthy woman, who often had ambitions beyond motherhood. The most important 1880s prototype of the New Woman was Olive Schreiner's Lyndall, in *The Story of an African Farm* (1883), whose ambition is to be an actress, regretting the decorative and domestic education she has received at a girls' boarding school. Wary of the claims of motherhood, she none the less acknowledges the significance of women's maternal role, describing the bringing up of children as 'The mightiest and noblest of human work'. A conflictual attitude towards motherhood is typical of a good deal of New Woman writing by women: Sarah Grand regarded it as central to women's self-identity, as did George Egerton, whereas Mona Caird was vehement in her opposition to the binding ties of maternity.

If the supporters of the New Woman did not always agree on the value of motherhood, then neither were they unanimous on the issue of women's sexual freedom: whilst Egerton's short stories celebrate it, all of Grand's writing prohibits the same. Feminists such as Grand represented the 'social purity' strand of feminism which was influential in the 1890s, and which is further represented by Laura Ormiston Chant in Chapter 3. What supporters of the New Woman did agree on was the necessity of a broader education for women as well as access to a wider cultural world than that deemed suitable for the bulk of middle-class Victorian women; such a commitment is powerfully evinced in the essays in this section by each of Hepworth Dixon, Eastwood, Grand, and Caird.

Not all strong-minded women of the period were feminists, as Mrs Humphry Ward's 'Appeal Against Female Suffrage' testifies. The measured response which closes this section was made by Millicent Garrett Fawcett, the leader of the late nineteenth-century women's movement.

Secondary reading: Ardis; Bland, *Banishing the Beast*; Ledger, *The New Woman*; Nelson; Pykett, *The Improper Feminine*; Showalter, *A Literature of their Own* and *Sexual Anarchy*.

1   from Mona Caird, 'Marriage' (1888)

It is not difficult to find people mild and easy-going about religion, and even politics may be regarded with wide-minded tolerance; but broach social subjects, and English men and women at once become alarmed and talk about the foundations of society and the sacredness of the home! Yet the particular form of social life, or of marriage, to which they are so deeply attached, has by no means existed from time immemorial; in fact, modern marriage, with its satellite ideas, only dates as far back as the age of Luther. Of course the institution existed long before, but our particular mode of regarding it can be traced to the era of the Reformation,[1] when commerce, competition, the great *bourgeois* class, and that remarkable thing called 'Respectability' also began to arise.

Before entering upon the history of marriage, it is necessary to clear the ground for thought upon this subject by a protest against the careless use of the words 'human nature,' and especially 'woman's nature.' History will show us, if anything will, that human nature has an apparently limitless adaptability, and that therefore no conclusion can be built upon special manifestations which may at any time be developed. Such development must be referred to certain conditions, and not be mistaken for the eternal law of being. With regard to 'woman's nature,' concerning which innumerable contradictory dogmas are held, there is so little really known about it, and its power of development, that all social philosophies are more or less falsified by this universal though sublimely unconscious ignorance. [. . .]

It is to Luther and his followers that we can immediately trace nearly all the notions that now govern the world with regard to marriage. Luther was essentially coarse and irreverent towards the oppressed sex; he placed marriage on the lowest possible platform, and, as one need scarcely add, he did not take women into counsel in a matter so deeply concerning them. In the age of chivalry the marriage-tie was not at all strict, and our present ideas of 'virtue' and 'honour' were practically non-existent. Society was in what is called a chaotic state; there was extreme licence on all sides, and although the standard of morality was far severer for the woman than for the man, still she had more or less liberty to give herself as passion dictated, and society tacitly accorded her a right of choice in matters of love. But Luther ignored all the claims of passion in a woman; in fact, she had no recognized claims whatever; she was not permitted to object to any part in life that might be assigned her; the notion of resistance to his decision never

---

[1] The Reformation was a religious and political movement of 16th-century Europe that began as an attempt to reform the Roman Catholic Church and resulted in the establishment of the Protestant churches, a movement in which Martin Luther (1483–1546) was a central figure.

occurred to him—her *role* was one of duty and of service; she figured as the legal property of a man, the safeguard against sin, and the victim of that vampire 'Respectability' which thenceforth was to fasten upon, and suck the life-blood of all womanhood. [. . .]

Now we come to the problem of to-day. This is extremely complex. We have a society ruled by Luther's views on marriage; we have girls brought up to regard it as their destiny; and we have, at the same time, such a large majority of women that they cannot all marry, even (as I think Miss Clapperton[2] puts it) if they had the fascinations of Helen of Troy and Cleopatra rolled into one. We find, therefore, a number of women thrown on the world to earn their own living in the face of every sort of discouragement. Competition runs high for all, and even were there no prejudice to encounter, the struggle would be a hard one; as it is, life for poor and single women becomes a mere treadmill. It is folly to inveigh against mercenary marriages, however degrading they may be, for a glance at the position of affairs shows that there is no reasonable alternative. We cannot ask every woman to be a heroine and choose a hard and thorny path when a comparatively smooth one (as it seems), offers itself, and when the pressure of public opinion urges strongly in that direction. A few higher natures will resist and swell the crowds of worn-out, underpaid workers, but the majority will take the voice of society for the voice of God, or at any rate of wisdom, and our common respectable marriage—upon which the safety of all social existence is supposed to rest—will remain, as it is now, the worst, because the most hypocritical, form of woman-purchase. Thus we have on the one side a more or less degrading marriage, and on the other side a number of women who cannot command an entry into that profession, but who must give up health and enjoyment of life in a losing battle with the world. [. . .]

The man who marries finds that his liberty has gone, and the woman exchanges one set of restrictions for another. She thinks herself neglected if the husband does not always return to her in the evenings, and the husband and society think her undutiful, frivolous, and so forth if she does not stay at home alone, trying to sigh him back again. The luckless man finds his wife so *very* dutiful and domesticated, and so *very* much confined to her 'proper sphere,' that she is, perchance, more exemplary than entertaining. Still, she may look injured and resigned, but she must not seek society and occupation on her own account, adding to the common mental store, bringing new interest and knowledge into the joint existence, and becoming thus a contented, cultivated and agreeable being. No wonder that while all this is forbidden we have so many unhappy wives and bored husbands. The more admirable the wives the more profoundly bored the husbands! [. . .]

[2] Jane Hume Clapperton was the socialist-feminist author of *Margaret Dunmore, or, A Socialist Home* (1888).

We come then to the conclusion that the present form of marriage—exactly in proportion to its conformity with orthodox ideas—is a vexatious failure. If certain people have made it a success by ignoring those orthodox ideas, such instances afford no argument in favour of the institution as it strands. We are also led to conclude that 'modern Respectability' draws its life-blood from the degradation of womanhood in marriage and in prostitution. But what is to be done to remedy these manifold evils? how is marriage to be rescued from a mercenary society, torn from the arms of 'Respectability,' and established on a footing which will make it no longer an insult to human dignity?

First of all we must set up an ideal, undismayed by what will seem its Utopian impossibility. Every good thing that we enjoy today was once the dream of a 'crazy enthusiast' mad enough to believe in the power of ideas and in the power of man to have things as he wills. The ideal marriage then, despite all dangers and difficulties, should be *free*. So long as love and trust and friendship remain, no bonds are necessary to bind two people together; life apart will be empty and colourless; but whenever these cease the tie becomes false and iniquitous, and no one ought to have power to enforce it. [. . .]

The economical independence of woman is the first condition of free marriage. She ought not to be tempted to marry, or to remain married, for the sake of bread and butter. But the condition is a very hard one to secure. Our present competitive system, with the daily increasing ferocity of the struggle for existence, is fast reducing itself to an absurdity, woman's labour helping to make the struggle only the fiercer. The problem now offered to the mind and conscience of humanity is to readjust its industrial organization in such a way as to gradually reduce this absurd and useless competition within reasonable limits, and to bring about in its place some form of co-operation, in which no man's interest will depend on the misfortune of his neighbour, but rather on his neighbour's happiness and welfare. It is idle to say that this cannot be done; the state of society shows quite clearly that it *must* be done sooner or later; otherwise some violent catastrophe will put an end to a condition of things which is hurrying towards impossibility. Under improved economic conditions the difficult problem of securing the real independence of women, and thence of the readjustment of their position in relation to men and to society would find easy solution. [. . .]

We see a limitless field of possibility opening out before us; [. . .] and we look forward steadily, hoping and working for the day when men and women shall be comrades and fellow-workers as well as lovers and husbands and wives, when the rich and many-sided happiness which they have the power to bestow one on another shall no longer be enjoyed in tantalizing snatches, but shall gladden and give new life to all humanity. That will be the day prophesied by Lewis Morris in *The New Order*—

> *'When man and woman in an equal union*
> *Shall merge, and marriage be a true communion.'*[3]

2   'Character Note: The New Woman' (1894)

'L'esprit de la plupart des femmes sert plus à fortifier leur folie que leur raison'[4] She is young, of course. She looks older than she really is. And she calls herself a woman. Her mother is content to be called a lady, and is naturally of small account. Novissima's chief characteristic is her unbounded self-satisfaction.

She is dark; and one feels that if she were fair she would be quite a different person. For fairness usually goes with an interest in children, and other gentle weaknesses of which Novissima is conspicuously innocent.

She dresses simply in close-fitting garments, technically known as tailor-made. She wears her elbows well away from her side. It has been hinted that this habit serves to diminish the apparent size of the waist. This may be so. Men do not always understand such things. It certainly adds to a somewhat aggressive air of independence which finds its birth in the length of her stride. Novissima strides in (from the hip) where men and angels fear to tread.

In the evening simplicity again marks her dress. Always close-fitting—always manly and wholly simple. Very little jewellery, and close-fitting hair. Which description is perhaps not technical. Her hands are steady and somewhat *en évidence*. Her attitudes are strong and independent, indicative of a self-reliant spirit.

With mild young men she is apt to be crushing. She directs her conversation and her glance above their heads. She has a way of throwing scraps of talk to them in return for their mild platitudes—crumbs from a well-stored intellectual table.

'Pictures—no, I do not care about pictures,' she says. 'They are all so pretty nowadays.'

She has a way of talking of noted men by their surnames *tout court* indicative of a familiarity with them not enjoyed by her hearer. She has a certain number of celebrities whom she marks out for special distinction—obscurity being usually one of their merits.

Prettiness is one of her pet aversions. Novissima is, by the way, not pretty herself. She is white. Pink girls call her sallow. She has a long face, with a discontented mouth, and a nose indicative of intelligence, and too large for feminine beauty as

---

[3] Sir Lewis Morris, 'The New Order', ll. 65–6. Morris (1833–1907) was a poet—a close associate of Alfred Tennyson—an educational reformer, and Welsh nationalist. His *Collected Works* had appeared in 1890.

[4] 'The spirit of the majority of women serves more to strengthen their madness than their reason'.

understood by men. Her equanimity, like her complexion, is unassailable. One cannot make her blush. It is the other way round.

In conversation she criticizes men and books freely. The military man is the object of her deepest scorn. His intellect, she tells one, is terribly restricted. He never reads—Reads, that is, with a capital. For curates she has a sneaking fondness—a feminine weakness too deeply ingrained to be stamped out in one generation of advancement.

Literary men she tolerates. They have probably read some of the books selected out of the ruck for her approval. But even to these she talks with an air suggestive of the fact that she could tell them a thing or two if she took the trouble. Which no doubt she could.

Novissima's mother is wholly and meekly under Novissima's steady thumb. The respectable lady's attitude is best described as speechless. If she opens her mouth, Novissima closes it for her with a tolerant laugh or a reference to some fictional character with whom the elder lady is fortunately unacquainted.

'Oh, Mother!' she will say, if that relative is mentioned. 'Yes; but she is hopelessly behind the times, you know.'

That settles Novissima's mother. As for her father—a pleasant, square-built man who is a little deaf—he is not either of much account. Novissima is kind to him as to an animal ignorant of its own strength, requiring management. She describes him as prim, and takes good care, in her jaunty way, that no deleterious fiction comes beneath his gaze.

'He would not understand it, poor old thing!' she explains.

And she is quite right.

Young Calamus, the critic, has had a better education than Novissima's father. He knows half-a-dozen countries, their language and their literature. And *he* does not understand Novissima's fiction.

The world is apt to take Novissima at her own valuation. When she makes a statement—and statements are her strong point—half the people in the room know better, but make the mistake of believing that they must be wrong, because she is so positive. The other half know better also, but are too wise or too lazy to argue.

While on a visit at a great country house Novissima meets young Calamus, of whom she has spoken with an off-hand familiarity for years. The genial hostess, who knows Novissima's standpoint, sends young Calamus down to dinner with her. He is clever enough for anybody, reflects my lady. And Novissima, who is delighted, is more than usually off-hand for the sake of his vanity. Calamus, as it happens, is perfectly indifferent as to what she may be thinking of him.

He is good-natured, and entirely free from self-consciousness. He is the real thing, and not the young man who is going to do something some day. He has begun doing it already. And there is a look in his keen, fair face which suggests that he intends going on.

Novissima's alertness of mind attracts him. Being a man, he is not above the influence of a trim figure and a pair of dark eyes. This is a study, and an entirely pleasant one, for Calamus is about to begin a new novel. He thinks that Novissima will do well for a side character, which is precisely that for which she serves in our daily life. She is not like the rest. But it is the rest that we fall in love with and marry.

Novissima has for the moment forced herself to the front of the stage; but in a few years she will only be a side character. Calamus knows this. He remembers the grim verdict of Dr. Kudos, his junior dean at Cambridge.

'Modern young women! Yes; interesting development of cheap education; but she proves nothing.'

Which is the worst of science. It looks upon us all as specimens, and expects us to prove something.

Novissima is pleased to approve of my lady's judgment in sending her down to dinner with Calamus. She feels that the other girls are a long way below his mental level—that they are wholly unfitted to manufacture conversation of a quality calculated to suit his literary taste.

Calamus happens to be rather a simple-minded young man. He has been everywhere. He has seen most things, and nothing seems to have touched a certain strong purity of thought which he probably acquired in the nursery. Men are thus. They carry heavier moral armour. Outward things affect them little. Novissima, on the other hand, is a little the worse for her reading.

She thinks she knows the style of talk that will suit him, and she is apparently wrong. For Calamus stares about him with speculative grey eyes. His replies are wholly commonplace and somewhat frivolous. Novissima is intensely earnest and in her desire to show him the depth of her knowledge, is not always discreet.

She talks of the future of women, of coming generations and woman's influence thereon.

'They had better busy themselves with the beginning of the future generation,' says Calamus, in his half-listening way.

'How do you mean?'

'Children,' explains Calamus in a single word.

Novissima mentions the name of one or two foreign authors not usually discussed in polite society in their own country, and Calamus frowns. She approaches one or two topics which he refuses to talk about with a simple bluntness.

He is hungry, having been among the turnips all day. He has no intention of treating Novissima to any of those delightfully original ideas which he sells to a foolish public at so much a line.

During the whole visit, Novissima and Calamus are considerably thrown together. Gossips say that she runs after him. He is superficially shallow, and refuses to be deep. She is superficially deep, and betrays her shallowness at every turn. He remembers Dr. Kudos, and makes himself very agreeable. She is only a side character. She proves nothing.

Then Calamus packs up his bag and goes back to town. There he presently marries Edith, according to a long-standing arrangement kept strictly to themselves.

Novissima is rather shocked. She feels, and says, that it is a pity. Edith is a tall girl, with motherly eyes and a clear laugh. She has no notion how clever Calamus is, and would probably care as much for him if he were a fool.

Novissima says that Mr. Calamus has simply thrown away his chance of becoming a great man. She says it, moreover, with all her customary assurance, from the high standpoint of critical disapproval that is hers. And Calamus proceeds to turn out the best work of his life-time, while Edith busies herself with mere household matters, and laughs her clear laugh over a cradle.

There is something wrong somewhere. It cannot, of course, be Novissima, for she is so perfectly sure of herself. Possibly it is Calamus who is wrong. But he is quite happy, and Edith is the same.

It is only Novissima who is not content. Dr. Kudos was right. She proves nothing. She has tried to prove that woman's mission is something higher than the bearing of children and the bringing them up. But she has failed.

---

3   Ella Hepworth Dixon, 'Why Women are
               Ceasing to Marry' (1899)

This question has been so often discussed from the strictly utilitarian aspect, that one may be pardoned for taking what, at the first blush, might be considered a somewhat flippant view of an alarming social phenomenon. It has been seriously argued—generally by masculine writers and elderly ladies who find themselves out of sympathy with the modern feminist movement—that women, nowadays, are disposed, from selfish reasons, to shirk the high privileges and duties of maternity and domestic life, to wish to compete with men, and undersell the market from motives of pure vanity, and to have so far unsexed themselves as to have lost the primordial instinct for conjugal life altogether.

Now, that any of these propositions are true can be denied by anyone even superficially acquainted with the modern movement, with those who lead it and with those who follow it. I forget which distinguished writer has said that 'every woman, in her heart, hankers after a linen-cupboard,' and this delightful aphorism may be truthfully applied, I take it, to every kind of modern woman, except the gypsy class of globe-trotters.

No. The reason why women are ceasing to marry must rather be attributed to a shifting feminine point of view, to a more critical attitude towards their masculine contemporaries. If, of late, they would seem to have shown a disposition to avoid the joys, cares, and responsibilities of the linen cupboard, it is chiefly, I think, because their sense of humour is often as keen as it was once supposed to be blunted. The proper adoring feminine attitude does not, it would seem, come naturally to the present generation, who are apt not so much—in Miltonic phrase—to 'see God' in their average suitors as to perceive in these young gentlemen certain of the least endearing qualities of the Anglo-Saxon race; those qualities, it may be whispered, which, though eminently suitable for the making of Empire, are not always entirely appreciated on the domestic hearth. This critical attitude among the womenfolk is no doubt mostly due to the enormous strides which have been made in feminine education during the last twenty years, though I hasten to add that that education has made them far more tolerant and broadminded, so that the average of domestic felicity will undoubtedly be higher as things progress. Indeed, the famous phrase, 'Tout comprendre, c'est tout pardonner,'[5] is most applicable of all to the eternal question of the sexes, and the man or woman who has mastered its significance is well on the way to make an ideal partner in marriage.

At present, however, we are in a transition stage, and there is a certain amount of misunderstanding nowadays between the sexes which make marrying and giving in marriage a somewhat hazardous enterprise.

This new and critical attitude on the part of the fair is a thing of quite recent growth. Before, and up to as late as, the mid-Victorian era, the recognised wifely pose was one of blind adoration. Directly a girl married she was supposed to think her husband perfect, unapproachable, wise and beautiful beyond all measure, and of a stupendous understanding. Most of the married ladies in the great mid-Victorian novels looked up to their spouses with admiration tempered by awe. Now that we have educated our womenfolk into a sense of humour—and there is no surer test of breadth of mind—this wifely meekness is no longer possible. Yet, seeing how the old masculine idols are shattered, and the heroes of ladies' novels are no longer Greek gods, or Guardsmen, or even men of blameless life, it is impossible not to sympathise with our masculine contemporaries, *Ces Rois en Exile*, who have lost a crown, and who have not yet made up their minds to swear 'Liberty, Equality, Fraternity!' with their feminine critics. It is possible, moreover, that the modern man has begun to see the humorous side of the question also. Occasionally he shows a disposition to step down from his pedestal,

---

[5] 'To understand everything is to forgive everything.'

and even to mix, on equal terms, with his more enlightened feminine friends. No less a modern person, for instance, than Mr. William Archer,[6] has publicly stated that he cannot sit in his stall at the theatre and listen to Katherine's abject speech about 'her lord, her king, her governor,' at the end of 'The Taming of the Shrew.'

> *'Then vail your stomachs, for it is no boot;*
> *And place your hands below your husband's foot;*
> *In token of which duty, if he please,*
> *My hand is ready, may it do him ease.'*[7]

This was the old idea of marriage. It will be readily seen that we have changed our ideals, and that if it is somewhat of an exaggeration to say that 'women are ceasing to marry,' it is certain that indiscriminate marrying has, to a certain extent, gone out. In short, *le premier venu* in no longer the successful wooer that he once was. Then, too, this shyness at being caught in the matrimonial net is largely a characteristic of the modern English maiden, for widows, like widowers, usually show an extraordinary eagerness to resume the fetters of the wedded state. Some recent amusing statistics on this subject proved that a man of forty remains a widower for two years only, while his feminine prototype shows even greater eagerness to console herself, for, under the age of thirty-five, she marries again within twenty months.

But we are at present concerned with bachelors and spinsters, of persons, in short, who have still the great experiment to make. It is certain that marriage—and its attendant responsibilities, the bringing up and starting in life of children—is looked upon far more seriously than our immediate forbears were wont to regard it. Elizabeth Barrett Browning (who, as the author of 'Aurora Leigh' undoubtedly proclaimed herself one of the earliest of the 'new women') was mortally afraid of marriage and did not attempt to conceal the fact from her adoring lover. In her recently published letters to Robert Browning, it is amusing to see how—just like any modern woman of 1899—she constantly threatens, that if they do not 'get on' when they are married, she will leave him and go to Greece. This question of 'going to Greece' becomes one of their principal humorous efforts, but there is just an acid flavour about it that makes one a little doubtful whether the distinguished author of 'Pippa Passes' appreciated the lady's constant references to such a contingency. In short, the invalid poetess who had lain for five years on a sofa, and whose knowledge of life must have been largely intuitive, was, in 1846,

---

[6] William Archer (1856–1924) was a Scottish drama critic, dramatist, translator, and promoter of the plays of Henrik Ibsen. Ibsen's plays contain a number of 'New Woman' characters, which is why Dixon approves him as a 'modern' man.

[7] Shakespeare, *The Taming of the Shrew*, v. ii. 176–9.

as timorous of entering on the adventure of marriage as the heroine of any modern problem novel.

The author of the 'Sonnets from the Portuguese' was probably alone in her generation. Then, indeed, was the happy-go-lucky time of Dan Cupid. A strictly brought-up young person was not supposed to have the only woman's privilege, the privilege of saying 'No.' She married, as a matter of course, the first young man who offered to settle down, pay taxes, and raise a family, and that family, unfortunately for her, sometimes assumed alarming proportions. This middle-class recklessness has brought, in this generation, its own Nemesis: an enormous number of young men who are obliged to seek a living in India, Africa, Canada, Australia, and New Zealand; a still larger number of young women who have to stay at home and partly earn their own livelihood.

It is in this way that we have got our young people not only separated by oceans and continents, but curiously afraid of making an experiment which their fathers and mothers entered upon—like the French in the war of 1870—with a light heart. The young girl of to-day, again, has read her 'Doll's House,' and is, it may be, firmly resolved to play the part of Nora in the conjugal duologue, and to refuse, in the now classic phrase, to be any man's 'squirrel.'[8] On his side, the modern young man shows a shrewd tendency to acquire in his wife not so much one of these engaging zoological specimens as a young person who will be able to pay the weekly bills and help him substantially in his career.

All these things, naturally, make for circumspection in marriage, and there are other reasons, chiefly owing to the amazing changes in the social life of women, which have gradually come abut during recent years. Someone has boldly laid it down that it is the bicycle which has finally emancipated women, but it is certain that there are other factors besides the useful and agreeable wheel.

For it is, primarily, the almost complete downfall of Mrs. Grundy[9] that makes the modern spinster's lot, in many respects, an eminently attractive one. Formerly, girls married in order to gain their social liberty; now, they more often remain single to bring about that desirable consummation. If young and pleasing women are permitted by public opinion to go to college, to live alone, to travel, to have a profession, to belong to a club, to give parties, to read and discuss whatsoever seems good to them, and to go to theatres without masculine escort, they have most of the privileges—and several others thrown in—for which the girl of twenty or thirty years ago was ready to barter herself to the first suitor who offered himself and the shelter of his name. Then, again, a capable woman who has begun

[8] Ibsen's *A Doll's House* was first staged in London in unexpurgated form in 1889; Nora, the heroine, leaves her husband and children at the close of the play, after a closing dialogue with her husband in which she verbally dissects their failed marriage.

[9] 'Mrs Grundy', a character in the play *Speed the Plough* (1798) by Thomas Morton (?1764–1838); Grundyism became synonymous in the 19th century with rigid conventional propriety.

a career and feels certain of advancement in it, is often as shy of entangling herself matrimonially as ambitious young men have ever shown themselves under like circumstances. Indeed, the disadvantages of marriage to a woman with a profession are more obvious than to a man, and it is just this question of maternity, with all its duties and responsibilities, which is, no doubt, occasionally the cause of many women forswearing the privileges of the married state. To be quite candid, however, I think this is very seldom the real cause of a girl's remaining single. Once her affections are involved, that bundle of nerves and emotions which we call woman is often capable of all the heroisms, and who has not numbered among their friends some delicate creature—the case of Mrs. Oliphant is one in point[10]—who has not only supported, by her own exertions, the children she bore, but the father of those children?

The modern woman, to be sure, is capable of supporting the father of her children, if she happens to be fond of that especial individual, but not (to put an extreme case) of marrying that father in order to regularise an anomalous position. The most successful German play of recent times treats, indeed, of this very subject. Herr Suderman's Magda, tyrannised over at home, goes out into the wide world and becomes a famous actress.[11] Meanwhile, during her Wanderjahre, she has had a lover, a priggish young man whom she has met in Berlin. Their relations were soon broken off, and the lover is not even aware that the beautiful young actress has had a child. On her return home, years after, she meets this man again, and he offers her marriage, providing their former *liaison* is kept secret, and the child kept away. Magda indignantly refuses, and goes back to her art, taking her little girl openly with her. The fact of her maternity, she holds, has ennobled her; her marriage with a hypocrite and a coward would degrade her in her own eyes.

This, it is true, may be described as the ultra-modern view of marriage and all that it entails, and it is one which obtains support only among the Teutonic races. The theory that a wedding ceremony mended all and ended all, is one which thoughtful Northern and Western peoples are nowadays inclined to dispute. Formerly, if there were a breath of scandal—sometimes totally unfounded—about two young people, well, you sent for the parson, rung the church-bells, and let the young couple make the best of this rash mating. Whether they were happy or not

[10] Margaret Oliphant (1828–97) was left pregnant and with two small children when her husband died of consumption. She famously supported these children as well as her brother and his family by writing nearly 125 books and working ceaselessly as a reviewer for *Blackwood's Magazine*. She was correcting proofs even on her deathbed, having tragically outlived all her children.

[11] A reference to the play *Heimat* (1893) by Hermann Sudermann (1857–1928). The play centres on the character of Magda Schwartze, an opera singer who confronts the father of her illegitimate child in a small provincial German town. Her exploits with other men are sufficient to result in the death from shock of her German lover. The play, often known as *Magda*, was widely performed in the 1890s: Magda was played by the famous actress, Sarah Bernhardt, to wide acclaim in London.

ever after, sad or merry, prosperous or unfortunate, was no affair of their neighbours. They were married; they had been sacrificed to society's rigorous demand
for the outward observance of the proprieties; and if they chafed and fumed, or,
finding themselves totally unsuited to each other, broke their spirits or their
hearts, why so did other excellent citizens, people whom Robert Louis Stevenson
quaintly calls 'respectable married people, with umbrellas,' who had bound
themselves with the same well-nigh indissoluble bonds.

It is just this general doubt of the institution of marriage, joined to that higher
ideal of the wedded state with which most educated women seem to be imbued,
that makes many people pause on the brink, and, choosing the known evil, remain
celibate rather than fly to others that they know not of. It is possible, indeed, that
a single woman of altruistic tendencies may argue that, if she is unhappy single,
only one person suffers; whereas, if she should marry, and the union turn out disagreeable, probably two people will be made miserable, and, in all probability
several people more.

Possibly it was better for the race (if quantity, and not quality, go to the making
of a nation) when its feminine half was troubled by no such doubts, but married
herself on the faintest provocation, and had no misgivings at rearing a numerous
progeny. On the other hand, it would seem certain that if woman continues to cultivate her critical faculties and her sense of humour—to exercise, in short, her
feminine prerogative of deliberate choice in the great affair of matrimony—that
the standard of human felicity will be steadily raised, and the wedded state will
shine forth in a different light to that in which it stands revealed to many thoughtful persons to-day.

In that golden age, indeed, when the equality of the sexes is reached, it is probable that the shrew, the nagging woman, and the jealous wife will all have become
curious specimens of a by-gone era. When a man marries, in short, it is to be
hoped that he will no longer 'domesticate the "Recording Angel,"' but will welcome to his hearth an agreeable companion, a gracious mistress, and a loyal
friend.

---

4   from Sarah Grand, 'The New Aspect of the
                    Woman Question' (1894)

It is amusing as well as interesting to note the pause which the new aspect of the
woman question has given to the Bawling Brothers who have hitherto tried to
howl down every attempt on the part of our sex to make the world a pleasanter
place to live in. That woman should ape man and desire to change places with him

was conceivable to him as he stood on the hearth-rug in his lord-and-master-monarch-of-all-I-survey attitude, well inflated with his own conceit; but that she should be content to develop the good material which she finds in herself and be only dissatisfied with the poor quality of that which is being offered to her in man, her mate, must appear to him to be a thing as monstrous as it is unaccountable. 'If women don't want to be men, what do they want?' asked the Bawling Brotherhood when the first misgiving of the truth flashed upon them; and then, to reassure themselves, they pointed to a certain sort of woman in proof of the contention that we were all unsexing ourselves.

It would be as rational for us now to declare that men generally are Bawling Brothers or to adopt the hasty conclusion which makes all men out to be fiends on the one hand and all women fools on the other. We have our Shrieking Sisterhood, as the counterpart of the Bawling Brotherhood. The latter consists of two sorts of men. First of all is he who is satisfied with the cow-kind of woman as being most convenient; it is the threat of any strike among his domestic cattle for more consideration that irritates him into loud and angry protests. The other sort of Bawling Brother is he who is under the influence of the scum of our sex, who knows nothing better than women of that class in and out of society, preys upon them or ruins himself for them, takes his whole tone from them, and judges us all by them. Both the cow-woman and the scum-woman are well within range of the comprehension of the Bawling Brotherhood, but the new woman is a little above him, and he never even thought of looking up to where she has been sitting apart in silent contemplation all these years, thinking and thinking, until at last she solved the problem and proclaimed for herself what was wrong with Home-is-the-Woman's-Sphere, and prescribed the remedy. [. . .]

We must look upon man's mistakes, however, with some leniency, because we are not blameless in the matter ourselves. We have allowed him to arrange the whole social system and manage or mismanage it all these ages without ever seriously examining his work with a view to considering whether his abilities and his motives were sufficiently good to qualify him for the task. We have listened without a smile to his preachments about our place in life and all we are good for, on the text that 'there is no understanding a woman.' We have endured most poignant misery for his sins, and screened him when we should have exposed him and had him punished. We have allowed him to exact all things of us, and have been content to accept the little he grudgingly gave us in return. We have meekly bowed our heads when he called us bad names instead of demanding proofs of the superiority which alone would give him a right to do so. We have listened much edified to man's sermons on the subject of virtue, and have acquiesced uncomplainingly in the convenient arrangement by which this quality has come to be altogether practised for him by us vicariously. [. . .]

The man of the future will be better, while the woman will be stronger and wiser. To bring this about is the whole aim and object of the present struggle, and with the discovery of the means lies the solution of the Woman Question. Man, having no conception of himself as imperfect from the woman's point of view, will find this difficult to understand, but we know his weakness, and will be patient with him, and help him with his lesson. It is the woman's place and pride and pleasure to teach the child, and man morally is in his infancy. There have been times when there was a doubt as to whether he was to be raised or woman was to be lowered, but we have turned that corner at last; and now woman holds out a strong hand to the child-man, and insists, but with infinite tenderness and pity, upon helping him up. [. . .]

5   from M. Eastwood, 'The New Woman in
              Fiction and in Fact' (1894)

As the novel heroine of the New Woman we have already been made extremely familiar with her. She has been flashed upon us in a rapid succession of such startling and vivid pictures, as to have thrown the dull, sober-tinted presentations of the old sort entirely into the shade. And to the modern mind, thirsting for whatever is novel and sensational, how sordid, how prosaic that other poor dead-level creature appears when, in the last chapter, she is left clinging fatuously to the male prop she has by dint of many pretty old-fashioned feminine dodges, succeeded in securing, or washing the baby in a nursing apron, compared with the flashing, dashing, ripping, tripping creation, yclept the New Woman.

Let us hasten to put the antiquated specimen on the shelf, with her insipid face to the wall, and forget her whilst we lose ourselves in the bewildering contemplation of the weirdly bewitching, the soulful, the mysterious, the tricksy, the tragic, the electrifying, the intensely-intense, and utterly unfathomable new one.

We observe her breathlessly, for she keeps us on the tenter-hooks of delightfully awful expectation. She is kaleidoscopic in the variety of her aspects. Her moods are like sudden gleams of electric fire, alternating with murky darkness, for at last—at last her soul has burst its fetters and is free!

That in the exuberance of a recently acquired freedom, after centuries of suppression by the tyrant man, this soul of hers should run somewhat amuck with her is a perfectly natural consequence. Like a riderless horse on the battle-field, it charges about with reckless abandon, unmindful of whom or what it may trample under foot. But mostly does the New Woman of fiction resemble a syren, luring the easy victim to his destruction. She has only to strike a vibrating 'key-note' on her seductive lyre, and behold he lies grovelling at her feet![12] And he likes it, for never does she let him feel bored a single minute. Whether in the capacity of lover or husband, she continues to hold him spell-bound. Usually, however, she begins by marrying him; he is easier to manage that way. And if she has kept him lively before the event, he now finds it grown infinitely livelier. His existence is one thrill of suspense. [. . .]

In short, she is 'Grand', every 'Iota' of her![13] Quite too much so, however, for the usages of our grossly practical, work-a-day world; therefore, much as she entertains him, it is a relief to the ordinary mortal to discover that she has no existence in it, but is rather a creation of the hyperbolically emancipated woman's riotous imagination.

None the less is the New Woman a positive and tangible fact. Only, she is altogether otherwise. Far from being unfitted for the world in which she lives, she is adapting herself with marvellous rapidity to its altered conditions. And why should she not? Why should the strong current of evolution which bears all else before it, leave woman alone behind? [. . .]

The New Woman of today will be the woman of the future. Only more so. At present she is passing through the ugly duckling stage. Like a growing girl, she has too many elbows. Her movements are spasmodic; her manners lack repose, and her voice has not yet acquired that rich and softly modulated cadence which is woman's most irresistible attribute. Her detractors would have us believe that those tender and endearing charms which ought to distinguish her gentler sex will be entirely wanting in her. As proof of the assertion they point to the audacious young person who, seated astride a bicycle, dressed in knickerbockers and peaked cap, shoots past them on the public road. Their grimly prejudiced humour sees in her the fast woman who cultivates man's pet vices, drives four-in-hand to the races and snaps her fingers in the face of respectable Mrs. Grundy.[14]

The abiding New Woman wears a very different aspect. Her brow is serious, for the brain behind is crammed as full of high projects as is the satchel she carries of pamphlets on the missions, rights, grievances and demands of her sex. She has neither the heart nor has she the time for fooling, and if she assumes certain articles of masculine garb on occasion, it is solely on account of their superior utility; if she rides out on a bicycle it is for the purpose of strengthening her muscles and expanding her lungs for the great work she has before her. Young as she

[12] A reference to George Egerton's collection of short stories, *Keynotes*, which inaugurated a series of 'Key-note' texts by New Woman writers. Each book cover incorporated initials of the writer into the design of a key: it symbolized the latch-key of freedom to enter and leave the family home without paternal authority.

[13] Playful references to fellow 'New Woman' writers: Sarah Grand (1854–1943) and 'Iota' (Kathleen Caffyn) (1853–1926).

[14] See n. 9 above.

is she talks fearlessly and authoritatively on all and every subject of social deprav-
ity, for there is nothing which was hitherto hidden from her which she has not
revealed. And since she knows the worst her soaring ambition will be content
with nothing less than the reformation of the entire male sex. There are those who
believe that the extreme remedy she is prepared to apply—that of refusing to unite
herself in wedlock to the man whose morals are not as pure as her own—cannot
fail in its salutary results. Her scheme of reform extends also beyond the fathers of
the coming race and includes the weak and foolish sisters who have obstinately
remained behind in their crumbling preserves. Observing how these laggards
have taken to tippling of late, the ardent reformer vows that she will never rest
until grocers' licences have been abolished. That she is herself a total abstainer is
not the least of her virtues. [. . .]

    Here has begun the radical change which is to effect the future generations.
She is fortifying its walls against the unworthy invader and has sworn to surrender only at the instance of disinterested love. Upon the strength of her purpose
depends the degree of her success.

---

6   from Mrs Humphry Ward *et al.*, 'An
             Appeal Against Female Suffrage' (1889)

We, the undersigned, wish to appeal to the common sense and the educated
thought of the men and women of England against the proposed extension of the
Parliamentary suffrage to women.

    1. While desiring the fullest possible development of the powers, energies,
and education of women, we believe that their work for the State, and their
responsibilities towards it, must always differ essentially from those of men, and
that therefore their share in the working of the State machinery should be different from that assigned to men. Certain large departments of the national life are of
necessity worked exclusively by men. To men belong the struggle of debate and
legislation in Parliament; the hard and exhausting labour implied in the administration of the national resources and powers; the conduct of England's relations
towards the external world; the working of the army and navy; all the heavy,
laborious, fundamental industries of the State, such as those of mines, metals,
and railways; the lease and supervision of English commerce, the management of
our vast English finance, the service of that merchant fleet on which our food
supply depends. In all these spheres women's direct participation is made impossible either by the disabilities of sex, or by strong formations of custom and habit

resting ultimately upon physical difference, against which it is useless to contend. [. . .]

The care of the sick and the insane; the treatment of the poor; the education of children: in all these matters, and others besides, [women] have made good their claim to larger and more extended powers. We rejoice in it. But when it comes to questions of foreign or colonial policy, or of grave constitutional change, then we maintain that the necessary and normal experience or women—speaking generally and in the mass—does not and can never provide them with such materials for sound judgement as are open to men. [. . .]

2. If we turn from the *right* of women to the suffrage—a right which on the grounds just given we deny—to the effect which the possession of the suffrage may be expected to have on their character and position and on family life, we find ourselves no less in doubt. It is urged that the influence of women in politics would tell upon the side of morality. We believe that it does so tell already, and will do so with greater force as women by improved education fit themselves to exert it more widely and efficiently. But it may be asked, On what does this moral influence depend? We believe that it depends largely on qualities which the natural position and functions of women as they are at present tend to develop, and which might be seriously impaired by their admission to the turmoil of active political life. These qualities are, above all, sympathy and disinterestedness. Any disposition of things which threatens to lessen the national reserve of such forces as these we hold to be a misfortune. It is notoriously difficult to maintain them in the presence of party necessities and in the heat of party struggle. Were women admitted to this struggle, their natural eagerness and quickness of temper would probably make them hotter partisans than men. [. . .]

3. Proposals for the extension of the suffrage to women are beset with grave practical difficulties. If votes are given to unmarried women on the same terms as they are given to men, large numbers of women leading immoral lives will be enfranchised on the one hand, while married women, who, as a rule, have passed through more of the practical experiences of life than the unmarried, will be excluded. [. . .]

4. A survey of the manner in which this proposal has won its way into practical politics leads us to think that it is by no means ripe for legislative solution. A social change of momentous gravity has been proposed: the mass of those immediately concerned in it are notoriously indifferent; there has been no serious and general demand for it, as is always the case if a grievance is real and reform necessary; the amount of information collected is quite inadequate to the importance of the issue; and the public has gone through no sufficient discipline of discussions on the subject. [. . .]

5. It is often urged that certain injustices of the law towards women would be easily and quickly remedied were the political power of the vote conceded to

them; and that there are many wants, especially among working women, which are now neglected, but which the suffrage would enable them to press on public attention. We reply that during the past half century all the principal injustices of the law towards women have been amended by means of the existing constitutional machinery; and with regard to those that remain, we see no signs of any unwillingness on the part of Parliament to deal with them. [. . .]

In conclusion: nothing can be further from our minds than to seem to depreciate the position or the importance of women. It is because we are keenly alive to the enormous value or their special contribution to the community, that we oppose what seems to us likely to endanger that contribution. We are convinced that the pursuit of a mere outward equality with men is for women not only vain but demoralising. It leads to a total misconception of woman's true dignity and special mission. It tends to personal struggle and rivalry, where the only effort of both the great divisions of the human family should be to contribute the characteristic labour and the best gifts of each to the common stock.

[The 104 signatories to the 'Appeal' comprised wives of politicians, scientists, men of letters and journalists, as well as titled ladies, novelists, female academics, school teachers and nurses. They included: Mrs Humphry Ward, Miss Beatrice Potter, Lady Randolph Churchill, Mrs T. H. Green, Mrs Leslie Stephen, Mrs Huxley, Mrs Lynn Linton, Mrs Rathbone Greg, Mrs H. H. Asquith, Mrs Matthew Arnold, Mrs Arnold Toynbee, and Mrs Max Müller.]

---

7   from Millicent Garrett Fawcett, 'The Appeal
         Against Female Suffrage: A Reply' (1889)

[. . .] The Protest speaks in congratulatory words of all recent changes which have extended opportunities of usefulness to women. [. . .] But, hardly any out of the hundred and four ladies who now rejoice in these changes have helped them while their issue was in any way doubtful. [. . .] The names of the women to whose unselfish and untiring labours we owe what has been done for women during the last twenty-five years in education, in social and philanthropic work, in proprietary rights, in some approach towards justice as regards the guardianship of children, in opening the means of medical education, are conspicuous by their absence, and for an excellent reason: they support the extension of the suffrage to duly qualified women. At the head of the educational movement for women are Miss Emily Davies, Miss Clough, Mrs Henry Sidgwick, Miss

Dorothea Beale of Cheltenham, Mrs William Grey, Miss Shirreff, Miss Buss, and Miss Eleanor Smith of Oxford [. . .] so are the Misses Davenport Hill, Miss Florence Nightingale, Miss Cons, Mrs Josephine Butler, Mrs Bright Lucas, Mrs Barnett, and Miss Irby, as representing the best women's work in philanthropy of various kinds; so are Dr Elizabeth Blackwell, Mrs Garrett Anderson, M.D., Dr Sophia Jex Blake, Miss Edith Pechey, M.D., and, I believe, all the women who have helped to open the medical profession to women.

A further consideration of the *Nineteenth Century* list of names shows that it contains a very large preponderance of ladies to whom the lines of life have fallen in pleasant places. There are very few among them of the women who have had to face the battle of life alone, to earn their living by daily hard work. [. . .]

[. . .] The ladies [. . .] mention the undoubted fact that married women must either be included or excluded in any women's suffrage Bill. [. . .] For my own part, it has always seemed for many reasons right to [. . .] support the measures which would enfranchise single women and widows, and not wives during the lifetime of their husbands. The case for the enfranchisement of women who are standing alone and bearing the burden of citizenship as ratepayers and taxpayers, seems unanswerable. If we have household suffrage, let the head of the house vote, whether that head be a man or a woman. The enfranchisement of wives is an altogether different question [. . .] If they were enfranchised, the effect, in ninety-nine cases out of a hundred, would be to give two votes to the husband. Wives are bound by law to obey their husbands. No other class in the community is in this position, and it seems inexpedient to allow political independence (which would only be nominal) to precede actual independence. [. . .]

[. . .] We do not want women to be bad imitations of men; we neither deny nor minimise the differences between men and women. The claim of women to representation depends to a large extent on those differences. Women bring something to the service of the state different from that which can be brought by men. Let this fact be frankly recognised and let due weight be given to it in the representative system of the country.

EDITORS' NOTES

1. Alison Mona Caird (1854–1931), daughter of the Scottish gentry, achieved notoriety with her essay 'Marriage' in 1888: the *Daily Telegraph* responded with a letters column entitled 'Is Marriage a Failure?' which elicited 27,000 letters from *Telegraph* readers, opening up the marriage debate to a wide public sphere. Her essays were eventually published as *The Morality of Marriage: And Other Essays on the Status and*

Destiny of Woman (1897). Caird was also a very successful author of New Woman novels: see especially *The Wing of Azrael* (1889) and *The Daughters of Danaus* (1894). She continued writing into the 1930s.

2. The high-cultural *Cornhill Magazine* (it was edited by Leslie Stephen, the father of Virginia Woolf, between 1871 and 1882) here helps to establish the popular stereotype of the New Woman as an unmaternal, superficially educated bore.

3. Ella Hepworth Dixon (1855-1932) was a fairly prolific journalist and travel writer as well as an author of New Woman fiction, most notably *The Story of a Modern Woman* (1894), a painful account of a young woman's attempt to forge a writing career. Her father William Hepworth Dixon was editor of the *Athenaeum*, which meant that she had many literary connections with, for example, Oscar Wilde, Henry James, and George Meredith—all of whom are discussed in her memoir *As I Knew Them*. She wrote occasionally for the *Yellow Book*. In the late 1890s she was editor of *The English-woman*, which became a clearing-house for advertising clerical and other jobs for a newly emergent women's labour market.

4. Sarah Grand (Frances Elizabeth McFall, née Clarke) (1854-1943) was an active suffrage campaigner and one of the most popular of the New Woman writers, famously locking horns with 'Ouida' on the subject in 1894. Grand horrified many readers with her frank treatment of sexually transmitted disease in her most popular novel, *The Heavenly Twins* (1893); she is also well known for her semi-autobiographical novel *The Beth Book* (1897). She differed from Mona Caird in her commitment to maternity as woman's highest function (Caird was far more sceptical).

5. M. Eastwood is notable for the subtle and important distinction she makes here between lampooning journalistic representations of the New Woman and her living and breathing feminist counterpart whose demands were far more reasonable.

6. 'An Appeal Against Female Suffrage' is important in its exposure of that sizeable body of successful middle-class women who did not support the campaign for women's suffrage. Mary Ward (1851-1920), who compiled the petition, was herself the author of a novel featuring a New Woman (*Marcella*, 1894), but is better known for her best-selling Christian-socialist novel, *Robert Elsmere* (1888). Beatrice Potter (1858-1943) later married Sydney Webb, became involved in Fabian socialism, and expressed regret at having signed the petition.

7. Millicent Garrett Fawcett (1847-1929) was the leader of the English women's suffrage movement in the 1890s and was involved in the movement from the start, being a member of the first women's suffrage committee established in 1867. She also laboured for married women's property rights.

5

LITERARY DEBATES

The literature of the fin de siècle is often associated with the Decadent movement, the 'Naughty Nineties' tag accentuating the importance to the period of writers such as Oscar Wilde, Ernest Dowson, Arthur Symons, and the many contributors to the 'Aesthetic' *Yellow Book*. The literary terrain was, though, much fought over: the New Woman fiction was in the ascendant, the rise of literary and dramatic naturalism was both condemned and defended, swashbuckling imperial adventure stories flooded the ever-expanding mass market, and literary Modernism was struggling to be born. Often presenting themselves as distinct, these literary and artistic 'movements' frequently nudged elbows with one another, jockeying for position in a rapidly transforming cultural landscape. The New Woman writing was lumped together by its opponents with the writing of the Decadent movement which was in turn designated as 'effeminate': Hugh Stutfield's reference to 'yellow lady novelists' was by no means an isolated incidence. Naturalism also frequently overlapped with proto-feminist writing, both being attacked for their 'candour' in sexual matters and their 'scientific' scrutiny of areas of human experience considered sordid by the literary establishment. The naturalist movement in the theatre, spearheaded by Ibsen, was self-consciously 'new'; it was at the same time a reaction against the nineteenth-century theatre's domination by popular dramatic forms; melodramas and romances formed the staple theatrical diet until Ibsen's 'serious' realistic dramas took the London stage by storm from 1889 onwards. The project of naturalist fiction was comparable: setting itself up in opposition both to the crippling prudery of the circulating libraries and to the demands of 'Grub Street', novels by George Moore, George Gissing, Jack London, and Margaret Harkness bear the hallmarks of Zola's naturalistic fictional techniques. Naturalist and 'Decadent' literature, although its proponents might not have recognized one another, were alike in their repudiation of the mass market and of 'Mrs Grundy'.

The 'modern spirit of revolt' and 'contempt for conventionalities' identified by Hugh Stutfield was partly enabled by the challenge to the circulating libraries in the 1890s. Throughout much of the second half of the nineteenth century, what writers of fiction could publish had depended on the guardians of such libraries: the standard 'three-decker' novels cost far too much to buy, so readers generally subscribed to a circulating library, the likes of which gradually gained a stranglehold over literary production; if publishers couldn't persuade the libraries to buy an author's book, then it would be a commercial failure. The proliferation of cheap single-volume novels in the 1890s, which reached a wider, less 'select' group of readers than that targeted by Mudie's and other middle-class circulating libraries, changed all this. Freed from the confining moral agenda laid down by the libraries, authors enjoyed a greater freedom of expression in the 1890s. This did not mean, though, that authors were not attacked when they overstepped the boundaries laid down by the literary establishment: Thomas Hardy was so discouraged by the moral outcry which ensued upon the publication of *Jude the Obscure* in 1895 that he never wrote another novel.

The growth of cheap single-volume editions, widely available at railway bookstalls, not only freed writers from Mudie's moral bondage, but also encouraged the growth of a huge popular market. One substantial part of this market comprised adventure stories and romances, and it is this popular field of literature which Andrew Lang defends in his essay 'Realism and Romance'. Politely rejecting the claims of 'serious' literature, Lang celebrates the virtues of 'swashbuckling' adventures and romances, claiming Malory's Arthurian romances and Homer's *Odyssey* as eminent romantic antecedents. Writers of masculine romances such as Rider Haggard, Stevenson, and Kipling were hugely popular, vying with female writers of romance such as 'Ouida' and Marie Corelli for their share of the popular fiction market.

Mass-produced fiction of the fin de siècle was a far cry from the project of literary Decadence. As described by Arthur Symons, such literature was avowedly 'aesthetic', appealing to a select audience and attempting to seek out 'the truth of spiritual things to the spiritual vision'. Symons's 'Decadent' canon—the Goncourts, Verlaine, Maeterlinck, Huysmans, and W. E. Henley—is, like Modernism, emphatically a European movement, led, like literary naturalism, by the French. Emphasizing the importance of 'nuance', the 'unsayability' of certain sensations, and the 'exquisite' nature of the feelings that Decadent writers try to express, Symons draws on musical and artistic analogies to attempt to define the Decadent movement in literature, notably making comparisons with the Impressionist and Symbolist schools. Literary

Modernism, then, usually associated with the 1920s and 1930s, in fact was 'born' amongst the writers of the Decadent school of the late nineteenth century, identified so acutely here by Symons.

Secondary reading: Beckson, Arthur Symons and London in the 1890s; Bristow, '"Sterile Ecstasies"' and Empire Boys; Dowling; Gagnier; Huyssen; Holbrook; Jackson; Miller; Pykett, Engendering Modernism and Reading Fin-de-Siècle Fictions; Showalter, Sexual Anarchy; Stokes, In the Nineties; Sturgis; Thornton; Trotter.

---

1   from Andrew Lang, 'Realism and Romance' (1886)

The question attributed to St. Bernard, 'Whither hast thou come?' is agitating critical and literary minds. There has seldom been so much writing about the value and condition of contemporary literature—that is, of contemporary fiction. In English journals and magazines a new Battle of the Books is being fought and they are the books of the circulating library. Literary persons have always revelled in a brawl, and now they are in the thick of the fray. Across the Atlantic the question of Novel or Romance—of Romance or Realism—appears to be taking the place of the old dispute about State Rights, and is argued by some with polished sarcasm, by others with libellous vigour. [. . .] Surely a superior person may be excused for thinking contemporary literature is rather overvalued, when all this pother is made about a few novels. [. . .] But the world will not take Mr. Matthew Arnold's advice about neglecting the works of our fleeting age. [. . .]

However much we may intellectually prefer the old books, the good books, the classics, we find ourselves reading the books of the railway stall. Here have we for travelling companions 'The History and Adventures of Joseph Andrews and his Friend, Mr Abraham Adams' (1743) on one side and 'Lady Branksmere' (1887) by the author of 'Phyllis,' on the other.[1] The diverting author of 'Phyllis' will pardon me for thinking Henry Fielding a greater author than she, but it is about the charming Margaret Daryl in her novel that I am reading just now and *not* about the brother of Pamela. We are all like that, we all praise the old and peruse the new; he who turns over this magazine is in no better case.

'Hypocrite lecteur, mon semblable, mon frère!'[2]

[1] *Lady Branksmere* and *Phyllis* were popular Victorian novels published anonymously by Margaret Wolfe Argles.

[2] 'You, hypocritical reader—my shadow, my brother!' Charles Baudelaire, last line from the opening poem, 'To the Reader', in *Les Fleurs du Mal* (1857), a key reference-point for late 19th-century literature.

After this confession and apology, one may enter the lists where critical lances are broken and knights unsaddled; where authors and reviewers, like Malory's men, 'lash at each other marvellously.' The dispute is the old dispute about the two sides of the shield. Fiction is a shield with two sides, the silver and the golden: the study of manners and of character, on one hand; on the other, the description of adventure, the delight of romantic narrative. Now, these two aspects blend with each other so subtly—and so constantly, that it really seems the extreme of perversity to shout for nothing but romance on one side, or for nothing but analysis of character and motive on the other. Yet for such abstractions and divisions people are clamouring and quarrelling. On one side, we are told that accurate minute descriptions of life as it is lived, with all its most sordid forms carefully elaborated, is the essence of literature; on the other, we find people maintaining that analysis is *ausgespielt* [. . .] and that the great heart of the people demands tales of swashing blows, of distressed maidens rescued, of 'murders grim and great', of magicians and princesses and wanderings in fairy lands forlorn. Why should we not have all sorts, and why should the friends of one kind of diversion quarrel with the lovers of another kind? [. . .] What can be more ludicrous than to excommunicate Thackeray, because we rejoice in Dickens; to boycott Daisy Miller because we admire Ayesha?[3] Upon my word, I hardly know which of these maidens I would liefer meet in the paradise of fiction, where all good novel readers hope to go: whether the little pathetic butterfly who died in Rome, or she who shrivelled away in the flame of Kor. Let us be thankful for good things and plenty of them; thankful for this vast and goodly assembly of people who never were; 'daughters of dreams and of stories,' among whom we may all make friends that will never be estranged. [. . .]

What is good, what is permanent may be found in fiction of every *genre*, and shall we 'crab' and underrate any *genre* because it chances not to be that which we are best fitted to admire? I, for one, admire M. Dostoieffsky so much, and so sincerely, that I pay him the supreme tribute of never reading him at all. Of 'Le Crime et le Chatiment,' some one has said that 'it is good—but powerful.'[4] That is exactly the truth; it is too powerful for me. I read in that book till I was crushed and miserable; so bitterly true it is, so dreadfully exact, such a quintessence of all the imaginable misery of man. Then, after reading the lowest deep of sympathetic abandonment (which I plumbed in about four chapters), I emerged, feeling that I had enough of M. Dostoieffsky for one lifetime. The novel, to my thinking, is simply perfect in its kind; only the kind happens to be too powerful for my con-

---

[3] Henry James, *Daisy Miller* (1879); Ayesha is the African goddess in Rider Haggard's *She* (1886). Lang co-wrote a novel with Haggard, *The World's Desire*, in 1890.

[4] Fyodor Dostoevsky's *Crime and Punishment* was originally published in Russian in 1866; most of his novels only appeared in English translation in the 1880s, where they were widely debated and disputed.

stitution. [. . .] No admiration however enthusiastic or personal, of modern stories of adventure can blind one to the merits of works of Realism like [. . .] 'Le Crime et le Chatiment,' or 'The Bostonians.'[5] These are real, they are excellent; and if one's own taste is better pleased by another kind of writing, none the less they are good for the people whom they suit; nay, they should be recognized as good by any one with an eye in his literary head. One only begins to object if it is asserted that this genre of fiction is the only permissible genre, that nothing else is of the nature of art. For it is evident that this kind of realism has a tendency to blink many things in life which are as real as jealous third-rate shrews and boozy pressmen. [. . .] [T]he tendency of Realism in fiction is often to find the Unpleasant Real in character much more abundant than the Pleasant Real. I am a pessimist myself, as the other Scot was a 'leear,' but I have found little but good in man and woman. Politics apart, men and women seem almost always to be kind, patient, courteous, good-humoured, and well-bred in all ranks of society when once you know them well. I think that the Realists, while they certainly show us the truth, are fondest of showing that aspect of it which is really the less common as well as the less desirable. Perhaps mean people are more easily drawn to generous people; at all events from the school of Realists we get too many mean people— even from a Realist who is as little a Realist as the king was a Royalist—from M. Zola.[6] These writers appear not to offer up Henry Fielding's prayer to the Muse, 'Fill my pages with humour, till mankind learn the good nature to laugh only at the follies of others, and the humility to grieve at their own.' There is not much humour in their works, and little good humour is bred of them. That is, the difference between work like Thackeray's, where there are abundant studies of the infinitely little in human nature, and work like that of many modern amateurs of Realism. 'It takes all sorts to make a world,' and all sorts, by virtue of his humour, Thackeray gives us. He gives us Captain Costigan and Harry Poker, as well as the crawling things in 'Lovel the Widower.' He gives us gentlemen and ladies as well as tuft-hunters and the George Brandons of this world. Fielding and Scott have this humour, this breadth, this greatness. Were I in a mood to disparage the modern Realists (whereas I have tried to show that their books are, in substance, about as good as possible, granting the genre), I might say that they not only use the microscope, and ply experiments, but ply them, too often, *in corpore vili.*[7] One does not dream of denying that they do exhibit noble and sympathetic

---

[5] Henry James, *The Bostonians* (1886). The character analysis of the 'morbid' Olive Chancellor would no doubt have distressed Lang, given the almost exclusively masculine concerns of the late Victorian adventure novel.

[6] Emile Zola (1840–1902) was the leading writer, theorist, and controversialist of a new mode of 'experimental' realism, known as Naturalism; his manifesto essay, 'The Experimental Novel', was written in 1884. For English conservatives, the form was associated with the investigation of immoral and sexual subjects.

[7] 'In matter of little value'.

characters now and then. But happy, and jolly, and humorous people they hardly ever show us; yet these have their place among realities. [. . .] If I were to draw up an indictment, I might add that some of them have an almost unholy knowledge of the nature of women. One would as lief explore a girl's room, and tumble about her little household treasures, as examine so curiously the poor secrets of her heart and tremors of her frame. [. . .] Such analysis makes one feel uncomfortable in the reading, makes one feel intrusive and unmanly. It is like overhearing a confession by accident. [. . .] Good it may be, clever it is; but it is not good for me. [. . .]

At this moment the strife is between the partisans of Realism thus understood and the partisans of stories told for the story's sake. [. . .] The 'Odyssey' is the typical example of a romance—as probable as 'The Arabian Nights,' yet unblemished—in the conduct of the plot, and peopled by men and women of flesh and blood. Are we to be told that we love the 'Odyssey' because the barbaric element has not died out of our blood, and because we have a childish love of marvels, miracles, man-eating giants, women who never die, 'murders grim and great,' and Homer's other materials. Very well. 'Public opinion,' in Boston, may condemn us, but we will get all the fun we can out of the ancestral barbarism of our natures. I only wish we had more of it. The Coming Man may be bald, toothless, highly 'cultured', and addicted to tales of introspective analysis. I don't envy him: when he has got rid of that relic of the ape, his hair; those relics of the age of combat, his teeth and nails; that survival of barbarism, his delight in the last battles of Odysseus, Laertes' son. [. . .] Not for nothing did Nature leave us all savages under our white skins; she has wrought thus that we might have many delights, among others 'the joy of adventurous living' and of reading about adventurous living. [. . .]

The advantage of our mixed condition, civilised at top with the old barbarian under our clothes, is just this, that we can enjoy all sorts of things. We can enjoy 'John Inglesant' (some of us), and others can revel in Buffalo Bill's Exhibition.[8] Do not let us cry that, because we are 'cultured,' there shall be no Buffalo Bill. Do not let us exclaim that, because we can read Paulus Silentiarius and admire Rufinus there shall be no broadside ballads nor magazine poetry.[9] If we will only be tolerant, we shall permit the great public also to delight in our few modern romances of adventure. They may be 'savage survivals,' but so is the whole of the

[8]   A contrast of high and low. J. H. Shorthouse's *John Inglesant*—an intense evocation of 17th-century Italy—was privately published in 1880, then issued to great intellectual acclaim the following year. William Cody (1846–1917) first brought his famous Buffalo Bill Wild West shows to Europe in the 1880s. They restaged famous battles with American Indian tribes: 6 million people attended the show at the Chicago World Fair in 1893.

[9]   Two late Roman poets: Paulus Silentiarius (6th century AD) survives in fragments and a couple of longer poems; Rufinus (4th century AD) was a convert to Christianity, who wrote commentaries and translations of the Bible, and studied in Jerusalem.

poetic way of regarding Nature. The flutter in the dovecots of culture caused by three or four boys' books is amazing. Culture is saddened at discovering that not only boys and illiterate people, but even critics not wholly illiterate, can be moved by a tale of adventure. 'Treasure Island' and 'Kidnapped' are boys' books written by an author of whose genius, for narrative, for delineation of character, for style, I hardly care to speak, lest enthusiasm should seem to border on fanaticism.[10] But, with all his gifts, Mr. Stevenson intended only a boys' book when he wrote 'Treasure Island' and restored Romance. He had shown his hand as a novelist of character and analysis in 'Prince Otto.' But he did not then use just the old immortal materials of adventure. As soon as he touched those, he made a boys' book which became a classic, and deserved to be a classic. 'Kidnapped' is still better, to my taste, and indeed Scott himself might have been the narrator of Alan Breck's battle, of his wanderings, of his quarrel with the other Piper. But these things are a little over the heads of boys who have not the literary taste. They prefer the adventures of Sir Harry and the other Allan in Kukuana-land or in Zu-Vendis.[11] We may not agree with their taste, but that *is* their taste. Probably no critic would venture to maintain that the discoverer of Kor has the same literary qualities as the historian of John Silver. It seems a pity, when we chance to have two good things, to be always setting one off against the other, and fighting about their relative merits. Mr. Stevenson and Mr. Rider Haggard have both written novels, have both written boys' books. Personally, I prefer their boys' books to their novels. They seem happier in their dealings with men than with women, and with war than with love. Of the two, Jess appears to me real, and the wife of Mr. Stevenson's Prince Otto shadowy. But Mr. Haggard's savage ladies are better than his civilised fair ones, while there is not a petticoat in 'Kidnapped' or 'Treasure Island.' As for 'She' herself, nobody can argue with a personal affection, which I entertain for that long-lived lady.

> 'The holy priests
> Bless her when she is riggish,'[12]

Shakespeare says of Cleopatra and, like the holy priests, I can pardon certain inconsequences in Ayesha. But other moralists must find her trying; poor Ayesha who 'was a true lover,' though she did not therefore, like Guinevere, 'make a good end.' Apparently female characters are not the strong point of either Mr. Haggard or Mr. Stevenson, as far as they have gone. [. . .]

---

[10] Lang is referring to the work of Robert Louis Stevenson (1850–94). *Treasure Island* (1883) was held to mark the renaissance of the traditional 'romance'; *Kidnapped* (1886), a historical romance based in Scotland, would have strongly appealed to Lang's love of Scottish folklore and history.

[11] References to lead characters in novels by H. Rider Haggard (1856–1925).

[12] Shakespeare, *Antony and Cleopatra*, II. ii. 239–40. This comes at the end of Enobarbus' famous description of Cleopatra on her 'burnish'd throne'.

Whatever the merits and demerits of modern English romance, one thing is certain. It is now undeniable that the love of adventure, and of mystery, and of a good fight lingers in the minds of men and women. [. . .] The moral is not that even the best boys' books are the highest class of fiction, but that there is still room for romance and love of romance in civilised human nature. Once more it is apparent that no single *genre* of novel is in future, or at least in the near future, to be a lonely literary sultan; lording it without rival over the circulating libraries. But to argue, therefore, that there is no more room for the novel of analysis and of minute study of character would be merely to make a new mistake. There will always, while civilised life endures, and while man is not yet universally bald and toothless—there will always be room for all kinds of fiction, *so long as they are good*. A new Jane Austen would be as successful as a new Charles Kingsley. More-over, it will always be possible to combine the interest of narrative and of adventure with the interest of character. [. . .] The lesson, then, is that it 'takes every sort to make a world', that all sorts have their chance, and that none should assert an exclusive right to existence. Do not let us try to write as if we were writing for *Homo Calvus*,[13] the bald-headed student of the future. Do not let us despise the day of small things, and of small people; the microscopic examination of the hearts of young girls and beery provincial journalists. These, too, are human, and not alien from us, nor unworthy of our interest. The dubitations of a Bostonian spinster may be made as interesting, by one genius, as a fight between a crocodile and a catawampus, by another genius. One may be as much excited in trying to discover whom a married American lady is really in love with, as by the search for the Fire of Immortality in the heart of Africa. But if there is to be no *modus vivendi*, if the battle between the crocodile of Realism and the catawampus of Romance is to be fought out to the bitter end—why, in that Ragnaruk, I am on the side of the catawampus.

---

2   from Arthur Symons, 'The Decadent Movement
          in Literature' (1893)

The latest movement in European literature has been called by many names, none of them quite exact or comprehensive—Decadence, Symbolism, Impressionism, for instance. It is easy to dispute over words, and we shall find that

---

[13] 'Hairless man'.

Verlaine[14] objects to being called a Decadent, Maeterlinck[15] to being called a Symbolist, Huysmans[16] to being called an Impressionist. These terms, as it happens, have been adopted as the badge of little separate cliques, noisy, brainsick young people who haunt the brasseries of the Boulevard Saint-Michel, and exhaust their ingenuities in theorizing over the works they cannot write. But, taken frankly as epithets which express their own meaning, both Impressionism and Symbolism convey some notion of that new kind of literature which is perhaps more broadly characterized by the word Decadence. The most representative literature of the day—the writing which appeals to, which has done so much to form, the younger generation—is certainly not classic, nor has it any relation with that old antithesis of the Classic, the Romantic. After a fashion it is no doubt a decadence: an intense self-consciousness, a restless curiosity in research, an over-subtilizing refinement upon refinement, a spiritual and moral perversity. If what we call the classic is indeed the supreme art—those qualities of perfect simplicity, perfect sanity, perfect proportion, the supreme qualities—then this representative literature of today, interesting, beautiful, novel as it is, is really a new and beautiful and interesting disease.

Healthy we cannot call it, and healthy it does not wish to be considered. The Goncourts,[17] in their prefaces, in their *Journal*, are always insisting on their own pet malady, *la nervose*. It is in their work, too, that Huysmans notes with delight 'le style tacheté et faisandé'—high-flavoured and spotted with corruption—which he himself possesses in the highest degree. 'Having desire without light, curiosity without wisdom, seeking God by strange ways, by ways traced by the hands of men; offering rash incense upon the high places to an unknown God, who is the God of darkness'—that is how Ernest Hello, in one of his apocalyptic moments, characterizes the nineteenth century.[18] And this unreason of the soul—of which Hello himself is so curious a victim—this unstable equilibrium, which has overbalanced so many brilliant intelligences into one form or another of spiritual confusion, is but another form of the *maladie*

[14] Paul Verlaine (1844–96), French poet, who was imprisoned in the 1870s for shooting and wounding his fellow-poet and lover, Arthur Rimbaud. Verlaine read in London in the 1890s, and he was a significant influence on British poets of the fin de siècle.

[15] Maurice Maeterlinck (1862–1949), a Belgian poet and dramatist who became one of the leading figures in the Symbolist movement.

[16] Joris-Karl Huysmans (1848–1907), a French novelist whose *À Rebours* (translated as either 'Against the Grain' or 'Against Nature') became the bible of decadence and aestheticism at the fin de siècle. This is the unnamed book that corrupts Dorian Gray in Wilde's *Picture of Dorian Gray* (1890).

[17] Edmond and Jules de Goncourt (1822–96 and 1830–70), French authors, brothers, who wrote in close collaboration. They are famous both for their painstakingly documented realist novels from the mid-century and for their *écriture artiste*, an impressionistic, highly mannered style, elaborate in syntax and vocabulary best anatomized in *Manette Salomon* (1867), a novel of artist life.

[18] Ernest Hello (1828–85), French Roman Catholic author and mystic. Given the complex relation to Catholicism in French and British decadence, authors like Hello were significant influences.

fin de siècle. For its very disease of form, this literature is certainly typical of a civilization grown over-luxurious, over-inquiring, too languid for the relief of action, too uncertain for any emphasis in opinion or in conduct. It reflects all the moods, all the manners, of a sophisticated society: its very artificiality is a way of being true to nature: simplicity, sanity, proportion—the classic qualities—how much do we possess them in our life, our surroundings, that we should look to find them in our literature—so evidently the literature of a decadence?

Taking the word Decadence, then, as most precisely expressing the general sense of the newest movement in literature, we find that the terms Impressionism and Symbolism define correctly enough the two main branches of that movement. Now Impressionist and Symbolist have more in common than either supposes; both are really working on the same hypothesis, applied in different directions. What both seek is not general truth merely, but *la vérité vraie*, the very essence of truth—the truth of appearances to the senses, of the visible world to the eyes that see it; and the truth of spiritual things to the spiritual vision. The Impressionist, in literature as in painting, would flash upon you in a new, sudden way so exact an image of what you have just seen, just as you have seen it, that you may say, as a young American sculptor, a pupil of Rodin, said to me on seeing for the first time a picture of Whistler's, 'Whistler seems to think his picture upon canvas—and there it is!'[19] Or you may find, with Sainte-Beuve, writing of Goncourt, the 'soul of the landscape'—the soul of whatever corner of the visible world has to be realized. The Symbolist, in this new, sudden way, would flash upon you the 'soul' of that which can be apprehended only by the soul—the finer sense of things unseen, the deeper meaning of things evident. And naturally, necessarily, this endeavour after a perfect truth to one's impression, to one's intuition—perhaps an impossible endeavour—has brought with it, in its revolt from ready-made impressions and conclusions, a revolt from the ready-made of language, from the bondage of traditional form, of a form become rigid. In France, where this movement began and has mainly flourished, it is Goncourt who was the first to invent a style in prose really new, impressionistic, a style which was itself almost sensation. It is Verlaine who has invented such another new style in verse.

The work of the brothers De Goncourt—twelve novels, eleven or twelve studies in the history of the eighteenth century, six or seven books about art, the art mainly of the eighteenth century and of Japan, two plays, some volumes of letters

---

[19] James Abbot McNeill Whistler (1834–1903), Impressionist painter and controversialist. Famed for his paintings, but also for the libel trial against the critic John Ruskin in 1878. Ruskin described Whistler's *The Falling Rocket, a Nocturne in Black and Gold* as 'throwing a pot of paint in the public's face'. Whistler sued, and was awarded damages of a farthing; as a result he declared bankruptcy in 1879. Later, he was a sparring partner and Chelsea neighbour of Oscar Wilde.

and of fragments, and a *Journal* in six volumes—is perhaps, in its intention and its consequences, the most revolutionary of the century. [. . .]

An opera-glass—a special, unique way of seeing things—that is what the Goncourts have brought to bear upon the common things about us; and it is here that they have done the 'something new', here more than anywhere. They have never sought 'to see life steadily, and see it whole': their vision has always been somewhat feverish, with the diseased sharpness of over-excited nerves. [. . .]

What Goncourt has done in prose—inventing absolutely a new way of saying things, to correspond with that new way of seeing things which he has found—Verlaine has done in verse. In a famous poem, 'Art Poétique', he has himself defined his own ideal of the poetic art:

> Car nous voulons la Nuance encore,
> Pas la Couleur, rien que la Nuance!
> Oh! la nuance seule fiance
> Le rêve au rêve et la flute au cor!

Music first of all and before all, he insists; and then, not colour, but *la nuance*, the last fine shade. Poetry is to be something vague, intangible, evanescent, a winged soul in flight 'toward other skies and other loves.' To express the inexpressible he speaks of beautiful eyes behind a veil, of the palpitating sunlight of noon, of the blue swarm of clear stars in a cool autumn sky; and the verse in which he makes this confession of faith has the exquisite troubled beauty—'sans rien en lui qui pèse ou qui pose'—which he commends as the essential quality of verse. [. . .]

Beginning his career as a Parnassian with the *Poèmes saturniens*, Verlaine becomes himself, in his exquisite first manner, in the *Fêtes galantes*, caprices after Watteau, followed, a year later, by *La Bonne Chanson*, a happy record of too confident a lover's happiness. *Romances sans paroles*, in which the poetry of Impressionism reaches its very highest point, is more *tourmenté*, goes deeper, becomes more poignantly personal. It is the poetry of sensation, of evocation; poetry which paints as well as sings, and which paints as Whistler paints, seeming to think the colours and outlines upon the canvas, to think them only, and they are there. [. . .] To fix the last fine shade, the quintessence of things; to fix it fleetingly; to be a disembodied voice, and yet the voice of a human soul: that is the ideal of Decadence, and it is what Paul Verlaine has achieved.

And certainly, so far as achievement goes, no other poet of the actual group in France can be named beside him or near him. But in Stéphane Mallarmé,[20] with his supreme pose as the supreme poet, and his two or three pieces of exquisite verse and delicately artificial prose to show by way of result, we have the prophet

---

[20] Stephane Mallarmé (1842–98), French poet, one of the founders of Modernist poetry.

and pontiff of the movement, the mystical and theoretical leader of the great emancipation. No one has ever dreamed such beautiful, impossible dreams as Mallarmé; no one has ever so possessed his soul in the contemplation of master-pieces to come. All his life he has been haunted by the desire to create, not so much something new in literature, as a literature which should itself be a new art. He has dreamed of a work into which all the arts should enter, and achieve them-selves by a mutual interdependence—a harmonizing of all the arts into one supreme art—and he has theorized with infinite subtlety over the possibilities of doing the impossible. [. . .] His early poems, 'L'Après-midi d'un Faune', 'Héro-diade', for example, and some exquisite sonnets, and one or two fragments of per-fectly polished verse, are written in a language which has nothing in common with every-day language—symbol within symbol within symbol, image within image; but symbol and image achieve themselves in expression without seeming to call for the necessity of a key. The latest poems (in which punctuation is some-times entirely suppressed for our further bewilderment) consist merely of a sequence of symbols, in which every word must be taken in a sense with which its ordinary significance has nothing to do. Mallarmé's contortion of the French lan-guage, so far as mere style is concerned, is curiously similar to the kind of depra-vation which was undergone by the Latin language in its decadence. It is, indeed, in part a reversion to Latin phraseology, to the Latin construction, and it has made, of the clear and flowing French language, something irregular, unquiet, expressive, with sudden surprising felicities, with nervous starts and lapses, with new capacities for the exact noting of sensation. [. . .]

Probably it is as a voice, an influence, that Mallarmé will be remembered. [. . .] But to find a new personality, a new way of seeing things, among the young writers who are starting upon every hand, we must turn from Paris to Brussels—to the so-called Belgian Shakespeare, Maurice Maeterlinck. [. . .] As a dramatist he has but one note, that of fear; he has but one method, that of repetition. [. . .] In *L'Intruse* and *Les Aveugles* the scene is stationary, the action but reflected upon the stage, as if from another plane. In *Les Sept Princesses* the action, such as it is, is 'such stuff as dreams are made of', and is literally, in great part, seen through a window.

This window, looking out upon the unseen—an open door, as in *L'Intruse*, through which death, the intruder, may come invisibly—how typical of the new kind of symbolistic and impressionistic drama which M. Maeterlinck has invented! [. . .] Partly akin to M. Maeterlinck by race, more completely alien from him in temper than it is possible to express, Joris Karl Huysmans demands a prominent place in any record of the Decadent movement. His work, like that of the Goncourts, is largely determined by the *maladie fin de siècle*—the diseased nerves that, in his case, have given a curious personal quality of pessimism to his outlook on the world, his view of life. Part of his work—*Marthe, Les Sœurs*

Vatard, En Ménage, À Vau-l'Eau—is a minute and searching study of the minor discomforts, the commonplace miseries of life, as seen by a peevishly disordered vision, delighting, for its own self-torture, in the insistent contemplation of human stupidity, of the sordid in existence. Yet these books do but lead up to the unique masterpiece, the astonishing caprice of *À Rebours*, in which he has concentrated all that is delicately depraved, all that is beautifully, curiously poisonous, in modern art. *À Rebours* is the history of a typical Decadent—a study, indeed, after a real man, but a study which seizes the type rather than the personality. In the sensations and ideas of Des Esseintes we see the sensations and ideas of the effeminate, over-civilized, deliberately abnormal creature who is the last product of our society: partly the father, partly the offspring, of the perverse art that he adores. Des Esseintes creates for his solace, in the wilderness of a barren and profoundly uncomfortable work, an artificial paradise. His Thébaïde raffinée is furnished elaborately for candle-light, equipped with the pictures, the books, that satisfy his sense of the exquisitely abnormal. [. . .] And at last, exhausted by these spiritual and sensory debauches in the delights of the artificial, he is left (as we close the book) with a brief, doubtful choice before him—madness or death, or else a return to nature, to the normal life.

Since *À Rebours*, M. Huysmans has written one other remarkable book, *Là-Bas*, a study in the hysteria and mystical corruption of contemporary Black Magic. But it is on that one exceptional achievement, *À Rebours*, that his fame will rest; it is there that he has expressed not merely himself, but an epoch. And he has done so in a style which carries the modern experiments upon language to their furthest development. Formed upon Goncourt and Flaubert, it has sought for novelty, *l'image peinte*, the exactitude of colour, the forcible precision of epithet, wherever words, images, or epithets are to be found. Barbaric in its profusion, violent in its emphasis, wearying in its splendour, it is—especially in regard to things seen—extraordinarily expressive, with all the shades of a painter's palette. Elaborately and deliberately perverse, it is in its very perversity that Huysmans' work—so fascinating, so repellent, so instinctively artificial—comes to represent, as the work of no other writer can be said to do, the main tendencies, the chief results, of the decadent movement in literature.

Such, then, is the typical literature of the Decadence—literature which, as we have considered it so far, is entirely French. But those qualities which we find in the work of Goncourt, Verlaine, Huysmans—qualities which have permeated literature much more completely in France than in any other country—are not wanting in the recent literature of other countries. [. . .] And in England, too, we find the same influences at work. The prose of Mr. Walter Pater,[21] the verse of

---

[21] Walter Pater (1839–94) strongly influenced the British Aesthetic movement at the fin de siècle, most notably in his *Studies in the History of the Renaissance* (1873). Attacked by some as unscholarly and morbid, Wilde lauded it as 'the holy writ of beauty'.

Mr. W. E. Henley[22]—to take two prominent examples—are attempts to do with the English language something of what Goncourt and Verlaine have done with the French. Mr. Pater's prose is the most beautiful English prose which is now being written; and, unlike the prose of Goncourt, it has done no violence to language, it has sought after no vivid effects, it has found a large part of mastery in reticence, in knowing what to omit. But how far away from the classic ideals of style is this style in which words have their colour, their music, their perfume, in which there is 'some strangeness in the proportion' of every beauty! The *Studies in the Renaissance* have made of criticism a new art—have raised criticism almost to the act of creation. And *Marius the Epicurean*, in its study of 'sensations and ideas' (the conjunction was Goncourt's before it was Mr. Pater's), and the *Imaginary Portraits*, in their evocations of the Middle Ages, the age of Watteau—have they not that morbid subtlety of analysis, that morbid curiosity of form, that we have found in the works of the French Decadents? A fastidiousness equal to that of Flaubert[23] has limited Mr. Pater's work to six volumes, but in these six volumes there is not a page that is not perfectly finished, with a conscious art of perfection. In its minute elaboration it can be compared only with goldsmith's work—so fine, so delicate is the handling of so delicate, so precious a material. Mr. Henley's work in verse has none of the characteristics of Mr. Pater's work in prose. Verlaine's definition of his own theory of poetical writing—'sincerity, and the impression of the moment followed to the letter'—might well be adopted as a definition of Mr. Henley's theory or practice. In *A Book of Verses* and *The Song of the Sword* he has brought into the traditional conventionalities of modern English verse the note of a new personality, the touch of a new method. The poetry of Impressionism can go no further, in one direction, than that series of rhymes and rhythms named *In Hospital*. The ache and throb of the body in its long nights on a rumbled bed, and as it lies on the operating-table, awaiting 'the thick, sweet mystery of chloroform', are brought home to us as nothing else that I know in poetry has ever brought the physical sensations. And for a sharper, closer truth of rendering, Mr. Henley has resorted (after the manner of Heine[24]) to a rhymeless form of lyric verse, which in his hands, certainly, is sensitive and expressive. Whether this kind of *vers libre* can fully compensate, in what it gains of freedom and elasticity, for what it loses of compact form and vocal appeal, is a difficult question. It is one that Mr. Henley's verse is far from solving in the affirmative, for, in his work, the finest things, to my mind, are rhymed. In the purely impressionistic way, do not the *London Voluntaries*, which are rhymed, surpass all the

---

[22]   William Ernest Henley (1849–1903) wrote, as a poet, ballads, lyrics, and impressionistic free verse, dedicating an evocation of the Thames ('Under a Stagnant Sky') to the impressionist painter Whistler, whose work he had consistently championed as a journalist.

[23]   Gustave Flaubert (1821–80), the first of the modern realists, whose *Madame Bovary* (1857) is notable for its rigorous psychological development, authenticity of detail, and 'impersonal' style.

[24]   Heinrich Heine (1797–1856), German poet, widely respected in Victorian Britain.

unrhymed vignettes and nocturnes which attempt the same quality of result? They flash before us certain aspects of the poet of London as only Whistler had ever done, and in another art. Nor is it only the poetry of cities, as here, nor the poetry of the disagreeable, as in *In Hospital*, that Mr. Henley can evoke; he can evoke the magic of personal romance. He has written verse that is exquisitely frivolous, daintily capricious, wayward and fugitive as the winged remembrance of some momentary delight. And, in certain fragments, he has come nearer than any other English singer to what I have called the achievement of Verlaine and the ideal of the Decadence: to be a disembodied voice, and yet the voice of a human soul.

------

3   from Walter Besant, Eliza Lynn Linton, and Thomas
     Hardy, 'Candour in English Fiction' (1890)

[1]

To those who ask why Fiction should be confined within certain bounds, why it should be forbidden to include this or that part of life, the reply is that there are no bounds whatever to the domain of Fiction. She may roam over the whole wide world: she may treat of men and women under any conditions: she may take up any subject. There is but the one condition of artistic fitness. Every artist is free, absolutely free, to exercise his own art in his own way. That is to say, in his own studio and in his own *cénacle*, he is free. It is when he works for exhibition: for the public: for pay or hire: that limitations come in. Then he finds bounds and hedges beyond which, if he chooses to stray, it is at his own peril. These limits are assigned by an authority known as Average Opinion. They may be narrow, because Average Opinion is generally a Philistine. Those who wish to enlarge these boundaries or to remove them altogether must educate and enlarge Average Opinion. In the matter of painting so much has lately been achieved in the enlargement of opinion that those who attempt a similar task in literature may be of good cheer. [. . .]

Those who demand a wider range for English Fiction desire chiefly, it is understood, a greater freedom in the treatment of Love. Certainly there is no other passion which yields to an artist such boundless possibilities. Without Love, the whole of life is insipid. Without Love, all Art perishes. In Love's escort march all the Emotions: they follow in pairs, each with its opposite. Tenderness with Rage: Truth with Treachery: Joy with Grief. Why should not writers, it is asked, treat of Love in freedom—Love according to the laws of Nature? Love existed before the Church invented a sacrament and called it marriage. The history of mankind is the history of Love. Why restrict those who ask for nothing but a free hand?

Here, however, Average Opinion says, or seems to say: 'If you treat of Love, save as Love obedient to the laws of Society, we will have none of you.' Average Opinion cannot explain this position. Were it more articulate it would be able to give its reasons. It would go on to say, in short: 'Modern Society is based upon the unit of the family. The family tie means, absolutely, that the man and the woman are indissolubly united and can only be parted by the shame and disgrace of one or the other. In order to protect the wife and the children, and to keep the family together, we have made stringent laws as to marriage. To make these laws more binding we have allowed the Church to invent for marriage so solemn and sacred a function that most women have come to believe that the Church ceremony constitutes true marriage. The preservation of the family is at the very foundation of our social system. As for the freedom of love which you want to treat in your books, it strikes directly at the family. If men and women are free to rove, there can be no family: if there is no fidelity in marriage, the family drops to pieces. Therefore, we will have none of your literature of free and adulterous Love.'

In fact, they will not have it. Average Opinion cannot be resisted. The circulating libraries refuse to distribute such books. They may be sold in certain shops, but not in those where the British Matron buys her books. The railway stalls will not display them. Worse than all, the author becomes liable to a criminal prosecution, which is painful and humiliating. Then those who demand greater freedom cry out upon the world for hypocrisy. 'Ye are like,' they say, 'unto whited sepulchres, which are indeed beautiful outward but are within full of all-uncleanness. The Press teems daily with proofs, open and manifest, of the existence of free and illegal Love: the very thing of which you will not suffer us to speak has seized upon every rank of society: nay, there has never been a time when the artificial restrictions of social and ecclesiastical law have been obeyed: there has never been any country in which they have been obeyed. You go on prating of social purity. It does not exist. It never has existed. And you think that men's mouths, or women's either, are to be stopped by your prudery and hypocrisy.'

Average Opinion is not credited with having much to say in reply. For these charges are partly true, though the exaggerations are indeed enormous. So far as we pretend to social purity as a nation we are indeed hypocrites. But to set up a standard of purity and to advocate it is not hypocrisy. This country, and the remnant still surviving of the New England stock, stand almost alone in the maintenance of such a standard. As for the widespread laxity alleged, it is not true. Certainly, there is a chapter in the lives of many men which they would not willingly publish. But in almost every such case the chapter is closed and is never reopened after the man has contracted the responsibilities of marriage. And as for the women—those above a certain level—there is never any closed chapter at all in their lives. When we talk of hypocrisies, let us not forget that the cultured class of British women—a vast and continually increasing class—are entirely to be trusted. Rare, indeed, is it that an Englishman of this class is jealous of his wife: never does he suspect his bride.

These considerations will perhaps explain the attitude of Average Opinion towards the literature of Free Love. Any novelist may write what he pleases: he may make an artistic picture of any materials he chooses; but he will not generally find, if he crosses certain boundaries, that his books will be distributed by Mudie or Smith. It is with him, then, if he desires to treat of things forbidden, a question of money—shall he restrict his pencil or shall he restrict his purse?

There is, however, one more answer to the accusation of narrowness. Is English Fiction narrow? Is the treatment of ungoverned passion absolutely forbidden? Then what of George Eliot, Charles Reade, Wilkie Collins, Nathaniel Hawthorne, Mrs. Gaskell—not to speak of living writers? Can any writer demand greater freedom than has been taken by the authors of *Adam Bede*, *A Terrible Temptation*, *Ruth*, or *The Scarlet Letter*? With these examples before him, no one, surely, ought to complain that he is not permitted to treat of Love free and disobedient. The author, however, must recognise in his work the fact that such Love is outside the social pale and is destructive of the very basis of society. He must. This is not a law laid down by that great authority, Average Opinion, but by Art herself, who will not allow the creation of impossible figures moving in an unnatural atmosphere. Those writers who yearn to treat of the adulteress and the courtesan because they love to dwell on images of lust are best kept in check by existing discouragements. The modern Elephantis may continue to write in French.

Walter Besant

[2]

Of all the writers of fiction in Europe or America the English are the most restricted in their choice of subjects. The result is shown in the pitiable poverty of the ordinary novel, the wearisome repetition of the same themes, and the consequent popularity of romances which, not pretending to deal with life as it is, at the least leave no sense of disappointment in their portrayal or of superficiality in their handling. The British Matron is the true censor of the Press, and exerts over fiction the repressive power she has tried to exert over Art. Things as they are—human nature as it is—the conflict always going on between law and passion, the individual and society—she will not have spoken of. She permits certain crimes to be not only described, but dilated on and gloated over. Murder, forgery, lies, and all forms of hate and malevolence she does not object to; but no one must touch the very fringes of uncertificated love under pain of the greater and the lesser excommunication. Hence, the subjects lying to the hand of the British novelist are woefully limited, and the permissible area of the conflict between humanity and society is daily diminishing. [. . .]

If a writer, disdaining the unwritten law, leaps the barriers set up by Mrs Grundy[25] and ventures into the forbidden Garden of Roses, he is boycotted by all respectable libraries and the severer kind of booksellers, and his works, though they sell in large numbers, are bought in a manner surreptitiously. [. . .]

All this is the outcome of the question: To whom ought Fiction to be addressed?—exclusively to the Young Person? or may not men and women, who know life, have their acre to themselves where the ingénue has no business to intrude? Must men go without meat because the babes must be fed with milk? Or, because men must have meat, shall the babes be poisoned with food too strong for them to digest? I, for one, am emphatically in favour of specialised literature. Just as we have children's books and medical books, so ought we to have literature fit for the Young Person and literature which gives men and women pictures of life as it is. Had the law which is in favour at the present day been the law of times past we should have lost some of our finest works; and the world would have been so much the poorer in consequence. But would any sane person propose to banish Fielding and Swift and Smollett and Richardson from our libraries, and Bowd-lerise all our editions of Shakespeare, and purify the Bible from passages which once were simple everyday facts, that no one was ashamed to discuss, and now are nameless indecencies impossible to be even alluded to, because these are not the fit kind of reading for boys and girls in their teens? With this excessive scrupulosity in fiction we publish the most revolting details in the daily Press; and we let our boys and girls read every paper that comes into the house. If even we debar them from these, with the large amount of uncompanioned liberty they have at the present day, and a penny or even a half-penny in their pockets, they may sup full of horrors and improprieties, as now the details of some ghastly murder, now those of some highly-coloured divorce suit, sell the papers in the streets and stir up the public imagination. And again, with the new development of education our young Girton girls may study Juvenal and Catullus in the original, and laugh over the plain speaking of Aristophanes; while French novels, of which the translation lands a man in prison, may be sold by their hundreds in the original language wherein every recently educated girl is a proficient.

The whole thing results from the muddle and the compromise which English morality so delights to make. The British Matron must have a scapegoat whom she sends into the desert laden with a few uncongenial sins, while she keeps all the rest in safe custody in her tents. She must have a whipping-boy for the

---

[25] 'Mrs Grundy' was the personification of prudish public opinion: she first appeared as a character in Thomas Morton's play, *Speed the Plough* (1798). 'Grundyism' became a common idiom in Victorian Britain for moral conventionalism and rigidity.

encouragement of her pupils. In literature this is the seventh commandment in all its forms and ramifications when discussed in the native tongue. Uncandid and also hypocritical, this attitude exposes us as a nation to both ridicule and blame. With a Press so rampantly unmuzzled—with editors of evening papers who go into the most disgusting and minute details of things which are, which have been done, and which, therefore, can be imitated—we fall foul of the writer who takes for his motive the subject of unlawful love, though he handles it with scrupulous delicacy and in the broadest manner of indication rather than description. [. . .]

In olden days, and I should imagine in all well-ordered houses still, the literature which was meant for men was kept on certain prohibited bookshelves of the library, or in the locked bookcase for greater security. The Young Person was warned off these shelves. If her discretion was not to be trusted and her word of honour was only a shaky security, the locked bookcase made all safe. Here the father kept his masculine literature; his translations of certain classical authors; his ethnological and some scientific books; his popular surgical, medical, and anatomical works; perhaps some speculative philosophies of an upsetting tendency; and all the virile work of the last and preceding centuries. To the Young Person were free Jane Austen and Sir Walter Scott, Miss Mitford and Miss Edgeworth, 'Evelina,' Fenimore Cooper, Marryat, G. P. R. James, and many others in the immediate past, with the largest proportion of the writers of fiction in the present day. If two or three here and there attempted the bow of Ulysses and tried on the mantle of Balzac, his, or more probably her books went into the closed compartment and the Young Person was no whit the worse. And this seems to me a better way all round and a finer kind of safeguarding than the emasculation of all fictitious literature down to the level of boys and girls; and the consequent presentation of human life in stories which are no truer to that human life than so many fairy tales dealing with griffins and flying dragons, good genii and malevolent old witches. The result of our present system of uncandid reticence, of make-believe innocence in one line with impossible villainies in others—the working response made to the demand of the British Matron for fairy tales, not facts—is that, with a few notable exceptions, our fictitious literature is the weakest of all at this present time, the most insincere, the most jejune, the least impressive, and the least tragic. It is wholly wanting in dignity, in grandeur, in the essential spirit of immortality. Written for the inclusion of the Young Person among its readers, it does not go beyond the schoolgirl standard. It may be charming, as the shy and budding miss is charming; but that smell of bread and butter spoils all quite as much as the smell of the apoplexy spoilt the Archbishop's discourse. Thus we have the queer anomaly of a strong-headed and masculine nation cherishing a feeble, futile, milk-and-water literature—of a truthful and straightforward race accepting the most transparent humbug as pictures of human life. A great king may make himself a hobby-horse for his children to ride on pickaback, but a great nation should be candid and truthful in art as well as in life, and mature men and women should not sacrifice truth and common-sense in literature for the sake of the Young Person. The locked bookcase is better.

E. Lynn Linton

[3]

[. . .] By a sincere school of Fiction we may understand a Fiction that expresses truly the views of life prevalent in its time, by means of a selected chain of action best suited for their exhibition. What are the prevalent views of life just now is a question upon which it is not necessary to enter further than to suggest that the most natural method of presenting them, the method most in accordance with the views themselves, seems to be by a procedure mainly impassive in its tone and tragic in its developments.

Things move in cycles; dormant principles renew themselves, and exhausted principles are thrust by. There is a revival of the artistic instincts towards great dramatic motives—setting forth that 'collision between the individual and the general'—formerly worked out with such force by the Periclean and Elizabethan dramatists, to name no other. More than this, the periodicity which marks the course of taste in civilised countries does not take the form of a true cycle of repetition, but what Comte, in speaking of general progress, happily characterises as 'a looped orbit': not a movement of revolution but—to use the current word—evolution.[26] Hence, in perceiving that taste is arriving anew at the point of high tragedy, writers are conscious that its revived presentation demands enrichment by further truths—in other words, original treatment: treatment which seeks to show Nature's unconsciousness not of essential laws, but of those laws framed merely as social expedients by humanity, without a basis in the heart of things; treatment which expresses the triumph of the crowd over the hero, of the commonplace majority over the exceptional few.

But originality makes scores of failures for one final success precisely because its essence is to acknowledge no immediate precursor or guide. It is probably to these inevitable conditions of further acquisition that may be attributed some developments of naturalism in French novelists of the present day, and certain crude results from meritorious attempts in the same direction by intellectual adventurers here and there among our own authors.

Anyhow, conscientious fiction alone it is which can excite reflective and abiding interest in the minds of thoughtful readers of mature age, who are weary of

---

[26] Auguste Comte (1798–1857), founder of the Positivist school of philosophy, which was an important source for the scientific naturalism (see Ch. 9) that informed Hardy's conception of the operations of fate and determinism.

puerile inventions and famishing for accuracy; who consider that, in representations of the world, the passions ought to be proportioned as in the world itself. This is the interest which was excited in the minds of the Athenians by their immortal tragedies, and in the minds of Londoners at the first performance of the finer plays of three hundred years ago. They reflected life, revealed life, criticised life. Life being a physiological fact, its honest portrayal must be largely concerned with, for one thing, the relations of the sexes, and the substitution for such catastrophes as favour the false colouring best expressed by the regulation finish that 'they married and were happy ever after,' of catastrophes based upon sexual relationship as it is. To this expansion English society opposes a well-nigh insuperable bar.

The popular vehicles for the introduction of a novel to the public have grown to be, from one cause and another, the magazine and the circulating library; and the object of the magazine and circulating library is not upward advance but lateral advance; to suit themselves to what is called household reading, which means, or is made to mean, the reading either of the majority in a household or of the household collectively. The number of adults, even in a large household, being normally two, and these being the members which, as a rule, have least time on their hands to bestow on current literature, the taste of the majority can hardly be, and seldom is, tempered by the ripe judgement which desires fidelity. However, the immature members of a household often keep an open mind, and they might, and no doubt would, take sincere fiction with the rest but for another condition, almost generally consistent: which is that adults who would desire true views for their own reading insist, for a plausible but questionable reason, upon false views for the reading of their young people.

As a consequence, the magazine in particular and the circulating library in general do not foster the growth of the novel which reflects and reveals life. They directly tend to exterminate it by monopolising all literary space. Cause and effect were never more clearly conjoined, though commentators upon the result, both French and English, seem seldom if ever to trace their connection. A sincere and comprehensive sequence of the ruling passions, however moral in its ultimate bearings, must not be put on paper—as the foundation of imaginative works, which have to claim notice through the above-named channels, though it is extensively welcomed in the form of newspaper reports. That the magazine and library have arrogated to themselves the dispensation of fiction is not the fault of the authors, but of circumstances over which they, as representatives of Grub Street,[27] have no control.

What this practically amounts to is that the patrons of literature—no longer Peers with a taste—acting under the censorship of prudery, rigorously exclude

---

[27] 'Grub Street' was a shorthand term for literary 'hack' work.

from the pages they regulate subjects that have been made, by general approval of the best judges, the bases of the finest imaginative compositions since literature rose to the dignity of an art.

The crash of broken commandments is as necessary an accompaniment to the catastrophe of a tragedy as the noise of drum and cymbals to a triumphal march. But the crash of broken commandments shall not be heard; or, if at all, but gently like the roaring of Bottom—gently as any sucking dove, or as 'twere any nightingale, lest we should fright the ladies out of their wits. More precisely, an arbitrary proclamation has gone forth that certain picked commandments of the ten shall be preserved intact—to wit the first, third, and seventh; that the ninth shall be infringed but gingerly; the sixth only as much as necessary; and the remainder alone as much as you please, in a genteel manner.

It is in the self-consciousness engendered by interference with spontaneity, and in aims at a compromise to square with circumstances, that the real secret lies of the charlatanry pervading so much of English fiction. It may be urged that abundance of great and profound novels might be written which should require no compromising, contain not an episode deemed questionable by prudes. This I venture to doubt. In a ramification of the profounder passions the treatment of which makes the great style, something 'unsuitable' is sure to arise; and then comes the struggle with the literary conscience. The opening scenes of the would-be great story may, in a rash moment, have been printed in some popular magazine before the remainder is written; as it advances month by month the situations develop, and the writer asks himself, what will his characters do next? What would probably happen to them, given such beginnings? On his life and conscience, though he had not foreseen the thing, only one event could possibly happen, and that therefore he should narrate, as he calls himself a faithful artist. But, though pointing a fine moral, it is just one of those issues which are not to be mentioned in respectable magazines and select libraries. The dilemma then confronts him, he must either whip and scourge those characters into doing something contrary to their natures, to produce the spurious effect of their being in harmony with social forms and ordinances, or, by leaving them alone to act as they will, he must bring down the thunders of respectability upon his head, not to say ruin his editor, his publisher, and himself.

What he often does, indeed can scarcely help doing in such a strait, is, belie his literary conscience, do despite to his best imaginative instincts by arranging a dénouement which he knows to be indescribably unreal and meretricious, but dear to the Grundyist and subscriber. If the true artist ever weeps it probably is then, when he first discovers the fearful price that he has to pay for the privilege of writing in the English language—no less a price than the complete extinction, in the mind of every mature and penetrating reader, of sympathetic belief in his personages.

To say that few of the old dramatic masterpieces, if newly published as a novel (the form which, experts tell us, they would have taken in modern conditions), would be tolerated in English magazines and libraries is a ludicrous understatement. Fancy a brazen young Shakespeare of our time—Othello, Hamlet, or Anthony and Cleopatra never having yet appeared—sending up one of those creations in narrative form to the editor of a London magazine, with the author's compliments, and his hope that the story will be found acceptable to the editor's pages; suppose him, further, to have the temerity to ask for the candid remarks of the accomplished editor upon his manuscript. One can imagine the answer that young William would get for his mad supposition of such fitness in any one of the gentlemen who so correctly conduct that branch of the periodical Press. [. . .]

Whether minors should read unvarnished fiction based on the deeper passions, should listen to the eternal verities in the form of narrative, is somewhat a different question from whether the novel ought to be exclusively addressed to those minors. The first consideration is one which must be passed over here; but it will be conceded by most friends of literature that all fiction should not be shackled by conventions concerning budding womanhood, which may be altogether false. It behoves us then to inquire how best to circumvent the present lording of nonage over maturity, and permit the explicit novel to be more generally written.

That the existing magazine and book-lending system will admit of any great modification is scarcely likely. As far as the magazine is concerned it has long been obvious that as a vehicle for fiction dealing with human feeling on a comprehensive scale it is tottering to its fall; and it will probably in the course of time take up openly the position that it already covertly occupies, that of a purveyor of tales for the youth of both sexes, as it assumes that tales for those rather numerous members of society ought to be written. There remain three courses by which the adult may find deliverance.

The first would be a system of publication under which books could be bought and not borrowed, when they would naturally resolve themselves into classes instead of being, as now, made to wear a common livery in style and subject, enforced by their supposed necessities in addressing indiscriminately a general audience.

But it is scarcely likely to be convenient to either authors or publishers that the periodical form of publication for the candid story should be entirely forbidden, and in retaining the old system thus far yet ensuring that the emancipated serial novel should meet the eyes of those for whom it is intended, the plan of publication as a feuilleton in newspapers read mainly by adults might be more generally followed, as in France. In default of this, or co-existent with it, there might be adopted what, upon the whole, would perhaps find more favour than any with those who have artistic interests at heart, and that is, magazines for adults; exclusively for adults, if necessary. As an offshoot there might be at least one magazine for the middle-aged and old.

There is no foretelling; but this (since the magazine form of publication is so firmly rooted) is at least a promising remedy, if English prudery be really, as we hope, only a parental anxiety. There should be no mistaking the matter, no half measures. *La dignité de la pensée*, in the words of Pascal,[28] might then grow to be recognised in the treatment of fiction as in other things, and untrammelled adult opinion on conduct and theology might be axiomatically appealed to. Nothing in such literature should for a moment exhibit lax views of that purity of life upon which the well-being of society depends; but the position of man and woman in nature, and the position of belief in the minds of man and woman—things which everybody is thinking but nobody is saying—might be taken up and treated frankly.

Thomas Hardy

---

4   from Hugh E. M. Stutfield, 'Tommyrotics' (1895)

A most excellent wag—quoted with approval by the grave and sedate 'Spectator'—recently described modern fiction as 'erotic, neurotic, and Tommyrotic'. Judging from certain signs of the times, he might have extended his description to the mental condition in our day of a considerable section of civilised mankind. Our restless, dissatisfied, sadly muddled, much inquiring generation seems to be smitten with a new malady, which so far bids fair to baffle the doctors. Society, in the limited sense of the word, still dreads the influenza and shudders at the approach of typhoid, but its most dangerous and subtle foes are beyond question: 'neurotics' and hysteria in their manifold forms.

A wave of unrest is passing over the world. Humanity is beginning to sicken at the daily round, the common task, of ordinary humdrum existence, and is eagerly seeking for new forms of excitement. Hence it is kicking over the traces all round. Revolt is the order of the day. The shadow of an immeasurable, and by no means divine, discontent broods over us all. Everybody is talking and preaching: one is distressed because he cannot solve the riddle of the universe, the why and the wherefore of human existence; another racks his brains to invent brand-new social or political systems which shall make everybody rich, happy, and contented at a bound. It is an age of individual and collective—perhaps I should say,

---

[28] 'The dignity of thought', as pursued in the maxims of French philosopher Blaise Pascal (1623–62).

collectivist fuss, and the last thing that anybody thinks of is settling down to do the work that lies nearest to him. Carlyle is out of fashion, for Israel has taken to stoning her older prophets who exhorted to duty, submission, and suchlike antiquated virtues, and the social anarchist and the New Hedonist bid fair to take their place as teachers of mankind.

It is thought by many that the hour brings forth the man; and just as the world seems most in need of him a new prophet has arisen to point out some of the dangers which lie in the path of modern civilisation. Like most prophets, he raves somewhat incoherently at times and is guilty of much exaggeration, but this is a fault common to nearly all men with a mission. And, when every allowance has been made on this score, we should still be grateful to Dr Max Nordau for his striking and powerful work, 'Degeneration.' The book has been violently assailed, and portions of it lend themselves readily to hostile criticism.[29] It is certainly not a book *virginibus puerisque*,[30] and it is exceedingly learned and long; but the wealth of epigram, the fecundity of illustration, and the brilliant incisiveness of its style, make it far from heavy reading. A perusal thereof forces one to 'devour much abomination,' as the Arabs say; but unsavoury topics are at any rate not handled sympathetically, as by decadent essayists and 'yellow' lady novelists, but rather in the spirit of fierce hatred and horror which characterise a Juvenal.[31]

And the sum of his matter is this—that ours may be an age of progress, but it is progress which, if left unchecked, will land us in the hospital or the lunatic asylum. [. . .] The causes of our mental disease are the wear-and-tear and excitement of modern life, and its symptoms are to be found in the debased emotionalism apparent in so many of the leading writers and thinkers of our day, who, together with their numerous followers and admirers, are victims of a form of mania whereof the scientific name is 'degeneration.' [. . .]

Continental influence upon our literature is more apparent now than for many years past. The predilection for the foul and repulsive, the puling emotionalism, and the sickly sensuousness of the French decadents, are also the leading characteristics of the nascent English schools. The former, to take a single example, are the direct intellectual progenitors of our aesthetes, whose doctrines Dr Nordau examines at quite unnecessary length. He takes far too seriously the intellectual clowning, their laboured absurdities and inane

---

[29] See the selections in Ch. 1: Stutfield's outburst needs to be read in the context of the debate around Nordau's *Degeneration*.

[30] This is a slighting reference to a collection of essays by Robert Louis Stevenson, bearing this title, and published in 1881, concerning marriage. Many critics have discussed the intense homoerotic adoration for Stevenson at the time: Stutfield would no doubt have disapproved at the very least of his foppish persona.

[31] Juvenal wrote a series of much-imitated satires on the corrupt state of the Roman empire in the 1st century AD.

paradoxes which the vulgar mistake for wit, as well as the assiduous literary and artistic mountebankery with which they have advertised themselves into notoriety. For a while sensible and healthy-minded people regarded with half-amused contempt their absurd claim to form a species of artistic aristocracy apart from the common herd, but the contempt has since deepened into disgust. Recent events, which shall be nameless,[32] must surely have opened the eyes even of those who have hitherto been blind to the true inwardness of modern aesthetic Hellenism,[33] and perhaps the less said on this subject now the better.

A somewhat similar, and scarcely less unlovely, offspring of hysteria and for-eign 'degenerate' influence is the neurotic and repulsive fiction which so justly incensed the 'Philistine' in the 'Westminster Gazette.'[34] Its hysterical origin shows itself chiefly in its morbid spirit of analysis. Judging from their works, the authors must be vivified notes of interrogation. Their characters are so dreadfully introspective. When they are not talking of psychology, they are discussing physi-ology. They search for new thrills and sensations, and they possess a maddening faculty of dissecting and probing their 'primary impulses'—especially the sexual ones. [. . .] They are oppressed with a dismal sense that everything is an enigma, that they themselves are 'playthings of the inexplicable'; or else they try to 'com-pass the whole physiological gamut of their being'—whatever that may be. I am quoting from Miss George Egerton's 'Discords,'[35] a fair type of English neurotic fiction, which some critics are trying to make us believe is very high-class litera-ture. I must confess that I find the characters in these books more agreeable when they are indulging in nebulous cackle like the above than when they are describ-ing their sexual emotions. [. . .]

It is noticeable that most of these profound psychological creations belong to that sex in which, according to Mrs Sarah Grand, 'the true spirit of God dwells,' and which, we are assured by another authority, 'constitutes the angelic portion of humanity.'[36] 'To be a woman is to be mad,' says the notorious and neurotic Mrs Ebbsmith.[37] Possibly, but the woman of the new Ibsenite neuro-

---

[32] The sentencing, in the early summer of 1895, of Oscar Wilde to two years' hard labour for 'acts of gross indecency'.

[33] Hellenism refers to the influence of ancient Greek civilization, language, art, and literature on the contemporary school of Aesthetes (of which Wilde was a representative). Hellenistic creative arts were characterized by a preference for delicate and highly decorated forms intended for connoisseurs. By the 1890s, 'Hellenic' was often coded as referring to forms of love between men: Wilde, for instance, had argued at his trial that his literature expressed a noble, Hellenic love for Alfred Lord Douglas, rather than physical desire.

[34] The *Westminster Gazette* was a conservative journal, which had been relaunched in 1893.

[35] A collection (1894) of sensuous, quasi-Decadent short stories by the New Woman writer, George Egerton (Mary Chavelita Dunne) (1859–1945).

[36] Grand (Frances Elizabeth McFall) (1854–1943) was one of the leading New Woman novelists. See Ch. 4 for one of her defining articles on the New Woman.

[37] *The Notorious Mrs Ebbsmith* (1895), by Arthur Wing Pinero, a playwright influenced by Henrik Ibsen.

pathic school is not only mad herself, but she does her best to drive those around her crazed also. As far as the husband is concerned, he is seldom deserving of much sympathy. In morbid novels and problem plays he is usually an imbecile, a bully, or a libertine. An even worse charge has recently been preferred against him: he is apt to snore horribly, thereby inducing insomnia—a disease to which our neuropaths are naturally subject. Indeed, the horrors of matrimony from the feminine point of view are so much insisted upon nowadays, and the Husband-Fiend is trotted out so often both in fiction and in drama, that one wonders how the demon manages still to command a premium in the marriage market. 'What brutes men are!' is the never-ceasing burden of the new woman's song, yet the 'choked up, seething pit' of matrimony (*vide* the 'Notorious Miss Ebbsmith') is still tolerably full. [. . .]

The physiological excursions of our writers of neuropathic fiction are usually confined to one field—that of sex. Their chief delight seems to be in making their characters discuss matters which would not have been tolerated in the novels of a decade or so ago. Emancipated woman in particular loves to show her independence by dealing freely with the relations of the sexes. Hence all the prating of passion, animalism, 'the natural workings of sex,' and so forth, with which we are nauseated. Most of the characters in these books seem to be erotomaniacs. Some are 'amorous sensitives,' others are apparently sexless, and are at pains to explain this to the reader. Here and there a girl indulges in what would be styled, in another sphere, 'straight talks to young men'. Those nice heroines of 'Iota's'[38] and other writers of the physiologico-pornographic school consort by choice with 'unfortunates,' or else describe at length their sensations in various interesting phases of their lives. The charming Gallia, in the novel of that name,[39] studies letters on the State Regulation of Vice,[40] and selects her husband on principles which are decidedly startling to the old-fashioned reader. Now this sort of thing may be very high art and wonderful psychology to some people, but to me it is garbage pure and simple, and such a dull garbage too. If anybody objects that I have picked out some of the extreme cases, I reply that these are just the books that sell. That morbid and nasty books are written is nothing: their popularity is what is disquieting. I have no wish to pose as a moralist. A book may be shameless and disgusting without being precisely immoral—like the fetid realism of Zola

---

[38] 'Iota' was the pen name of Kathleen Caffyn (1853–1926). Her novel of 1894, *The Yellow Aster*, was influenced by Ibsen and Zola, and achieved notoriety to the extent that 'Iota' became a byword for the New Woman in anti-feminist circles.

[39] *Gallia* (1895), by Menie Muriel Dowie (1866–1945), another classic of the New Woman school of fiction.

[40] A reference to the Contagious Disease Acts of the 1860s, which became a focus for feminist campaigners. The Acts allowed for the imprisonment of prostitutes in the notorious 'Lock Hospitals' where they could be forcibly examined and treated for venereal disease.

and Mr George Moore[41]—and the novels I allude to are at any rate thoroughly unhealthy. [. . .]

Some critics are fond of complaining of the lack of humour in the 'new' fiction. But what in heaven's name do they expect? In this age of sciolism, or half-knowledge, of smattering and chattering, we are too much occupied in improving our minds to be mirthful. In particular the New Woman, or 'the desexualised half-man,' as a character in 'Discords' unkindly calls her, is a victim of the universal passion for learning and 'culture,' which, when ill-digested, are apt to cause intellectual dyspepsia. With her head full of all the 'ologies and 'isms, with sex-problems and heredity, and other gleanings from the surgery and the lecture-room, there is no space left for humour, and her novels are for the most part merely pamphlets, sermons, or treatises in disguise. [. . .]

Along with its diseased imaginings—its passion for the abnormal, the morbid, and the unnatural—the anarchical spirit broods over all literature of the decadent and 'revolting' type. It is rebellion all along the line. Everybody is to be a law unto himself. The restraints and conventions which civilised mankind have set over their appetites are absurd, and should be dispensed with. Art and morality have nothing to do with one another (twaddle borrowed from the French Parnassians);[42] there is nothing clean but the unclean; wickedness is a myth, and morbid impressionability is the one cardinal virtue. Following their French masters, our English 'degenerates' are victims of what Dr Nordau calls ego-mania. They are cultivators of the 'I'—moral and social rebels, like Ibsen, whose popularity rests far less on his merits as a writer than on the new evangel of revolt which he preaches, or like Ola Hansson, whose aim is to go one better than Ibsen.[43] By the way, the 'triumphant doctrine of the ego,' which Miss George Egerton finds so comforting, appears to be the theory of a German imbecile who, after several temporary detentions, was permanently confined in a lunatic asylum.[44] His writings being thoroughly hysterical and abnormal, he naturally had a crowd of foolish disciples who considered him a very great philosopher. [. . .]

---

[41] George Moore (1852–1933) was the most prominent English exponent of Naturalism; see his novels, *A Modern Lover* (1883), *A Mummer's Wife* (1885), and *Esther Waters* (1894).

[42] The Parnassians were a group of Paris-based poets dedicated to 'objectivism' and elaborately formal poetry, their name deriving from three collections, *Le Parnasse Contemporain*, in 1866, 1871, and 1876. It was an influential movement in British versions of decadence in the 1890s, praised by Edmund Gosse and W. E. Henley. The best English proponent was Austin Dobson (1840–1921), whose poetry was well regarded in the 1890s.

[43] [Stutfield's footnote:] 'Young Oleg's Ditties,' translated by George Egerton. I have just been reading these 'beautiful prose poems,' as Miss Egerton calls them, together with Mr Punch's excellent skit thereon, and I am not sure whether the original or the travesty is the more absurd. The author's confused and idiotic babblings mark him out as a worthy disciple and expositor of the mad Nietzsche, whose works Dr Nordau analyses at length. If this be the literature of the future, heaven help poor humanity!

[44] A reference to Friedrich Nietzsche (1844–1900), who was committed to an asylum in 1889. His work was translated into English in the 1890s.

It would appear, then, that we are approaching an era of what somebody has called 'holy, awful, individual freedom.' Life is henceforth to be ordered on the go-as-you-please principle. Novelists and essayists denounce the 'disgusting slavery' of wedlock, and minor poets may be heard twittering about free-love and the blessedness of 'group-marriages.' [. . .] [Mr Grant Allen] is [. . .] the inventor of the phrase 'New Hedonism.'[45] Where the newness comes in, by the way, I have never been able to see. That the realisation of oneself through pleasure ought to be the chief aim of life, was said by the Greeks more than two thousand years ago. Of late years the doctrine has been consistently preached and practised by our late prophet of the aesthetes, who are beyond question the real modern representatives of Hedonism. Nevertheless, Mr Grant Allen is of opinion that 'the New Hedonist should take the high ground and speak with authority.' He should uphold 'the moral dignity of his creed' against the 'low ideals of narrow and vulgar morality.' And his creed is, of course, the old anarchical one which teaches that asceticism and self-sacrifice are not only a bore, but positively disgusting. The one duty of the ego is to itself, and its mission on this sinful earth is to enjoy itself to its utmost capacity. Let us, then, follow Mr Grant Allen and the erotomaniac authors, and take our appetites for sign-posts, and follow where the passions lead. If they land mankind, as they have in the past, in moral abysses and abnormalities that cannot be named, what matter if only we find our pleasure. Let us cease to worship the beauty of holiness, and glorify the sexual instinct in its stead. 'Everything high and ennobling in our nature,' says Mr Grant Allen, 'springs from the sexual instinct.' 'Its subtle aroma pervades all literature.' It does, indeed, and a very unpleasant aroma it is becoming. [. . .]

Concerning marriage, Mr Allen considers the desire of a man to keep to himself a wife whose affection has cooled 'the vilest, the deepest-seated, the most barbaric' of all the hateful monopolist instincts. 'She is not yours: she is her own. Unhand her!' he melodramatically exclaims. *La propriété c'est le vol*,[46] and in the good times that are coming no doubt we shall have a community of all things— free land, free love, free spoons and forks, free everything. The sacredness of the marriage-tie is apparently mere old-fashioned Tory twaddle in the eyes of our *révoltés*, and the grasping dotard of a husband who fondly and selfishly hopes to retain the 'monopoly' of the wife of his bosom must learn sounder, because newer, doctrine. Our wives henceforth are to be the partners, of our joys possibly, but of our sorrows only if they so desire it. The lady will take her husband, like her sewing-machine, on approval or on the three-years'-hire system. If he turns out

---

[45] Grant Allen (1848–99), novelist and polymath, who gained instant notoriety (and considerable wealth) in 1895 with the publication his anti-marriage novel, *The Woman Who Did.*

[46] 'Property is theft'—an anarchist slogan derived from Pierre Joseph Prondhon (1809–1865), whose *Qu'est-ce que la propriété* was published in 1840.

vicious or a bore—or perhaps if he snores unduly—like Ibsen's Nora, she will bang the door and develop her personality apart. [. . .]

Here we have the social *vox Tommyrotica* pitched in its loudest key, and sensible people will not be greatly moved by the din. [. . .]

What we lack nowadays is a school of sound, fearless, and vigorous criticism. The public, who in things literary and artistic largely resemble a flock of sheep, know not where to look for guidance. [. . .]

If public opinion should prove powerless to check the growing nuisance, all the poor Philistine can do is to stop his ears and hold his nose until perhaps finally the policeman is called in to his aid. [. . .]

Much of the modern spirit of revolt has its origin in the craving for novelty and notoriety that is such a prominent feature of our day. A contempt for conventionalities and a feverish desire to be abreast of the times may be reckoned among the first-fruits of decadentism. Its subtle and all-pervading influence is observable nowadays in the affectations and semi-indecency of fashionable conversation. [. . .] Effeminacy and artificiality of manner are so common that they have almost ceased to appear ridiculous. Table-talk is garnished with the choice flowers of new woman's speech or the jargon of our shoddy end-of-the-century Renaissance. In certain sections of society it requires some courage to be merely straightforward and natural. Personally, I esteem it rather a distinction to be commonplace. Affectation is not a mark of wit, nor does the preaching of a novel theory or crack-brained social fad argue the possession of a great intellect. Whence, then, sprang the foolish fear of being natural, the craving to attitudinise in everything? The answer is plain. It was Oscar Wilde who infected us with our dread of the conventional, with the silly straining after originality characteristic of a society that desires above all things to be thought intellectually smart. [. . .] But let the Philistine take heart of grace. He is not alone in his fight for common sense and common decency. That large number of really cultivated people whose instincts are still sound and healthy, who disbelieve in 'moral autonomy,' but cling to the old ideals of discipline and duty, of manliness and self-reliance in men, and womanliness in women; who sicken at Ibsenism and the problem play, at the putrid eroticism of a literature that is at once hysterical and foul; who, despising the apes and mountebanks of the new culture, refuse to believe that to be 'modern' and up-to-date is to have attained to the acme of enlightenment—all these will be on his side.

5   from Editorial Comment, *Daily Telegraph* (14 March 1891)

Dramatic art never, in our deliberate judgement, had enemies more deadly than those who have recently clubbed together to bolster up the reputation of the Norwegian writer Henrik Ibsen, and who yesterday evening produced upon a semi-private stage his positively abominable play entitled *Ghosts*. These, beyond doubt, are strong expressions to employ, but they are adopted calmly and after due study of the works of the Scandinavian 'moralist' in question, as well as of the explanations and vindications of them freely forthcoming from his passionate admirers. A band of these strange people, deriving encouragement apparently from the licence lately accorded by the Lord Chamberlain to three previous plays by the same author, *The Pillars of Society*, *A Doll's House*, and *Rosmersholm*, have conspired—for their method is really semi-secret—to put upon a kind of surreptitious stage a further series of Ibsen's social dramas, and others of like kind. Our columns report this morning how the Royalty Theatre, which is a house licensed by the Lord Chamberlain, witnessed last night what was called a 'private invitation performance' on behalf of what is also styled 'The Independent Theatre of London'.[47] Is it by these appellations that the promoters of the disgusting representation seen and heard yesterday at the Royalty propose to escape the reprobation due to such as aim at infecting the modern theatre with poison after desperately inoculating themselves and others? We gravely doubt whether even technically the organisers of this imitation of the French Théâtre Libre can put themselves outside the Act of Parliament governing this department of public morals. As has been already pointed out, they collect funds for the series of performances under the furtive title of 'terms of membership', albeit no money is actually taken at the doors of their theatre. [. . .] Mr. Grein, manager of the Independent Theatre, [. . .] poses altogether as a reformer and friend of high dramatic art.

Much (he says) has been done in speech and writing to misinterpret my intentions, to accuse me of a craving for the ugly. But let me assure everyone that I have but one aim—to serve Art, to show the budding dramatists how powerful plays can be evolved by the simplest means. My programme will plead my cause, and I hope it will be convincing that I worship, above all, the beautiful and the artistic. *Ghosts*, I may add, is not beautiful—in the ordinary

---

[47] A non-commercial avant-gardist theatre committed to performing modern plays which did not necessarily coincide with the popular taste. Modelled on the contemporary French 'Théâtre Libre'.

sense—but it is artistic, because it is a powerful play, written in human language, because it is as simple as a tragedy of the Greeks.

Ay! the play performed last night is 'simple' enough in plan and purpose, but simple only in the sense of an open drain; of a loathsome sore unbandaged; of a dirty act done publicly; or of a lazar-house with all its doors and windows open. It is no more 'Greek', and can no more be called 'Greek' for its plainness of speech and candid foulness, than could a dunghill at Delphi, or a madhouse at Mitylene. It is not 'artistic' even, in the sense of the anatomical studies of the Great Masters; because they, in carefully drawing the hidden things of life and nature, did it in the single and steadfast worship of truth and Beauty, the subtle framework and foundation of which they thus reverently endeavoured to seize. The framework theory of the Norwegian's 'inspiration' however, is said, by his own panegyrists, to be expressed in his play, *An Enemy of the People*, where the hero, Dr. Stockmann—declared, by the way, to be the portrait of Dr. Ibsen himself—observes, 'The great discovery I have made within the last few years is the discovery that all our sources of spiritual life are poisoned, and that our whole society rests upon a pestilential basis of falsehood.' Truly, the aim and object of Ibsen's social plays seem to be to make this good by plots, situations, and dialogues about as 'Greek' as was the clout of Diogenes, and about as 'artistic' as the wrapper on a quack-medicine bottle. [. . .] In Ibsen's melancholy and malodorous world the ghosts that walk seem all of them, moreover, evil and miserable. He loves to make his heroes stand in the strong sun of public favour and estimation, only in order to throw beside them a dark shadow of baseness and hypocrisy which he makes out to be their real personalities. Human society itself is for him but a vile crowd of actors and actresses walking shamefully on the thin crust of a quagmire called 'Law and Order'. There is nothing new, and nothing true, and it does not signify. Until we learn at the feet, forsooth, of this Scandinavian playwright to laugh at honour, to disbelieve in love, to mock at virtue, to distrust friendship, and to deride fidelity, we have learned nothing. This new favourite of a foolish school, who is to set aside Shakespeare and Sheridan, and to teach the hitherto fairly decent genius of the modern English stage a better and a darker way, seems, to our judgement, to resemble one of his own Norwegian ravens emerging from the rocks with an insatiable appetite for decayed flesh rather than any Aeschylus of the North, [. . .] or even any new and dramatic Schopenhauer[48] full of the sadness of human life, and blind to its gladness. Any healthy-minded critic will rise, we think, from the perusal of this so-called 'master's' works with the conclusion that Henrik Ibsen of Skien is what Zola would have been without his invention and analysis, Carlyle

[48] Arthur Schopenhauer (1788–1860), pessimist German philosopher whose work greatly influenced a number of fin-de-siècle writers.

without his genius and piety, or the 'melancholy Jacques' without his culture and wit, if they also had been born of a seafaring family in a poor fishing village upon the Western Fjords.

---

6   from Arthur Symons, 'Henrik Ibsen' (1889)

One of the truly most notable books published in England for some time past [. . .] is [. . .] the volume entitled *The Pillars of Society, and Other Plays*, by Henrik Ibsen. [. . .]

The art of Ibsen in his social dramas is of that essentially modern kind which is not content with holding the mirror up to nature, but desires to drive in certain reformatory ideas over and above the impression conveyed by an impartial reflection of life. [. . .] Ibsen's grip on his subject-matter is prodigious, and his subject-matter is modern life—life and the abuses of life. To read one of his plays is to pass an hour in a centre of existence—in a great city, where the crowds have their passions and agitations, or, better still, in some small place, a selected corner out of all this bustle, in which the action, more circumscribed, can be concentrated, and thus strike home with a deeper intensity. The action of one of the greatest of his dramas, *Ghosts*, takes place in a country house by one of the western fjords during the hours of a single day from noon to sunset; but in its scope it embraces humanity, and speaks to universal nature. Here again the 'purpose' with which he writes justifies itself: it is because he has a purpose—because, that is, he is a thinker who goes right down to Nature, who weighs, and finds wanting, a society which does not grow out of that one true soil—that his art becomes universal: his purpose is the life-blood of his art. [. . .]

His fundamental demand is for individual liberty [. . .] 'To revolutionise people's minds', as he himself has said, 'that is the one thing that avails'. Thus his plays are no party-pamphlets, but a gospel of real light: they illuminate, they do not merely argue. Nor is Ibsen an idealist in the contemptuous sense which people often give to the word—an unpractical visionary. He is directly and steadily practical, full of common sense, shrewdness, attention to fact, to detail. He can found a play on a sanitary question; nothing is trivial, common, uninteresting to him. [. . .]

But Ibsen is not only a great thinker, he is a great artist. Nothing shows us better than Ibsen's social dramas the true meaning of the word realism—a word which has unhappily come to be associated with pictures of life which are necessarily sordid, frequently unclean. The connection between the realistic and the abominable is a question I have never been able to fathom. Realism is a picture of life as it really is, and in life as it really is the element of grossness is only one of many elements. Ibsen's realism stifles nothing; it is daring to discuss matters over which society draws a veil, but it is never gross, never unhealthy, it 'sees life steadily, and sees it whole'. Ibsen paints ordinary life; his people are (if I may speak in terms of another nationality) the people one meets in the City, one's lawyer, one's banker, the men one hears discussing stocks and shares, business people; or, again, the officials of a country town, the clergyman, the ladies who work for charitable institutions, the doctor, the newspaper editor, the printer. All these people meet, talk over their own affairs, speak of their business, go to and fro, just as if they were really living their parts. Every character, down to the merest 'walking gentleman', is carefully finished; we get from all the same impression of reality. It is life, and yet life from a point of view which is not the point of view of the crowd. Everywhere there is a deep undercurrent of irony. [. . .] And [. . .] conventional people everywhere hate Ibsen—because they fear him; he shocks them—because he tells the inconvenient truth. A caricaturist is never feared, but in Ibsen you never lose the lesson in the laugh. [. . .]

Ghosts [. . .] has roused a violent opposition. It is a tragedy which encroaches as far as art can well go in the direction of physical horror, and the prolonged anguish of its action is unrelieved by even a momentary ray of really cheerful light. The play shows, in its few intense hours of crisis, the working of the relentless law of heredity. It is the final triumph of nature over conventionality, and Ibsen has not spared the morality of conventional suppression one drop of the bitter cup. The play is certainly very painful reading, but the painfulness is justified, from the moral point of view, by the 'purpose', from the artistic point of view by the unquestionable power of it. I know nothing in any play so complete in its mastery over the springs of horror and sympathetic suffering as the last scene, the expected and dreaded climax—the final flowering of the latent germ of madness in the innocent Osvald. The horror of *The Cenci* is less dreadful than this.[49] [. . .]

Ibsen's art, [. . .] as Mr. Ellis well says in the powerful and thoughtful introduction to [the plays] [. . .], 'is the expression of a great soul crushed by the weight of an antagonistic social environment into utterance that has caused him to be regarded as the most revolutionary of modern writers'. [. . .]

EDITORS' NOTES

1. Andrew Lang (1844–1912) was one of the most prolific and versatile writers in late nineteenth-century London—the British Library catalogue lists nearly 350 works,

[49] A reference to Shelley's verse drama, *The Cenci* (1819), in which a daughter accused of the murder of her father reveals the incestuous horrors of family life that drove her to violence.

ranging through poetry, anthropology, Greek myth and history, literary criticism, psychical research (see Chapter 11), melodramatic novels, literary reminiscences, historical monographs, folk-tales, and fairy-tales. He was a close friend of many in the intellectual elite, like the editor Leslie Stephen, but also champion of new popular culture, co-writing works with Rider Haggard, and being the first to bring to British attention the early Indian stories of Rudyard Kipling.

2. Arthur Symons (1865–1945): for a biographical note see Chapter 3. Following the Wilde trials of April 1895, Symons changed the title of the essay included here: the 'Decadent' movement was now associated with homosexuality and vice; 'Symbolism' was a less loaded term.

3. Sir Walter Besant (1836–1901) is now best remembered for his novel *All Sorts and Conditions of Men* (1882) which draws attention to the dreadful living and working conditions of the inhabitants of London's East End and stimulated the foundation of the People's Palace in Mile End (1887) for rational amusement and intellectual improvement. In 1884 he founded the Society of Authors.

Eliza Lynn Linton (1822–98) was a pioneering female journalist who, ironically, became a leading opponent of the women's movement. A successful novelist as well as journalist who was able to support herself and her family, Linton is now best remembered for her famous articles in the *Saturday Review* in 1868, which attacked the 'Girl of the Period' and 'The Shrieking Sisterhood' for their unfeminine (as she saw it) social and cultural aspirations.

Thomas Hardy (1840–1928) later gained some notoriety as a 'candid' writer of fiction: his *Tess of the D'Urbervilles* (1891) and *Jude the Obscure* (1895), published after this article, were both fiercely attacked for their apparently liberal attitude towards female sexuality and the Marriage Question.

4. 'Tommyrotics' is written in the vein of, and clearly owes a debt to, Max Nordau's *Degeneration*, which had only just been translated into English. This article—along with its author Hugh Stutfield—has become synonymous with anti-Decadent, anti-naturalist, anti-feminist, and generally anti-modern reaction at the fin de siècle.

5 and 6. The moral and cultural debate provoked by the plays of Henrik Ibsen was so intense at the fin de siècle that we have included two typical opposing views here. The vitriolic tone of the *Telegraph* leader was characteristic of establishment responses to *Ghosts*, whose English première led to a flood of more than 500 reviews. The *Telegraph* editorial was almost certainly written by its theatre critic, Clement Scott, who was one of Ibsen's bitterest opponents in England. Symons's response is characteristic of the so-called 'Ibsenite' school, the Norwegian's followers including such progressives and radicals as George Bernard Shaw, Edmund Gosse, Eleanor Marx, Edward Aveling, Olive Schreiner, and Havelock Ellis.

6

THE NEW IMPERIALISM

Between 1870 and 1900, the British empire was extended by 4.75 million square miles, annexing thirty-nine separate areas and adding 88 million new 'subjects' for Queen and Empress Victoria, taking her tally to 420 million people. This astonishing expansion is a key phenomenon of the fin de siècle, saturating British culture in the 1880s and 1890s, and its multiform effects have made this our longest set of selections. In three sections, we will try to evoke the arrival of a new 'official' policy of forward expansion, discuss the changing popular representation of imperial affairs, and represent the marginalized but persistent voices of critique from within the era.

The New Imperialism was as much a puzzle to contemporary commentators as it has been disputed by subsequent historians—what caused this change in policy? It is clear from Seeley's hugely influential views in *The Expansion of England*, extracted below, that empire was conceived at the beginning of the 1880s largely as colonies of white emigrants sharing blood kinship with England. India had been a historical accident, and a worrying dependant, not part of the organic conception of a 'natural' expansion of Greater Britain. Within three years, however, Britain had occupied Egypt, consolidated its South African colonies, and was engaging with Germany, France, Portugal, and Belgium in the 'scramble for Africa'. What produced this change? Economists suggest that commercial competition with Germany and America forced the British to seek new protected markets and raw materials, since informal 'spheres of influence' no longer operated. Robinson and Gallagher sparked controversy by suggesting that competition was merely the spur to an accidental, reluctant, and largely strategic occupation of territory. Marxist historians disagree and point to the emergence of truly international capitalism, arguing that governments proved powerless against the huge wealth of entrepreneurs like Cecil Rhodes, and preferred to share the profits that resulted. Some propose that a relatively benign liberal British attitude to colonies, genuinely believing in the 'civilizing mission', was dismantled by a succession of rebellions and native violence, leading to an ideological hardening and a 'scientific racism' that rendered the African population an unimportant detail in occupying 'wasted land' (scientific views of the 'savage' are investigated in more detail in Chapter 13). A more cultural approach posits that empire became a new locus for making the nation cohere—Victoria's status as empress, conferred in 1876, constituted a way of providing a set of compelling representations that might bind a riven population together. It is this which may explain a pervasive sense of panic, of impending doom and imperial decline, that accompanies this era of seemingly unstoppable expansion. All of these approaches contain useful ways of orienting a reading of the documents we present here.

The heroes of empire—General 'Chinese' Gordon, standing alone against Muslim fanatics in Khartoum in 1885, Lord 'Bobs' Roberts leading the relief party in May 1900 to free Robert 'B-P' Baden-Powell from the siege of Mafeking in the Boer War—were products of a transformed print media and popular culture. It is the flags and cheap portraits, the advertisements for Bovril and Pears' Soap, that can convey the ways in which the New Imperialism saturated British culture. Here, newspaper reports move from the anonymity and distance of the early 1880s to the bestseller narratives of the dastardly Muslims and the personality-driven reportage of George Steevens. Steevens was the voice of the new popular and imperialist press—writing for the *Daily Mail* when it was first launched in 1896 in a dashing, breathless style from the midst of battle. The speed with which his reports reached home—by telegraph—reflected important technological changes driving mass print culture. On Steevens's death during the Boer War Vernon Blackburn was not exaggerating when he claimed 'What Mr. Kipling has done for fiction, Mr. Steevens did for fact.' Texts like these, as much as Kipling or Haggard, produced the defining representations of the British empire.

Critiques of the New Imperialism came from distinct sources. Economic arguments are the main drive behind Olive Schreiner's analysis of the elements making war in South Africa inevitable, and these are best stated in the classic socialist reading of imperialism by J. A. Hobson. The hypocrisy of deploying the Christian rhetoric of the 'civilizing mission' is the target of Cunninghame Graham's marvellous mock-sermon on the troublesome 'nigger'. A passionate Christian sense of brotherhood with the native could still motivate antipathy to the violent 'pacification' of African tribes. The most successful campaign against the murderous logic of imperial expansion was against the Congo Free State (where an estimated 8 million natives were killed by forced labour, war, and disease between 1885 and 1908), and was led by Edmund Morel of the Congo Reform Association, a society that emerged from the humanitarian traditions of the Aborigines' Protection Society and the Anti-Slavery Society. The atrocities in the Congo, as mediated by Joseph Conrad's *Heart of Darkness* (1899), are the images that now dominate the understanding of the New Imperialism of the fin de siècle. It is worth remembering, however, how belatedly news from the Congo arrived—a brief report we have reproduced from *The Times* in 1897 was among the first to suggest the atrocities to a British public largely swept up in the mechanisms of jingoistic fervour.

Secondary reading. General histories: Harlow and Carter; Hobsbawm, *The Age of Empire*; Hyam; Morris; Pakenham, *The Boer War* and *The Scramble for Africa*; Robinson and Gallagher. For the Boer War: Tabitha Jackson; Pakenham, *The Boer War*. For cultural representations of empire: Brantlinger, *Rule of Darkness*; McClintock; MacDonald; John MacKenzie; Said. For critiques: Ascherson; Bernard Porter; Schneer.

I. THE 'FORWARD' POLICY

1   from Sir John Seeley, *The Expansion of England* (1883)

TENDENCY IN ENGLISH HISTORY

History ought to look at things from a greater distance and more comprehensively. If we stand aloof a little and follow with our eyes the progress of the English State, the great governed society of English people, in recent centuries, we shall be much more struck by another change, which is not only far greater but even more conspicuous, though it has always been less discussed, partly because it proceeded more gradually, partly because it excited less opposition. I mean the simple obvious fact of the extension of the English name into other countries of the globe, the foundation of Greater Britain.

There is something very characteristic in the indifference which we show towards this mighty phenomenon of the diffusion of our race and the expansion of our state. We seem, as it were, to have conquered and peopled half the world in a fit of absence of mind. While we were doing it, that is in the eighteenth century, we did not allow it to affect our imaginations or in any degree to change our ways of thinking; nor have we even now ceased to think of ourselves as simply a race inhabiting an island off the northern coast of the Continent of Europe. We constantly betray by our modes of speech that we do not reckon our colonies as really belonging to us; thus if we are asked what the English population is, it does not occur to us to reckon in the population of Canada and Australia. [. . .]

Let us consider what this Greater Britain at the present day precisely is. Excluding certain small possessions, which are chiefly of the nature of naval or military stations, it consists besides the United Kingdom of four great groups of territory, inhabited either chiefly or to a large extent by Englishmen and subject to the Crown, and a fifth great territory also subject to the Crown and ruled by English officials, but inhabited by a completely foreign race. The first four are the Dominion of Canada, the West Indian Islands, among which I include some territories on the continent of Central and Southern America, the mass of South African possessions of which Cape Colony is the most considerable, and fourthly the Australian group, to which, simply for convenience, I must here add New Zealand. The dependency is India. [. . .]

But of course it strikes us at once that this enormous Indian population does not make part of the Greater Britain in the same sense as those ten millions of Englishmen who live outside of the British Islands. The latter are of our own blood, and are therefore united with us by the strongest tie. The former are of alien race and religion, and are bound to us only by the tie of conquest. It may be fairly questioned whether the possession of India does or ever can increase our power or security, while there is no doubt that it vastly increases our dangers and responsibilities. Our colonial Empire stands on a quite different footing; it has some of the fundamental conditions of stability. There are in general three ties by which states are held together, community of race, community of religion, community of interest. By the first two our colonies are evidently bound to us, and this fact by itself makes the connection strong. It will grow indissolubly firm if we come to recognise also that interest bids us maintain the connection, and this conviction seems to gain ground. When we inquire then into the Greater Britain of the future we ought to think much more of our Colonial than of our Indian Empire. [. . .]

Whether good or bad then, the growth of Greater Britain is an event of enormous magnitude. Evidently as regards the future it is the greatest event. But an event may be very great, and yet be so simple that there is not much to be said about it, that it has scarcely any history. It is thus that the great English Exodus is commonly regarded, as if it had happened in the most simple, inevitable manner, as if it were merely the unopposed occupation of empty countries by the nation which happened to have the greatest surplus population and the greatest maritime power. I shall show this to be a great mistake. I shall show that this Exodus makes a most ample and a most full and interesting chapter in English history. [. . .]

The great central fact in this chapter of history is that we have had at different times two such Empires. So decided is the drift of our destiny towards the occupation of the New World that after we had created one Empire and lost it, a second grew up almost in our own despite. The figures I gave you refer exclusively to our second Empire, to that which we still possess. When I spoke of the ten millions of English subjects who live beyond the sea, I did not pause to mention that a hundred years ago we had another set of colonies which had already a population of three millions, that these colonies broke off from us and formed a federal state, of which the population has in a century multiplied more than sixteenfold, and is now equal to that of the mother country and its colonies taken together. It is an event of prodigious magnitude, not only that this Empire should have been lost to us, but that a new state, English in race and character, should have sprung up, and that this state should have grown in a century to be greater in population than every European state except Russia. But the loss we suffered in the secession of the American colonies has left in the English mind a doubt, a misgiving, which affects our whole forecast of the future of England.

For if this English Exodus has been the greatest English event of the eighteenth and nineteenth centuries, the greatest English question of the future must be, what is to become of our second Empire, and whether or no it may be expected to go the way of the first. In the solution of this question lies that moral which I said ought to result from the study of English history. [. . .]

But though we must not prejudge the question whether we ought to retain our Empire, we may fairly assume that it is desirable after due consideration to judge it.

With a view to forming such a judgment, I propose in these lectures to examine historically the tendency to expansion which England has so long displayed. We shall learn to think of it more seriously if we discover it to be profound, persistent, necessary to the national life, and more hopefully if we can satisfy ourselves that the secession of our first colonies was not a mere normal result of expansion, like the bursting of a bubble, but the result of temporary conditions, removable and which have been removed.

2   Joseph Chamberlain, 'The True Conception
of Empire' (1897)

The following speech was delivered on March 31, 1897, at the Hotel Métropole, when Mr. Chamberlain presided at the annual dinner of the Royal Colonial Institute:—

I have now the honour to propose to you the toast of 'Prosperity to the Royal Colonial Institute.' (Cheers.) The Institute was founded in 1868, almost exactly a generation ago, and I confess that I admire the faith of its promoters, who, in a time not altogether favourable to their opinions, sowed the seeds of Imperial patriotism—(hear, hear)—although they must have known that few of them could live to gather the fruit and to reap the harvest. (Cheers.) But their faith has been justified by the result of their labours, and their foresight must be recognised in the light of present experience.

It seems to me that there are three distinct stages in our Imperial history. We began to be, and we ultimately became, a great Imperial Power in the eighteenth century, but, during the greater part of that time, the colonies were regarded, not only by us, but by every European Power that possessed them, as possessions valuable in proportion to the pecuniary advantage which they brought to the mother country, which, under that order of ideas, was not truly a mother at all, but appeared rather in the light of a grasping and absentee landlord desiring to take from his tenants the utmost rents he could exact. The colonies were valued and maintained because it was thought that they would be a source of profit—of direct profit—to the mother country.

That was the first stage, and when we were rudely awakened by the War of Independence in America from this dream, that the colonies could be held for our profit alone, the second chapter was entered upon, and public opinion seems then to have drifted to the opposite extreme; and, because the colonies were no longer a source of revenue it seems to have been believed and argued by many people that their separation from us was only a matter of time, and that that separation should be desired and encouraged lest haply they might prove an encumbrance and a source of weakness.

It was while those views were still entertained, while the little Englanders—(laughter)—were in their full career, that this Institute was founded to protest against doctrines so injurious to our interests—(cheers)—and so derogatory to our honour; and I rejoice that what was then, as it were, 'a voice crying in the wilderness' is now the expressed and determined will of the overwhelming majority of the British people. (Loud cheers.) Partly by the efforts of this Institute and similar organisations, partly by the writings of such men as Froude and Seeley[1]—(hear, hear)—but mainly by the instinctive good sense and patriotism of the people at large, we have now reached the third stage in our history, and the true conception of our Empire. (Cheers.)

What is that conception? As regards the self-governing colonies we no longer talk of them as dependencies. The sense of possession has given place to the sen-

---

[1] J. A. Froude, like Seeley, was an imperialist historian, as in *Oceana, or England and her Colonies* (1886), which advocated the colonization of 'wasted' land by mass emigration of England's surplus populations.

timent of kinship. We think and speak of them as part of ourselves—(cheers)—as part of the British Empire, united to us, although they may be dispersed throughout the world, by ties of kindred, of religion, of history, and of language, and joined to us by the seas that formerly seemed to divide us. (Cheers.)

But the British Empire is not confined to the self-governing colonies and the United Kingdom. It includes a much greater area, a much more numerous population in tropical climes, where no considerable European settlement is possible, and where the native population must always vastly outnumber the white inhabitants; and in these cases also the same change has come over the Imperial idea. Here also the sense of possession has given place to a different sentiment—the sense of obligation. We feel now that our rule over these territories can only be justified if we can show that it adds to the happiness and prosperity of the people—(cheers)—and I maintain that our rule does, and has, brought security and peace and comparative prosperity to countries that never knew these blessings before. (Cheers.)

In carrying out this work of civilisation we are fulfilling what I believe to be our national mission, and we are finding scope for the exercise of those faculties and qualities which have made of us a great governing race. (Cheers.) I do not say that our success has been perfect in every case, I do not say that all our methods have been beyond reproach; but I do say that in almost every instance in which the rule of the Queen has been established and the great *Pax Britannica* has been enforced, there has come with it greater security to life and property, and a material improvement to the condition of the bulk of the population. (Cheers.) No doubt, in the first instance, when these conquests have been made, there has been bloodshed, there has been loss of life among the native populations, loss of still more precious lives among those who have been sent out to bring these countries into some kind of disciplined order, but it must be remembered that that is the condition of the mission we have to fulfil. There are, of course, among us— there always are among us, I think—a very small minority of men who are ready to be the advocates of the most detestable tyrants, provided their skin is black—men who sympathise with the sorrows of Prempeh and Lobengula,[2] and who denounce as murderers those of their countrymen who have gone forth at the command of the Queen, and who have redeemed districts as large as Europe from the barbarism and the superstition in which they had been steeped for centuries. I remember a picture by Mr. Selous[3] of a philanthropist—an imaginary

[2] Prempeh I (1871–1931), king of Asante, crowned in 1894, and whose rule was then systematically destroyed by the British forces 'pacifying' West Africa. Lobengula (1833–94), chief of Ndebele, who negotiated the lease of gold reserves to Cecil Rhodes in 1888. This agreement was betrayed and his army destroyed during Rhodes's annexation of Matabeleland in 1893-4.

[3] Frederick Selous (1851–1917), big-game hunter and frontier imperialist, who assisted Cecil Rhodes in securing Matabele annexation, and the man who planted the British flag on the territory that became Rhodesia. He was killed in action in Africa in First World War.

philanthropist, I will hope—sitting cosily by his fireside and denouncing the methods by which British civilisation was promoted. This philanthropist complained of the use of Maxim guns and other instruments of warfare, and asked why we could not proceed by more conciliatory methods, and why the impis of Lobengula could not be brought before a magistrate, fined five shillings, and bound over to keep the peace. (Loud laughter.)

No doubt there is humorous exaggeration in this picture, but there is gross exaggeration in the frame of mind against which it was directed. You cannot have omelettes without breaking eggs; you cannot destroy the practices of barbarism, of slavery, of superstition, which for centuries have desolated the interior of Africa, without the use of force; but if you will fairly contrast the gain to humanity with the price which we are bound to pay for it, I think you may well rejoice in the result of such expeditions as those which have recently been conducted with such signal success—(cheers)—in Nyassaland, Ashanti, Benin, and Nupé—expeditions which may have, and indeed have, cost valuable lives, but as to which we may rest assured that for one life lost a hundred will be gained, and the cause of civilisation and the prosperity of the people will in the long run be eminently advanced. (Cheers.) But no doubt such a state of things, such a mission as I have described, involve heavy responsibility. In the wide dominions of the Queen the doors of the temple of Janus are never closed—(hear, hear)—and it is a gigantic task that we have undertaken when we have determined to wield the sceptre of empire. Great is the task, great is the responsibility, but great is the honour—(cheers); and I am convinced that the conscience and the spirit of the country will rise to the height of its obligations, and that we shall have the strength to fulfil the mission which our history and our national character have imposed on us. (Cheers.)

In regard to the self-governing colonies our task is much lighter. We have undertaken, it is true, to protect them with all the strength at our command against foreign aggression, although I hope that the need for our intervention may never arise. (Hear, hear.) But there remains what then will be our chief duty—that is, to give effect to that sentiment of kinship to which I have referred and which I believe is deep in the heart of every Briton. We want to promote a closer and a firmer union between all members of the great British race, and in this respect we have in recent years made great progress—so great that I think sometimes some of our friends are apt to be a little hasty, and to expect even a miracle to be accomplished. I would like to ask them to remember that time and patience are essential elements in the development of all great ideas. (Cheers.) Let us, gentlemen, keep our ideal always before us. For my own part, I believe in the practical possibility of a federation of the British race—(loud cheers)—but I know that it will come, if it does come, not by pressure, not by anything in the nature of dictation from this country, but it will come as the realisation of the dearest wish of our colonial fellow-subjects themselves. (Hear, hear.)

That such a result would be desirable, would be in the interest of all our colonies as well as of ourselves, I do not believe any sensible man will doubt. It seems to me that the tendency of the time is to throw all power into the hands of the greater Empires, and the minor kingdoms—those which are non-progressive—seem to be destined to fall into a secondary and subordinate place. But, if Greater Britain remains united, no empire in the world can ever surpass it in area, in population, in wealth, or in the diversity of its resources. (Cheers.)

Let us, then, have confidence in the future. (Hear, hear.) I do not ask you to anticipate with Lord Macaulay the time when the New Zealander will come here to gaze upon the ruins of a great dead city. There are in our present condition no visible signs of decrepitude and decay. (Cheers.) The mother country is still vigorous and fruitful, is still able to send forth troops of stalwart sons to people and occupy the waste spaces of the earth; but yet it may well be that some of these sister nations whose love and affection we eagerly desire may in the future equal and even surpass our greatness. A trans-oceanic capital may arise across the seas, which will throw into shade the glories of London itself; but in the years that must intervene let it be our endeavour, let it be our task, to keep alight the torch of Imperial patriotism, to hold fast the affection and the confidence of our kinsmen across the seas, so that in every vicissitude of fortune the British Empire may present an unbroken front to all her foes, and may carry on even to distant ages the glorious traditions of the British flag. (Loud cheers.) It is because I believe that the Royal Colonial Institute is contributing to this result that with all sincerity I propose the toast of the evening.

---

3   from Cecil Rhodes, speech at Drill Hall, Cape Town (18 July 1899)

Mr. Mayor, Ladies, and Gentlemen,—I have to thank you for the great reception that you have given me here tonight. I recognise what it is for; it is for the work, the idea. We must dismiss the personal. I listened tonight to the various addresses; they carry encouragement towards the completion of the great idea. When the thought came to get through the continent it was a mad thought, it was the idea of a lunatic. That is what they said; but it has grown, and it has advanced, and you greet me here tonight because you see that it has passed from the era of imagination to practical completion. It is now not a question, sir, of the lunacy of the project; it is merely a question of the years that it will take to complete. The only awkward thing is the progress of time. We do get older, and we do become a little hurried in our ideas because of that terrible time. You can conquer anything. You can conquer, if you will allow me to say it, even raids,[4] but time you can never interfere with; and so we have to complete, with all the rapidity we can, the project that is before us, that is the project of uniting the North and the South of Africa. You have been good enough to ask me how, or rather what success has been achieved. Thanks to the goodness of our people, when the politicians were rather timid, I may tell you that I was fortunate enough to obtain four millions of money to extend the railway from Bulawayo in the direction of Egypt. That sum will carry us to the borders of the German sphere, that is, to Tanganyika. It means four or five years of work, but during these subsequent five years one will not be bothered with pounds, shillings, and pence, because the money is subscribed. Then I hope to get the engineers to proceed with their work with the greatest rapidity possible.

Then we arrive at the borders of the German territory, and as I notice you have referred in the kindest way to the actions of the German emperor towards myself, I can only tell you that, in my humble opinion, he is a big man. He allowed me to understand that he would be pleased to see me, and I discussed with him the question of passing through his territory by telegraph and railway, and he met me in the fairest way, and gave me, through his Ministers, every assistance. There will be no difficulty with the German territory, and I can only add that I think the German people are very fortunate in having such an emperor, who spends his whole day in efforts for his people. We have the private satisfaction of knowing that he is half an Englishman. Well, sir, you can see we are getting on.

And then, sir, I had the good luck to meet Lord Kitchener in London. We met very frequently, and we rode in the morning together. I think horse exercise increases the activity of the brain. And we came to a distinct understanding, and I think you will hear before very long that funds have been provided for Lord Kitchener to proceed from Khartoum to Uganda. I had the opportunity of meeting him on several occasions. [. . .] I did not think for one moment in the times that are past that I should have had a meeting like this. It is because of the past trouble, of the necessity of support, and because, if you may look at it from this point of view, of the persistency of one's action, that you have forgiven the faults for the greater purpose.

And, sir, my people have changed. I speak of the English people, with their marvellous common sense, coupled with their powers of imagination—all thoughts of Little England are over. They are tumbling over each other, Liberals and Conservatives, to show which side are the greater and most enthusiastic Imperialists. The people have changed, and so do all the parties, just like the

---

[4] An oblique reference to the 'Jameson Raid'; see Editors' Note 3 at the end of this chapter for further details.

Punch and Judy show at a country fair. The people have found out that England is small, and her trade is large, and they have also found out that other people are taking their share of the world, and enforcing hostile tariffs. The people of England are finding out that 'trade follows the flag,' and they have all become Imperialists. They are not going to part with any territory. And the bygone ideas of nebulous Republics are over. The English people intend to retain every inch of land they have got, and perhaps, sir, they intend to secure a few more inches. And so the thought of my country has changed. When I began this business of annexation, both sides were most timid. They would ask one to stop at Kimberley, then they asked one to stop at Khama's country. I remember Lord Salisbury's Chief Secretary imploring me to stop at the Zambesi. Mr. Mayor, excuse me for using the word 'I,' but unfortunately I have been alone in these efforts. Now, sir, they won't stop anywhere; they have found out that the world is not quite big enough for British trade and the British flag; and the operation of even conquering the planets is only something which has yet to be known. I have little doubt about the Colonial people, and in saying so, I cover in the Colonial people the Dutch as well as the English. Notwithstanding my past little temporary difficulty, if we were all to accept equal rights, I feel convinced that we should all be united on the proposition that Africa is not, after all, big enough for us. [. . .]

We must try, if possible, to keep the continent together. It is perfectly possible. I must not touch on politics tonight, but if we could only get a united feeling, Africa would be united to Tanganyika. That is number two we have to work for. I personally have to work for my railway to Egypt, and my telegraph to Egypt, and you have to work with me for that greater object, the union of the country. I have often stated it, but if you were to go up in a balloon, how ridiculous it would appear to you to see all these divided States, divided tariffs, divided peoples; the Almighty made them one, and it is our work also to unite them. [. . .]

Once the competition between us is on the basis of the best man coming to the front, be he a German, or be he a Frenchman, or be he a Russian, or be he a Dutchman, or be he an Englishman, the question is over. I remember some years ago when I was the Prime Minister, being present at Stellenbosch, and at the college there I saw the young men with their intelligent faces, and I felt that they had nothing to fear from the question of equal rights on an equal basis. I felt that they had nothing to fear. I felt that they had nothing to fear, on account of the domination, and the vigour, and the physical energy of my race. I don't think that they have much to fear if we can only accept that programme, which covers everything. You need not then talk of this law or of that law if you can get the thought impressed into the minds of those who share this country with us that all we want is equal rights; that the Almighty has made this country one, and you cannot make divisions. You can draw imaginary lines, but we are all one, and I would say, sir, it is no good my trying to go to Egypt, or thinking out thoughts of union if we are not all one.

II. REPORTAGE

4   from 'General Gordon', *The Illustrated London News* (14 February 1885)

On Wednesday last, six days after the news of the capture or surrender of Khartoum and its occupation by the Mahdi's forces[5] had reached London, the mournful intelligence of General Gordon's death was published upon the authority of information obtained by Sir Charles Wilson and Lieutenant Stuart Wortley, who arrived on Monday evening at Korti, the head-quarters of Lord Wolseley. It was stated that General Gordon died on the 4th inst., at Khartoum, apparently from a wound inflicted upon him by assassins who stabbed him, on the morning of the 27th ult., as he was coming out of the Government House or Palace, the gates of the city having been opened to the enemy, during the night, by the teacherous officers of the garrison. We fear that the announcement of his death is but too true; it had seemed very possible that he might have been able, with a few personal followers, to escape from the city and to get up the Nile, where he could easily have found a place of safety; and if, on the other hand he had been taken prisoner by the Mahdi, there is every reason to believe that his life would have been spared, in order that he might be kept for a hostage, or to exact a ransom for his liberation. There does not seem to have been any considerable fighting in Khartoum upon this occasion; and we can only regard the killing of General Gordon as an act of murder, which may have been perpetrated by some of his own revolted native soldiery, or by Mussulman fanatics, or perhaps by the perfidious officers and local chiefs who had gone over to the enemy's side. [. . .]

General Gordon seems to have felt confident of the effect of his personal influence among the native tribes, and of his ability to dissuade them from joining the Mahdi. Although he vehemently protested against the abandonment of Soudan, the policy which had been announced by the British Government and accepted by the Khedive,[6] it was hastily resolved to send Gordon out upon a special mission, 'to report on the military situation there, to provide in the best manner for

[5]   The Mahdi—'the Guide'—is a figure from Islamic eschatology, a mystical being whose appearance among men would signify the return of the Messiah. Mohammed Ahmed adopted the title of Mahdi, and declared religious war on British forces in the Sudan.

[6]   Turkish title of the appointed ruler of Egypt, when British and Ottoman empires competed for influence over the territory.

the safety of the European population of Khartoum, and of the Egyptian garrisons throughout the country, as well as for the evacuation of the Soudan, with the exception of the seaboard.' [. . .] He distinctly understood that he was not to expect, under any circumstances, the support of a military force; and this he fully acknowledged in his official communications to our Government, before proceeding from Cairo. [. . .]

This is a sad and tragical story; and we wish it could be shown that adequate measures had been taken to communicate to the Mahdi, and to the insurgent tribes of the Soudan, while Khartoum was yet safe, the conciliatory intentions of our Government. [. . .] The forcible repression of the Soudan revolt has been pursued with results hitherto unavailing, at an enormous sacrifice of life, accompanied by the fall of Khartoum and the death of General Gordon.

---

5   from Major F. R. Wingate from the original manuscripts
     of Father Joseph Ohrwalder, *Ten Years' Captivity in
     the Mahdi's Camp 1882–92* (1893)

The surging mass threw itself on the palace, overflowed into the lovely garden, and burst through the doors in wild search of their prey; but Gordon went alone to meet them. As they rushed up the stairs, he came towards them and tried to speak to them; but they could not or would not listen, and the first Arab plunged his huge spear into his body. He fell forward on his face, was dragged down the stairs, many stabbed him with their spears, and his head was cut off and sent to the Mahdi.

Such was the end of the brave defender of Khartum. When I came from El Obeid to Omdurman I visited Khartum, and went to the palace, where I was shown some black spots on the stairs which they told me were the traces of Gordon's blood.

On Gordon's head being brought to the Mahdi, he appeared to have been much displeased at his death—not because he felt any pity for him, but he believed that Gordon might join his army. Had he not done so, he would have imprisoned him and reduced him to slavery. It was much better that Gordon should have died when he did than have remained a captive in the hands of these cruel and fanatical Arabs. Gordon's head was hung on a tree in Omdurman, and the wild multitude rejoiced in heaping curses on it and insulting it. [. . .]

All this success increased the adulation and worship of the Mahdi to an extraordinary extent, and as for himself, although he was continually warning his followers to despise the good things of this world, and to abandon all luxurious modes of life, he surrounded himself with every sort of comfort and luxury, appreciating to the utmost the very pleasures which he declaimed so violently. He urged moderation in eating and drinking, yet he secured for himself every dainty which Khartum could possibly produce. He now wore shirts and trousers of the finest material, and, before putting them on, his wives were obliged to perfume them with incense and other costly fragrances. His wives attended on him in turns, but no regularity was preserved. They anointed his body with all sorts of precious unguents, but his speciality was the expensive 'Sandalia' (a perfume prepared from sandal-wood and oil), and so saturated was he with these perfumes that when he went forth the air was laden with sweet-smelling odours.

The courtyard of his harem was full of women, from little Turkish girls of eight years old to the pitch-black Dinka negress or copper-coloured Abyssinian; almost every tribe in the Sudan supplied its representative, so that one might say the entire Sudanese woman-world was to be seen here. [. . .]

But all this good living and unbridled sensuality were to be the cause of his speedy dissolution. He grew enormously fat. The two visitors, whom I mentioned above, saw him only eight days before his death, and told me that they believed then he could not live much longer. Early in Ramadan he fell sick, and soon became dangerously ill. The hand of God's justice fell heavily upon him; and it was decreed that he should no longer enjoy the empire which he had raised on the dead bodies of thousands of the victims to his wretched hypocrisy and deceit.

It is, indeed, terrible to think of the awful misery and distress brought upon his own country by this one man. His disease grew rapidly worse; he complained of pain in the heart, and died, on the 22nd of June, 1885, of fatty degeneration of the heart. Some say that he was a victim to the vengeance of a woman who had lost husband and children in the fall of Khartum, and who repaid the Mahdi outrage on her own person by giving him poison in his food. This may be so; and it is true, poison is generally used in the Sudan to put people out of the way; but I am rather inclined to think that it was outraged nature that took vengeance on its victim; and that it was the Mahdi's debauched and dissolute mode of life which caused his early death.

———

6   from G. W. Steevens, 'The Battle of Omdurman',
        With Kitchener to Khartum (1898)

A trooper rose out of the dimness from behind the shoulder of Gebel Surgham, grew larger and plainer, spurred violently up to the line and inside. A couple more were silhouetted across our front. Then the electric whisper came racing down the line; they were coming. The Lancers came in on the left; the Egyptian mounted troops drew like a curtain across us from left to right. As they passed a flicker of white flags began to extend and fill the front in their place. The noise of something began to creep in upon us; it cleared and divided into the tap of drums and far-away surf of raucous war-cries. A shiver of expectancy thrilled along our army, and then a sigh of content. They were coming on. Allah help them! they were coming on.

It was now half-past six. The flags seemed still very distant, the roar very faint, and the thud of our first gun was almost startling. It may have startled them too, but it startled them into life. The line of flags swung forward, and a mass of white flying linen swung forward with it too. They came very fast, and they came very straight; and then presently they came no farther. With a crash the bullets leaped out of the British rifles. It began with the Guards and Warwicks—section volleys at 2,000 yards; then, as the Dervishes edged rightward, it ran along to the High-landers, the Lincolns, and to Maxwell's Brigade. The British stood up in double rank behind their zariba; the blacks lay down in their shelter-trench; both poured out death as fast as they could load and press trigger. Shrapnel whistled and Maxims growled savagely. From all the line came perpetual fire, fire, fire, and shrieked forth in great gusts of destruction.

And the enemy? No white troops would have faced that torrent of death for five minutes, but the Baggara and the blacks came on. The torrent swept into them and hurled them down in whole companies. You saw a rigid line gather itself up and rush on evenly; then before a shrapnel shell or a Maxim the line suddenly quivered and stopped. The line was yet unbroken, but it was quite still. But other lines gathered up again, again, and yet again; they went down, and yet others rushed on. Sometimes they came near enough to see single figures quite plainly. One old man with a white flag started with five comrades; all dropped, but he alone came bounding forward to within 200 yards of the 14th Sudanese. Then he folded his arms across his face, and his limbs loosened, and he dropped sprawling to earth beside his flag.

It was the last day of Mahdism, and the greatest. They could never get near, and they refused to hold back. By now the ground before us was all white with dead men's drapery. Rifles grew red-hot; the soldiers seized them by the slings and dragged them back to the reserve to change for cool ones. It was not a battle, but an execution. [. . .]

We waited half an hour or so, and then the sudden bugle called us to our feet. 'Advance,' it cried; 'to Omdurman!' added we. Slowly the force broke up, and expanded. [. . .] Movement was slow, since the leading brigades had to wait till the others had gone far enough inland to take their positions. We passed over a corner of the field of fire, and saw for certain what awful slaughter we had done. The bodies were not in heaps—bodies hardly ever are; but they spread evenly over acres and acres. And it was very remarkable, if you remembered the Atbara,[7] that you hardly saw a black; nearly all the dead had the high forehead and taper cheeks of the Arab. The Baggara had been met at last, and he was worth meeting. Some lay very composedly, with their slippers placed under their heads for a last pillow; some knelt, cut short in the middle of a last prayer. Others were torn to pieces, vermilion blood already drying on brown skin, killed instantly beyond doubt. Others, again, seemingly as dead as these, sprang up as we approached, and rushed savagely, hurling spears at the nearest enemy. They were bayoneted or shot. Once again the plain seemed empty, but for the advancing masses and the carpet of reddened white and broken bodies underfoot. [. . .]

Thus much for the right; on the left the British cavalry were in the stress of an engagement, less perfectly conducted, even more hardily fought out. [. . .] Four squadrons in line, the 21st Lancers swung into their first charge.

Knee to knee they swept on till they were but 200 yards from the enemy. Then suddenly—then in a flash—they saw the trap. Between them and the 300 there yawned suddenly a deep ravine; out of the ravine there sprang instantly a cloud of dark heads and a brandished lightning of swords, and a thunder of savage voices. Mahmud smiled when he heard the tale in prison at Halfa, and said it was their favourite stratagem. It had succeeded. Three thousand, if there was one, shot to a short four hundred; but it was too late to check now. Must go through with it now! The blunders of British cavalry are the fertile seed of British glory: knee to knee the Lancers whirled on. One hundred yards—fifty—knee to knee—

Slap! 'It was just like that,' said a captain, bringing his fist hard into his open palm. Through the swordsmen they shore without checking—and then came the khor. The colonel at their head, riding straight through everything without sword or revolver drawn, found his horse on its head, and the swords swooping about his own. He got the charger up again, and rode on straight, unarmed, through everything. The squadrons followed him down the fall. Horses plunged, blundered, recovered, fell; dervishes on the ground lay for the hamstringing cut; officers pistolled them in passing over, as one drops a stone into a bucket; troopers thrust till lances broke, then cut; everybody went on straight, through everything.

And through everything clean out the other side they came—those that kept up or got up in time. The others were on the ground—in pieces by now, for the cruel swords shore through soldier and thigh, and carved the dead into fillets. Twenty-four of these, and of those that came out over fifty had felt sword or bullet or spear. Few horses stayed behind among the swords, but nearly 130 were wounded. Lieutenant Robert Grenfell's troop came on a place with a jump out as well as a jump in; it lost officer, centre guide, and both flank guide, ten killed,

---

[7] Battle of Atbara, 8 Apr. 1898, when Kitchener's forces annihilated the majority of the Mahdi forces.

eleven wounded. Yet, when they burst straggling out, their only thought was to rally and go in again. 'Rally, No. 2!' yelled a sergeant, so mangled across the face that his body was a cascade of blood, and nose and cheeks flapped hideously as he yelled. 'Fall out, sergeant, you're wounded,' said the subaltern of his troop. 'No, no, sir; fall in!' came the hoarse answer; and the man reeled in his saddle. 'Fall in, No. 2; fall in. Where are the devils? Show me the devils!' And No. 2 fell in—four whole men out of twenty.

They chafed and stamped and blasphemed to go through them again, though the colonel wisely forbade them to face the pit anew. There were gnashings of teeth and howls of speechless rage—things half theatrical, half brutal to tell of when blood has cooled, yet things to rejoice over, in that they show the fighting devil has not, after all, been civilised out of Britons. Also there are many and many deeds of self-abandoning heroism; of which tale the half will never be told. Take only one. Lieutenant de Montmorency missed his troop-sergeant, and rode back among the slashes to look for him. There he found the hacked body of Lieutenant Grenfell. He dismounted, and put it up on his horse, not seeing, in his heat, that life had drained out long since by a dozen channels. The horse bolted under the slackened muscles, and De Montmorency was left alone with his revolver and 3,000 screaming fiends. Captain Kenna and Corporal Swarbrick rode out, caught his horse, and brought it back; the three answered the fire of the 3,000 at fifty yards, and got quietly back to their own line untouched.

---

7   'Relief of Mafeking' and 'London's Roar of Jubilation',
     Daily Mail (19 May 1900)

RELIEF OF MAFEKING

THE BESIEGERS' CORDON BROKEN BY THE FLYING COLUMN

HEAVY BOMBARDMENT AND FLIGHT OF THE BOERS

THE UNKNOWN BRITISH FORCE TRIUMPHANTLY ENTERS THE TOWN

UNPARALLELED SCENES OF REJOICING

Mafeking is relieved; after a seige lasting 216 days. The southern relief force has come up in time, and, after hard fighting, driven on the Boers.

Lord Roberts has kept his word. He requested the garrison to hold out until May 18. On May 18 it was announced from Pretoria that the relief had arrived.

The following telegrams give all the news that is known on the subject. They emanate from Pretoria, but the Boers have never acknowledged defeat without its being not only true, but very much worse than they have admitted.

PRETORIA, Friday, May 18 (11.35am.).
It is officially announced that when the laagers and forts around Mafeking had been severely bombarded the siege was abandoned by the Boers. A British force advancing from the south then took possession of the town.—Reuter.

To the above telegram Reuter's Agency adds the following note:—
'From the wording of the above telegram, and notably the use of the word "laagers," it may be inferred that the British relief force vigorously attacked the Boer laagers and forts around the town and compelled the Boers to raise the siege.'

PRETORIA, Wednesday, May 16.
There has been heavy fighting again along the Bechuanaland Railway.— Laffan.

MOLOPO, Thursday, May 17 (via Lorenco Marques, Friday, May 18)
Sharp fighting was resumed today around Mafeking, but it is still without decisive results.—Laffan.

These two brief telegrams show that the Boers round Mafeking did not raise the siege of their own free will, but were routed by the southern relief column.

PRIVATE CORROBORATION

The Press Association states the Colonel Baden-Powell's brother in London yesterday received a telegram from a Dutch friend in Pretoria announcing the relief of Mafeking.

THE HISTORY OF THE SIEGE

When the history of the siege comes to be written there will be no brighter episode for the pen of the recorder than the heroic defence by Colonel Baden-Powell and his tiny band of the little town of Mafeking, out on the lone veldt.

Cut off from all communication with the outside, save by the chance and dangerous trade of native siege runners, the little force through good and through all report hung on like grim death to the town which they had been told off to defend, and never for one solitary moment did it enter into the head of a single defender to suggest aught, but resistance to the last. As one of the garrison put it early in February, 'If the Boers do enter, they will enter a cemetery. We will never see Pretoria.'

The investment of Mafeking was the earliest move in the war; the Boers expected to take it with little resistance, though they sent a force for the work which outnumbered the garrison six times in strength and ten times in point of artillery. The siege practically began on October 15; it has ended, so far as is known, on Thursday last, May 17, or possibly yesterday only, May 18.

The siege was altogether unlike that of Ladysmith or of Kimberley. The firing was almost incessant, save on Sundays, from dawn to eve. It was one continual life in the trenches for the garrison, wet or fine, always during the day, and often at night. There was no relaxation, and for many weary months there was hardly food enough to support life.

The garrison attempted sorties during the earlier weeks of the investment for two reasons. First because they thought it might be possible to drive a wedge into the Boer defence and thereby render the general scheme of attack untenable, and secondly because they thought that severe 'hammerings' might render the attackers disinclined for further losses of the kind, with the result that they would raise the siege.

These anticipations were not fulfilled. The sorties were brilliantly carried out, and they caused the Boers much loss, but what was the loss, severe as it was, to so great a force as the Boers constantly kept round the town.

Consequently the garrison had nothing to do but to wait on in the hopes of being relieved some day.

It is an open secret that at one time—before Magersfontein[8]—it was trusted that Lord Methuen would be able to bring relief: this hope proved illusory; then the garrison saw Colonel Plumer advance and retire, his force being mighty of courage but too few in numbers; then came the rumours of relief from the south, which were mere rumours to the garrison for fully six weary weeks before they crystallised into the present advance.

From time to time the garrison received reassuring messages, words of hope from the Queen, from Lord Roberts, from friends. They husbanded their ammunition, they economised their food till they endured hardships which have fallen to the lot of few garrisons in the whole annals of warfare, and they steeled their hearts to hold out till help came.

The story of the last and desperate Boer failure to storm the town last Saturday will probably prove one of the most dramatic ever written. It failed, and the British flag now flies over Mafeking, where it has flown since that eventful day when London heard that the Boers had wrecked the armoured train south of Kraalpan, and that 'war had begun.'

Heroes all, women and children, the living and the dead, they have been, and the Empire will ever remember it.

---

[8] Battle of Magersfontein Hill, December 1900, in which 1,000 British troops were killed.

LONDON'S ROAR OF JUBILATION

WILD FRENZY THAT SURPASSES DESCRIPTION

LORD MAYOR SPEAKS TO A VAST MULTITUDE

THOUSANDS SERENADE MRS. BADEN-POWELL

Mafeking is free! No more doubt, no more anxiety, no more hours of weary waiting for the glad news. It has come.

At 9.30 last night the announcement came that the Boers had abandoned the siege. It is not possible to gauge the rapidity with which the news spread through the metropolis and throughout the country, for almost immediately, from all parts, came inquiries by telephone asking if it was true.

London simply went wild with delight.

Fleet-street, which, on ordinary nights, contains only its usual number of pedestrians was, as if by magic, transformed into a thoroughfare crowded and jammed with an excited throng of cheering, shouting, gesticulating, happy people. Whistles were blown, even the innocent shovel that is used to stoke the May-day fireplace was utilised for demonstrative purposes. Hawkers were on the scene with that rapidity which is only equalled by the vulture when it sees its prey. They were bereft of their 'B-P' buttons, their Union Jacks, and their paper hats, sometimes receiving pay for them and as often not. In front of the newspaper offices the crowd became thick and impassable. The police were there, but that is all, for they were as atoms in a mighty sea.

No pen can describe the wildness, the enthusiasm, the glee of that Fleet-street gathering. It was unparalleled in its mad, frenzied happiness over the relief of that heroic little band. And it was not a momentary enthusiasm, but late into the night the crowds became greater and greater, and the cheering wilder and wilder. Where these people all came from will ever be a mystery.

A great crowd came down from the West-end, where the news had also then been received, and added fresh fuel to the fire of enthusiasm. The 'Evening News' War Edition, with its tricolour poster, was bought up with marvellous avidity. Even the contents bills were appropriated by the gleeful celebrators. Men in silk hats took the posters from the boys and suspended them over their shoulders like sandwichmen. [. . .]

ROAR IN THE STRAND

It came like a hurricane in the Strand, with a whisper that grew in a moment into a roar that lasted far into the night. How it began no one can tell. One shrill cry from a newsboy, one flash of the red, white, and blue 'Evening News' bill, and the Strand burst into cheers.

A man with a cornet was atop of an omnibus as the first boy rushed by shouting 'Mafeking is relieved!' He never waited to consider, but clapped his instrument to his lips, and with all the wind in him blew out 'Rule Britannia' over the heads of the people.

The cheering thousands made their way to Trafalgar-square. Never was such a sight in London. The square was running over with people—men, women, young, old.

'Union Jacks' fetched 10s on the spot. By eleven o'clock traffic was all but suspended. Thousands of people—hundreds with guns on their shoulders—were marching round and round the square, singing, babbling with joy.

Hundreds of flags waved in the air, hundred of hats swung round men's heads, hundreds of women shook their handkerchiefs and cried 'Hurrah for Mafeking!' Round and round they marched, a dozen abreast arm in arm, gloriously happy, nearly drunk with the excitement of the hour—no one had time to imbibe anything but the news. [. . .]

THE WILD WEST

In the West-end the announcement was received with the same wild enthusiasm. At first no one would believe it. 'We have heard that story too often before,' they said to each other. But the rich men rushed to their clubs and the poor men to Fleet-street to see if it were true.

And then suddenly the scene in the streets changed. Every main roadway became packed with dense crowds of wild, cheering people. Men climbed on the tops of four-wheeled cabs, waved flags aloft and shouted themselves hoarse. A band of the Endell-Street Boys Brigade marching down Shaftesbury-avenue became the centre of a great demonstration. Girls of eight or nine from the slums of Soho and Drury-lane drew up in lines in front of it and danced along the streets, oblivious to all around them.

Red lights flashed from windows, tin horns tooted, guns were fired, and pandemonium was let loose. Everywhere was the sound of jubilation and steam whistles.

An American standing in the crush at Piccadilly-circus, calmly chewing half of a dry cigar, said: 'Well, this beats Manilla night in New York all hollow. I thought that these Britishers were a soulless people, but, bless me, if this ain't the worst I ever saw!'

AT THE WAR OFFICE

The war office was surrounded by a crowd which grew like a mountain torrent after a deluge of rain. The doors were closed and placarded 'No news!' And it is doubtful if the belated official announcement will be made until some time today.

Many important personages called and asked for information, but the clerk in charge had none to give. Soon the 'Evening News' bill came along in a cab, and the crowd relieved itself by cheering and shouting for 'B-P' and 'Bobs' who had kept his word in saying that Mafeking would be relieved by the 18th.

The great clubs in Pall Mall were filled to overflowing, and the 'Rag' opposite the War Office, with its great stone steps, looked as if there were an open-air meeting at its doors. The street was barely passable.

In front of Marlborough House there was such a cheering, howling crowd as there has never been before. St. James's-street was black, and far up Piccadilly London let itself loose as it did everywhere, in paeans of joy.

---

8   'Affairs on the Upper Congo', *The Times* (14 May 1897)

A representative of Reuter's Agency has had an interview with the Rev. K V Sjöblom, a Danish missionary on the staff of the American Baptist Mission, who has returned from Equatorville, 1800 miles up the river, after five years' residence on the Upper Congo.

After giving other instances of the reluctance of the highest Congo State officials to investigate charges of inhuman treatment of natives brought to their notice by himself and other missionaries, Mr. Sjöblom quoted the following case:—

'At the end of last year a force of State soldiers at the order of the commissaire of the district entered the village of Mandaka Vajigo, near my station, and, seeing the natives run away as usual at their approach, held out a quantity of brass rods with which they trade, indicating that they were not there to fight, but to buy food. Meanwhile a portion of the troops were sent down to the other end of the village, the natives were surrounded, the State soldiers opened fire upon them, and about 50 were killed. This being reported to us by the soldiers and the natives, Mr. Banks rode out to inquire into it. He himself counted 20 or 30 dead bodies, and the natives wanted him to go into the bush, where they said many more were lying. Mr. Banks, having seen the bodies in the village and a heap of hands that had been cut off, concluded that he had ample proof without going into the bush. He seemed surprised that the hands had not been sent to the State station to be counted, but was told that it was not necessary to show them to the State officer; they were counted by the native sergeant. A few days later Governor Wahis on his return down river called in at our station and asked Mr. Banks if any further atrocities had taken place since his last visit. Mr. Banks detailed what he had heard, and M. Wahis, answered that it was impossible. He told the Governor that he had seen it himself, whereupon M. Wahis summoned the commandant in charge—the officer who had ordered the raid had already gone elsewhere—and asked him in French if the story was true. The Belgian officer assured M. Wahis that it was, but the latter, thinking Mr. Banks did not understand French, said, "After all, you may have seen this, but you have no witnesses." "Oh," said Mr. Banks, "I can call the commandant, who has just told you it is true." M. Wahis then tried to minimize the matter, when to his great surprise Mr. Banks added, "In any case I have at his own request furnished to the British Consul who passed through here lately a signed statement concerning it."

'M. Wahis rose from his chair, saying, "Oh, then it is all over Europe." Then for the first time he said that the responsible commissaire must be punished. Some time after the Governor's departure we were surprised to hear that the guilty officer had been sentenced to five years' imprisonment. As the officer was all this time waging warfare in the interior we failed to understand what it meant. We afterwards learnt that he had been sentenced to remain for five years on the Congo without furlough.'

Mr. Sjöblom went on to show that 'the curse of the Congo is its forced labour,' especially in connexion with the collection of rubber. 'Native armed sentinels chosen from the wildest tribes are placed in the towns to force the people to bring in rubber.' In illustration of the horrors of this system, Mr. Sjöblom related the following incidents, of which he had been an eyewitness:—

'In February, 1895, while I was preaching to a number of natives at a place called Ebira, where a white man had never been seen before, some of these sentinels rushed forward and seized an old man because he had been away fishing instead of collecting rubber. The old man was thrown to the ground and dragged a few yards aside. The sentinel then pointed the gun at his head and shot him there before my eyes. Then, putting another cartridge into his gun, he pointed it at the crowd and they immediately fled. Next he told a little boy, eight or nine years old, to cut off the old man's right hand, which he did. The dying man, not yet quite insensible, attempted to withdraw his hand when he felt the knife, but in vain. The hand was then placed on a fallen tree, where already four others were displayed, so that all might see them and take warning. The others had previously been smoked, and shortly this, too, was laid on the fire and smoked, in order to preserve them for the commissaire—trophies of civilization. Besides what I have seen on my journeys, sentinels have often passed the mission station carrying smoked hands, which were being taken to the commissaire with the rubber.

The latest date on which this occurred in my sight was December 14, 1895, when I, together with two other missionaries, saw a sentinel pass carrying a basket containing 18 right hands. The hands were placed on the ground and counted. "There were 19 hands," exclaimed the sentinel, turning in anger to the woman who carried the basket, "how is it you have lost one?" The woman had been captured for the purpose of carrying the basket, which very likely contained the hands of her own relatives. We could not understand how it was that these murders were still going on when we had heard that no more people were to be killed on account of the rubber business. But on my last journey, December, 1895, I discovered the secret. One Monday night a sentinel, having just delivered his amount of rubber to the commissaire, came to me asking my advice. "What are we to do?" he said. "When all the people are gathered together the commissaire openly tells us sentinels not to kill any more people for the rubber. 'If you do I will kill you, or send you to Boma,' but afterwards he calls us aside and privately tells us 'If the people do not bring plenty of rubber kill some, but do not bring any more hands to me; never mind my command.'"

'Other sentinels came to me in the same perplexity. They were simply the commissaire's tools, and liable to be put to death for killing others, as a means of justifying himself; and in equal danger of losing their lives for not bringing in the full amount of rubber at the cost of bloodshed.'

III. CRITIQUES

9 from R. B. Cunninghame Graham, ' "Bloody Niggers" ' (1897)

That the all-wise and omnipresent God, to whom good people address their prayers, and for whose benefit, as set forth in the sustenation of his clergy, they hoard their threepenny bits all through the week, is really but a poor, anthropomorphous animal, is day by day becoming plainer and more manifest. He (Jahvé)[9] created all things, especially the world in which we live, and which is really the centre of the universe, in the same way as England is the centre of the planet, and as the Stock Exchange is the real centre of England, despite the dreams of the astronomers and the economists. He set the heavens in their place, bridled the sea, disposed the tides the phases of the moon, made summer, winter, and the seasons in their due rotation, showed us the constant resurrection of the

---

[9] Version of the Hebrew 'Jehovah'.

day after the death of night, sent showers, hail, frost, snow, thunder and lightning, and the other outward manifestations of his power to serve, to scourge, or to affright us, according to his will. [. . .]

Alps, Himalayas, Andes, La Plata, and Vistula, Amazon, with Mississippi, Yangtsekiang and Ganges, Volga, Rhine, Elbe and Don; Hecla and Stromboli, Pichincha, and Cotopaxi, with the Istachihuatl and Lantern of Maracaibo; seas, White and Yellow, with Oceans, Pacific and Atlantic; great inland lakes as Titicaca, Ladoga, all the creeks, inlets, gulfs and bays, the plains, the deserts, the geysers, hot springs on the Yellowstone, Pitch Lake of Trinidad, and, to be brief, the myriad wonders of the world were all awaiting newly created man, waiting his coming forth from out of the bridal chamber between the Tigris and Euphrates, like a mad bridegroom to run his frenzied course. Then came the (apparent) lapsus in the creator's scheme. That the first man in the fair garden by the Euphrates was white, I think, we take for granted. True that we have no information on the subject, but in this matter of creation we have entered, so to speak, into a tacit compact with the creator, and it behoves us to concur with him and help him when a difficulty looms.

Briefly I leave the time when man contended with the mastodon, hunted the mammoth, or was hunted in his turn by the plesiosaurus or by pterodactyl. Scanty indeed are the records which survive of the Stone Age, the Bronze, or of the dwellers in the wattled wigwams on the lakes. Suffice it, that the strong preyed on the weak as they still do today in Happy England, and that early dwellers upon earth seem to have thought as much as we do, how to invent appliances with which to kill their fellows.

The Hebrew Scriptures and the record of crimes, of violence, and bad faith committed by the Jews on other races, need not detain us, as they resemble so entirely our own exploits among the 'niggers' of today. I take it that Jahvé was little taken up with any of his creatures, except the people who inhabited the countries from which the Aryans came. Assyrians, Babylonians, Egyptians, Persians, and the rest were no doubt useful and built pyramids, invented hanging gardens, erected towers, observed the stars, spoke truth (if their historians lie not), drew a good bow, and rode like centaurs or like Gauchos. What did it matter when all is said and done? They were all 'niggers,' and whilst they fought and conquered, or were conquered, bit by bit the race which God had thought of from the first slowly developed. [. . .]

Thus, through the mist of time, the Celto-Saxon race emerged from heathendom and woad and, in the fulness of the creator's pleasure, became the tweed-clad Englishman. Much of the earth was his, and in the skies he had his mansion already, well aired, with every appliance known to modern sanitary science waiting for him with a large bible on the chest of drawers in every room. Australia, New Zealand, Canada, India, and countless islands, useful as coaling stations and depots where to stack his bibles for diffusion amongst the heathen, all owned his sway. Races, as different from his own as is a rabbit from an elephant, were ruled by tweed-clad satraps expedited from the public schools, the universities, or were administered by the dried fruits culled from the Imperial Bar. But whilst God's favoured nation thus had run its course, the French, the Germans, Austrians, Spaniards, Dutch, Greeks, Italians, and all the futile remnant of mankind outside 'our flag' had struggled to equal them. True that in most particulars they were inferior. Their beer was weak, their shoddy not so artfully diffused right through their cloth, their cottons less well 'sized,' the Constitution of their realm less nebulous, or the Orders of their Churches better authenticated, than were our own. No individual of their various nationalities, by a whole life of grace was ever half so moral, as the worst of us is born. And so I leave them, weltering in their attempts to copy us, and turn to those of whom I wished to write when I sat down, but the exordium, which of course I had to write, had stood so long between us that I fear my readers, if I happen to attain to such distinction, are wondering where the applicability of the title may be described.

I wished to show, as Moses told us, that God made the earth and made it round, planted his trees, his men and beasts upon it, and let it simmer slowly till his Englishmen stood forth. It seemed to me that his state was become almost anthropomorphous, and I doubted, if, after all, he was so wise as some folks say. In other portions of the earth as Africa, America, Australia, and in the myriad islands of the South Seas people called 'niggers' live.

What is a 'nigger'? Now this needs some words in order to explain his just position. Hindus, as Brahmins, Bengalis, dwellers in Bombay, the Cingalese, Sikhs and Pathans, Rajpoots, Parsis, Afghans, Kashmiris, Beluchis, Burmese, with all the dwellers from the Caspian Sea to Timur Laut, are thus described. Arabs are 'niggers.'

So are Malays, the Malagasy, Japanese, Chinese, Red Indians, as Sioux, Comanches, Nàvajos, Apaches with Zapatecas, Esquimaux, and in the south are 'niggers' though their hair is straight. Turks, Persians, Levantines, Egyptians, Moors, and generally all those of almost any race whose skins are darker than our own, and whose ideas of faith, of matrimony, banking, and therapeutics differ from those held by the dwellers of the meridian of Primrose Hill, cannot escape. Men of the Latin races, though not born free, can purchase freedom with a price, that is, if they conform to our ideas, are rich and wash, ride bicycles, and gamble on the Stock Exchange. If they are poor, then woe betide them, let them paint their faces white with all the ceruse which ever Venice furnished, to the black favour shall they come. A plague on pigments, blackness is in the heart, not in the face, and poverty, no matter how it washes, still is black.

In the consideration of the 'nigger' races which God sent into the world for whites (and chiefly Englishmen) to rule, 'niggers' of Africa occupy first place. I take it Africa was brought about in sheer ill-humour. No one can think it possible that an all-wise God (had he been in his sober senses) would create a land and fill it full of people destined to be replaced by other races from across the seas. Better, by far, to have made the 'niggers' white and let them by degrees all become Englishmen, than put us to the trouble of exterminating whole tribes of them, to carry out his plan. At times a thinking man knows scarcely what to think, and sometimes doubts whether he is the God we took him for and if he is a fitting Deity for us to worship, and if we had not better once for all, get us a God of our own race and fitted for our ways. 'Niggers' who have no cannons, and cannot construct a reasonable torpedo, have no rights. 'Niggers' whose lot is placed outside our flag, whose lives are given over to a band of money-grubbing miscreants (chartered or not) have neither rights nor wrongs. Their land is ours, their cattle, fields, their houses, their poor utensils, arms, all that they have; their women, too, are ours to use as concubines, to beat, exchange, to barter for gunpowder or gin, or any of the circulating media that we employ with 'niggers'; ours to infect with syphilis, leave with child, outrage, torment, and make consort with the vilest of our vile, more vile than beasts. Cretans, Armenians, Cubans, Macedonians, we commiserate, subscribe, feel for, our tender hearts are wrung when 'Outlanders' cannot get votes. Bishops and Cardinals and statesmen, with philanthropists and pious ladies, all go wild about the Turks. Meetings are held and resolutions passed, articles are written, lectures delivered, and the great heart of Britain stirred as if stocks were down. But 'niggers,' 'bloody niggers,' have no friends. Witness 'Fraudesia,' where Selous cants and Colenbrander hangs, whilst Rhodes plays 'bonnet,' and Lord Grey and Co. add empires to our sway, duly baptised in blood.

So many rapes and robberies, hangings and murders, blowings up in caves, pounding to jelly with our maxim guns, such sympathy for Crete, such coyness to express opinion on our doings in Matabeleland; our clergy all dumb dogs, our politicians dazed about Armenia; 'land better liked than niggers,' 'stern justice meted out'—can England be a vast and seething mushroom bed of base hypocrisy, and our own God, Jahvé Sabboath, an anthropomorpous fool?

---

10   from Olive Schreiner, *An English-South African's View of the Situation* (1899)

[. . .] South Africa is a young country, and taken as a whole it is an arid, barren country agriculturally. Our unrivalled climate, our sublime and rugged natural scenery,

The Joy and Pride

of the South African heart, is largely the result of this very aridity and rockiness. Parts are fruitful, but we have no vast corn-producing plains, which for generations may be cultivated almost without replenishing, as in Russia and America; we have few facilities for producing those vast supplies of flesh which are poured forth from Australia and New Zealand; already we import a large portion of the grain and flesh we consume. We may, with care, become a great fruit-producing country, and create some rich and heavy wines, but, on the whole, agriculturally, we are, and must remain, as compared with most other countries, a poor nation. Nor have we any great inland lakes, seas, and rivers, or great arms of the sea, to enable us to become a great maritime or carrying people. One thing only we have which saves us from being the poorest country on earth, and should make us the richest. We have our vast stores of mineral wealth, of gold and diamonds, and probably of other wealth yet unfound. This is all we have. Nature has given us nothing else; we are a poor people but for these. Out of the veins running through rocks and hills, and the mud-beds, heavy with jewels, that lie in our arid plains, must be reared and created our great national institutions, our colleges and museums, our art galleries and universities; by means of these our system of education must be extended; and on the national side, out of these must the great future of South Africa be built up—or not at all. The discovery of our mineral wealth came somewhat suddenly upon us. We were not prepared for its appearance by wise legislative enactments, as in New Zealand or some other countries. Before the people of South Africa as a whole had had time to wake up to the truth and to learn the first

Great and Terrible Lesson

our diamonds should have taught us, the gold mines of the Transvaal were discovered.

We South Africans, Dutch and English alike, are a curious folk, strong, brave, with a terrible intensity and perseverance, but we are not a sharp people well versed in the movements of the speculative world. In a few years the entire wealth of South Africa, its mines of gold and diamonds, its coalfields, and even its most intractable lands from the lovely Hex River Valley to Magaliesberg, had largely passed into the hands of a very small knot of speculators. In hardly any instances are they South Africans. That they were not South Africans born would in itself matter less than nothing, had they thrown in their lot with us, if in sympathies, hopes, and fears they were one with us. They are not. It is not merely that the wealth which should have made us one of the richest peoples in the world has left us one of the poorest, and is exported to other countries, that it builds palaces in Park Lane, buys yachts in the Mediterranean, fills the bags of the croupiers at Monte Carlo, decks foreign women with jewels, while our citizens toil in poverty;

this is a small matter. But those men are not of us! That South Africa we love whose great fortune is dearer to us than our own interests, in the thought of whose great and noble destiny lies the source of our patriotism and highest inspiration, for whose good in a far-distant future we, Dutch and English alike would sacrifice all in the present—this future is no more to them than the future of the Galapago Islands. We are a hunting ground to them, a field for extracting wealth, for

Building up Fame and Fortune;

nothing more. This matter does not touch the Transvaal alone; from the lovely Hex River Valley, east, west, north, and south, our lands are being taken from us, and passing into the hands of men who not only care nothing for South Africa, but apply the vast wealth they have drawn from South African soil in an attempt to corrupt our public life, and put their own nominees into our parliaments, to grasp the reins of power, that their wealth may yet more increase. Is it strange that from the hearts of South Africans, English and Dutch alike, there is arising an exceedingly great and bitter cry, 'We have sold our birthright for a mess of pottage!' [. . .]

Might generally conquers, and there is no doubt that England might send out sixty or a hundred thousand hired soldiers to South Africa, and they could bombard our towns and destroy our villages; they could shoot down men in the prime of life, and old men and boys, till there was hardly a kopje in the country without its stain of blood, and the Karoo bushes grew up greener on the spot where men from the midlands who had come to help their fellows fell, never to go home. I suppose it would be quite possible for the soldiers to shoot all male South Africans who appeared in arms against them. It might not be easy, a great many might fall, but a great Empire could always import more to take their places; *we* could not import more, because it would be our husbands and sons and fathers who were falling, and when they were done we could not produce more. Then the war would be over. There would not be a house in Africa—where African-born men and women lived—without its mourners, from Sea Point to the Limpopo; but South Africa would be pacified. [. . .]

Do not think that when imported soldiers walk across South African plains to take the lives of South African men and women that it is only African sand and African bushes that are cracking beneath their tread; at each step they are breaking the fibres, invisible as air but strong as steel, which bind the hearts of South Africans to England. Once broken they can never be made whole again; they are living things; broken they will be dead. Each bullet which a soldier sends to the heart of a South African to take his life wakes up another who did not know he was an African. You will not kill us with your Lee-Metfords; you will make us. There are men who do not know they love a Dutchman, but the first three hundred that fall, they will know it.

Do not say, 'But you are English, you have nothing to fear; we have no war with you.' There are hundreds of us, men and women who have loved England; we would have given our lives for her; but rather than strike down one South African man fighting for freedom, we would take this right hand and hold it in the fire, till nothing was left of it but a charred and blackened bone.

---

11   from J. A. Hobson, *Imperialism: A Study* (1902)

ECONOMIC PARASITES OF IMPERIALISM

I

[. . .] Although the new Imperialism has been bad business for the nation, it has been good business for certain classes and certain trades within the nation. The vast expenditure on armaments, the costly wars, the grave risks and embarrassments of foreign policy, the stoppage of political and social reforms within Great Britain, though fraught with great injury to the nation, have served well the present business interests of certain industries and professions.

It is idle to meddle with politics unless we clearly recognise this central fact and understand what these sectional interests are which are the enemies of national safety and the commonwealth. We must put aside the merely sentimental diagnosis which explains wars or other national blunders by outbursts of patriotic animosity or errors of statecraft. Doubtless at every outbreak of war not only the man in the street but the man at the helm is often duped by the cunning with which aggressive motives and greedy purposes dress themselves in defensive clothing. There is, it may be safely asserted, no war within memory, however nakedly aggressive it may seem to the dispassionate historian, which has not been presented to the people who were called upon to fight as a necessary defensive policy, in which the honour, perhaps the very existence, of the State was involved.

The disastrous folly of these wars, the material and moral damage inflicted even on the victor, appear so plain to the disinterested spectator that he is apt to despair of any State attaining years of discretion, and inclines to regard these natural cataclysms as implying some ultimate irrationalism in politics. But careful analysis of the existing relations between business and politics shows that the aggressive Imperialism which we seek to understand is not in the main the product of blind passions of races or of the mixed folly and ambition of politicians. It is far more rational than at first sight appears. Irrational from the standpoint of the whole nation, it is rational enough from the standpoint of certain classes in the nation. A completely socialist State which kept good books and presented regular balance-sheets of expenditure and assets would soon discard Imperialism; an intelligent *laissez-faire* democracy which gave duly proportionate weight in its policy to all economic interests alike would do the same. But a State in which certain well-organised business interests are able to outweigh the weak, diffused interest of the community is bound to pursue a policy which accords with the pressure of the former interests.

In order to explain Imperialism on this hypothesis we have to answer two questions. Do we find in Great Britain today any well-organised group of special commercial and social interests which stand to gain by aggressive Imperialism and the militarism it involves? If such a combination of interests exists, has it the power to work its will in the arena of politics?

What is the direct economic outcome of Imperialism? A great expenditure of public money upon ships, guns, military and naval equipment and stores, growing and productive of enormous profits when a war, or an alarm of war, occurs; new public loans and important fluctuations in the home and foreign Bourses; more posts for soldiers and sailors and in the diplomatic and consular services; improvement of foreign investments by the substitution of the British flag for a foreign flag; acquisition of markets for certain classes of exports, and some protection and assistance for trades representing British houses in these manufactures; employment for engineers, missionaries, speculative miners, ranchers and other emigrants.

Certain definite business and professional interests feeding upon imperialistic expenditure, or upon the results of that expenditure, are thus set up in opposition to the common good, and, instinctively feeling their way to one another, are found united in strong sympathy to support every new imperialist exploit.

If the £60,000,000 which may now be taken as a minimum expenditure on armaments in time of peace were subjected to a close analysis, most of it would be traced directly to the tills of certain big firms engaged in building warships and transports, equipping and coaling them, manufacturing guns and rifles, and ammunition, supplying horses, wagons, saddlery, food, clothing for the services, contracting for barracks, and for other large irregular needs. Through these main channels the millions flow to feed many subsidiary trades, most of which are quite aware that they are engaged in executing contracts for the services. Here we have an important nucleus of commercial Imperialism. Some of these trades, especially the shipbuilding, boiler-making, and gun and ammunition making trades, are conducted by large firms with immense capital, whose heads are well aware of the uses of political influence for trade purposes.

These men are Imperialists by conviction; a pushful policy is good for them.
[. . .]

II

By far the most important economic factor in Imperialism is the influence relating to investments. The growing cosmopolitanism of capital is the greatest economic change of this generation. Every advanced industrial nation is tending to place a larger share of its capital outside the limits of its own political area, in foreign countries, or in colonies, and to draw a growing income from this source. [. . .]

The statistics of foreign investments, however, shed clear light upon the economic forces which are dominating our policy. While the manufacturing and trading classes make little out of their new markets, paying, if they knew it, much more in taxation than they get out of them in trade, it is quite otherwise with the investor.

It is not too much to say that the modern foreign policy of Great Britain is primarily a struggle for profitable markets of investment. To a larger extent every year Great Britain is becoming a nation living upon tribute from abroad, and the classes who enjoy this tribute have an ever-increasing incentive to employ the public policy, the public purse, and the public force to extend the field of their private investments, and to safeguard and improve their existing investments. This is, perhaps, the most important fact in modern politics, and the obscurity in which it is wrapped constitutes the gravest danger to our State.

What is true of Great Britain is true likewise of France, Germany, the United States, and of all the countries in which modern capitalism has placed large surplus savings in the hands of a plutocracy or of a thrifty middle class. [. . .]

Aggressive Imperialism, which costs the tax-payer so dear, which is of so little value to the manufacturer and trader, which is fraught with such grave incalculable peril to the citizen, is a source of great gain to the investor who cannot find at home the profitable use he seeks for his capital, and insists that his Government should help him to profitable and secure investments abroad.

If, contemplating the enormous expenditure on armaments, the ruinous wars, the diplomatic audacity of knavery by which modern Governments seek to extend their territorial power, we put the plain, practical question, *Cui bono?*[10] the first and most obvious answer is, The investor. [. . .]

III

If the special interest of the investor is liable to clash with the public interest and to induce a wrecking policy, still more dangerous is the special interest of the financier, the general dealer in investments. In large measure the rank and file of the investors are, both for business and for politics, the cat's-paws of the great financial houses, who use stocks and shares not so much as investments to yield

---

[10] 'Who gains?'

them interest, but as material for speculation in the money market. In handling large masses of stocks and shares, in floating companies, in manipulating fluctuations of values, the magnates of the Bourse find their gain. These great businesses—banking, broking, bill discounting, loan floating, company promoting—form the central ganglion of international capitalism. United by the strongest bonds of organisation, always in closest and quickest touch with one another, situated in the very heart of the business capital of every State, controlled, so far as Europe is concerned, chiefly by men of a single and peculiar race, who have behind them many centuries of financial experience, they are in a unique position to control the policy of nations. No great quick direction of capital is possible save by their consent and through their agency. Does any one seriously suppose that a great war could be undertaken by any European State, or a great State loan subscribed, if the house of Rothschild and its connections set their forces against it? [. . .]

The wealth of these houses, the scale of their operations, and their cosmopolitan organisation make them the prime determinants of imperial policy. They have the largest definite stake in the business of Imperialism, and the amplest means of forcing their will upon the policy of nations.

In view of the part which the non-economic factors of patriotism, adventure, military enterprise, political ambition, and philanthropy play in imperial expansion, it may appear that to impute to financiers so much power is to take a too narrowly economic view of history. And it is true that the motor-power of Imperialism is not chiefly financial: finance is rather the governor of the imperial engine, directing the energy and determining its work: it does not constitute the fuel of the engine, nor does it directly generate the power. Finance manipulates the patriotic forces which politicians, soldiers, philanthropists, and traders generate; the enthusiasm for expansion which issues from these sources, though strong and genuine, is irregular and blind; the financial interest has those qualities of concentration and clear-sighted calculation which are needed to set Imperialism to work. An ambitious statesman, a frontier soldier, an over-zealous missionary, a pushing trader, may suggest or even initiate a step of imperial expansion, may assist in educating patriotic public opinion to the urgent need of some fresh advance, but the final determination rests with the financial power. The direct influence exercised by great financial houses in 'high politics' is supported by the control which they exercise over the body of public opinion through the Press, which, in every 'civilised' country, is becoming more and more their obedient instrument. [. . .]

Such is the array of distinctively economic forces making for Imperialism, a large loose group of trades and professions seeking profitable business and lucrative employment from the expansion of military and civil services, from the expenditure on military operations, the opening up of new tracts of territory and trade with the same, and the provision of new capital which these operations require, all these finding their central guiding and directing force in the power of the general financier.

The play of these forces does not openly appear. They are essentially parasites upon patriotism, and they adapt themselves to its protecting colours. In the mouths of their representatives are noble phrases, expressive of their desire to extend the area of civilisation, to establish good government, promote Christianity, extirpate slavery, and elevate the lower races. Some of the business men who hold such language may entertain a genuine, though usually a vague, desire to accomplish these ends, but they are primarily engaged in business, and they are not unaware of the utility of the more unselfish forces in furthering their ends. Their true attitude of mind is expressed by Mr. Rhodes in his famous description of 'Her Majesty's Flag' as 'the greatest commercial asset in the world.'

---

12   from E. D. Morel, 'The Story of the
            Congo Free State' (1920)

From 1891 until 1912, the paramount object of European rule in the Congo was the pillaging of its natural wealth to enrich private interests in Belgium. To achieve this end, a specific, well-defined System was thought out in Brussels and applied on the Congo. Its essential features were known to the Belgian Government from 1898 onwards. They were defended in principle, and their effects denied, by successive Belgian Ministries, some of whose members were actively concerned in the working of the System, and even personal beneficiaries from it, for twelve years; although the Belgian Government did not govern the Congo, and, while apologising for and acclaiming the methods of the administration there pursued, washed its hands of responsibility for the actions of what it termed 'a foreign State.' The System had its European side and its African side. In Europe—the formulation of a Policy which should base itself upon the claim of sovereign right and be expounded in decrees, promulgations and *pièces justificatives*; in whose support should be enlisted the constitutional machinery of Belgium, including the diplomatic and consular representatives of Belgium in foreign countries, buttressed by a body of international legal authorities well remunerated for the purpose. In Africa—the execution of that Policy.

The Policy was quite simple. Native rights in land were deemed to be confined to the actual sites of the town or village, and the areas under food cultivation around them. Beyond those areas no such rights would be admitted. The land was 'vacant,' i.e. without owners. Consequently the 'State' was the owner. The

'State' was Leopold II, not in his capacity of constitutional Monarch of Belgium, but as Sovereign of the 'Congo Free State.' Native rights in nine-tenths of the Congo territory being thus declared non-existent, it followed that the native population had no proprietary right in the plants and trees growing on that territory, and which yielded rubber, resins, oils, dyes, etc.: no right, in short, to anything animal, vegetable, or mineral which the land contained. [. . .] A 'State' required revenue. Revenue implied taxation. The only articles in the Congo territory capable of producing revenue were the ivory, the rubber, the resinous gums and oils; which had become the property of the 'State.' The only medium through which these articles could be gathered, prepared and exported to Europe—where they would be sold and converted into revenue—was native labour. Native labour would be called upon to furnish those articles in the name of 'taxation.' [. . .]

[E]very official in the country had to be made a partner in the business of getting rubber and ivory out of the natives in the guise of 'taxation.' Circulars, which remained secret for many years, were sent out, to the effect that the paramount duty of Officials was to make their districts yield the greatest possible quantity of these articles; promotion would be reckoned on that basis. [. . .] 'Concessionaire' Companies were created to which the King farmed out a large proportion of the total territory, retaining half the shares in each venture. These privileges were granted to business men, bankers, and others with whom the King thought it necessary to compound. They floated their companies on the stock market. The shares rose rapidly. [. . .]

These various measures at the European end were comparatively easy. The problem of dealing with the natives themselves was more complex. A native army was the pre-requisite. The years which preceded the Edicts of 1891–2 were employed in raising the nucleus of a force of 5,000. It was successively increased to nearly 20,000 apart from the many thousands of 'irregulars' employed by the Concessionaire Companies. This force was amply sufficient for the purpose, for a single native soldier armed with a rifle and with a plentiful supply of ball cartridge can terrorise a whole village. The same system of promotion and reward would apply to the native soldier as to the Official—the more rubber from the village, the greater the prospect of having a completely free hand to loot and rape. A systematic warfare upon the women and children would prove an excellent means of pressure. They would be converted into 'hostages' for the good behaviour, in rubber collecting, of the men. [. . .] The whole territory would thus become a busy hive of human activities, continuously and usefully engaged for the benefit of the 'owners' of the soil thousands of miles away, and their crowned Head, whose intention, proclaimed on repeated occasions to an admiring world, was the 'moral and material regeneration' of the natives of the Congo.

Such was the Leopoldian 'System,' briefly epitomised. It was conceived by a master brain.

EDITORS' NOTES

1. Sir John Robert Seeley (1834–95). Religious thinker, historian, and classicist, famed for *Ecce Homo* (1865), his controversial life of a very human Christ. He succeeded Charles Kingsley as Professor of Modern History at Cambridge, 1869. The *Dictionary of National Biography* suggests his lectures, published as *The Expansion of England* in 1883, 'contributed perhaps more than any other single utterance to the change of feeling respecting the relations between Great Britain and her colonies'. He was knighted in 1894 on the recommendation of Lord Rosebery. He opposed Irish Home Rule, and was an important figure in the Imperial Federation League, a society which dissolved in 1894 but was reformed by Joseph Chamberlain and others as the British Empire League in 1895.

2. Joseph Chamberlain (1836–1914) was a successful Birmingham businessman, who retired a wealthy man in order to pursue a political career. He led Birmingham City Council, and introduced radical reformist policies, leading, for instance, the National Education League, which achieved the introduction of compulsory state education from 1870. MP for Birmingham from 1876, he rapidly rose through Liberal ranks to become President of the Board of Trade. His radical reformist policies at home were matched by an aggressive imperialism on foreign issues, as he was an active member of the Imperial Federation League. Chamberlain was at the centre of the split in the Liberal Party over the issue of Home Rule for Ireland. As a Liberal Unionist, he served as Colonial Secretary in alliance with the Conservative administration under Lord Salisbury from 1895. He was mainly responsible for the extension of empire in West Africa, the Royal Niger Company becoming a Crown Colony under his direction. The policy of 'pacification' of recalcitrant tribes led to a public conflict with the traveller and anthropologist Mary Kingsley (see Chapter 13).

3. Cecil Rhodes (1853–1902). An arch-imperialist, he dreamed of the Cape Town to Cairo railway that would symbolize British rule over the whole of Africa; he also famously dreamed of returning America to the British empire, and even of colonizing the stars. Sent out to Natal in 1870 due to ill health, in ten years he was the majority owner of De Beers diamond mine. From 1880 his wealth made him a central political figure both in the Cape Colony and in the formation of British imperial policy, although his transparent rapaciousness always embarrassed the rhetoric of the 'civilizing mission'. Reliance on private capital, rather than on the public purse, to fuel territorial advances, was a typical nineteenth-century strategy. Rhodes annexed Bechuanaland in 1884 and pushed north; he negotiated a Royal Charter from British government to form what became Rhodesia in 1889. Prime Minister of the Cape Colony from 1890, his policy aim was to unite the different South African republics,

both English and Dutch. In 1895 his desire to control the Kimberley diamond mines, situated in the Boer Transvaal, led to the disastrous 'Jameson Raid', in which Rhodes's ally Jameson failed to foment a rebellion in Kimberley. Rhodes resigned, but his actions prompted more moves towards the Anglo-Boer War (1899–1902). The speech reprinted here was made on his return to the Cape after a visit to London and Oxford (in order to be given a controversial honorary doctorate), and to Germany, to negotiate money and passages through European 'spheres of influence' for his beloved railway project.

4. General Charles 'Chinese' Gordon (1833–85) was constructed as *the* iconic servant of the British empire. His death at the hands of Muslim nationalists, the last Englishman left in Khartoum after a siege of 317 days, was a key event in turning public attitudes towards a more aggressive imperialist stance. Gladstone had refused to fund a relief army to 'rescue' Gordon, considering Gordon's actions a deliberate attempt to force the occupation of Sudan. Public campaigns to demand his rescue (led by W. T. Stead in the *Pall Mall Gazette*, who had been instrumental in sending Gordon to the Sudan) forced Gladstone's hand, and the relief party left in November 1884. It arrived two days too late. Gordon was immediately mythologized as a sacrificial hero. In life, he had been an eccentric and volatile figure—Lytton Strachey's portrait of him in *Eminent Victorians* is a vicious demolition of the imperial class. He made his career first in the Crimean War, and then, between 1860 and 1865, as leader of the Chinese 'Ever Victorious Army'. He led them from the front, unarmed but for a baton with which to 'conduct' the offensive, in thirty-three engagements, putting down rebel armies for the emperor, and thus securing British influence in China until the 1890s. From 1874 to 1877, he served as governor of equatorial Central Africa, and from 1877 to 1880 as governor of the Sudan—driven by a Christian faith that supported the suppression of Muslim slave-traders, fully in accord with missionary and humanitarian programmes of 'civilizing' Africa. During a year in Jerusalem in 1883–4, he sought out holy sites, developing his theory that if God spoke in Jerusalem, hell was likely to be located somewhere in the South Pacific. This trip was curtailed by his fateful appointment to oversee the withdrawal of British troops from Sudan—a policy which, by remaining in Khartoum, Gordon rejected.

5. *Ten Years' Captivity* went through ten editions in the year it was published—it represents the first details from a Western source from the Sudan after Gordon's death and the British retreat. It was translated by Sir Francis Reginald Wingate (1861–1953), who had been a soldier in the relief party, before becoming director of Military Intelligence in Egypt in 1889, and, once Sudan had been reoccupied, governor of Sudan from 1899.

6. The Battle of Omdurman was understood by the British public as the final revenge against the Mahdist movement that had slaughtered Gordon. Kitchener (1850–1916) led a modern, technological army force, laying down the Sudan military railway as it went, annihilating Mahdist forces over three years. On completion of his mission he became Lord Kitchener of Khartoum—George Steevens's book ends with a description of a belated Christian service for the heroic Gordon in the grounds of the palace where he had been killed. Steevens (1869–1900) enjoyed amazing fame in his brief

career as a journalist for the *Daily Mail*. *With Kitchener to Khartoum* went through thirteen editions in a matter of weeks. His death from enteric fever during the siege of Ladysmith in the Boer War led to outpourings of grief.

7. Mafeking represented, like Gordon, the pluck and courage of the British at the colonial frontier. A small garrison army was bombarded and besieged for 216 days before the relief army, led by Buller's replacement, Lord Roberts, arrived on 18 May. The last siege to be broken, this restored British faith in their military superiority—hence the extraordinary London scenes described by the *Daily Mail*. By 6 June, Pretoria, the Boer capital of the Transvaal, had been gained by Roberts's forces, marking an end to the first phase of the war. Mafeking is inscribed in British culture via its commanding officer—Robert Baden-Powell (1857–1941)—whose ingenuity in survival modulated into the Boy Scout movement. *Scouting for Boys* (1908) provided various means to 'Be Prepared', and contained chapters such as 'Our Empire: How it Grew—How it Must be Held'. Survival in Mafeking depended on black messengers and scouts as well as the starvation of the black population; this did do something to undermine his reputation.

9. Robert Bontine Cunninghame Graham (1852–1936) was a traveller and scholar of Spanish South America, a poet, and a politician. His political trajectory shifted from being a Liberal MP (1886–92), passionately supportive of Irish Home Rule and anti-imperialist, to the socialism of his friend William Morris. He was arrested during the Trafalgar Square socialist riots of 1887, and imprisoned briefly, his case taken up by fellow radical W. T. Stead in the *Pall Mall Gazette*. Later in life he became a Labour MP in 1922 before becoming the first president of the National Party of Scotland (the 'Cunninghame' and the 'Graham' marked a distinguished lineage, and he could reasonably claim to be the rightful king of Scotland).

10. Olive Schreiner (1855–1920). Born in South Africa, to a missionary, but a convert to scientific naturalism on reading Herbert Spencer. She arrived in England in 1881, complete with a novel in manuscript. *The Story of an African Farm* was published pseudonymously in 1883, and is regarded as an important precursor text for the New Woman of the 1890s. She moved in bohemian and radical circles in the 1880s, having abortive relationships with Karl Pearson (see Chapters 9 and 13) and Havelock Ellis (see Chapter 12). She returned to South Africa in 1889, writing short fiction and political and feminist works, particularly *Woman and Labour* (1911). Her attack on the economics driving the English and Boers to war was particularly close to home: her brother was president of the Cape Colony from 1898, arguing for peace and resigning when the war began.

11. John Atkinson Hobson (1858–1940) lecturer and journalist, who worked for liberal papers like the *Nation* and the *Manchester Guardian*. His analysis of the forces of capital in the prosecution of imperialism is a classic left-wing document, influencing Lenin's argument in *Imperialism: The Highest Stage of Capitalism* (1917). It is also of its time, regarding the evils of capitalism and Jewish bankers as synonymous. Internationalist in perspective, however, he was involved in early attempts to found the League of Nations.

12. Edmund Morel (1873–1924) began his career as a shipping clerk in Liverpool. He

became increasingly interested in the shipments arriving from the Congo, and suspected that the figures could only conceal a system of major exploitation. The Congo
Free State had been the product of the need of the European powers for a buffer zone
to avoid conflict during the 'scramble for Africa'. The Berlin Conference of 1885
assigned the area of the Congo Basin to the 'International Association of the Congo',
ostensibly a humanitarian organization dedicated to eradicating slavery. It was, in
fact, a cover for the Belgian king, Leopold II (Queen Victoria's uncle), who set about
amassing a personal fortune by the most brutal means necessary. Little information
emerged from the Congo until the end of the century; most of it was from Christian
missionaries. Morel, active in the Anti-Slavery Society (which published details of
alleged atrocities in its journal), formed the Congo Reform Association in 1903, and
began to pour out a sequence of documents detailing the vicious system. It was only
retrospectively that the nature of the system could be understood—Morel's best
summary comes from his last book, *The Black Man's Burden* (1920). This was a
successful campaign, in part because the 'humanitarian' and 'civilizing' appeals
associated with the British empire could be contrasted favourably with the evils of
the Congo. The Congo was eventually 'nationalized' by Belgium in 1908, Leopold
dying in 1909.

7

SOCIALISM

Socialism was one of the new, regenerative cultural and political forces of the British fin de siécle. Since the official death of Chartism in 1858 it had been the trade union movement which had represented the interests of working men; it was not until the 1880s that specifically socialist political parties began to emerge. Socialism hardly took Britain by storm in the 1880s: the total combined membership of the Social Democratic Federation (SDF), the Socialist League, the Hammersmith Socialist Society, and the Fabian Society was something in the order of 2,000 people. It was the 1890s which witnessed the most remarkable growth of socialism in Britain, with the establishment of the Independent Labour Party (ILP) in 1893 and of the Labour Representation Committee (later the Labour Party) in 1900. The gradual formation of socialism in the last two decades of the nineteenth century was not a smooth process: a multitude of competing political and economic discourses was circulated and hotly debated, and in the 1880s ideological disagreements within the SDF led to the formation of various splinter groups. Anarchists crossed swords with parliamentarians, and individualists balked at the full-blooded statism of some sectors of the emergent socialist movement in Britain.

The Social Democratic Federation, formed in 1881, was the largest of the new socialist societies of the 1880s and was Marxist in orientation. At its second annual conference in 1883 it adopted nationalization of the means of production as its central aim. The SDF was officially antipathetic to the trade union movement, which it deemed to be too reformist and insufficiently socialist; under the leadership of the anti-Semitic Henry Hyndman it was also intensely nationalistic and imperialist (although this was by no means always the case at grass-roots level). Crucially, the SDF espoused the seeking of state socialism through political action. It failed to become the major political force it could have been because of its failure to recognize the significance of the trade unions in Britain, whose support it failed to court.

The Socialist League, objecting to Hyndman's nationalism and xenophobia, seceded from the SDF in December 1884 and included members such as William Morris, Eleanor Marx, Edward Aveling, E. Belfort Bax, and Andrea Scheu. The League was more internationalist in outlook than the SDF, but it hardly represented a uniform view. Not all of its members agreed with the likes of William Morris (the League's leader), who wanted to abolish parliament altogether, as outlined in his utopian fiction *News from Nowhere* (1890). In his anti-parliamentary stance Morris had certain affinities with the anarchists who also comprised a section of the Socialist League; but he differed from them in his emphasis on co-operation and communitarianism as opposed to individual anarchism. The Socialist League was unified in its desire that the existing political and economic system in Britain should be overthrown by force: Morris was scornful of the SDF's putting up of socialist candidates in the 1885 general election.

The Fabian Society was formed in January 1884 and, middle-class in orientation, it generally favoured a gradualist parliamentary approach to socialism. The *Fabian Essays in Socialism* (1889), of which Shaw's 'Economic Basis' is one, catapulted the Fabians into the public limelight, selling 25,500 copies between the end of 1889 and the spring of 1893.

Into the 1890s the newly formed Independent Labour Party took upon itself the difficult task of marrying an individualist brand of socialism, with its emphasis on the ways in which individual lives could be culturally transformed by socialism, to the collectivism of the trade union movement, which it wisely perceived to be central to the labour movement in Britain at the end of the century. Oscar Wilde's highly individualistic 'Soul of Man Under Socialism' may at first sight seem characteristically maverick, but it does coincide with certain aspects of ILP thought in its emphasis on socialism as a means of promoting a richer cultural life for individuals. Philip Snowden, in his lecture and pamphlet, *The Individual Under Socialism* (1905), almost seems to be rehearsing the core of Wilde's essay in an argument which denies the view that socialism would sacrifice individual liberty, maintaining instead that by releasing the individual from capitalist exploitation socialism would establish the moral conditions necessary for the development of a true individuality and the exercise of true liberty. Written in response to hearing Shaw's lecture 'The Economic Basis of Socialism', Wilde's 'Soul of Man' accepts the desirability of a redistribution of wealth whilst utterly rejecting the incipient statism of Shaw's stance (Shaw's analysis implies an extension of state control). Wilde and Morris can also be distinguished one from the other in that whilst Wilde anarchistically insists 'Every man must be left quite free to choose his own work. No form of compulsion must be exercised over him', Morris acknowledges the need for co-operation between men, and that 'if I am a member of a Socialist community I must do my due share of rougher work'.

All of the new socialist societies and parties of the fin de siècle included women members, many at grass-roots level as well as more notable cultural luminaries such as Olive Schreiner (see Chapter 6) in the SDF and Eleanor Marx in the Socialist League. Relations between socialists and feminists at the fin de siècle were by no means always smooth, but feminists such as Isabella Ford, who had made a name for herself with her New Woman novel from 1895, *On the Threshold*, carried out important work in their insistence on the significant correlations between feminism and socialism in Britain. Ford was a high-profile member of the ILP, a party which, unlike the Tory and Liberal parties, allowed women to be full branch members.

Secondary reading: Alexander; Crick; Laybourn; Mackenzie and Mackenzie; Saville; Thompson.

---

1   from William Morris, 'How We Live and How We Might Live' (1887)

The word Revolution, which we Socialists are so often forced to use, has a terrible sound in most people's ears, even when we have explained to them that it does not necessarily mean a change accompanied by riot and all kinds of violence, and cannot mean a change made mechanically and in the teeth of opinion by a group of men who have somehow managed to seize on the executive power for the moment. Even when we explain that we use the word revolution in its etymological sense, and mean by it a change in the basis of society, people are scared at the idea of such a vast change, and beg that you will speak of reform and not revolution. As, however, we Socialists do not at all mean by our word revolution what these worthy people mean by their word reform, I can't help thinking that it would be a mistake to use it, whatever projects we might conceal beneath its harmless envelope. So we will stick to our word which means a change of the basis of society. [. . .]

How do we live, then, under our present system? Let us look at it a little.

And first, please to understand that our present system of Society is based on a state of perpetual war. Do any of you think that this is as it should be? I know that

you have often been told that competition, which is at present the rule of all production, is a good thing, and stimulates the progress of the race; but the people
who tell you this should call competition by its shorter name of *war* if they wish
to be honest, and you would then be free to consider whether or no war stimulates
progress, otherwise than as a mad bull chasing you over your own garden may do.
War, or competition, whichever you please to call it, means at the best pursuing
your own advantage at the cost of some one else's loss. [. . .]

Now let us look at this kind of war a little closer, run through some of the forms
of it, that we may see how the 'burn, sink, and destroy' is carried on in it. First,
you have that form of it called national rivalry, which in good truth is nowadays
the cause of all gunpowder and bayonet wars which civilised nations wage. For
years past we English have been rather shy of them, except on those happy occasions when we could carry them on at no sort of risk to ourselves, when the killing
was all on one side, or at all events when we hoped it would be. We have been shy
of gunpowder war with a respectable enemy for a long while, and I will tell you
why: it is because we have had the lion's share of the world-market; we didn't
want to fight for it as a nation, for we had got it; but now this is changing in a most
significant, and, to a Socialist, a most cheering way; we are losing or have lost
that lion's share; it is now a desperate 'competition' between the great nations of
civilisation for the world-market, and to-morrow it may be a desperate war for
that end. [. . .]

[. . .] That is how we live now with foreign nations, prepared to ruin them
without war if possible, with it if necessary, let alone meantime the disgraceful
exploiting of savage tribes and barbarous peoples on whom we force at once our
shoddy wares and our hypocrisy at the cannon's mouth.

Well, surely Socialism can offer you something in the place of all that. It can; it
can offer you peace and friendship instead of war [. . .] so that any citizen of one
community could fall to work and live without disturbance of his life when he was
in a foreign country, and would fit into his place quite naturally; so that all
civilised nations would form one great community, agreeing together as to the
kind and amount of production and distribution needed; working at such and
such production where it could be best produced; avoiding waste by all means.
Please to think of the amount of waste which they would avoid, how much such a
revolution would add to the wealth of the world! [. . .]

Meantime let us pass from this 'competition' between nations to that between
'the organisers of labour,' great firms, joint-stock companies; capitalists in short,
and see how competition 'stimulates production' among them: indeed it does do
all that; but what kind of production? Well, production of something to sell at a
profit, or say production of profits: and note how war commercial stimulates that:
a certain market is demanding goods; there are, say, a hundred manufacturers
who make that kind of goods, and every one of them would if he could keep that

market to himself, and struggles desperately to get as much of it as he can, with the obvious result that presently the thing is overdone, and the market is glutted, and all that fury of manufacture has to sink into cold ashes.

Doesn't that seem something like war to you? Can't you see the waste of it—waste of labour, skill, cunning, waste of life in short? Well you may say, but it cheapens the goods. In a sense it does; and yet only apparently, as wages have a tendency to sink for the ordinary worker in proportion as prices sink; and at what a cost do we gain this appearance of cheapness! [. . .]

The manufacturer, in the eagerness of his war, has had to collect into one neighbourhood a vast army of workers, he has drilled them till they are as fit as may be for his special branch of production, that is, for making a profit out of it, and with the result of their being fit for nothing else: well, when the glut comes in that market he is supplying, what happens to this army, every private in which has been depending on the steady demand in that market, and acting, as he could not choose but act, as if it were to go on for ever? You know well what happens to these men: the factory door is shut on them; on a very large part of them often, and at the best on the reserve army of labour, so busily employed in the time of infla-tion. What becomes of them? Nay, we know that well enough just now. But what we don't know, or don't choose to know, is that this reserve army of labour is an absolute necessity for commercial war; if *our* manufacturers had not got these poor devils whom they could draft on to their machines when the demand swelled, other manufacturers in France, or Germany, or America, would step in and take the market from them.

So you see, as we live now, it is necessary that a vast part of the industrial population should be exposed to the danger of periodical semi-starvation, and that, not for the advantage of the people in another part of the world, but for their degradation and enslavement. [. . .] Why have the profit makers got all this power, or at least why are they able to keep it?

That takes us to the third form of war commercial: the last, and the one which all the rest is founded on. We have spoken first of the war of rival nations; next of that of rival firms: we have now to speak of rival men. As nations under the present system are driven to compete with one another for the markets of the world, and as firms or the captains of industry have to scramble for their share of the profits of the markets, so also have the workers to compete with each other—for liveli-hood; and it is this constant competition or war amongst them which enables the profit-grinders to make their profits, and by means of the wealth so acquired to take all the executive power of the country into their hands. But here is the differ-ence between the position of the workers and the profit-makers: to the latter, the profit-grinders, war is necessary; you cannot have profit-making without compe-tition, individual, corporate, and national; but you may work for a livelihood without competing; you may combine instead of competing.

I have said war was the life-breath of the profit-makers; in like manner, combination is the life of the workers.

Now observe, I said that to the existence of the workers it was combination, not competition, that was necessary, while to that of the profit-makers combination was impossible, and war necessary. The present position of the workers is that of the machinery of commerce, or in plainer words its slaves; when they change that position and become free, the class of profit-makers must cease to exist; and what will then be the position of the workforce? Even as it is they are the one necessary part of society, the life-giving part; the other classes are but hangers-on who live on them. But what should they be, what will they be, when they, once for all, come to know their real power, and cease competing with one another for livelihood? I will tell you: they will be society, they will be the community. And being society—that is, there being no class outside them to contend with—they can then regulate their labour in accordance with their own real needs. [. . .]

Now, to get closer to details: [. . .]

What is it that I need, therefore, which my surrounding circumstances can give me—my dealings with my fellow-men—setting aside inevitable accidents which co-operation and forethought cannot control, if there be such?

Well, first of all I claim good health; and I say that a vast proportion of people in civilisation scarcely even know what that means. To feel mere life a pleasure; to enjoy the moving one's limbs and exercising one's bodily powers; to play, as it were, with sun and wind and rain; to rejoice in satisfying the due bodily appetites of a human animal without fear of degradation or sense of wrong-doing: yes, and therewithal to be well-formed, straight-limbed, strongly knit, expressive of countenance—to be, in a word, beautiful—that also I claim. If we cannot have this claim satisfied, we are but poor creatures after all; and I claim it in the teeth of those terrible doctrines of asceticism, which, born of the despair of the oppressed and degraded, have been for so many ages used as instruments for the continuance of that oppression and degradation. [. . .]

Now the next thing I claim is education. And you must not say that every English child is educated now; that sort of education will not answer my claim, though I cheerfully admit it is something: something, and yet after all only class education. What I claim is liberal education; opportunity, that is, to have my share of whatever knowledge there is in the world according to my capacity or bent of mind, historical or scientific; and also to have my share of skill of hand which is about in the world, either in the industrial handicrafts or in the fine arts; picture-painting, sculpture, music, acting, or the like: I claim to be taught, if I can be taught, more than one craft to exercise for the benefit of the community. [. . .]

But I also know that this claim for education involves one for public advantages in the shape of public libraries, schools, and the like, such as no private person, not even the richest, could command: but these I claim very confidently, being sure that no reasonable community could bear to be without such helps to a decent life.

Again, the claim for education involves a claim for abundant leisure, which once more I make with confidence; because when once we have shaken off the slavery of profit, labour would be organized so unwastefully that no heavy burden would be laid on the individual citizens; every one of whom as a matter of course would have to pay his toll of some obviously useful work. [. . .]

But now, in order that my leisure might not degenerate into idleness and aimlessness, I must set up a claim for due work to do. Nothing to my mind is more important than this demand, and I must ask your leave to say something about it. I have mentioned that I should probably use my leisure for doing a good deal of what is now called work; but it is clear that if I am a member of a Socialist Community I must do my due share of rougher work than this—my due share of what my capacity enables me to do, that is; no fitting of me to a Procrustean bed; but even that share of work necessary to the existence of the simplest social life must, in the first place, whatever else it is, be reasonable work; that is, it must be such work as a good citizen can see the necessity for; as a member of the community, I must have agreed to do it.

To take two strong instances of the contrary, I won't submit to be dressed up in red and marched off to shoot at my French or German or Arab friend in a quarrel that I don't understand; I will rebel sooner than do that.

Nor will I submit to waste my time and energies in making some trifling toy which I know only a fool can desire; I will rebel sooner than do that.

However, you may be sure that in a state of social order I shall have no need to rebel against any such pieces of unreason; only I am forced to speak from the way we live to the way we might live.

Again, if the necessary reasonable work be of a mechanical kind, I must be helped to do it by a machine, not to cheapen my labour, but so that as little time as possible may be spent upon it, and that I may be able to think of other things while I am tending the machine. And if the work be specially rough or exhausting, you will, I am sure, agree with me in saying that I must take turns in doing it with other people; I mean I mustn't, for instance, be expected to spend my working hours always at the bottom of a coal-pit. [. . .]

The last claim I make for my work is that the places I worked in, factories or workshops, should be pleasant, just as the fields where our most necessary work is done are pleasant. [. . .]

Well. So much for my claims as to my *necessary* work, my tribute to the community. [. . .] Then would come the time for the new birth of art, so much talked of, so long deferred. [. . .]

And, again, that word art leads me to my last claim, which is that the material surroundings of my life should be pleasant, generous, and beautiful; that I know is a large claim, but this I will say about it, that if it cannot be satisfied, if every civilized community cannot provide such surroundings for all its members, I do not want the world to go on; it is a mere misery that man has ever existed. [. . .]

As to what extent it may be necessary or desirable for people under social order to live in common, we may differ pretty much according to our tendencies towards social life. For my part I can't see why we should think it a hardship to eat with the people we work with; I am sure that as to many things, such as valuable books, pictures, and splendour of surroundings, we shall find it better to club our means together; and I must say that often when I have been sickened by the stupidity of the mean idiotic rabbit warrens that rich men build for themselves in Bayswater and elsewhere, I console myself with visions of the noble communal hall of the future, unsparing of materials, generous in worthy ornament, alive with the noblest thoughts of our time, and the past, embodied in the best art which a free and manly people could produce; such an abode of man as no private enterprise could come anywhere near for beauty and fitness, because only collective thought and collective life could cherish the aspirations which would give birth to its beauty, or have the skill and leisure to carry them out. [. . .]

Well, I will now let my claims for decent life stand as I have made them. To sum them up in brief, they are: First, a healthy body; second, an active mind in sympathy with the past, the present, and the future; thirdly, occupation fit for a healthy body and an active mind; and fourthly, a beautiful world to live in. [. . .]

And how? Chiefly, I think, by educating people to a sense of their real capacities as men, so that they may be able to use to their own good the political power which is rapidly being thrust upon them; to get them to see that the old system of organizing labour for *individual profit* is becoming unmanageable, and that the whole people have now got to choose between the confusion resulting from the break up of that system and the determination to take in hand the labour now organized for profit, and use its organization for the livelihood of the community: [. . .] and then at last it will only be a step over the border, and the civilized world will be socialized; and, looking back on what has been, we shall be astonished to think of how long we submitted to live as we live now.

---

2   from George Bernard Shaw,
        'The Economic Basis of Socialism' (1889)

[. . .] If a railway is required, all that is necessary is to provide subsistence for a sufficient number of labourers to construct it. If, for example, the railway requires the labour of a thousand men for five years, the cost to the proprietors of the site is the subsistence of a thousand men for five years. This subsistence is technically called capital. It is provided for by the proprietors not consuming the whole excess over wages of the produce of the labour of their other wage workers, but setting aside enough for the subsistence of the railway makers. In this way capital can claim to be the result of saving, or, as one ingenious apologist neatly put it, the reward of abstinence, a gleam of humour which still enlivens treatises on capital. The savers, it need hardly be said, are those who have more money than they want to spend: the abstainers are those who have less. At the end of the five years, the completed railway is the property of the capitalists; and the railway makers fall back into the labour market as helpless as they were before. [. . .]

The introduction of the capitalistic system is a sign that the exploitation of the labourer toiling for a bare subsistence wage has become one of the chief arts of life among the holders of tenant rights. It also produces a delusive promise of endless employment which blinds the proletariat to those disastrous consequences of rapid multiplication which are obvious to the small cultivator and peasant proprietor. But indeed the more you degrade the workers, robbing them of all artistic enjoyment, and all chance of respect and admiration from their fellows, the more you throw them back, reckless, on the one pleasure and the one human tie left to them—the gratification of their instinct for producing fresh supplies of men. You will applaud this instinct as divine until at last the excessive supply becomes a nuisance: there comes a plague of men; and you suddenly discover that the instinct is diabolic, and set up a cry of 'overpopulation.' But your slaves are beyond caring for your cries: they breed like rabbits; and their poverty breeds filth, ugliness, dishonesty, disease, obscenity; drunkenness, and murder. In the midst of the riches which their labour piles up for you, their misery rises up too and stifles you. You withdraw in disgust to the other end of the town from them; you appoint special carriages on your railways and special seats in your churches and theatres for them; you set your life apart from theirs by every class barrier you can devise; and yet they swarm about you still: your face gets stamped with your habitual loathing and suspicion of them: your ears get so filled with the language of the vilest of them that you break into it when you lose your self-control: they poison your life as remorselessly as you have sacrificed theirs heartlessly. You begin to believe intensely in the devil. Then comes the terror of their revolting; the drilling and arming of bodies of them to keep down the rest; the prison, the hospital, paroxysms of frantic coercion, followed by paroxysms of frantic charity. And in the meantime, the population continues to increase!

It is sometimes said that during this grotesquely hideous march of civlization from bad to worse, wealth is increasing side by side with misery. Such a thing is eternally impossible: wealth is steadily decreasing with the spread of poverty. But riches are increasing, which is quite another thing. The total of the exchange values produced in the country annually is mounting perhaps by leaps and bounds. But the accumulation of riches, and consequently of an excessive purchasing power, in the hands of a class, soon satiates that class with socially useful wealth, and sets them offering a price for luxuries. The moment a price is to be had for a luxury, it acquires exchange value, and labour is employed to produce it. A New York lady, for instance, having a nature of exquisite sensibility, orders an elegant rosewood and silver coffin, upholstered in pink satin, for her dead dog. It is made; and meanwhile a live child is prowling barefooted and hunger-stunted in the frozen gutter outside. The exchange value of the coffin is counted as part of the national wealth; but a nation which cannot afford food and clothing for its children cannot be allowed to pass as wealthy because it has provided a pretty coffin for a dead dog. Exchange value itself, in fact, has become bedevilled like everything else, and represents, no longer utility, but the cravings of lust, folly, vanity, gluttony, and madness, technically described by genteel economists as 'effective demand.' Luxuries are not social wealth: the machinery for producing them is not social wealth: labour skilled only to manufacture them is not socially useful labour: the men, women, and children who make a living by producing them are no more self-supporting than the idle rich for whose amusement they are kept at work. It is the habit of counting as wealth the exchange values involved in these transactions that makes us fancy that the poor are starving in the midst of plenty. They are starving in the midst of plenty of jewels, velvets, laces, equipages, and racehorses; but not in the midst of plenty of food. In the things that are wanted for the welfare of the people we are abjectly poor; and England's social policy today may be likened to the domestic policy of those adventuresses who leave their children half-clothed and half-fed in order to keep a carriage and deal with a fashionable dressmaker. But it is quite true that whilst wealth and welfare are decreasing, productive power is increasing; and nothing but the perversion of this power to the production of socially useless commodities prevents the apparent wealth from becoming real. The purchasing power that commands luxuries in the hands of the rich would command true wealth in the hands of all. Yet private property must still heap the purchasing power upon the few rich and withdraw it from the many poor. So that, in the end, the subject of the one boast that private property can make—the great accumulation of so-called 'wealth' which it points so proudly to as the result of its power to scourge men and women daily to prolonged and intense toil—turns out to be a simulacrum. With all its energy, its Smilesian 'self-help,' its merchant-princely enterprise, its ferocious sweating and slave-driving, its prodigality of blood, sweat and tears, what has it heaped up, over and above the pittance of its slaves? Only a monstrous pile of frippery, some tainted class literature and class art, and not a little poison and mischief.

This, then, is the economic analysis which convicts Private Property of being unjust even from the beginning, and utterly impossible as a final solution of even the individualist aspect of the problem of adjusting the share of the worker in the distribution of wealth to the labour incurred by him in its production. All attempts yet made to construct true societies upon it have failed: the nearest things to societies so achieved have been civilizations, which have rotted into centres of vice and luxury, and eventually been swept away by uncivilized races. That our own civilization is already in an advanced stage of rottenness may be taken as statistically proved. That further decay instead of improvement must ensue if the institution of private property be maintained, is economically certain. Fortunately, private property in its integrity is not now practicable. Although the safety valve of emigration has been furiously at work during this century, yet the pressure of population has forced us to begin the restitution to the people of the sums taken from them for the ground landlords, holders of tenant rights, and capitalists, by the imposition of an income tax, and by compelling them to establish out of their revenues a national system of education, besides imposing restrictions—as yet only of the forcible-feeble sort—on their terrible power of abusing the wage contract. [. . .]

On Socialism the analysis of the economic action of Individualism bears as a discovery, in the private appropriation of land, of the source of those unjust privileges against which Socialism is aimed. It is practically a demonstration that public property in land is the basic economic condition of Socialism. But this does not involve at present a literal restoration of the land to the people. The land is at present in the hands of the people: its proprietors are for the most part absentees. The modern form of private property is simply a legal claim to take a share of the produce of the national industry year by year without working for it. It refers to no special part or form of that produce; and in process of consumption its revenue cannot be distinguished from earnings, so that the majority of persons, accustomed to call the commodities which form the income of the proprietor his private property, and seeing no difference between them and the commodities which form the income of a worker, extend the term private property to the worker's subsistence also, and can only conceive an attack on private property as an attempt to empower everybody to rob everybody else all round. But the income of a private proprietor can be distinguished by the fact that he obtains it unconditionally and gratuitously by private right against the public weal, which is incompatible with the existence of consumers who do not produce. Socialism involves discontinuance of the payment of these incomes, and addition of the wealth so saved to incomes derived from labour.

As we have seen, incomes derived from private property consist partly of economic rent; partly of pensions, also called rent, obtained by the subletting of tenant rights; and partly of a form of rent called interest, obtained by special adaptations of land to production by the application of capital: all these being finally paid out of the difference between the produce of the worker's labour and the price of that labour sold in the open market for wages, salary fees, or profits.[1] The whole, except economic rent, can be added directly to the incomes of the workers by simply discontinuing its reaction from them. Economic rent, arising as it does from variations of fertility or advantages of situation, must always be held as common or social wealth, and used, as the revenues raised by taxation are now used, for public purposes, among which Socialism would make national insurance and the provision of capital matters of the first importance.

The economic problem of Socialism is thus solved; and the political question of how the economic solution is to be practically applied does not come within the scope of this essay. But if we have got as far as intellectual conviction that the source of our social misery is no eternal well-spring of confusion and evil, but only an artificial system susceptible of almost infinite modification and readjustment—nay, of practical demolition and substitution at the will of Man—then a terrible weight will be lifted from the minds of all except those who are, whether avowedly to themselves or not, clinging to the present state of things from base motives. [. . .]

But Socialism now challenges individualism, scepticism, pessimism, worship of Nature personified as a devil, on their own ground of science. The science of the production and distribution of wealth is Political Economy. Socialism appeals to that science, and, turning on Individualism its own guns, routs it in incurable disaster. Henceforth the bitter cynic who still finds the world an eternal and unimprovable doghole, with the placid person of means who repeats the familiar misquotation, 'the poor ye shall have always with you,' lose their usurped place among the cultured, and pass over to the ranks of the ignorant, the shallow and the superstitious. As for the rest of us, since we were taught to revere proprietary respectability in our unfortunate childhood, and since we found our childish hearts so hard and unregenerate that they secretly hated and rebelled against respectability in spite of that teaching, it is impossible to express the relief with which we discover that our hearts were all along right, and that the current respectability of today is nothing but a huge inversion of righteous and scientific social order weltering dishonesty, uselessness, selfishness, wanton misery, and idiotic waste of magnificent opportunities for noble and happy living. It was terrible to feel this, and yet to fear that it could not be helped—that the poor must starve and make you ashamed of your dinner—that they must shiver and make you ashamed of your warm overcoat. It is to economic science—once the Dismal, now the Hopeful—that we are indebted for the discovery that though the evil is

---

[1] [Shaw's note:] This excess of the product of labour over its price is treated as a single category with impressive effect by Karl Marx, who called it 'surplus value.'

enormously worse than we knew, yet it is not eternal—not even very long lived, if we only bestir ourselves to make an end of it.

---

3   from Oscar Wilde, 'The Soul of
Man Under Socialism' (1891)

The chief advantage that would result from the establishment of Socialism is, undoubtedly, the fact that Socialism would relieve us from that sordid necessity of living for others which, in the present condition of things, presses so hardly upon almost everybody. In fact, scarcely any one at all escapes.

Now and then, in the course of the century, a great man of science, like Darwin; a great poet like Keats; a fine critical spirit like M. Renan;[2] a supreme artist like Flaubert, has been able to isolate himself, to keep himself out of reach of the clamorous claims of others, to stand 'under the shelter of the wall,' as Plato puts it, and so to realise the perfection of what was in him, to his own incomparable gain, and to the incomparable and lasting gain of the whole world. These, however, are exceptions. The majority of people spoil their lives by an unhealthy and exaggerated altruism—are forced, indeed, so to spoil them. They find themselves surrounded by hideous poverty, by hideous ugliness, by hideous starvation. It is inevitable that they should be strongly moved by all this. The emotions of man are stirred more quickly than man's intelligence; and as I pointed out some time ago in an article on the function of criticism, it is much more easy to have sympathy with suffering than it is to have sympathy with thought. Accordingly, with admirable, though misdirected intentions, they very seriously and very sentimentally set themselves to the task of remedying the evils that they see. But their remedies do not cure the disease: they merely prolong it. Indeed, their remedies are part of the disease.

They try to solve the problem of poverty, for instance, by keeping the poor alive; or, in the case of a very advanced school, by amusing the poor.

But this is not a solution; it is an aggravation of the difficulty. The proper aim is to try and reconstruct society on such a basis that poverty will be impossible. And the altruistic virtues have really prevented the carrying out of this aim. Just as the worst slave-owners were those who were kind to their slaves, and so prevented the horror of the system being realised by those who suffered from it, and understood by those who contemplated it, so, in the present state of things in England,

---

[2] Ernst Renan (1823–92), philologist and historian of Christianity, whose *Life of Jesus* (1863) caused great controversy across Europe. He was considered one of the most important essayists of his time.

the people who do most harm are the people who try to do most good; and at last we have had the spectacle of men who have really studied the problem and know the life—educated men who live in the East End—coming forward and imploring the community to restrain its altruistic impulses of charity, benevolence, and the like. They do so on the ground that such charity degrades and demoralises. They are perfectly right. Charity creates a multitude of sins.[3]

There is also this to be said. It is immoral to use private property in order to alleviate the horrible evils that result from the institution of private property. It is both immoral and unfair.

Under Socialism all this will, of course, be altered. There will be no people living in fetid dens and fetid rags, and bringing up unhealthy, hunger-pinched children in the midst of impossible and absolutely repulsive surroundings. The security of society will not depend, as it does now, on the state of the weather. If a frost comes we shall not have a hundred thousand men out of work, tramping about the streets in a state of disgusting misery, or whining to their neighbours for alms, or crowding round the doors of loathsome shelters to try and secure a hunch of bread and a night's unclean lodging. Each member of the society will share in the general prosperity and happiness of the society, and if a frost comes no one will practically be anything the worse.

Upon the other hand, Socialism itself will be of value simply because it will lead to Individualism.

Socialism, Communism, or whatever one chooses to call it, by converting private property into public wealth, and substituting Cupertino for competition, will restore society to its proper condition of a thoroughly healthy organism, and ensure the material well-being of each member of the community. It will, in fact, give Life its proper basis and its proper environment. But, for the full development of Life to its highest mode of perfection, something more is needed. What is needed is Individualism. If the Socialism is Authoritarian; if there are Governments armed with economic power as they are now with political power; if, in a word, we are to have Industrial Tyrannies, then the last state of man will be worse than the first. At present, in consequence of the existence of private property, a great many people are enabled to develop a certain very limited amount of Individualism. They are either under no necessity to work for their living, or are enabled to choose the sphere of activity that is really congenial to them, and gives them pleasure. These are the poets, the philosophers, the men of science, the men of culture—in a word, the real men, the men who have realised themselves, and in whom all Humanity gains a partial realisation. Upon the other hand, there are a great many people who, having no private property of their own, and being

[3] This argument clearly responds to philanthropic ventures and proposals for dealing with the problem of poverty such as those proposed by William Booth and the Salvation Army. Excerpts from Booth's *In Darkest England* appear in Ch. 2.

always on the brink of sheer starvation, are compelled to do the work of beasts of burden, to do work that is quite uncongenial to them, and to which they are forced by the peremptory, unreasonable, degrading Tyranny of want. These are the poor; and amongst them there is no grace of manner, or charm of speech, or civilisation or culture, or refinement in pleasures, or joy of life. From their collective force Humanity gains much in material prosperity. But it is only the material result that it gains, and the man who is poor is in himself absolutely of no importance. He is merely the infinitesimal atom of a force that, so far from regarding him, crushes him: indeed, prefers him crushed, as in that case he is far more obedient.

Of course it might be said that the Individualism generated under conditions of private property is not always, or even as a rule, of a fine or wonderful type, and that the poor, if they have not culture and charm, have still many virtues. Both these statements would be quite true. The possession of private property is very often extremely demoralising, and that is, of course, one of the reasons why Socialism wants to get rid of the institution. In fact, property is really a nuisance. Some years ago people went about the country saying that property has duties. They said it so often and so tediously that, at last, the Church has begun to say it. One hears it now from every pulpit. It is perfectly true. Property not merely has duties, but has so many duties that its possession to any large extent is a bore. It involves endless claims upon one, endless attention to business, endless bother. If property had simply pleasures, we could stand it; but its duties make it unbearable. In the interest of the rich we must get rid of it. The virtues of the poor may be readily admitted, and are much to be regretted. We are often told that the poor are grateful for charity. Some of them are, no doubt, but the best amongst the poor are never grateful. They are ungrateful, discontented, disobedient, and rebellious. They are quite right to be so. Charity they feel to be a ridiculously inadequate mode of partial restitution, or a sentimental dole, usually accompanied by some impertinent attempt on the part of the sentimentalist to tyrannise over their private lives. Why should they be grateful for the crumbs that fall from the rich man's table? [. . .]

It is clear, then, that no Authoritarian Socialism will do. For while under the present system a very large number of people can lead lives of a certain amount of freedom and expression and happiness, under an industrial-barrack system, or a system of economic tyranny, nobody would be able to have any such freedom at all. It is to be regretted that a portion of our community should be practically in slavery, but to propose to solve the problem by enslaving the entire community is childish. Every man must be left quite free to choose his own work. No form of compulsion must be exercised over him. If there is, his work will not be good for him, will not be good in itself, and will no be good for others. And by work I simply mean activity of any kind.

I hardly think that any Socialist, nowadays, would seriously propose that an inspector should call every morning at each house to see that each citizen rose up and did manual labour for eight hours. Humanity has got beyond that stage, and reserves such a form of life for the people whom, in a very arbitrary manner, it chooses to call criminals. But I confess that many of the socialistic views that I have come across seem to me to be tainted with ideas of authority, if not of actual compulsion. Of course authority and compulsion are out of the question. All association must be quite voluntary. It is only in voluntary associations that man is fine. [. . .]

Individualism, then, is what through Socialism we are to attain. As a natural result the State must give up all idea of government. It must give it up because, as a wise man once said many centuries before Christ, there is such a thing as leaving mankind alone; there is no such thing as governing mankind. All modes of government are failures. Despotism is unjust to everybody, including the despot, who was probably made for better things. Oligarchies are unjust to the many, and ochlocracies are unjust to the few. High hopes were once formed of democracy; but democracy means simply the bludgeoning of the people by the people for the people. It has been found out. I must say that it was high time, for all authority is quite degrading. It degrades those who exercise it, and degrades those over whom it is exercised. When it is violently, grossly, and cruelly used, it produces a good effect, by creating, or at any rate bringing out, the spirit of revolt and Individualism that is to kill it. When it is used with a certain amount of kindness, and accompanied by prizes and rewards, it is dreadfully demoralising. People, in that case, are less conscious of the horrible pressure that is being put on them, and so go through their lives in a sort of coarse comfort, like petted animals, without ever realising that they are probably thinking other people's thoughts, living by other people's standards, wearing practically what one may call other people's second-hand clothes, and never being themselves for a single moment. 'He who would be free [. . .] must not conform.' And authority, by bribing people to conform, produces a very gross kind of over-fed barbarism amongst us. [. . .]

Now as the State is not to govern, it may be asked what the State is to do. The State is to be a voluntary manufacturer and distributor of necessary commodities. The State is to make what is useful. The individual is to make what is beautiful. And as I have mentioned the word labour, I cannot help saying that a great deal of nonsense is being written and talked nowadays about the dignity of manual labour. There is nothing necessarily dignified about manual labour at all, and most of it is absolutely degrading. It is mentally and morally injurious to man to do anything in which he does not find pleasure, and many forms of labour are quite pleasureless activities, and should be regarded as such. To sweep a slushy crossing for eight hours on a day when the east wind is blowing is a disgusting occupation. To sweep it with mental, moral, or physical dignity seems to me to be impossible. To sweep it with joy would be appalling. Man is made for something better than disturbing dirt. All work of that kind should be done by a machine. [. . .]

The fact is, that civilisation requires slaves. The Greeks were quite right there. Unless there are slaves to do the ugly, horrible, uninteresting work, culture and contemplation become almost impossible. Human slavery is wrong, insecure, and demoralising. On mechanical slavery, on the slavery of the machine, the future of the world depends. And when scientific men are no longer called upon to go down to a depressing East End and distribute bad cocoa and worse blankets to starving people, they will have delightful leisure in which to devise wonderful and marvellous things for their own joy and the joy of every one else. There will be great storages of force for every city, and for every house if required, and this force man will convert into heat, light, or motion, according to his needs. Is this Utopian? A map of the world that does not include Utopia is not worth even glancing at, for it leaves out the one country at which Humanity is always landing. And when Humanity lands there, it looks out, and, seeing a better country, sets sail. Progress is the realisation of Utopias.

Now, I have said that the community by means of organisation of machinery will supply the useful things, and that the beautiful things will be made by the individual. This is not merely necessary, but it is the only possible way by which we can get either the one or the other. An individual who has to make things for the use of others, and with reference to their wants and their wishes, does not work with interest, and consequently cannot put into his work what is best in him. Upon the other hand, whenever a community or a powerful section of a community, or a government of any kind, attempts to dictate to the artist what he is to do, Art either entirely vanishes, or becomes stereotyped, or degenerates into a low and ignoble form of craft. A work of art is the unique result of a unique temperament. Its beauty comes from the fact that the author is what he is. It has nothing to do with the fact that other people want what they want. Indeed, the moment that an artist takes notice of what other people want, and tries to supply the demand, he ceases to be an artist, and becomes a dull or an amusing craftsman, an honest or a dishonest tradesman. He has no further claim to be considered as an artist. Art is the most intense mood of Individualism that the world has known. I am inclined to say it is the only real mode of Individualism that the world has known. [. . .]

And it is to be noted that it is the fact that Art is this intense form of Individualism that makes the public try to exercise over it an authority that is as immoral as it is ridiculous, and as corrupting as it is contemptible.[4] It is not quite their fault. The public has always, and in every age, been badly brought up. They are

---

[4] Wilde is again writing in reaction to contextual debates: see the debate concerning morality and censorship of the novel, explored in 'Candour in English Fiction' in Ch. 5.

continually asking Art to be popular, to please their want of taste, to flatter their absurd vanity, to tell them what they have been told before, to show them what they ought to be tired of seeing, to amuse them when they feel heavy after eating too much, and to distract their thoughts when they are wearied of their own stupidity. Now Art should never try to be popular. The public should try to make itself artistic. [. . .]

Of course, we have to a very great extent got rid of any attempt on the part of the community, or the Church, or the Government, to interfere with the individualism of speculative thought, but the attempt to interfere with the individualism of imaginative art still lingers. It fact, it does more than linger; it is aggressive, offensive, and brutalising.

In England, the arts that have escaped best are the arts in which the public take no interest. Poetry is an instance of what I mean. We have been able to have fine poetry in England because the public do not read it, and consequently do not influence it. [. . .]

It is evident, then, that all authority in such things is bad. People sometimes inquire what form of government is most suitable for an artist to live under. To this question there is only one answer. The form of government that is most suitable to the artist is no government at all. Authority over him and his art is ridiculous. It has been stated that under despotism artists have produced lovely work. This is not quite so. Artists have visited despots, not as subjects to be tyrannised over, but as wandering wonder-makers, as fascinating vagrant personalities, to be entertained and charmed and suffered to be at peace and allowed to create. There is this to be said in favour of the despot, that he, being an individual, may have culture, while the mob, being a monster, has none. One who is an Emperor and King may stoop down to pick up a brush for a painter, but when the democracy stoops down it is merely to throw mud. And yet the democracy have not so far to stoop as the emperor. In fact, when they want to throw mud they have not to stoop at all. But there is no necessity to separate the monarch from the mob; all authority is equally bad.

There are three kinds of despots. There is the despot who tyrannises over the body. There is the despot who tyrannises over the soul. There is the despot who tyrannises over the soul and body alike. The first is called the Prince. The second is called the Pope. The third is called the People. [. . .]

. . . [I]t is through joy that the Individualism of the future will develop itself. [. . .]

Man has sought to live intensely, fully, perfectly. When he can do so without exercising restraint on others, or suffering it ever, and his activities are all pleasurable to him, he will be saner, healthier, more civilised, more himself. Pleasure is Nature's test, her sign of approval. When man is happy, he is in harmony with himself and his environment. The new Individualism, for whose service Socialism, whether it wills it or not, is working, will be perfect harmony. It will be what the Greeks sought for, but could not, except in Thought, realise completely because they had slaves, and fed them; it will be what the Renaissance sought for, but could not realise completely except in Art, because they had slaves, and starved them. It will be complete, and through it each man will attain to his perfection. The new Individualism is the new Hellenism.

---

4   from Isabella O. Ford, *Women and Socialism* (1907)

At this moment, when the woman's movement has reached its present advanced stage, and when certainly the justice, if not always the expediency, of granting women's claim to possess equal political power with men is admitted by all intelligent persons, it may seem a little unnecessary to write further pamphlets, or revise old ones, on the subject. But it appears to me extremely important that just at this acute stage of the battle the absolute expediency for the welfare of the State, as well as the justice, of granting the vote to women should be made perfectly clear, and most particularly to those who desire to understand the Labour movement and what it really stands for, because unless the relation of the Labour movement—or perhaps it is better to use the wider term of the Socialist movement—to the Women's Movement, be clearly recognised, the real inner meaning of Socialism itself cannot be understood, for the two movements have the same common origin and the same aims.

THE MEANING OF SOCIALISM

There are many people, even those in the Socialist ranks, who apparently forget, or perhaps have never quite realised, that Socialism demands more than that we should merely import Socialistic institutions into our midst, such as free meals for children, municipalisation, &c., and consider that they will regenerate society and turn us all into Socialists. It insists on a moral regeneration of society of the most complete and searching kind in order to make a lasting foundation for the political and social changes we many of us long to see.

Justice is to be the foundation on which we must build, not the kind of justice we have hitherto considered as sufficient for us, and which many countries pride themselves is their watchword and standard, but a justice that demands freedom for all. 'All men are free and equal,' declares the United States of America, but in only four of those States are women free, the industrial condition of the workers is not by any means one of freedom, and in the South the race question is still in a state of frightful chaos. Socialism, when it says that in order to have a great nation we must build on this sound foundation, also says that so long as any section of a State be left ignorant and fettered, and therefore powerless to help this immense work forward, that State will be incomplete, for its foundation will be incomplete, for since each and all of us alike are members of the State, it demands from us all an equal share of service. All hands must be on deck if we would save the ship. [. . .]

THE IMPORTANCE OF THE HOME

Now the relationship between men and women forms the core, the centre round which society grows, for the family, the home, is the very heart of a nation. If that relationship be founded on justice such as I have described above, then we shall have a knowledge growing fuller and more complete as experience teaches each generation, of how to build our state out of this moral regeneration which Socialism calls for, since the two who form the home, understanding it equally in their own lives will teach each other and their families how to undertake it. As things are now, neither understands it,—(the man as occupying the more ignoble position, that of the oppressor, even less perhaps than the woman,)—for they stand in a false position of inequality towards each other, and that falseness spreads, as a fungus spreads its evil growth, into their relationship to others. Hence we have the world as we now see it: founded not on justice, not on freedom, but on a make-believe of both.

Socialism goes straight to the home, to the heart of the world, in its cry for freedom. Free the home, let the woman be no longer in political subjection, and free the worker, it says; bring light into all the dark homes of the earth so that each one like a torch may spread the light throughout all the world, and by that light we shall then see wisely and clearly how to bring about the social changes we so ardently desire. Reforms coming thus from the heart of a nation, must be and will be, of the strongest and most enduring kind.

CONNECTION BETWEEN THE WOMAN'S MOVEMENT AND THE LABOUR MOVEMENT

But now how is the woman's movement and the labour movement connected besides in this common demand for a State founded on the highest justice and the consequent reform of the home? They both arise from the common evil of economic dependence, or rather, economic slavery. They represent two sides of the very same question. [. . .]

At the present moment the connection between the women's movement and the Socialist movement seems closer than ever. Before the last general election the ruling classes extended the antagonism they have always shown to the woman's cause, in an even more decided manner than usual to the Trade Union cause, and whole Labour movement. The woman's cause received several blows too of a worse character than it had received for several previous years. Now, in Parliament, the Labour Party has definitely and decidedly espoused the cause of women's political enfranchisement, and the two causes are, therefore, in the House of Commons at least, distinctly joined together. Partly through the spread of the socialist trend of thought, partly through the slow upward growth of the women themselves, and the public work which they have achieved under immense difficulties, but chiefly through the terrible economic conditions which women wage earners have now to endure, the Labour Party realises that there can be no economic freedom for a country in which one half of the workers have no political freedom. The denial of such freedom to any one class must of necessity, as explained at the beginning, act disastrously on the progress of the whole community, and the more so when, as in this case, this class includes half the whole nation. [. . .]

WOMEN'S REFORM WORK

The next point we come to is to show that women by their public work, both in countries where they have the vote and in those where they have not, make the same demands and have the same objects in view as the Labour Party.

In England on all public bodies on which women sit, they are insisting on proper cottage accommodation and a good water supply in rural and urban districts. They are urging that the lives of those who live in workhouses shall be made happy and useful, and that the children there must be trained to be good citizens, and that no 'taint of pauperism' be attached to them hereafter. They are asking that women shall receive equal pay with men for equal work. They have refused on more than one important occasion to support a candidate whose moral character was known to be bad.

These are all part of the Socialist creed.

If we turn to countries where women possess full political power we shall find this resemblance between the aims of Woman and Labour even still more apparent.

In Wyoming, where women have exercised the suffrage since 1869, in Utah and Idaho, where they were enfranchised in 1896, and in Colorado, in 1893, the women's vote raised the age of consent to 18. In this country it is still 16. In Wyoming women teachers must (by law) receive equal pay for equal work and when equally qualified, as men teachers receive. Excellent legislation against gambling has been passed. The employment of boys and girls in mines, and of children under 14 in public exhibitions is also forbidden there. Free

Libraries, free Kindergartens, the proper treatment of children, and also of animals, the cleanliness of streets, and the care of the aged, the feeble-minded and insane, industrial conditions, and a host of other matters equally important, including temperance measures, have all been traced to the women's vote.

In New Zealand, as we all know, Old Age Pensions were obtained in 1898, *i.e.*, five years after women had obtained the franchise, and, as everyone agrees, it was their vote mostly which passed it. Industrial reforms also of an important kind, both there and in Australia, have resulted from the women's vote. The presence too of women at the polling booth in those countries has been productive of nothing but good, as all the authorities combine in telling us; men have taken more interest in recording their votes, the public houses are closed on the election day in some parts, and neither the husband's shirt buttons nor the baby have been in the least neglected. Sir John Cockburn says, in referring to South Australia,[5] and the effect of the women's vote there, 'In the first place, legislators have to lead decent lives. Women won't put up with any nonsense. [. . .] The woman's vote in South Australia has been a vote for health, physical and moral, in the highest possible sense.'

Everywhere in England we see women fighting for reforms of the same kind as those for which the Labour Party is fighting, and arousing therefore the same opposition from those who prefer stagnation to reform. The women are, of course, generally unconscious as yet of the connection between their cause and the labour cause, and of the similarity of their respective aims, and doubtless, the larger reforms we in the Socialist ranks desire, they do not always understand or wish for. [. . .] Women's work is awakening people to see that society must be responsible for the welfare of the individual, because the individual, each one of us who fulfils a duty to the State, is the State (each for all, all for each, we say), and I am convinced they have thus helped immensely, even though unconsciously, to prepare the way for the growth of a Socialism of the best and most enduring kind. [. . .]

Women are called conservative, but has there been any great struggle or revolution in which women have not taken a prominent and important part? What would the Russian revolution be without the women: whose women stood more nobly beside their men, even in the trenches, than the Boer women? Politicians know that when once the women of a nation come into political power, their day of quiet slumber or gentle obstruction is over, for, as Sir John Cockburn puts it, 'women won't put up with any nonsense.' The extension of men's vote, even if it

[5] Sir John Cockburn (1850–1929), politician in the state of South Australia, variously education secretary, chief secretary, and prime minister. He was a key figure in the eventual federation of Australia. He served as President of the International Alliance for Women's Suffrage (although he was also active in the Freemasons, which somewhat calls into question any 'feminist' credentials).

be to manhood suffrage, they apparently do not dread at all, and one supposes they must argue from experience.

At the heart of every woman who now asks for the vote in all seriousness, lies the conviction that until women possess this power, the deepest moral evils against which the world is perpetually battling, can never be crushed or even touched. This is chiefly due to the increasing knowledge of industrial life and conditions which women have gained through their work as Guardians, Factory Inspectors, Sanitary Inspectors, and so forth. It has shown them with a fearful distinctness, that the barbarous state of our marriage and divorce laws, of our laws concerning the custody of children, illegal motherhood and fatherhood, the condition of our streets and factories, etc: all press most heavily on the lives of *poor* women. It is this knowledge which has stirred in so many women's minds an enthusiasm strong as a religion—to many it is a religion—and a desperate determination that these things shall no longer continue, and, therefore they have brought the question forward in such a manner that it now has acquired a position of enormous importance in all thinking minds.

The Labour Party has found its political voice, the women insist that theirs be heard, too. The Labour Party, understanding economic slavery as no other class can, understands the women's need, and the two stand together now, in this demand for political freedom, which alone brings economic freedom. [. . .]

In the past, and indeed in some measure at the present day too, there has been a prejudice against the woman's movement amongst Socialists on the ground that it owes its origin and growth, mostly, if not entirely, to middle-class women. Surely it is anti-Socialistic and futile to argue this position. Our present Socialist party was in the beginning formed chiefly by middle-class men and women. William Morris was a middle-class man. Lord Shaftesbury was not of the 'Working Class,' as we term it, but the Factory Acts he initiated nevertheless marked the beginning of a Socialistic industrial era.[6] The very reason why the Labour movement of the present day is superior to all similar movements in the past, and why it has before it a future of endless growth and development, is because it has swept into its great current followers of all classes. It has got beyond the earlier stages of mere class warfare, it has lost that old provincial spirit, and is now international, cosmopolitan in its demands. It aims at binding the workers of all nations, regardless of sex or race or caste into one great whole, and in that word Workers, it includes all who contribute their share of service to the world. Mutual service is an imperative condition. It appeals to all who join its ranks, solely on this condition.

---

[6] Lord Shaftesbury (1801–85) steered a series of Factory Acts through parliament—in 1833, to ban child workers under 9 from employment, and restrict the hours of those between 9 and 13, and appointing factory inspectors to oversee the legislation. The 1840 Act banned child chimney-sweeps; the 1844 Act restricted women's hours of work.

Just so is the women's movement now expanding out of its narrow origin and appealing to all classes of women to take their share in the crusade. The Trade Union woman sees that she is entitled to political representation in return for her political fund levy. Discontent is everywhere spreading amongst women workers, and they are desiring to put their case themselves before the world, in their own way. Their standard of living has been slowly raised by the sanitary and housing and factory reforms the middle-class woman has been ceaselessly advocating since she attained a place in the local government of the country, and they are therefore beginning to wish for better conditions in their lives.

The middle-class woman, as I have pointed out, bases her demand for justice, primarily on the needs of the working woman, now that her knowledge of those needs has grown clearer.

It is impossible, therefore, any longer to brand the woman's movement as only a middle-class affair. [. . .]

RESULT OF THE TWO MOVEMENTS WORKING TOGETHER

We must I think, surely gather from a clear understanding of the common origin and aims of these two movements, that the more they work alongside or together, the more each will strengthen the other. The Labour party will always keep the economic side well to the front, and this is a side women are apt to overlook since all women do not yet grasp the intimate connection between morals and economics. Women will help to keep more clearly before our eyes, than is perhaps always possible now, those great ideals for the accomplishment of which Labour representation is only a means. History shows us that no cause can be far reaching or eternal that has not within it a religious enthusiasm, using the word in its very widest sense. The loyalty of women to priest and parson, for which they are continually ridiculed, has its foundation (distorted as is its shape at present) in a dim, unconscious recognition of this. Turned into wide and wholesome channels this enthusiasm will be invaluable to the Labour movement.

We think now that we understand and worship love, justice and compassion, but our present understanding of them is a mere blurred vision compared with what, in the future, it will be when men and women stand together, helping and teaching one another as equals and friends, instead of as now often living alongside one another as strangers, sometimes even as enemies. Our lives at present are mostly quite different from our ideals, poor as our ideals are,—we worship poverty in our churches, and we scorn it in our daily life and our laws, which class the lunatic and the pauper together; we reverence women and motherhood in our poetry, whilst we underpay and enslave women, and motherhood leads to untold misery and degradation in the lives of innumerable women; we talk much about the beauty of compassion for the weak and helpless, and at the same time we think we are justified in torturing animals, of all things the most helpless, for our own use and comfort. All this, and infinitely more of a like nature, we do in a stupid, blind fashion, not knowing that we do it. Slowly our eyes are opening and we begin to feel our lives are wrong, and we long to do better: but it is not until woman, strong and free, stands beside man, helping him to reach this better life, and not as now often holding him back from it, that we shall begin in real earnest to walk towards the full light of day.

May it not be that this very subjection has in itself so chastened, so trained her (woman) to think of others rather than of herself, that after all it may have acted more as a blessing than as a curse to the world? May it not bring her to the problems of the future with a purer aim and a keener insight than is possible for man?

EDITORS' NOTES

1. William Morris (1834–96) joined the Social Democratic Federation in 1883, but seceded to form the Socialist League in 1884. His narrative poem 'The Pilgrims of Hope' (1885), centres on the Paris Commune of 1871 and was first published in the League's own magazine, *Commonweal*. Most of his later work, except for *Poems by the Way* (1891) and *Chants for Socialists* (1884–5), was in prose, and the politically most significant of these were the utopian socialist dream-fantasies *A Dream of John Ball* (1888) and *News from Nowhere* (1890). 'How We Live and How We Might Live' started out as a lecture delivered to the Hammersmith Branch of the SDF at Kelmscott House, on 30 November 1884. Morris sees war as the foundational principle of capitalist society: wars between nations and rival capitalists; wars against colonized peoples; and wars between classes. Socialist revolution, he believed, would bring an end to all such wars.

2. George Bernard Shaw (1856–1950) moved to London from Dublin in 1876, and set out on a literary career. As well as writing novels and, more successfully, plays, Shaw was a music, art, and literary critic for the *Dramatic Review* (1885–6), *Our Corner* (1885–6), the *Pall Mall Gazette* (1885–8), and *The Star* (1888–90). He was later drama critic for the influential *Saturday Review* (1895–8), and was one of Ibsen's leading acolytes in the fin-de-siècle years; his *Quintessence of Ibsenism* was published in 1891. Shaw joined the Fabian Society in May 1884, and was initially Marxist in orientation before committing himself to land reform and state control. Shaw diverged from Marx after reading an article by the Revd Philip Wicksteed, a disciple of the English economist Stanley Jevons, who in the October 1884 issue of *Today* challenged Marx's Labour Theory of Value on the grounds that labour could not be the sole determinant of value, since differences in the fertility of soil and consequent land values could be crucial in determining the value of a commodity. Subsequently, the recognition of rent as a value not reducible to individual human labour began to dominate Fabian thinking.

Shaw's contribution to the *Fabian Essays on Socialism* (1889), included here, was to become a central feature of Fabian philosophy, defining its attitudes to policy and action. He suggests in the essay that there are at least three rents that contribute to 'surplus value', and that the most obvious is the rent accruing to land according to its fertility. He called this 'economic rents' and suggested that surplus value was also gained from rent of ability, a product of the fertility of the brain, and rent of capital, produced by an employer putting someone to work on the land. The implication of the article seems to be that there are many levels of rent and that many individuals of all classes obtain the surplus value, so that it is not simply a matter of one class exploiting another class, for many people of all classes are involved in the production of surplus value. Such an economic model downgrades the importance of class conflict and suggests that all that was needed was a change in the structure of society. A redistribution of income, according to Shaw, could be achieved by state ownership of the land and progressive taxation; and that such a redistribution would produce economic growth. Shaw's essay contributed importantly to the Fabians' playing down of class conflict and stress on the need gradually to extend state control and the power of municipal authorities with the aim of redressing economic imbalances. See also the Editors' note on Shaw at the end of chapter 1.

3. Oscar Wilde (1854–1900) is best known as a dramatist, novelist, Aesthete, and Decadent. His imprisonment in 1895 for 'acts of gross indecency' meant that in the late twentieth century he was often understood in the context of the formation of homosexual identities at the fin de siècle. Here, though, he is writing a plea for artistic freedom and individualism, a state of being which he believed, after hearing Bernard Shaw speak, could best be achieved through socialism. Wilde's essay has been translated into many languages and is based on the paradox that we should not waste energy in sympathizing with those who suffer needlessly, and that only socialism can free us to cultivate our personalities. Wilde is opposed to authoritarianism, for that would mean the enslavement of the whole of society instead of the part that is at present enslaved. In his opposition to any form of government or social coercion, Wilde seems here in some ways to be more of an anarchist than a socialist: he is reported by Richard Ellmann to have told an interviewer in 1894 that 'I am something of an anarchist' (*Oscar Wilde* (New York: Knopf, 1984), 328).

4. Isabella Ford (1855–1924) was the daughter of a wealthy Leeds Quaker family. She joined the Fabian Society in 1883, at the same time as her friend, the bohemian socialist and homosexual Edward Carpenter. She established the Leeds Tailoresses' Union in 1889, and in 1890 helped form the Leeds Women's Suffrage Society. Three years later she was instrumental in forming a Leeds branch of the Independent Labour Party, and the two organizations worked closely together. In 1903 Ford became a member of the national executive committee of the ILP, and played an important role in persuading leaders of the ILP to support women's suffrage. Always convinced of the link between women's emancipation and the socialist movement, she achieved some fame with her New Woman novel, *On the Threshold* (1895).

8

ANARCHISM

Central to late nineteenth-century anarchist thought was the conviction that the state, and indeed all forms of government, should be abolished, to be replaced by a system of voluntary co-operation between individuals and between small groups. At loggerheads with the state socialism favoured by the Fabian socialists in England, by German followers of Marx and, later, by the British Labour Party, anarchism was a thoroughly international, if radically splintered movement. Represented in this chapter are a Russian who lived in France and England, a German who emigrated to the USA, a Frenchman who lived variously in London, Paris, and America, and a Russian woman who emigrated first to America and then to England before supporting the Spanish republican movement during the Spanish Civil War. The internationalism of the anarchist movement is important, for it was the 'foreign' profile of anarchism which provoked the British characterization of anarchists as violent, degenerate revolutionaries intent on sabotaging the British constitution. That constitution became represented metonymically by the Royal Observatory at Greenwich, which was the apparent target of an anarchist bomb attack in April 1894. Overlapping discourses on racial difference and degeneration led *The Times* to present the blond, underdeveloped, effeminate, and definitively 'foreign' body of Martial Bourdin, the Greenwich bomber, as a generalized trope for anarchism. The British cultural imagination had a horrible fascination for anarchism, with Conrad's *The Secret Agent* (1906) being joined by numerous other (anti-) anarchist fictions, including Henry James's *The Princess Casamassima* (1887), Robert Louis Stevenson's *The Dynamiters* (1894), L. T. Meade and R. Eustace's *The Brotherhood of the Seven Kings* (1899), and George Sims's 'Alec the Actor' (1913). In *The Secret Agent* Karl Yundt, the burnt-out anarchistic advocate of murder, is apparently based on the German anarchist John Most (1846–1906), who, although he urged violent deeds, never actually undertook any. Michaelis, in the same novel, has been identified variously with the federalist anarchist Mikhail Bakunin (1814–76), his follower Peter Kropotkin (1842–1921), and even William Morris (1834–96).

Cultural responses to anarchism in Britain bore an uneven relationship to the reality of the political movement itself. Certainly a number of apparently anarchist-inspired incidents gathered momentum in the early 1890s: in 1892 Jean-François Ravachol (1859–92) was guillotined after several explosions in Paris; in October 1892 the mayor of Chicago was assassinated; in 1893 in Barcelona, a bomb was thrown in the Liceo Theatre, killing about twenty of the audience; and various other incidents in Spain, Italy, and France caught public attention. None the less, the general condemnation of anarchists as destructive and murderous revolutionaries which prevailed in Britain was a crude and in most cases an inaccurate response. There were several strands within anarchist political thought in the nineteenth century, and they sometimes conflicted with one another. Pierre Joseph Proudhon (1809–65), whose famous 'property is theft' slogan led to his unofficial crowning as the father of anarchism, was a so-called philosophic anarchist, advocating peaceful change and the gradual evolution of an anarchist society. Very different from Proudhon were those anarchists (of whom John Most was a prime example) who advocated 'propaganda by deed', whereby individual acts of protest (sometimes theft, sometimes physical violence) were urged as a means of raising the political profile of anarchism. The anarchist belief that the individual should be freed from all forms of authority meant that a strong individualist vein ran through anarchist thought, and this was at odds with the collectivism of leading anarchists such as Peter Kropotkin, whose *Mutual Aid* (1902) emphasized co-operation. Kropotkin, essentially a moderate, was concerned with the co-operative rather than the competitive aspect of natural evolution, especially the place of 'mutual aid' in the 'struggle for existence'. The tension between individualism and collectivism within anarchist thought is captured by Emma Goldman's essay, in which she argues that anarchism's 'economic arrangements must consist of voluntary productive and distributive associations, gradually developing into free communism. [. . .] Anarchism, however, also recognizes the right of the individual, or numbers of individuals, to arrange at all times for other forms of work in harmony with their tastes and desires.' It is this tension which William Morris found irresolvable. As anti-statist as any anarchist could be, Morris all the same had a problem with the individualism of anarchism, which he thought favoured 'the rule of the strongest individual, taking for their motto "To each one according to their deeds"' (Letter to *Commonweal*, 17 August 1889, p. 261). Morris believed that

individuals had to submit to collective decisions, which is why he ultimately opposed his anarchist comrades in the Socialist League, eventually abandoning the League to them in November 1890.

Secondary Reading: Marsh; Nettlau; Oliver; Trautmann.

---

1   from Peter Kropotkin, *Words of a Rebel* (1885)

'THE PARIS COMMUNE'[1]

On the 18th of March, 1871, the people of Paris rose against a rule that was generally detested and despised, and proclaimed the city of Paris independent, free
and belonging only to itself.

This overthrow of central power was made without the usual scenes of a revolutionary uprising: on that day there were neither volleys of shot nor floods of
blood shed behind the barricades. The rulers were eclipsed by an armed people
going out into the street; the soldiers evacuated the city, the bureaucrats hastened
towards Versailles, taking with them everything they could carry. The government evaporated like a puddle of stinking water under the breath of a spring
wind, and by the 19th, having shed hardly a drop of its children's blood, Paris
found itself free of the past that had contaminated the great city.

At the same time, the revolution that had been accomplished in this way
opened up a new era in the series of revolutions, by which the people march forward from slavery to freedom. Under the name of The Paris Commune a new
idea was born, destined to become the point of departure for future revolutions.

As is always the case with great ideas, it was not a product of the conceptions
of an individual philosopher. It was born of the collective intelligence; it sprang
from the heart of an entire people. But it was vague in the beginning, and many
among those who helped to realize it and who even gave their lives for it, did not
imagine the event as we conceive it today; they did not fully understand the revolution they were inaugurating, nor the fecundity of the new principle which they

---

[1] The Paris Commune—a revolutionary social order led by the proletariat—was established in Paris
on 17–18 March 1871 and fell to French government troops on 28 May 1871. A majority of the so-called
Communards (members of the Commune) were followers of Auguste Blanqui, a revolutionist held
prisoner in Versailles; many other Communards either supported the school of socialist anarchism
expounded by Pierre Joseph Proudhon or were members of the International Workingmen's Association, of which Karl Marx was a corresponding secretary. The Paris Commune became a heroic source of
inspiration for many late 19th-century socialists and anarchists, including not only Kropotkin but also
William Morris, who used it as the subject for his poem 'The Pilgrims of Hope' (1886).

were seeking to put into execution. It was only in the working out of the thought from this time onwards that the new principle became more and more specific and clear, and appeared in all its lucidity, all its beauty, its justice and the importance of its results. [. . .]

At that time two great currents of ideas confronted each other [. . .]: the Popular State on the one hand and Anarchy on the other.

According to the German socialists, the State should take possession of all accumulated wealth and give it to workers' associations; it should organize production and exchange, and keep watch over public life, over the functioning of society.

To this the majority of socialists of Latin race, replied that such a State—even admitting that by some impossible chance it could exist—would be the worst of tyrannies, and they opposed this ideal with a new ideal copied from the past; anarchy, that is to say, the complete abolition of States, and reorganization from the simple to the complex through the free federation of the popular forces of producers and consumers.

It was soon admitted, even by 'statists' less imbued with government prejudices, that Anarchy indeed represented a greatly superior form of organization than that envisaged in the popular State; but, they declared, the anarchist ideal is so far beyond us that we cannot concern ourselves with it at the present time. At the same time, anarchist theory lacked a concrete and simple formula with which to define its point of departure, to give body to its aims, and to show that they were based on a conception that had a real existence among the people. The federation of workers' corporations and groups of consumers across the frontiers and apart from the existing States, still seemed too vague a concept; and at the same time, it was easy to perceive that they could not comprehend the whole diversity of human manifestations. A clearer formula, one that was easier to comprehend, and which had its basic elements in the reality of things, was needed. [. . .]

For five months while it was isolated by the siege, Paris had lived its own life and it had come to understand the vast economic, intellectual and moral powers at its disposal; it had glimpsed and understood the strength of its initiatives. At the same time, it had seen that the band of brigands who had seized power did not know how to organize anything—either the defence of France or the development of the interior. It had seen how this central government had set itself against all that the intelligence of a great city might bring to fruition. It had seen more than that: the powerlessness of any government to ward off great disasters or to assist positive evolution when it is ripe for fulfilment. During the siege it had suffered frightful poverty, the poverty of the workers and defenders of the town, beside the indolent luxury of the idlers. And it had seen the failure, thanks to the central power, of all its attempts to put an end to this scandalous regime. Each time the people wished to take a free initiative, the government doubled its fetters, and the idea was born quite naturally that Paris should turn itself into an independent Commune, able to realize within its walls the will of the people.

Suddenly, the word Commune, began to emerge from every mouth.

The Commune of 1871 could not be any more than a first sketch. Born at the end of a war, surrounded by two armies ready to give a hand in crushing the people, it dared not declare itself openly socialist, and proceeded neither to the expropriation of capital nor to the organization of work, nor even to a general inventory of the city's resources. Nor did it break with the tradition of the State, of representative government, and it did not attempt to achieve within the Commune that organization from the simple to the complex it adumbrated by proclaiming the independence and free federation of Communes. But it is certain that if the Commune of Paris had lived a few months longer, the strength of events would have forced it towards these two revolutions. We should not forget that [in the French Revolution] the bourgeoisie devoted four years of the revolutionary period to proceed from a moderate monarchy to a bourgeois republic;[2] it should not surprise us that the people of Paris could not overleap in a single day the gulf that separated the anarchist Commune from the rule of bandits. But we must also realize that the revolution, in France and certainly also in Spain, will be communalist. It will take up the work of the Paris Commune where it was halted by the assassinations perpetrated by the men of Versailles.[3] [. . .]

After having surrounded the people of Paris and cut off all their exits, the rulers released on them soldiers brutalized by barrack life and wine, and said to them openly in the Assembly: 'kill the wolves, the she-wolves, and the cubs!' And to the people they said:

'Whatever you do, you will perish! If you are taken with arms in your hands—death! If you beg for mercy—death! To whatever side you turn your eyes, left, right, before, behind, above, below—death! You are not only out-side the law; you are outside humanity. Neither age nor sex will be able to save you, either you or yours. You will die, but before that you will savour the agony of your wife, of your sister, of your mother, of your daughter, of your son, even down to the cradle! Before your eyes they will drag the wounded from the ambulances to slash them with sword-bayonets and bludgeon them with rifle butts. They will drag them, still alive, by their broken legs or bleeding arms, and throw them into the river like bags of ordure that scream and suffer.

'Death! Death! Death!'

[2] Kropotkin is referring here to the French Revolution of 1789.
[3] More than 20,000 Communards were slaughtered by French government troops when the Commune fell on 28 May 1871.

And after this frantic orgy upon a pile of corpses, after the mass exterminations, a vengeance both mean and atrocious was to continue—floggings, thumbscrews, unendurable fetters, blows of prison guards, insults, hunger, all the refinements of cruelty.

Are the people likely to forget these great deeds?

'Down, but not out,' the Commune is being reborn today. This is not merely a dream of the conquered caressing in their imagination a beautiful mirage of hope. No! The Commune today becomes the precise and visible aim of the revolution that already rumbles near us. The idea penetrates the masses, gives them a flag to march behind, and we firmly count on the present generation to accomplish the social revolution of the Commune, and in this way put an end to the ignoble exploitation by the bourgeoisie, rid the people of the tutelage of the new State, and inaugurate in the evolution of the human species a new era of liberty, equality and solidarity.

2   from Johann [John] Most, 'Anarchy' (1888)

Anarchy is said to be general confusion, wild turmoil, which every civilization scorns. Since this condition renders both government and law unthinkable, anarchy means the atomization of society into isolated individuals, who with impunity attack others, until the strong subject the weak in a slavery more terrible than the world has ever seen. Abominable and absurd, the goal of the anarchist! Foul the means by which it is to be attained, namely theft, murder, arson, and all kinds of destruction! Anarchy is therefore a mixture of idiocy and crime. Against it society must defend with all power—legally so far as possible, violently when necessary. At all events, every lover of order is obliged to nip anarchy in the bud as well as eradicate anarchists root and branch from the face of the earth. [. . .]

Now if people would only think [. . .] they would see: anarchy (autonomy or freedom) really means, not the criminal chaos just referred to, but the absence of the criminal chaos that archy (subjugation or government) has brought to mankind. Archy springs from the desire of the strong to oppress the weak; and up to the present day, whatever its form, oppression has been its goal. Archy, always the tool of the propertied, has forever put the screws to the unpropertied. The more barbaric the society, the harsher and more flagrant the archy. The higher the civilization, the more refined the cleverness of the archists in hiding the usurpation of power—without weakening the exercise of power. [. . .]

If archy in all forms has brought mankind grief, it follows that the remedy is repudiation. The repudiation of archy is anarchy. Anarchy is therefore the goal of freedom-seeking mankind. Whoever seeks freedom, advances anarchy. If, among freedom-seekers, a multitude want no part of anarchy (having a false notion of it), that fact does not demean anarchy. The multitude simply do not know that, regardless of the route taken in the search for the rights of man, every route leads to anarchy. It cannot be otherwise; for either one accepts archy or one fights it and advances its opposite, anarchy. Something in between is unthinkable. [. . .]

The truth that government (archy) is instituted to exploit the poor is a truth the opponents of anarchy blink at; and, counting on the ignorance they have created in the masses, they adduce a hundred bagatelles in archy's favour. They emphasize crime. Were government and law abolished, they say, unpunished crime would peril life and property until chaos rendered existence disagreeable at best.

These sorcerers! In broad daylight they ascribe to anarchy aberrations of their society, when the basis of anarchy is the absence of such aberrations. All crimes— except misbehaviour of madmen, which, by definition, is the symptom of an illness—all crimes are notoriously the offspring of the system of private property, archy's reason for being. This system mandates a struggle for existence, by all, against all. Greed and the lust for power flourish in the propertied and goad the propertied to crimes that as a rule go unpunished because archy enforces its laws against another kind of 'crime': those deeds done out of necessity and in response to brutality. Turn the pages of the so-called civil law: the topic is 'yours and mine'; the civil law is the natural result of a society of individuals who want to cheat as much as possible because cheating is the only way to power and wealth. Today's society considers such behaviour normal.

Freedom and equality, the conditions of anarchy, would end this ruinous struggle for existence. [. . .] Law, purposeless, would no longer be needed, nor government [. . .] and they would disappear.

More important than the arguments of the archists are the arguments from a side that should have the least reason to oppose anarchy. Unconscious anarchists, particularly those called socialists, expend untold time and effort attacking anarchy, even though their goals are freedom and equality (anarchy). [. . .] These people maintain: anarchy is opposite to socialism. In truth, anarchy is socialism perfected. Because anarchists seek freedom for the individual—the greatest human happiness—other socialists say the anarchists contradict the brother-hood of man. As if the brotherhood of man did not presuppose the freedom of the individual! [. . .]

This wrongheadedness goes so far as to claim that the anarchists ignore tech-nology and favour cottage industry. [. . .] But [. . .] no anarchist wants to reverse technological advances; every anarchist wants more such advances. Accordingly, anarchists recognize, labour and production must be organized, their powers united. And since the lack of freedom today results from private property's control of the factors of production [. . .] those who want freedom (anarchy) want these things owned in common; that is, they want communism. [. . .]

Contrary to the old-style communists, however, the anarchists declare for the organization with the greatest validity, federalism. [. . .] From it, 'over-and under' structure—that is, authority concentrated in economic and political hierarchies, and power centralized in the state—would be excluded. Instead, voluntary association would give rise to thousands of special organizations, interconnected horizontally according to purpose or necessity. [. . .]

Organization is paramount. Indeed, the enemies of the proletariat are so well organized, so unified, that the proletariat commit crime by not gathering all forces and directing them at once at the destruction of the status quo by all possible means. For whether the propertied and ruling classes call themselves conservative or liberal, clerical or free-thinking, protectionist or free-trade, aristocrat or democrat, imperialist or republican—their differences hinder them not from seeing themselves as the propertied against the unpropertied. [. . .] Nor should be overlooked the monstrous police, military, and legal apparatus that stands at the disposal of the bourgeoisie. Nor should be forgotten the machinations of the black constabulary of priests and the reactionary press; the bourgeoisie can turn them to its purpose, too. [. . .]

If the rich stick together, why can't the poor stick together? Unfortunately, the cause of discord among those who should be of one heart and a single mind, and who need the profoundest of unity to achieve victory, is nothing but fear of the word anarchy. Yet all that a socialist has to get rid of, to be an anarchist, is the idea of the political state, to which socialists who are terrified hold fast, even though Marx and Engels taught that in a truly free society, the state would wither away.

What is the supreme joy of mankind? It is the greatest freedom possible, i.e., the opportunity to realize intellectual and physical potential. Of course, such freedom must not go beyond the point at which it hurts someone, for then a domination of some by others occurs. At the same time, in a civilized society, many goals are not attainable by individuals; they can be reached only by associations with a common purpose. But is that to say: a system must exist in which an individual has by dictate to exist tucked away in the bureau of a centralized state, put there by a higher power and told what to do from birth to death? [. . .]

What is needed to produce a system in which the freedom of one and all is guaranteed is simply an agreement for a free society! No need for a Providence directing from above; it is only necessary that things are handled correctly from below. [. . .]

What is the issue? Is it not whether besides society a state is needed? The answer, you see, is simpler than many think. We need only imagine what the state has been hitherto. Is it natural, an eternal verity? It is a creature of circumstance, used by a clique to dominate the masses. Let us therefore smash the state to bits. [. . .] Nothing less must be the climax of the Revolution.

---

3   William Morris, letter to *Commonweal* (18 May 1889)

In answer to our comrade Blackwell's suggestion and in default of someone else beginning that free discussion he speaks of, I wish to note down a few thoughts suggested by reading the clauses of the Anarchist Congress at Valentia, as stated by our comrade; premising that I do so in no polemical spirit, but simply by giving my own thoughts and hopes for the future for what they may be worth.[4]

I will begin by saying that I call myself a Communist, and have no wish to qualify that word by joining any other to it. The aim of Communism seems to me to be the complete equality of condition for all people; and anything in a Socialist direction which stops short of this is merely a compromise with the present condition of society, a halting-place on the road to the goal. This is the only logical outcome of any society which is other than a close company sustained by violence for the express purpose of 'exploitation of man by man' in the interest of the strongest. Our present 'society' dominated by capitalism, the society of contract, is a form of this class-society which has been forced upon those who hold the slave ideal by the growth of knowledge and the acquirement by man of mastery over the forces of nature. The history of 'society' since the fall of feudalism has been the gradual freeing of class or slave-society from the fetters of superstition, so that it might develop naturally within its prescribed limits of 'exploitation of man by man,' and that stupendous and marvellously rapid growth in power and resources of modern slave-society is due to this shaking off of superstition.

Communism also will have to keep itself free of superstition. Its ethics will have to be based on the recognition of natural cause and effect, and not on rules derived from a priori ideas of the relation of man to the universe or some imagined ruler of it; and from these two things, the equality of condition and the recognition of the cause and effect of material nature, will grow all Communistic life. So far I think I can see clearly; but when I try to picture to myself the forms which that life will take, I confess I am at fault, and I think we must all be so. Most people who

---

[4] In the 13 Apr. 1889 edition of *Commonweal*, James Blackwell, an anarchist comrade in the Socialist League, had written a letter to initiate a discussion of 'communist anarchism', and quoted with sympathy some of the resolutions passed at the Anarchist Congress in Valencia, Spain. See the editors' notes below for further details.

can be said to think at all are now beginning to see that the realization of Social-ism is certain; although many can see no further than a crude and incomplete State Socialism, which very naturally repels many from Socialism altogether. All genuine Socialists admit that Communism is the necessary development of Socialism; but I repeat, further than this all must be speculative; and surely in speculating on the future of society we should try to shake ourselves clear of mere phrases: especially as many of them will cease to have a meaning when the change comes that we all of us long for. And here I join issue with our Anarchist-Communist friends, who are somewhat authoritative on the matter of authority, and not a little vague also. For if freedom from authority means the assertion of the advisability or possibility of an individual man doing what he pleases always and under all circumstances, this is an absolute negation of society, and makes Communism as the highest expression of society impossible; but when you begin to qualify this assertion of the right to do as you please by adding 'as long as you don't interfere with other people's rights to do the same,' the exercise of some kind of authority becomes necessary. If individuals are not to coerce others, there must somewhere be an authority which is prepared to coerce them not to coerce; and that authority must clearly be collective. And there are other difficulties besides this crudest and most obvious one.

The bond of Communistic society will be voluntary in the sense that all people will agree in its broad principles when it is fairly established, and will trust to it as affording mankind the best kind of life possible. But while we are advocating equality of condition—i.e. due opportunity free to everyone for the satisfaction of his needs—do not let us forget the necessary (and beneficent) variety of tempera-ment, capacity and desires which exists amongst men about everything outside the region of the merest necessaries; and though many, or, if you will, most of these different desires could be satisfied without the individual clashing with collective society, some of them could not be. Any community conceivable will sometimes determine on collective action which, without being in itself immoral or oppressive, would give pain to some of its members; and what is to be done then if it happens to be a piece of business which must be either done or left alone? would the small minority have to give way or the large majority? A con-crete example will be of use here, especially as it affects my temperament. I have always believed that the realization of Socialism would give us an opportunity of escaping from that grievous flood of utilitarianism which the full development of the society of contract has cursed us with; but that would be in the long run only; and I think it quite probable that in the early days of Socialism the reflex of the terror of starvation, which so oppresses us now, would drive us into excesses of utilitarianism. Indeed, there is a school of Socialists now extant who worship utilitarianism with a fervour of fatuity which is perhaps a natural consequence of their assumption of practicality. So that it is not unlikely that the public opinion of a community would be in favour of cutting down all the timber in England, and turning the country into a big Bonanza farm or a market-garden under glass. And in such a case what could we do? who objected 'for the sake of life to cast away the reasons for living,' when we had exhausted our powers of argument? Clearly we should have to submit to authority. And a little reflection will show us many such cases in which the collective authority will weigh down individual opposition, however reasonable, without a hope for its being able to assert itself immediately; in such matters there must be give and take: and the objectors would have to give up the lesser for the greater. In short, experience shows us that wherever a dozen thoughtful men shall meet together there will be twelve different opinions on any subject which is not a dry matter of fact (and often on that too); and if those twelve men want to act together, there must be give and take between them, and they must agree on some common rule of conduct to act as a bond between them, or leave their business undone. And what is this common bond but authority—that is, the conscience of the association voluntarily accepted in the first instance.

Furthermore, when we talk of the freedom of the individual man, we must not forget that every man is a very complex animal, made up of many different moods and impulses; no man is always wise, or wise in all respects. Philip sober needs protection against Philip drunk, or he may chance to wake up from his booze in a nice mess. Surely we all of us feel that there is a rascal or two in each of our skins besides the other or two who want to lead manly and honourable lives, and do we not want something to appeal to on behalf of those better selves of ours? and that something is made up of the aspirations of our better selves, and this is the social conscience without which there can be no true society, and which even a false society is forced to imitate, and so have a sham social conscience—what we sometimes call hypocrisy.

Now I don't want to be misunderstood. I am not pleading for any form of arbitrary or unreasonable authority, but for a public conscience as a rule of action: and by all means let us have the least possible exercise of authority. I suspect that many of our Communist-Anarchist friends do really mean that, when they pronounce against all authority. And with equality of condition assured for all men, and our ethics based on reason, I cannot think that we need fear the growth of a new authority taking the place of the one which we should have destroyed, and which we must remember is based on the assumption that equality is impossible and that slavery is an essential condition of human society. By the time it is assumed that all men's needs must be satisfied according [to] the measure of the common wealth, what may be called the political side of the question would take care of itself.

4   'Anarchist', letter to *Commonweal* (22 June 1889)

William Morris, in continuing the discussion initiated by comrade Blackwell, says, 'When you begin to qualify this assertion of the right to do as you please by adding "as long as you don't interfere with other people's rights to do the same," the exercise of some kind of authority becomes necessary.' If by 'authority' comrade Morris merely means, what also he thinks the Communist-Anarchists mean, a public conscience, I, individually, should have no objection to his statement. But in these discussions the word should, I think, be given a more restricted meaning. It should mean, in my opinion, the authority of compulsory representative institutions, such as parliaments, county and municipal councils, school boards, etc. With this meaning I should deny the necessity for the exercise of authority.

Very clearly there are two kinds of association, the voluntary and the compulsory; exemplified, the one by trade unions and the other by government, whether representative or otherwise; the one supported by voluntary contributions, the other by rates and taxes, neither more nor less than a compulsory service rendered to those who have the power to compel it. Of these two forms of association it is necessary, I think, to make a choice. The society of the future must be either of one or the other. If completely free, then it seems absurd to advocate parliamentary methods for its realisation. Our business should be to begin the destruction of the compulsory kind of association at once in all its forms; to withdraw from elections and to rely solely upon voluntary society. This free association is the only guarantee of the due observance of our equal liberty, now as in the future, and much might be done to hasten the advent of Anarchy, which is the final hope of even the State Socialists themselves, by a greater insistence on the rigid observance of this principle under existing conditions, and none the less because they are economically bad. Taking this course, we may reasonably hope that by the time all forms of compulsion, economic and political, which are at present the all-important ones, are ended, the William Morrisses of the future will not be called upon to endure the uglinesses of an excess of utilitarianism.

5   'The Explosion in Greenwich Park' and
     'Bourdin's Antecedents', *The Times* (17 February 1894)

(From Our Special Correspondent)

It is not surprising that the police authorities should be reticent with regard to the extent of their knowledge concerning the explosion in Greenwich Park on Thursday afternoon. Their position is that while Parliament is sitting it is their duty to give to the Home Office such information as may be at their disposal, while it is the duty of the Home Secretary to exercise his discretion and to give to the public, through the House of Commons, such information as may seem to him advisable from the point of view of the public interest. The answer of the Home Secretary in the House of Commons last night may be taken to express his opinion that the knowledge presumably in the hands of the police ought not, for the present at any rate, to be made public. Some things, however, are certain, and amongst them is the fact that Martial Bourdin, the man who died in the Seamen's Hospital at Greenwich on Thursday, was in his lifetime an Anarchist and the well-known associate of Anarchists in their English headquarters in the neighbourhood of Tottenham-court-road.[5] The plain facts told below will, it is believed, go far to prove that the vigilance shown by the police in watching the foreign Anarchists in London lately has terrified those against whom that vigilance was directed; that Bourdin, one of the most intrepid spirits among them, having been notoriously indigent a day or two before he came to his death, was provided with funds wherewith to escape from this country; that when he entered Greenwich Park on Thursday afternoon he was not merely seeking out a place in which to hide a store of explosives of the most dangerous character, but was armed with a carefully-manufactured bomb, fragments of which were eventually lodged in his own person. Whether his actual intention was to blow up the Conservatory at Greenwich or not is one of those questions which can be judged from probabilities only, since the person who could have spoken with certainty upon the point is dead; but the facts certainly show that he intended some serious mischief when he entered Greenwich Park; and the path which he followed, a narrow, zigzag, and secluded path, leads practically nowhere except to the Observatory.

The facts actually known are these:—Martial Bourdin, an out-of-work French tailor, who has been in America and was a well-known member of the dovecote of Anarchists having the Autonomie Club as its headquarters, was discovered at exactly a quarter to 5 rather less than half-way up the zigzag path referred to. To

---

[5] *The Times* greatly overstates both Bourdin's and the Autonomie Club's significance to the international anarchist movement.

find this path it is necessary only to enter the park by the main entrance at the bottom of Royal-hill, and to pursue the straight avenue leading upwards from that gate until the Observatory appears directly upon the left at the top of a knoll. Up that knoll in the manner described runs the path and at about the second corner from the bottom Bourdin was found by Sullivan, one of the park-keepers who had been attracted by the sound of the explosion. When found he was kneeling on the ground in a pool of blood, with his body slanting backwards, but his head bowed forward upon his chest. He cried or moaned, in good English but with a French accent, 'Take me home', but when interrogated as to his address he was unable to do more than repeat the words he had already uttered. He was, of course, treated with humanity. Sullivan held him up by the arms, while another keeper went for the nearest doctor, and some of the officials at the Observatory brought brandy. But the doctor, when he came, seeing clearly that the case was hopeless, could do nothing more than order the immediate removal of the man to the Seamen's Hospital below.

The spot where Bourdin was found, albeit only 60 or 70 yards from the Observatory, was not the place where the explosion took place. For some 20 yards more up the tortuous path, at a point nearer to the Observatory by some ten yards in a direct line—for the direction of the path to and fro must be taken into consideration—the path was soaked with blood and the railings which border it were spattered with portions of flesh. Bourdin, therefore, was dangerously near the Observatory when the infernal machine which he carried exploded.

Still living, but apparently unconscious—so senseless, indeed, that one of his bearers believed him to be dead—Bourdin was carried down towards the Seamen's Hospital, and such was the general horror of the scene that the park-keepers may readily be forgiven for the exaggeration which appears to have coloured their description of his wounds, for, as a matter of plain fact, his body was not ripped and torn in the manner which has been described, although the wounds were terrible enough. Just before the park gate was reached the stretcher was lowered, Sullivan moistened the wretched man's lips with brandy, and the eyes opened. But that was all. He was then carried into the hospital, where the house-surgeon and Mr Smith did all that was in their power for him; but the case was hopeless, and notwithstanding statements to the effect that he opened his lips to say, 'I feel very cold,' the fact is that he died, exactly 50 minutes after the explosion had taken place, without saying another word.

Bourdin's clothes were handed over to the police, and it is stated upon the authority of a Press agency that they contained, in addition to something like £13 in money, directions concerning the proper combinations of explosive materials of the most dangerous quality, a card of membership of the Autonomie Club, a ball ticket securing admission to a ball to be given in support of Freedom next week, and sundry other documents. Upon this point it is impossible for me to speak with personal knowledge; but for the rest I speak only of that which I saw, and I trust that it may never be my duty to look again upon a sight so horrible. Bourdin's body lies on a slate slab in the underground mortuary of the Seamen's Hospital. It is that of a remarkably short man, 5ft. 1in. by measurement, well nourished, and proportioned, but inadequately developed. The man, said one competent to judge, could hardly have been more than 22. The hair and moustache are silky and fair: there is no beard; the eyes are blue. The left hand is absolutely gone. The right hand is small and delicate. Upon the trunk there is no wound at all until the abdominal region is reached. There on the right side of the body is a wound of considerable depth, and on the left side of the body are some smaller wounds with hard substances within. In the very centre of the body is a large wound, and on the thighs, particularly on the left side, are sundry wounds of a sufficiently serious character, but not sufficiently maiming to prevent the man from staggering backwards, with his right hand clutching the railings, down the hill to the place at which he was found, kneeling and facing the Observatory, by Sullivan. It was the wound in the centre of the body which was the most certain cause of death, for that wound went absolutely through to the back, close to the spine.

From this wound, late yesterday afternoon, dropped an all-important piece of iron; which put an end completely to any theory that this was an accidental explosion of materials intended to be hidden out of harm's way, and showed it to be a premature explosion of an infernal machine deliberately constructed to work out an infernal purpose. It was a curved piece of iron, with five parallel grooves upon the inner side, roughly cast upon the outside, and splashed with a streak of brass where, possibly, it had impinged upon a button of the man's garments before entering his body. The curve, if completed in a circle, would have on the inner side a space rather larger than that occupied by a penny piece. The ends were broken off roughly in a fresh fracture: the thickness of the iron was between an eighth and a quarter of an inch at the thickest part, and it tapered off at the smooth top, so to speak, in much the same manner as the lip of a stone bottle such as is used to contain ginger beer. Whether the curve of the bomb was part of an ellipse, it is impossible to say at present. Possibly the fragments, which are undoubtedly contained within the body, and which will be brought to light when the *post mortem* is made, may fill up the curve; but among the few persons who have seen the fragment there exists little doubt that this piece of iron, with its freshly broken ends, was part of the neck of the bomb which killed Bourdin.

For the rest, there is little or nothing to be said. The police are using anxious care in investigation, and Colonel Majendio has, in due course, visited the scene

of the explosion in order to make such inquiries as may be necessary towards discovering the exact nature of the explosive used; but the inquest will not be held
until Monday next in all probability, and it is not reasonable to expect specific
information on this point before that date.

'BOURDIN'S ANTECEDENTS'

The Press Association yesterday had an interview with the brother of Martial
Bourdin. M. Henri Bourdin is a tailor by occupation, and rents a small workshop
at 18, Great Tichfield Street, W.C. He is a small, demure-looking man, of fair
complexion and frail physique, and in height and build is said greatly to resemble
the dead man. 'This event,' said M. Henri Bourdin, 'is a terrible shock to me and
to other members of my family. My brother Martial was a quiet and reserved man,
and never conversed with me about any but the most trifling things. He had
numerous references from his employers describing him as a good workman and
quite honest. I had no idea that he was in any way, either here or abroad, associated with societies holding extreme political views. My brother was 26 years of
age, and was born in Tours.[6] He was a tailor, but had, unfortunately, been out of
work. Occasionally he visited me for the purpose of obtaining work. I last saw him
about noon yesterday when he entered my workshop and told me he had no work
to do. I told him I could not help him, for at present I had nothing to do myself.
He did not ask for money, and I had noticed that, whenever on previous occasions he has visited me, he has had at least a small sum of money in his possession.
He was a bachelor, and whenever he had work he could earn very good wages. I
do not know why he should have gone to Greenwich. So far as I am aware, he had
no friends there. He occasionally attended political gatherings in this neighbourhood, and sometimes listened to political lectures; but he never said anything to
me to lead me to suppose that he held Anarchist views. I do not think he believed
much in politics, but he was very reticent. I brought my brother over to England
about six years ago, but subsequently he returned to Paris. He recrossed to
London, and then went to America. I know nothing of his life in the States. He
returned from America to France, and came over again to London about four
months ago.'

---

[6] A town in the Loire area of western France.

6   from Emma Goldman, 'Anarchism: What it Really Stands For' (1911)

Anarchy

Ever reviled, accursed, ne'er understood,
  Thou art the grisly terror of our age.
'Wreck of all order,' cry the multitude,
  'Art thou, and war and murder's endless rage.'
O, let them cry. To them that ne'er have striven
  The truth that lies behind a word to find,
To them the word's right meaning was not given.
  They shall continue blind among the blind.
But thou, O word, so clear, so strong, so pure,
  Thou sayest all which I for goal have taken.
I give thee to the future! Thine secure
  When each at least unto himself shall waken.
Come it in sunshine? In the tempest's thrill?
  I cannot tell—but it the earth shall see!
I am an Anarchist! Wherefore I will
  Not rule, and also ruled I will not be!

John Henry Mackay[7]

The history of human growth and development is at the same time the history of the terrible struggle of every new idea heralding the approach of a brighter dawn. In its tenacious hold on tradition, the Old has never hesitated to make use of the foulest and cruellest means to stay the advent of the New, in whatever form or period the latter may have asserted itself. Nor need we retrace our steps into the distant past to realize the enormity of opposition, difficulties, and hardships placed in the path of every progressive idea. The rack, the thumbscrew, and the knout are still with us; so are the convict's garb and the social wrath, all conspiring against the spirit that is serenely marching on.

Anarchism could not hope to escape the fate of all other ideas of innovation. Indeed, as the most revolutionary and uncompromising innovator, Anarchism must needs meet with the combined ignorance and venom of the world it aims to reconstruct.

To deal even remotely with all that is being said and done against Anarchism would necessitate the writing of a whole volume. I shall therefore meet only two of the principal objections. In so doing, I shall attempt to elucidate what Anarchism really stands for. [. . .]

---

[7] Mackay (1864–1913) was a German Scottish individualist anarchist, poet, and writer.

What, then, are the objections? First, Anarchism is impractical, though a beautiful ideal. Second, Anarchism stands for violence and destruction, hence it must be repudiated as vile and dangerous. Both the intelligent man and the ignorant mass judge not from a thorough knowledge of the subject, but either from hearsay or false interpretation.

A practical scheme, says Oscar Wilde, is either one already in existence, or a scheme that could be carried out under the existing conditions; but it is exactly the existing conditions that one objects to, and any scheme that could accept these conditions is wrong and foolish.[8] The true criterion of the practical, therefore, is not whether the latter can keep intact the wrong or foolish; rather it is whether the scheme has vitality enough to leave the stagnant waters of the old, and build, as well as sustain, new life. In the light of this conception, Anarchism is indeed practical. More than any other idea, it is helping to do away with the wrong and foolish; more than any other idea, it is building and sustaining new life.

The emotions of the ignorant man are continuously kept at a pitch by the most blood-curdling stories about Anarchism. Not a thing too outrageous to be employed against this philosophy and its exponents. Therefore Anarchism represents to the unthinking what the proverbial bad man does to the child,— a black monster bent on swallowing everything; in short, destruction and violence.

Destruction and violence! How is the ordinary man to know that the most violent element in society is ignorance; that its power of destruction is the very thing Anarchism is combating? Nor is he aware that Anarchism, whose roots, as it were, are part of nature's forces, destroys, not healthful tissue, but parasitic growths that feed on the life's essence of society. It is merely clearing the soil from weeds and sagebrush, that it may eventually bear healthy fruit.

Someone has said that it requires less mental effort to condemn than to think. The widespread mental indolence, so prevalent in society, proves this to be only too true. Rather than go to the bottom of any given idea, to examine into its origin and meaning, most people will either condemn it altogether, or rely on some superficial or prejudicial definition of non-essentials.

Anarchism urges man to think, to investigate, to analyze every proposition; but that the brain capacity of the average reader be not taxed too much, I also shall begin with a definition, and then elaborate on the latter.

anarchism:—The philosophy of a new social order based on liberty unrestricted by man-made law; the theory that all forms of government rest on violence, and are therefore wrong and harmful, as well as unnecessary.

---

[8] A reference to Oscar Wilde's *Soul of Man Under Socialism* (see Ch. 7 above), which could just as readily have been included in this chapter.

The new social order rests, of course, on the materialistic basis of life; but while all Anarchists agree that the main evil today is an economic one, they maintain that the solution of that evil can be brought about only through the consideration of every phase of life,—individual, as well as the collective; the internal, as well as the external phases. [. . .]

Religion, the dominion of the human mind; Property, the dominion of human needs; and Government, the dominion of human conduct, represent the stronghold of man's enslavement and all the horrors it entails. Religion! How it dominates man's mind, how it humiliates and degrades his soul. God is everything, man is nothing, says religion. But out of that nothing God has created a kingdom so despotic, so tyrannical, so cruel, so terribly exacting that naught but gloom and tears and blood have ruled the world since gods began. Anarchism rouses man to rebellion against this black monster. Break your mental fetters, says Anarchism to man, for not until you think and judge for yourself will you get rid of the dominion of darkness, the greatest obstacle to all progress. [. . .]

'Property is robbery,' said the great French Anarchist Proudhon.[9] Yes, but without risk and danger to the robber. Monopolizing the accumulated efforts of man, property has robbed him of his birthright, and has turned him loose a pauper and an outcast. [. . .]

Real wealth consists in things of utility and beauty, in things that help to create strong, beautiful bodies and surroundings inspiring to live in. But if man is doomed to wind cotton around a spool, or dig coal, or build roads for thirty years of his life, there can be no talk of wealth. What he gives to the world is only gray and hideous things, reflecting a dull and hideous existence,—too weak to live, too cowardly to die. [. . .]

Anarchism cannot but repudiate such a method of production: its goal is the freest possible expression of all the latent powers of the individual. Oscar Wilde defines a perfect personality as 'one who develops under perfect conditions, who is not wounded, maimed, or in danger.'[10] A perfect personality, then, is only possible in a state of society where man is free to choose the mode of work, the conditions of work, and the freedom to work. One to whom the making of a table, the building of a house, or the tilling of the soil, is what the painting is to the artist and the discovery to the scientist,—the result of inspiration, of intense longing, and deep interest in work as a creative force. That being the ideal of Anarchism, its economic arrangements must consist of voluntary productive and distributive associations, gradually developing into free communism, as the best means of producing with the least waste of human energy. Anarchism, however, also recognizes the right of the individual, or numbers of individuals, to

<hr/>

[9] Pierre Joseph Prondhon (1809–65), a French socialist who came to be regarded as the 'father' of international anarchism. His *Qu'est-ce que La propriété?* was published in 1840.

[10] Another reference to Wilde's *Soul of Man Under Socialism*.

arrange at all times for other forms of work, in harmony with their tastes and desires.

Such free display of human energy being possible only under complete individual and social freedom, Anarchism directs its forces against the third and greatest foe of all social equality; namely, the State, organized authority, or statutory law,—the dominion of human conduct.

Just as religion has fettered the human mind, and as property, or the monopoly of things, has subdued and stifled man's needs, so has the State enslaved his spirit, dictating every phase of conduct. 'All government in essence,' says Emerson, 'is tyranny.'[11] It matters not whether it is government by divine right or majority rule. In every instance its aim is the absolute subordination of the individual. [. . .]

The most absurd apology for authority and law is that they serve to diminish crime. Aside from the fact that the State is itself the greatest criminal, breaking every written and natural law, stealing in the form of taxes, killing in the form of war and capital punishment, it has come to an absolute standstill in coping with crime. It has failed utterly to destroy or even minimize the horrible scourge of its own creation.

Crime is naught but misdirected energy. So long as every institution of today, economic, political, social, and moral, conspires to misdirect human energy into wrong channels; so long as most people are out of place doing the things they hate to do, living a life they loathe to live, crime will be inevitable, and all the laws on the statutes can only increase, but never do away with, crime. [. . .]

Anarchism, then, really stands for the liberation of the human mind from the dominion of religion; the liberation of the human body from the dominion of property; liberation from the shackles and restraint of government. Anarchism stands for a social order based on the free grouping of individuals for the purpose of producing real social wealth; an order that will guarantee to every human being free access to the earth and full enjoyment of the necessities of life, according to individual desires, tastes, and inclinations. [. . .]

Will it not lead to a revolution? Indeed, it will. No real social change has ever come about without a revolution. People are either not familiar with their history, or they have not yet learned that revolution is but thought carried into action.

Anarchism, the great leaven of thought, is today permeating every phase of human endeavour. Science, art, literature, the drama, the effort for economic betterment, in fact every individual and social opposition to the existing disorder of things, is illumined by the spiritual light of Anarchism. It is the philosophy of the

[11] Ralph Waldo Emerson (1803–82), American transcendentalist essayist and poet who inspired many anarchists.

sovereignty of the individual. It is the theory of social harmony. It is the great, surging, living truth that is reconstructing the world, and that will usher in the Dawn.

EDITORS' NOTES

1. Peter Kropotkin (1842–1921) was a Russian prince who became one of the leading exponents of communistic anarchism in France and in England. He was imprisoned in Russia in 1874 for handing out anarchist propaganda to peasants and workers. Escaping in 1876 he joined an international anarchist society, the Jurassic Federation. Subsequently settling in France, in 1883 he was sentenced to five years in gaol for his anarchist activism. He was released after three years, and lived and worked in England for the next three decades. Whilst in England he edited the anarchist journal *Freedom* from 1886 to 1907. He returned to Russia after the Bolshevik Revolution of 1917, but took no part in Soviet political life. Central to Kropotkin's communist anarchism, clearly demonstrated here in his response to the Paris Commune of 1871, is a belief that all forms of government must be abandoned in favour of a federation of communistic societies operating on the principle of mutual aid and co-operation rather than through governmental institutions. He was vehemently anti-parliamentarian and anti-statist.

2. Johann [John] Most (1846–1906) was a German bookbinder, then a Social Democrat deputy in parliament, and finally a social revolutionary and anarchist. Imprisoned for his revolutionary activities in 1878, he was released after five months and expelled from Berlin whence he travelled to London as a political refugee. In London he set up and edited the most influential German anarchist newspaper of the late nineteenth century, *Freiheit* (1879–1910), which was distributed from Britain from 1879 to 1882. Most left London for the USA in 1882, where he spent the rest of his life lecturing and making speeches in the cause of anarchism. He was repeatedly imprisoned for his anarchist activism and was refused US citizenship. Most is an important representative of militant anarchism: he was a chief advocate of so-called 'propaganda by the deed' whereby acts of individual violence (including murder) were urged to raise the political profile of the anarchist movement. Most met Kropotkin in the USA in 1897 and 1901; William Morris supported Most when the latter was persecuted by the Liberal government of 1891 for praising the assassins of Tsar Alexander II in *Freiheit*. Emma Goldman spoke at Most's memorial in Grand Central Palace, New York City, on 1 April 1906 after his death in March of that year.

3 and 4. William Morris (1834–96) is here responding to James Blackwell's enthusiastic quotations from the resolutions passed at the Anarchist Congress in Valentia, Spain, published in a letter to *Commonweal* on 13 April 1889. The resolutions included:

1. By Anarchism we understand a social state in which there is no necessity for government [. . .] Whilst the principle of authority exists, there will be no guarantee for the

liberty of all members of society. The principle of authority [. . .] always degenerates into tyranny. [. . .]

2. Since we recognize that a society will never be completely Anarchist whilst there remains in it the least authoritarianism or subjection, we must also recognize as a guarantee of liberty the abolition of the principle of private property and of the exploitation of man by man. [. . .]

Subsequent responses to Morris's letter include the one presented here from an anonymous 'anarchist' who tries to persuade Morris that his own position is akin to that of the communist anarchists (never entirely the case). Morris's utopian society of the future presented in his *News from Nowhere* (1890) does, though, seem to have been partially shaped by communist-anarchist thought of the period.

For a biographical note on Morris see Chapter 7.

5. Martial Bourdin (1867–94), an out-of-work tailor, was a French member of the anarchist Autonomie Club in London who blew himself up on his way to destroy (it was supposed) the Royal Observatory at Greenwich. Although this incident both attracted and appalled the fevered political imagination of late Victorian London, Bourdin was not a significant figure: he is not even mentioned in Max Nettlau's encyclopedic *Short History of Anarchism* (1934). Nettlau (1865–1944), himself a communist anarchist, was a member of the Socialist League in London in the 1890s and would have known about the Bourdin incident, which he clearly did not think worthy of comment. Bourdin's death did, though, elicit a memorial essay in *Commonweal* (the official journal of the Socialist League) on 10 March 1894, as well as this report from *The Times*.

6. Emma Goldman (1869–1940), a Russian anarchist who emigrated to the USA in 1885, where she worked in close association with the Polish-born anarchist Alexander Berkman (1870–1936). She was imprisoned in New York City in 1893 for incitement to riot. Released in 1894 she lectured in Europe, and also undertook regular lecture tours in the USA. From 1906 to 1917 she edited and published *Mother Earth*, an anarchist monthly. Imprisoned in the USA once more in 1917 for trying to violate the US conscription laws (she was a pacifist in the First World War), she and Berkman were deported to Russia on their release in 1919. At first she admired the Soviet regime, but later voiced vehement criticisms of its policies and was expelled from the country. Coming to Britain she married a Welsh miner in 1926, so becoming a British subject. During the Spanish Civil War (1936–9) she worked for the Spanish republican government in London and Madrid. She died in Toronto.

9

SCIENTIFIC NATURALISM

One of the most marked features of the fin de siècle is the authority given to science. Notions of developmental progress or degenerative and entropic decline insistently inform discussions of the individual, the city, and the nation-state, as we have seen. The wide currency of scientific thought in the late Victorian period is remarkable, given that before 1870 it was a marginal part of formal education, there was no state funding of science, and no conception of a scientific profession. The 'scientist' did not exist until the twentieth century, and knowledge had hitherto been organized through Classical and Christian sources.

The fin-de-siècle enthusiasm for translating all problems into scientific terminology was the product, in the main, of a group of brilliant workers in science, most of whom, after years of poorly paid teaching and hack journalism, finally moved into positions of power in the early 1870s. Through an endless stream of speeches, public disputes, books, Royal Commissions, and institutional restructurings, this group contested theological explanations of the natural world with an unapologetically secular scientific naturalism. The key statements of this group, which would dominate the intellectual sphere of the late Victorian period, include T. H. Huxley's *Lay Sermons* (1870), Darwin's *The Descent of Man* (1871), John Tyndall's *Fragments of Science* (1871), Edward Tylor's *Primitive Culture* (1871), Francis Galton's *Hereditary Genius* (1872), G. H. Lewes's *Problems of Life and Mind* (1875-9), and Herbert Spencer's 'synthetic philosophy', which he began in the 1860s and completed in 1897. The influential editors John Morley and Leslie Stephen were also part of the group, thus ensuring vectors of publication for their ideas. 'Scientific naturalism' was secular, rationalist, anti-clerical, and anti-authoritarian. It was monistic, arguing that all phenomena in the universe operated on determinable, mechanical laws,

rendering any supernatural intervention or 'spiritual' entities impossible. It was also thoroughly empiricist, arguing only from experience, dis-
missing as 'unknowable' any questions of metaphysics and first causes
and thus restricting legitimate knowledge to the phenomenal realm
(Huxley coined the term 'agnostic' for this position in 1869). The persistent locus of attack was 'natural theology', the subordination of natural
knowledge to a religious frame—a position that was still rigorously
argued by many prominent figures well into the 1890s, whether
scientists like Sir William Thomson (Lord Kelvin) or the politicians
William Gladstone and Arthur Balfour. It is important to emphasize,
then, that this is not a chapter on 'science' but on a specific scientific
ideology.

Our selections include early influential statements of scientific naturalism, including the most famously provocative utterance, Tyndall's
'Belfast Address', with its declaration that 'all religious theories must
submit to the control of science, and relinquish all thought of controlling
it'. Tyndall, a Protestant Irishman, was declaring war on the Catholic
authorities that had refused to include physical sciences in the university
syllabus—Tyndall's speech caused a major outcry across the country,
and produced an enormous volume of responses. Reading these early
texts, however, it is important to note how anxious Huxley, Clifford,
and Tyndall are to differentiate their naturalism from the 'bugbear' of
materialism, which tended to be associated with godless, revolutionary
European thought.

The two later selections, from the 1890s, show significant
changes. Karl Pearson's *Grammar of Science* remained a popular
assertion of the value of scientific thought into the 1930s. Science is now
discussed in terms of government funding and universal education;
it is also tied to questions of responsible citizenship. Although Pearson
argues that scientific thinking allows citizens disinterested objectivity
to exercise their newly ascribed democratic rights, the reader is
invited to turn to Pearson's contributions to eugenic thought in the
last chapter of this anthology to reflect on just how ideological this
form of 'scientific naturalism' had become. Indeed, the attempt to
'shape' society according to the strict laws of evolution in the thinking of
either eugenicists or socialist thinkers led Huxley to part company
from the majority of his fellow scientific naturalists in his last major
lecture, *Evolution and Ethics* in 1893. The ageing Huxley now pitted
humanity and its fragile systems of ethics and community against a
harsh and indifferent 'cosmic process'; gone was the utopian promise
of organizing society in harmony with the laws that scientific thought
had articulated.

Secondary reading: Barton, 'The X-Club' and 'John Tyndall, Pantheist'; Cardwell; Desmond; Lightman *Origins of Agnosticism* and *Victorian Science*; Nye; Paradis; Postlethwaite; Turner, *Between Science and Religion* and *Contesting Cultural Authority*.

---

1 from T. H. Huxley, 'On the Physical Basis of Life' (1870)

Let us suppose that knowledge is absolute, and not relative, and therefore, that our conception of matter represents that which it really is. Let us suppose, further, that we do not know more of cause and effect than a certain definite order of succession among facts, and that we have a knowledge of the necessity of that succession—and hence, of necessary laws—and I for my part, do not see what escape there is from utter materialism and necessarianism. For it is obvious that our knowledge of what we call the material world is, to begin with, at least as certain and definite as that of the spiritual world, and that our acquaintance with law is of as old a date as our knowledge of spontaneity. Further, I take it to be demonstrable that it is utterly impossible to prove that anything whatever may not be the effect of a material and necessary cause, and that human logic is equally incompetent to prove that any act is really spontaneous. A really spontaneous act is one which, by the assumption, has no cause; and the attempt to prove such a negative as this is, on the face of the matter, absurd. And while it is thus a philosophical impossibility to demonstrate that any given phenomenon is not the effect of a material cause, any one who is acquainted with the history of science will admit, that its progress has, in all ages, meant, and now, more than ever, means, the extension of the province of what we call matter and causation, and the concomitant gradual banishment from all regions of human thought of what we call spirit and spontaneity.

I have endeavoured [. . .] to give you a conception of the direction towards which modern physiology is tending; and I ask you, what is the difference between the conception of life as the product of a certain disposition of material molecules, and the old notion of an Archaeus governing and directing blind matter within each living body, except this—that here, as elsewhere, matter and law have devoured spirit and spontaneity? And as surely as every future grows out of past and present, so will the physiology of the future gradually extend the realm of matter and law until it is co-extensive with knowledge, with feeling, and with action.

The consciousness of this great truth weighs like a nightmare, I believe, upon many of the best minds of these days. They watch what they conceive to be the progress of materialism, in such fear and powerless anger as a savage feels, when, during an eclipse, the great shadow creeps over the face of the sun. The advancing tide of matter threatens to drown their souls; the tightening grasp of law impedes their freedom; they are alarmed lest man's moral nature be debased by the increase of wisdom.

If the 'New Philosophy' be worthy of the reprobation with which it is visited, I confess their fears seem to me to be well founded. While, on the contrary, could David Hume be consulted, I think he would smile at their perplexities, and chide them for doing even as the heathen, and falling down in terror before the hideous idols their own hands have raised.[1]

For, after all, what do we know of this terrible 'matter,' except as a name for the unknown and hypothetical cause of states of our own consciousness? And what do we know of that 'spirit' over whose threatened extinction by matter a great lamentation is arising, like that which was heard at the death of Pan, except that it is also a name for an unknown and hypothetical cause, or condition, of states of consciousness? In other words, matter and spirit are but names for the imaginary sub-strata of groups of natural phenomena.

And what is the dire necessity and 'iron' law under which men groan? Truly, most gratuitously invented bugbears. I suppose if there be an 'iron' law, it is that of gravitation; and if there be a physical necessity, it is that a stone, unsupported, must fall to the ground. But what is all we really know, and can know, about the latter phenomenon? Simply, that, in human experience, stones have fallen to the ground under these conditions; that we have not the smallest reason for believing that any stone so circumstanced will not fall to the ground; and that we have, on the contrary, every reason to believe that it will so fall. It is very convenient to indicate that all the conditions of belief have been fulfilled in this case, by calling the statement that unsupported stones will fall to the ground, 'a law of nature.' But when, as commonly happens, we change *will* into *must*, we introduce an idea of necessity which most assuredly does not lie in the observed facts, and has no warranty that I can discover elsewhere. For my part, I utterly repudiate and anathematize the intruder. Fact I know; and Law I know; but what is this Necessity, save an empty shadow of my own mind's throwing?

But if it is certain that we can have no knowledge of the nature of either matter or spirit, and that the notion of necessity is something illegitimately thrust into the perfectly legitimate conception of law, the materialistic position that there is nothing in the world but matter, force, and necessity, is as utterly devoid of justification as the most baseless of theological dogmas. The fundamental doctrines of materialism, like those of spiritualism, and most other 'isms,' lie outside 'the

---

[1]   David Hume (1711–76), Scottish philosopher, whose sceptical, secular method for the foundation of a science of man was a major influence on Huxley. Hume's refutation of miracles was constantly invoked by Victorian scientific naturalists.

limits of philosophical inquiry,' and David Hume's great service to humanity is his irrefragable demonstration of what these limits are. [. . .]

If a man asks me what the politics of the inhabitants of the moon are, and I reply that I do not know; that neither I, nor any one else, have any means of knowing; and that, under these circumstances, I decline to trouble myself about the subject at all, I do not think he has any right to call me a sceptic. [. . .]

Why trouble ourselves about matters of which, however important they may be, we do know nothing, and can know nothing? We live in a world which is full of misery and ignorance, and the plain duty of each and all of us is to try to make the little corner he can influence somewhat less miserable and somewhat less ignorant than it was before he entered it. To do this effectually it is necessary to be fully possessed of only two beliefs: the first, that the order of nature is ascertainable by our faculties to an extent which is practically unlimited; the second, that our volition counts for something as a condition of the course of events.

Each of these beliefs can be verified experimentally, as often as we like to try. Each, therefore, stands upon the strongest foundation upon which any belief can rest, and forms one of our highest truths. If we find that the ascertainment of the order of nature is facilitated by using one terminology, or one set of symbols, rather than another, it is our clear duty to use the former; and no harm can accrue, so long as we bear in mind, that we are dealing merely with terms and symbols.

In itself it is of little moment whether we express the phenomena of matter in terms of spirit; or the phenomena of spirit, in terms of matter: matter may be regarded as a form of thought, thought may be regarded as a property of matter— each statement has a certain relative truth. But with a view to the progress of science, the materialistic terminology is in every way to be preferred. For it connects thought with the other phenomena of the universe, and suggests inquiry into the nature of those physical conditions, or concomitants of thought, which are more or less accessible to us, and a knowledge which may, in future, help us to exercise the same kind of control over the world of thought, as we already possess in respect of the material world; whereas, the alternative, or spiritualistic, terminology is utterly barren, and leads to nothing but obscurity and confusion of ideas.

2   from W. K. Clifford, 'On the Aims and
           Instruments of Scientific Thought' (1872)

[. . .] It seems to me that the difference between scientific and merely technical thought [. . .] is just this: Both of them make use of experience to direct human action; but while technical thought or skill enables a man to deal with the same circumstances that he has met with before, scientific thought enables him to deal with different circumstances that he has never met with before. But how can experience of one thing enable us to deal with another quite different thing? To answer this question we shall have to consider more closely the nature of scientific thought.

Let us take another example. You know that if you make a dot on a piece of paper, and then hold a piece of Iceland spar over it, you will see not one dot but two. A mineralogist, by measuring the angles of a crystal, can tell you whether or no it possesses this property without looking through it. He requires no scientific thought to do that. But Sir William Rowan Hamilton, the late Astronomer-Royal of Ireland, knowing these facts and also the explanation of them which Fresnel had given, thought about the subject, and he predicted that by looking through certain crystals in a particular direction we should see not two dots but a continuous circle. Mr. Lloyd made the experiment, and saw the circle, a result which had never been even suspected.[2] This has always been considered one of the most signal instances of scientific thought in the domain of physics. It is most distinctly an application of experience gained under certain circumstances to entirely different circumstances. [. . .]

The step, then, from past experience to new circumstances must be made in accordance with an observed uniformity in the order of events. This uniformity has held good in the past in certain places; if it should also hold good in the future and in other places, then, being combined with our experience of the past, it enables us to predict the future, and to know what is going on elsewhere; so that we are able to regulate our conduct in accordance with this knowledge.

The aim of scientific thought, then, is to apply past experience to new circumstances; the instrument is an observed uniformity in the course of events. By the use of this instrument it gives us information transcending our experience, it enables us to infer things that we have not seen from things that we have seen; and the evidence for the truth of that information depends on our supposing that the uniformity holds good beyond our experience. [. . .]

[2] In 1832 the mathematician and astronomer Hamilton made this theoretical prediction, which was then confirmed in the laboratory by the Professor of Physics at Trinity College, Dublin, Humphrey Lloyd, building on the work of French pioneer of optics Jean Fresnel. At the time, this prediction of phenomena in the real world was seen as a major triumph for scientific methodology.

We have, then, come somehow to the following conclusions. By scientific thought we mean the application of past experience to new circumstances by means of an observed order of events. By saying that this order of events is exact we mean that it is exact enough to correct experiments by, but we do not mean that it is theoretically or absolutely exact, because we do not know. The process of inference we found to be in itself an assumption of uniformity, and we found that, as the known exactness of the uniformity became greater, the stringency of the inference is increased. By saying that the order of events is reasonable we do not mean that everything has a purpose, or that everything can be explained, or that everything has a cause; for neither of these is true. But we mean that to every reasonable question there is an intelligible answer, which either we or posterity may know *by the exercise of scientific thought*.

For I specially wish you not to go away with the idea that the exercise of scientific thought is properly confined to the subjects from which my illustrations have been chiefly drawn tonight. When the Roman jurists applied their experience of Roman citizens to dealings between citizens and aliens, showing by the difference of their actions that they regarded the circumstances as essentially different, they laid the foundations of that great structure which has guided the social progress of Europe. That procedure was an instance of strictly scientific thought. When a poet finds that he has to move a strange new world which his predecessors have not moved; when, nevertheless, he catches fire from their flashes, arms from their armoury, sustentation from their footprints, the procedure by which he applies old experience to new circumstances is nothing greater or less than scientific thought. When the moralist, studying the conditions of society and the ideas of right and wrong which have come down to us from a time when war was the only chance of survival, evolves from them the conditions and ideas which must accompany a time of peace, when the comradeship of equals is the condition of national success; the process by which he does this is scientific thought and nothing else. Remember, then, that it is the guide of action; that the truth which it arrives at is not that which we can ideally contemplate without error, but that which we may act upon without fear; and you cannot fail to see that scientific thought is not an accompaniment or condition of human progress, but human progress itself. And for this reason the question of what its characters are, of which I have inadequately endeavoured to give you some glimpse, is the question of all questions for the human race.

3   from John Tyndall, 'Belfast Address' (1874)

[. . .] An impulse inherent in primeval man turned his thought and questionings betimes towards the sources of natural phenomena. The same impulse, inherited and intensified, is the spur of scientific action today. Determined by it, a process of abstraction from experience we form physical theories which lie beyond the pale of experience, but which satisfy the desire of the mind to see every natural occurrence resting upon a cause. In forming their notions of the origin of things, our earliest historic (and doubtless, we might add, our prehistoric) ancestors pursued, as far as their intelligence permitted, the same course. They also fell back upon experience, but with this difference—that the particular experiences which furnished the weft and woof of their theories were drawn, not from the study of nature, but from what lay much closer to them, the observation of men. Their theories accordingly took an anthropomorphic form. To supersensual beings, which, 'however potent and invisible, were nothing but a species of human creatures, perhaps raised from among mankind, and retaining all human passions and appetites,' were handed over the rule and governance of natural phenomena.

Tested by observation and reflection, these early notions failed in the long run to satisfy the more penetrating intellects of our race. Far in the depths of history we find men of exceptional power differentiating themselves from the crowd, rejecting these anthropomorphic notions, and seeking to connect natural phenomena with their physical principles. But long prior to these purer efforts of the understanding the merchant had been abroad, and rendered the philosopher possible; commerce had developed, wealth amassed, leisure for travel and for speculation secured, while races educated under different conditions, and therefore differently formed and endowed, had been stimulated and sharpened by mutual contact. In those regions where the commercial aristocracy of ancient Greece mingled with its eastern neighbours, the sciences were born, being nurtured and developed by freethinking and courageous men. The state of things to be displaced may be gathered from a passage of Euripides quoted by Hume. 'There is nothing in the world; no glory, no prosperity. The gods toss all into confusion; mix everything with its reverse, that all of us, from our ignorance and uncertainty, may pay them the more worship and reverence.' Now, as science demands the radical extirpation of caprice and the absolute reliance upon law in nature, there grew with the growth of scientific notions a desire and determination to sweep from the field of theory this mob of gods and demons, and to place natural phenomena on a basis more congruent with themselves. [. . .]

In our day great generalisations have been reached. The theory of the origin of species is but one of them. Another, of still wider grasp and more radical significance, is the doctrine of the Conservation of Energy, the ultimate philosophical issues of which are as yet but dimly seen—that doctrine which 'binds nature fast in fate' to an extent not hitherto recognised, exacting from every antecedent its equivalent consequent, from every consequent its equivalent antecedent, and bringing vital as well as physical phenomena under the dominion of that law of causal connection which, as far as the human understanding has yet pierced, asserts itself everywhere in nature. Long in advance of all definite experiment upon the subject, the constancy and indestructibility of matter had been affirmed; and all subsequent experience justified the affirmation. Later researches extended the attribute of indestructibility to force. This idea, applied in the first instance to inorganic, rapidly embraced organic nature. The vegetable world, though drawing almost all its nutriment from invisible sources, was proved incompetent to generate anew either matter or force. Its matter is for the most part transmuted air; its force transformed solar force. The animal world was proved to be equally uncreative, all its motive energies being referred to the combustion of its food. The activity of each animal as a whole was proved to be the transferred activities of its molecules. The muscles were shown to be stores of mechanical force, potential until unlocked by the nerves, and then resulting in muscular contractions. The speed at which messages fly to and fro along the nerves was determined, and found to be, not as had been previously supposed, equal to that of light or electricity, but less than the speed of a flying eagle.

This was the work of the physicist: then came the conquests of the comparative anatomist and physiologist, revealing the structure of every animal, and the function of every organ in the whole biological series, from the lowest zoophyte up to man. The nervous system had been made the object of profound and continued study, the wonderful and, at bottom, entirely mysterious controlling power which it exercises over the whole organism, physical and mental, being recognised more and more. Thought could not be kept back from a subject so profoundly suggestive. Besides the physical life dealt with by Mr. Darwin, there is a psychical life presenting similar gradations, and asking equally for a solution. How are the different grades and orders of mind to be accounted for? What is the principle of growth of that mysterious power which on our planet culminates in Reason? These are questions, which, though not thrusting themselves so forcibly upon the attention of the general public, had not only occupied many reflecting minds, but had been formally broached [. . .] before the 'Origin of Species' appeared. [. . .]

The *origination* of life is a point lightly touched upon, if at all, by Mr. Darwin and Mr. Spencer. Diminishing gradually the number of progenitors, Mr. Darwin comes at length to one 'primordial form'; but he does not say, as far as I remember, how he supposes this form to have been introduced. He quotes with satisfaction the words of a celebrated author and divine who had 'gradually learnt to see that it is just as noble a conception of the Deity to believe He created a few original forms, capable of self-development into other and needful forms, as to believe that He required a fresh act of creation to supply the voids caused by the action of His laws.' What Mr. Darwin thinks of this view of the introduction of life I do not know. Whether he does or does not introduce his 'primordial form' by a creative act, I do not know. But the question will inevitably be asked, 'How came the form there?' With regard to the diminution of the number of created forms, one does not see that much advantage is gained by it. The anthropomorphism, which it seemed the object of Mr. Darwin to set aside, is as firmly associated with the creation of a few forms as with the creation of a multitude. We need clearness and thoroughness here. Two courses, and two only are possible. Either let us open our doors freely to the conception of creative acts, or, abandoning them, let us radically change our notions of matter. If we look at matter as pictured by Democritus,[3] and as defined for generations in our scientific text-books, the absolute impossibility of any form of life coming out of it would be sufficient to render any other hypothesis preferable; but the definitions of matter given in our text-books were intended to cover its purely physical and mechanical properties. And taught as we have been to regard these definitions as complete, we naturally and rightly reject the monstrous notion that out of *such* matter any form of life could possibly arise. But are the definitions complete? Everything depends on the answer to be given to this question. Trace the line of life backwards, and see it approaching more and more to what we call the purely physical condition. We reach at length those organisms which I have compared to drops of oil suspended in a mixture of alcohol and water. We reach the *protogenes* of Haeckel,[4] in which we have 'a type distinguishable from a fragment of albumen only by its finely granular character.' Can we pause here? We break a magnet and find two poles in each of its fragments. We continue the process of breaking, but however small the parts, each carries with it, though enfeebled, the polarity of the whole. And when we can break no longer, we prolong the intellectual vision to the polar molecules. Are we not urged to do *something* similar in the case of life? Is there not a temptation to close to some extent with Lucretius, when he affirms that 'Nature is seen to do all things spontaneously of herself without the meddling of the gods?' or with Bruno, when he declares that matter is not 'that mere empty *capacity* which philosophers have pictured her to be, but the universal mother who brings forth

---

[3] Democritus, 5th-century BC Greek philosopher, and founder of atomic theory—that all phenomena are explicable in terms of the properties and actions of ultimate or elementary particles.

[4] Ernst Haeckel (1834–1919), German zoologist, whose *General Morphology* was an important statement of scientific naturalism and evolutionary theory. The *Morphology* contained evolutionary trees, tracing the divergence of varieties and species. *Protogenes* was postulated as the original primary material from which all life might be derived—rather like the 'protoplasm' which was the main subject of Huxley's 'On the Physical Basis of Life.'

all things as the fruit of her own womb?'[5] The questions here raised are inevitable. They are approaching us with accelerated speed, and it is not a matter of indifference whether they are introduced with reverence or irreverence. Abandoning all disguise, the confession that I feel bound to make before you is that I prolong the vision backward across the boundary of the experimental evidence, and discern in that matter, which we in our ignorance, and notwithstanding our professed reverence for its Creator, have hitherto covered with opprobrium, the promise and potency of every form and quality of life.

The 'materialism' here enunciated may be different from what you suppose, and I therefore crave your gracious presence to the end. 'The question of an external world,' says Mr. J. S. Mill, 'is the great battle-ground of metaphysics.' Mr. Mill himself reduces external phenomena to 'possibilities of sensation.'[6] Kant, as we have seen, made time and space 'forms' of our own intuitions. Fichte, having first by the inexorable logic of his understanding proved himself to be a mere link in that chain of eternal causation which holds so rigidly in nature, violently broke the chain by making nature, and all that it inherits, an apparition of his own mind. And it is by no means easy to combat such notions.[7] For when I say I see you, and that I have not the least doubt about it, the reply is, that what I am really conscious of is an affection of my own retina. And if I urge that I can check my sight of you by touching you, the retort would be that I am equally transgressing the limits of fact; for what I am really conscious of is, not that you are there, but that the nerves of my hand have undergone a change. All we hear, and see, and touch, and taste, and smell, are, it would be urged, mere variations on our own condition, beyond which, even to the extent of a hair's breadth, we cannot go. That anything answering to our impressions exists outside of ourselves is not a *fact*, but an *inference*, to which all validity would be denied by an idealist like Berkeley, or by a sceptic like Hume. Mr. Spencer takes another line. With him, as with the uneducated man, there is no doubt or question as to the existence of an external world. But he differs from the uneducated, who think that the world really *is* what consciousness represents it to be. Our states of consciousness are mere *symbols* of an outside entity which produces them and determines the order of their succession, but the real nature of which we can never know. In fact the whole process of evolution is the manifestation of a Power absolutely inscrutable to the intellect of man. As little

[5] Lucretius (98–55 BC), Roman poet and theorist of the natural world, who argued that the study of nature can free man of false superstitions: an important point of reference for scientific naturalism therefore. Giordano Bruno (1548–1600) was a Renaissance scholar, scientist, and mystic, burnt at the stake as a Catholic heretic. One of the most widely discussed Renaissance figures in the 19th century.

[6] John Stuart Mill (1806–73), political theorist and philosopher, whose *System of Logic* (1843) was a foundational text for scientific naturalism in its formulations of the empirical method.

[7] Immanuel Kant (1724–1804) and Johann Fichte (1762–1814): idealists arguing, in different ways, for the primacy of the subjective over the objective world. Idealism was frequently tinged with theistic arguments (Bishop Berkeley's English idealism is mentioned later in the paragraph), and became a target for scientific naturalists.

in our day as in the days of Job can man by searching find this Power out. Considered fundamentally, it is by the operation of an insoluble mystery that life is evolved, species differentiated, and mind unfolded from their prepotent elements in the immeasurable past. There is, you will observe, no very rank materialism here.[8]

The strength of the doctrine of evolution consists, not in an experimental demonstration (for the subject is hardly accessible to this mode of proof), but in its general harmony with the method of nature as hitherto known. From contrast, moreover, it derives enormous relative strength. On the one side we have a theory (if it could with any propriety be so called) derived, as were the theories referred to at the beginning of this address, not from the study of nature, but from the observation of men—a theory which converts the Power whose garment is seen in the visible universe into an Artificer, fashioned after the human model, and acting by broken efforts as man is seen to act. On the other side we have the conception that all we see around us, and all we feel within us—the phenomena of physical nature as well as those of the human mind—have their unsearchable roots in a cosmical life, if I dare apply the term, an infinitesimal span of which only is offered to the investigation of man. And even this span is only knowable in part. We can trace the development of a nervous system, and correlate it with the parallel phenomena of sensation and thought. We see with undoubting certainty that they go hand in hand. But we try to soar in a vacuum the moment we seek to comprehend the vacuum between them. An Archimedean fulcrum is here required which the human mind cannot command; and the effort to solve the problem, to borrow an illustration from an illustrious friend of mine, is like the effort of a man trying to lift himself by his own waistband. All that has been here said is to be taken in connection with this fundamental truth. When 'nascent senses' are spoken of, when 'the differentiation of a tissue at first vaguely sensitive all over' is spoken of, and when these processes are associated with 'the modification of an organism by its environment,' the same parallelism, without contact, or even approach to contact, is implied. There is no fusion possible between the two classes of facts—no motor energy in the intellect of man to carry it without logical rupture from the one to the other.

Further, the doctrine of evolution derives man, in his totality, from the interaction of organism and environment through countless ages past. The human understanding, for example—the faculty which Mr. Spencer has turned so skilfully round upon its own antecedents—is itself a result of the play between organism and environment through cosmic ranges of time. Never surely did prescription plead so irresistible a claim. But then it comes to pass that, over and

---

[8]   Tyndall summarizes the argument from Herbert Spencer's *First Principles* (1862), which formulates a divide between science and its unknowable antithesis—'nescience'. This was another key reference-point for scientific naturalism, and informs Tyndall's argument over the next few paragraphs.

above his understanding, there are many other things appertaining to man whose prescriptive rights are quite as strong as that of the understanding itself. It is a result, for example, of the play of organism and environment that sugar is sweet and aloes are bitter, that the smell of henbane differs from that of a rose. Such facts of consciousness (for which, by the way, no adequate reason has ever been rendered) are quite as old as the understanding itself; and many other things can boast an equally ancient origin. Mr. Spencer at one place refers to that most powerful of passions—the amatory passion—as one which, when it first occurs, is antecedent to all relative experience whatever; and we may pass its claim as being at least as ancient and as valid as that of the understanding itself. Then there are such things woven into the texture of man as the feeling of awe, reverence, wonder—and not alone the sexual love just referred to, but the love of the beautiful, physical and moral, in nature, poetry, and art. There is also that deep-set feeling which, since the earliest dawn of history, and probably for ages prior to all history, incorporated itself in the religions of the world. You who have escaped from these religions in the high-and-dry light of the understanding may deride them; but in so doing you deride accidents of form merely, and fail to touch the immovable basis of the religious sentiment in the emotional nature of man. To yield this sentiment reasonable satisfaction is the problem of problems at the present hour. And grotesque in relation to scientific culture as many of the religions of the world have been and are—dangerous, nay, destructive, to the dearest privileges of freemen as some of them undoubtedly have been, and would, if they could, be again—it will be wise to recognise them as the forms of force, mischievous, if permitted to intrude on the region of *knowledge*, over which it holds no command, but capable of being guided by liberal thought to noble issues in the region of *emotion*, which is its proper sphere. It is vain to oppose this force with a view to its extirpation. What we should oppose, to the death if necessary, is every attempt to found upon this elemental bias of man's nature a system which should exercise despotic sway over his intellect. I do not fear any such consummation. Science has already to some extent leavened the world, and it will leaven it more and more. I should look upon the mild light of science breaking in upon the minds of the youth of Ireland, and strengthening gradually to the perfect day, as a surer check to any intellectual or spiritual tyranny which might threaten this island, than the laws of princes or the swords of emperors. Where is the cause of fear? We fought and won our battle even in the Middle Ages: why should we doubt the issue of a conflict now?

The impregnable position of science may be described in a few words. All religious theories, schemes, and systems, which embrace notions of cosmogony, or which otherwise reach into its domain, must, in so far as they do this, submit to the control of science, and relinquish all thought of controlling it. Acting otherwise proved disastrous in the past, and it is simply fatuous today. Every system which would escape the fate of an organism too rigid to adjust itself to its environment, must be plastic to the extent that the growth of knowledge demands. When this truth has been thoroughly taken in, rigidity will be relaxed, exclusiveness diminished, things now deemed essential will be dropped, and elements now rejected will be assimilated. The lifting of the life is the essential point; and as long as dogmatism, fanaticism, and intolerance are kept out, various modes of leverage may be employed to raise life to a higher level. Science itself not unfrequently derives motive power from an ultra-scientific source. Whewell[9] speaks of enthusiasm of temper as a hindrance to science; but he means the enthusiasm of weak heads. There is a strong and resolute enthusiasm in which science finds an ally. [. . .]

I have touched on debatable questions, and led you over dangerous ground—and this partly with the view of telling you, and through you the world, that as regards these questions science claims unrestricted right of search. It is not to the point to say that the views of Lucretius and Bruno, of Darwin and Spencer, may be wrong. Here I should agree with you, deeming it indeed certain that these views will undergo modification. But the point is, that, whether right or wrong, we claim the freedom to discuss them. The ground which they cover is scientific ground; and the right claimed is one made good enough through tribulation and anguish, inflicted and endured in darker times than ours, but resulting in the immortal victories which science has won for the human race. I would set forth equally the inexorable advance of man's understanding in the path of knowledge, and the unquenchable claims of his emotional nature which the understanding can never satisfy. The world embraces not only a Newton, but a Shakespeare—not only a Boyle, but a Raphael—not only a Kant, but a Beethoven—not only a Darwin, but a Carlyle. Not in each of these, but in all, is human nature whole. They are not opposed, but supplementary—not mutually exclusive, but reconcilable. And if, still unsatisfied, the human mind, with the yearning of a pilgrim for his distant home, will turn to the mystery from which it has emerged, seeking so to fashion it as to give unity to thought and faith, so long as this is done, not only without intolerance or bigotry of any kind, but with the enlightened recognition that ultimate fixity of conception is here unattainable, and that each succeeding age must be held free to fashion the mystery in accordance with its own needs—then, in opposition to all the restrictions of Materialism, I would affirm this to be a field for the noblest exercise of what, in contrast with the *knowing* faculties, may be called the *creative* faculties of man. Here, however, I must quit a theme too great for me to handle, but which will be handled by the loftiest minds ages after

---

[9] William Whewell (1794–1866), Cambridge scholar and man of science, was centrally involved in the professionalization of science in England in the 1830s and 1840s.

you and I, like streaks of morning cloud, shall have melted into the infinite azure of the past.

---

4   from Karl Pearson, *A Grammar of Science* (1892)

INTRODUCTORY—THE SCOPE AND METHOD OF SCIENCE

1. SCIENCE AND THE PRESENT

Within the past forty years so revolutionary a change has taken place in our appreciation of the essential facts in the growth of human society, that it has become necessary not only to rewrite history, but to profoundly modify our theory of life and gradually, but none the less certainly to adapt our conduct to the novel theory. The insight which the investigations of Darwin, seconded by the suggestive but far less permanent work of Spencer, have given us into the development of both individual and social life, has compelled us to remodel our historical ideas and is slowly widening and consolidating our moral standards. The slowness ought not to dishearten us, for one of the strongest factors of social stability is the inertness, nay, rather active hostility, with which human societies receive all new ideas. It is the crucible in which the dross is separated from the genuine metal, and which saves the body-social from a succession of unprofitable and possibly injurious experimental variations. That the reformer should be also the martyr is, perhaps, a not over-great price to pay for the caution with which society as a whole must move; to replace an individual man may require years, but a stable and efficient society is the outcome of centuries of development. [. . .]

It is very difficult for us who live in the last quarter of the nineteenth century to rightly measure the relative importance of our age in the history of civilization. [. . .] The contest of opinion in nearly every field of thought—the struggle of old and new standards in every sphere of activity, in religion, in commerce, in social life—touch the spiritual and physical needs of the individual far too nearly for us to be dispassionate judges of the age in which we live. That we live in an era of rapid social variation can scarcely be doubted by any one who regards attentively the marked contrasts presented by our modern society. It is an era alike of great self-assertion and of excessive altruism; we see the highest intellectual power accompanied by the strangest recrudescence of superstition; there is a strong socialist drift and yet not a few remarkable individualist teachers; the extremes of religious faith and of unequivocal freethought are found jostling with each other. Nor do these opposing traits exist only in close social juxtaposition. The same individual mind, unconscious of its own want of logical consistency, will often exhibit our age in microcosm. [. . .]

The wide extension of the franchise in both local and central representation has cast a greatly increased responsibility on the individual citizen. He is brought face to face with the most conflicting opinions and with the most diverse party cries. The state has become in our day the largest employer of labour, the greatest dispenser of charity, and, above all, the schoolmaster with the biggest school in the community. Directly or indirectly the individual citizen has to find some reply to the innumerable social and educational problems of the day. He requires some guide in the determination of his own action or in the choice of fitting representatives. He is thrust into an appalling maze of social and educational problems; and if his tribal conscience has any stuff in it, he feels that these problems ought not to be settled, so far as he has the power of settling them, by his own personal interests, by his individual prospects of profit or loss. He is called upon to form a judgment apart from his own feelings and emotions if it possibly may be—a judgment in what he conceives to be the interests of society at large. It may be a difficult thing for the large employer of labour to form a right judgment in matters of factory legislation, or for the private schoolmaster to see clearly the questions of state-aided education. None the less we should probably all agree that the tribal conscience ought for the sake of social welfare to be stronger than private interest, and that the *ideal* citizen, if he existed, would form a judgment free from personal bias.

2. SCIENCE AND CITIZENSHIP

How is such a judgment—so necessary in our time with its hot conflict of personal opinion and its increased responsibility for the individual citizen—how is such a judgment to be formed? In the first place it is obvious that it can only be based on a clear knowledge of the facts, an appreciation of their sequence and relative significance. The facts once classified, once understood, the judgment based upon them ought to be independent of the individual mind which examines them. Is there any other sphere, outside that of ideal citizenship, in which there is habitual use of this method of classifying facts and forming judgments upon them? For if there be, it cannot fail to be suggestive as to methods of eliminating personal bias; it ought to be one of the best training grounds for citizenship. The classification of facts and the formation of absolute judgments upon the basis of this classification—judgments independent of the idiosyncrasies of the individual mind—is peculiarly *the scope and method of modern science*. The scientific man has above all things to aim at self-elimination in his own judgments, to provide an argument which is as true for each individual mind as for his own. *The classification of facts, the recognition of their sequence and relative significance is the function of science,* and the habit of forming a judgment upon these facts unbiased by personal feeling is characteristic of what we shall term the scientific frame of mind. The scientific method of examining facts is not peculiar to one class of phenomena and to one class of workers; it is applicable to social as well as to physical problems, and we must carefully guard ourselves against supposing that the scientific frame of mind is a peculiarity of the professional scientist.

Now this frame of mind seems to me an essential of good citizenship, and of the several ways in which it can be acquired few surpass the careful study of some one branch of natural science. The insight into method and the habit of dispassionate investigation which follow from acquaintance with the scientific classification of even some small range of natural facts, give the mind an invaluable power of dealing with many other classes of facts as the occasion arises. The patient and persistent study of some one branch of natural science is even at the present time within the reach of many. In some branches a few hours' study a week, if carried on earnestly for two or three years, would be not only sufficient to give a thorough insight into scientific method, but would also enable the student to become a careful observer and possibly an original investigator in his chosen field, thus adding a new delight and a new enthusiasm to his life. The importance of a just appreciation of the scientific method is so great, that I think the state may be reasonably called upon to place instruction in pure science within the reach of all its citizens. Indeed, we ought to look with extreme distrust on the large expenditure of public money on polytechnics and similar institutions, if the manual instruction which it is proposed to give at these places be not accompanied by efficient teaching in pure science. The scientific habit of mind is one which may be acquired by all, and the readiest means of attaining to it ought to be placed within the reach of all.

The reader must be careful to note that I am only praising the scientific habit of mind, and suggesting one of several methods by which it may be cultivated. No assertion has been made that the man of science is necessarily a good citizen, or that his judgment upon social or political questions will certainly be of weight. It by no means follows that, because a man has won a name for himself in the field of natural science, his judgments on such problems as Socialism, Home Rule, or Biblical Theology will necessarily be sound. They will be sound or not according as he has carried his scientific method into these fields. He must properly have classified and appreciated his facts, and have been guided by them, and not by personal feeling or class bias in his judgments. It is the scientific habit of mind as an essential for good citizenship, and not the scientist as sound politician that I wish to emphasize.

5   from T. H. Huxley, *Evolution and Ethics* (1893)

The propounders of what are called the 'ethics of evolution,' when the 'evolution of ethics' would usually better express the object of their speculations, adduce a number of more or less interesting facts and more or less sound arguments, in favour of the origin of moral sentiments, in the same way as other natural phenomena, by a process of evolution. I have little doubt, for my own part, that they are on the right track; but as the immoral sentiments have no less been evolved, there is, so far, as much natural sanction for the one as the other. The thief and the murderer follow nature just as much as the philanthropist. Cosmic evolution may teach us how the good and evil tendencies of man may have come about; but, in itself, it is incompetent to furnish any better reason why what we call good is preferable to what we call evil than we had before. Some day, I doubt not, we shall arrive at an understanding of the evolution of the aesthetic faculty; but all the understanding in the world will neither increase nor diminish the force of the intuition that this is beautiful and that is ugly.

There is another fallacy which appears to me to pervade the so-called 'ethics of evolution.' It is the notion that because, on the whole, animals and plants have advanced in perfection of organization by means of the struggle for existence and the consequent 'survival of the fittest'; therefore men in society, men as ethical beings, must look to the same process to help them towards perfection. I suspect that this fallacy has arisen out of the unfortunate ambiguity of the phrase 'survival of the fittest.' 'Fittest' has the connotation of 'best'; and about 'best' there hangs a moral flavour. In cosmic nature, however, what is 'fittest' depends upon the conditions. Long since, I ventured to point out that if our hemisphere were to cool again, the survival of the fittest might bring about, in the vegetable kingdom, a population of more and more stunted and humbler and humbler organisms, until the 'fittest' that survived might be nothing but lichens, diatoms, and such microscopic organisms as those which give red snow its colour; while, if it became hotter, the pleasant valleys of the Thames and Isis might be uninhabitable by any animated beings save those that flourish in the tropical jungle. They, as the fittest, the best adapted to changed conditions, would survive.

Men in society are undoubtedly subject to the cosmic process. As among other animals, multiplication goes on without cessation, and involves the severe competition for the means of support. The struggle for existence tends to eliminate those less fitted to adapt themselves to the circumstances of their existence. The strongest, the most self-assertive, tend to tread down the weaker. But the influence of the cosmic process on the evolution of society is the greater the more rudimentary its civilization. Social progress means a checking of the cosmic process at every step and the substitution for it of another, which may be called the ethical process; the end of which is not the survival of those who may happen to be the fittest, in respect of the whole of the conditions which obtain, but of those who are ethically the best.

As I have already urged, the practice of that which is ethically best—what we call goodness or virtue—involves a course of conduct which, in all respects, is opposed to that which leads to success in the cosmic struggle for existence. In place of ruthless self-assertion it demands self-restraint; in place of thrusting aside, or treading down, all competitors, it requires that the individual shall not merely respect, but shall help his fellows; its influence is directed, not so much to the survival of the fittest, as to the fitting of as many as possible to survive. It repudiates the gladiatorial theory of existence. It demands that each man who enters into the enjoyment of the advantages of a polity shall be mindful of his debt to those who have laboriously constructed it; and shall take heed that no act of his weakens the fabric in which he has been permitted to live. Laws and moral precepts are directed to the end of curbing the cosmic process and reminding the individual of his duty to the community, to the protection and influence of which he owes, if not existence itself, at least the life of something better than a brutal savage.

It is from neglect of these plain considerations that the fanatical individualism of our time attempts to apply the analogy of cosmic nature to society. Once more we have a misapplication of the stoical injunction to follow nature; the duties of the individual to the state are forgotten, and his tendencies to self-assertion are dignified by the name of rights. It is seriously debated whether the members of a community are justified in using their combined strength to constrain one of their number to contribute his share to the maintenance of it; or even to prevent him from doing his best to destroy it. The struggle for existence, which has done such admirable work in cosmic nature, must, it appears, be equally beneficent in the ethical sphere. Yet if that which I have insisted upon is true; if the cosmic process has no sort of relation to moral ends; if the imitation of it by man is inconsistent with the first principles of ethics; what becomes of this surprising theory?

Let us understand, once and for all, that the ethical progress of society depends, not on imitating the cosmic process, still less in running away from it, but in combating it. It may seem an audacious proposal thus to pit the microcosm against the macrocosm and to set man to subdue nature to his higher ends; but I venture to think that the great intellectual difference between the ancient times with which we have been occupied and our day, lies in the solid foundation we have acquired for the hope that such an enterprise may meet with a certain measure of success.

The history of civilization details the steps by which men have succeeded in building up an artificial world within the cosmos. Fragile reed as he may be, man, as Pascal says,[10] is a thinking reed: there lies within him a fund of energy, operating intelligently and so far akin to that which pervades the universe, that it is competent to influence and modify the cosmic process. In virtue of his intelligence, the dwarf bends the Titan to his will. In every family, in every polity that has been established, the cosmic process in man has been restrained and otherwise modified by law and custom; in surrounding nature, it has been similarly influenced by the art of the shepherd, the agriculturist, the artisan. As civilization has advanced, so has the extent of this interference increased; until the organized and highly developed sciences and arts of the present day have endowed man with a command over the course of non-human nature greater than that once attributed to the magicians. The most impressive, I might say startling, of these changes have been brought about in the course of the last two centuries; while a right comprehension of the process of life and of the means of influencing its manifestations is only just dawning upon us. We do not yet see our way beyond generalities; and we are befogged by the obtrusion of false analogies and crude anticipations. But Astronomy, Physics, Chemistry, have all had to pass through similar phases, before they reached the stage at which their influence became an important factor in human affairs. Physiology, Psychology, Ethics, Political Science, must submit to the same ordeal. Yet it seems to me irrational to doubt that, at no distant period, they will work as great a revolution in the sphere of practice.

The theory of evolution encourages no millennial anticipations. If, for millions of years, our globe has taken the upward road, yet, some time, the summit will be reached and the downward route will be commenced. The most daring imagination will hardly venture upon the suggestion that the power and the intelligence of man can ever arrest the procession of the great year.

Moreover, the cosmic nature born with us and, to a large extent, necessary for our maintenance, is the outcome of millions of years of severe training, and it would be folly to imagine that a few centuries will suffice to subdue its masterfulness to purely ethical ends. Ethical nature may count upon having to reckon with a tenacious and powerful enemy as long as the world lasts. But, on the other hand, I see no limit to the extent to which intelligence and will, guided by sound principles of investigation, and organized in common effort, may modify the conditions of existence, for a period longer than that now covered by history. And much may be done to change the nature of man himself. The intelligence which has converted the brother of the wolf into the faithful guardian of the flock ought to be able to do something towards curbing the instincts of savagery in civilized men.

But if we may permit ourselves a larger hope of abatement of the essential evil

[10] Blaise Pascal (1623–62), scientist and theistic thinker.

of the world than was possible to those who, in the infancy of exact knowledge, faced the problem of existence more than a score of centuries ago, I deem it an essential condition of the realization of that hope that we should cast aside the notion that the escape from pain and sorrow is the proper object of life.

We have long since emerged from the heroic childhood of our race, when good and evil could be met with the same 'frolic welcome'; the attempts to escape from evil, whether Indian or Greek, have ended in flight from the battle-field; it remains to us to throw aside the youthful over-confidence and the no less youthful discouragement of nonage. We are grown men, and must play the man

> strong in will
> To strive, to seek, to find, and not to yield,

cherishing the good that falls in our way, and bearing the evil, in and around us, with stout hearts set on diminishing it. So far, we all may strive in one faith towards one hope:

> It may be that the gulfs will wash us down,
> It may be we shall touch the Happy Isles,
>
> . . . but something ere the end,
> Some work of noble note may yet be done.[11]

EDITORS' NOTES

1. Thomas Henry Huxley (1825–95). The most prominent public advocate for the profession and ideology of science in nineteenth-century England. The son of a London schoolteacher, he trained in medicine during the political upheavals of the 1840s. Between 1846 and 1850 he was ship's surgeon on HMS *Rattlesnake*, writing successful zoological papers during and after the trip. Although he was elected Fellow of the Royal Society in 1851 it was nearly two years before he found a lecturing appointment—an unemployment shared with his fellow advocate of science, John Tyndall. He was lecturer at the Royal School of Mines in 1854, and held various professorships at the Royal Institution, the College of Surgeons, and the Royal School of Science to eke out his precarious finances. From the mid-1860s he was at the heart of the scientific establishment, sitting on the important Royal Commission on Scientific Instruction and the Advancement of Science, which produced eight reports between 1870 and 1875 and which shaped (after much delay) the institutions, profession, and public funding of science in Britain. 'On the Physical Basis of Life' was delivered as a Sunday lecture in Edinburgh in 1869; when published in the *Fortnightly Review*, the issue

[11] Huxley cites Tennyson, *Ulysses*, but in reverse order: lines 69–70, 62–3, and 51–2.

went through seven editions, and the editor John Morley termed it the most influential article of his generation.

2. William Kingdon Clifford (1845–79). Gifted mathematician and writer, whose early death from consumption was mourned by fellow advocates of scientific naturalism as the loss of a highly promising spokesman and polemicist. His collected *Lectures and Essays* were edited by the scientific naturalist and editor Leslie Stephen and the Postivist thinker Frederick Pollock in 1879. Trained at King's College London and Trinity College, Cambridge, he became Professor of Applied Mathematics in 1871. This speech was delivered to the British Association for the Advancement of Science in 1872.

3. John Tyndall (1820–93). Professor of Physics at the Royal Institution from 1867 to 1887, during which time his research, brilliant public lectures, and popular science writing made him one of the key proponents of science in the nineteenth century. He was born in Ireland into a dissenting Protestant family, and worked for the Ordnance Survey and on the railways as an engineer before funding his own studies in physics in Germany from 1848 to 1850 (the superiority of German technical education was a constant anxiety and complaint amongst under-funded and despised workers in science in England). On his return to England his work in electricity and magnetism attracted the attention of the revered scientist Michael Faraday; Tyndall lectured under Faraday from 1853, succeeding his master as professor in 1867. He was a close ally of Huxley, although his work was read more enthusiastically by Aesthetes and theists (even spiritualists) as providing space for the imagination and sublime possibilities in excess of 'mechanistic' models of humanity—his most popular works derived from his love of Alpine mountain-climbing, which combined research into glacial formation with evocations of the sublime. The furore caused by the Belfast Address has erased this Romantic side of Tyndall's appeal to a wide Victorian public.

4. Karl Pearson (1857–1936). Educated in Cambridge before beginning a legal career at the Bar in 1882. He rapidly abandoned this for a professorship in applied mathematics at University College London. He was a member of radical freethinking groups in the 1880s (writing *The Ethic of Free Thought* in 1888). He founded the Men and Women's Club in July 1885 in order to discuss issues related to marriage, sexuality, and gender from a 'scientific' viewpoint, and it drew leading intellectuals like Havelock Ellis, Eleanor Marx Aveling, Olive Schreiner, and Annie Besant (for an absorbing history of the Club, see Walkowitz, *City of Dreadful Delight*). Pearson was elected Fellow of the Royal Society for work in statistics in 1896. *A Grammar of Science* was to exert a great influence up to the Second World War, although Pearson is now largely remembered as the founder of the Eugenics Laboratory and as the first Professor of Eugenics at University College (see Chapter 13).

10

PSYCHOLOGY

The 'mad-doctors' of the large system of asylums that rapidly expanded as a result of the Lunacy Laws of the 1840s and 1850s were the lowest of a lowly profession. They required no medical training, and were widely held to be little more than prison guards. Stories of abuses of committal procedures fed a good deal of the Sensation fiction genre of the 1860s, and real-life cases of women imprisoned in asylums by dastardly husbands and corrupt mad-doctors continued into the late nineteenth century (see Alex Owen on Louisa Lowe, or Judith Walkowitz, in *City of Dreadful Delight*, on Georgina Weldon—two women who won legal cases against their committals). Many see the history of nineteenth-century psychiatry as a struggle for professional legitimacy against surgeons and medical doctors on the one hand, and popular demonologies on the other.

By the 1880s and 1890s psychology had achieved a degree of respectable scientific standing and 'alienists' a certain level of cultural authority. This was the result of two developments. The first was the growing importance of psychology on the Continent: in Germany, Wundt established a basis for an experimental psychology; in France, the eminent neurologist Jean-Martin Charcot turned his skills to the study of hysteria and mental disorders from the late 1870s. His Salpêtrière hospital, a complex of buildings with over 5,000 inmates, became world-famous: he gave weekly lectures and demonstrations up to his death in 1894. The second development was the rise of scientific naturalism and the cultural diffusion of evolutionary ideas in Britain. Darwin had concluded *On the Origin of Species* with the promise that 'Psychology will be based on a new foundation, that of the necessary acquirement of each mental power and capacity by gradation', and Herbert Spencer and George Lewes had begun the attempt to fulfil that promise with book-length studies.

Both Charcot's work and the Darwinian model saw mental states as efflorescences of the body, in accordance with a naturalism that wished to ground the *psyche* (Greek for 'soul') in the physical world. The interplay of mind and body meant that somatic illnesses and lesions would produce mental equivalents, whilst treatment focused on reasserting mental willpower over the unruly and primitive body. What is most interesting about the psychology of the 1890s, however, is the proliferation of very different theories of the psyche as these more 'mechanical' models of psychophysiology began to break down. Our selections, taken from a very brief period, try to reflect that diversity.

Horatio Bryan Donkin was doctor to Karl Marx's family, and to Olive Schreiner, and was a member of Karl Pearson's circle. He lectured on women's health and served on the Royal Commission on the Feeble Minded. His article on hysteria is a complicated mix of enlightened realization that social and sexual restrictions on women produce mental illness alongside treatments which suggest electric shock and the Weir Mitchell 'cure' of forced feeding and isolation (a treatment fictionalized to devastating effect in Charlotte Perkins Gilman's *The Yellow Wallpaper*). Donkin veers between social factors and an anxiety to locate physiological sources for the disease. Two young Viennese doctors, Breuer and Freud, first communicated their very different findings in a seminal article of 1893. Here, the insight that hysteria might be caused by repressed traumatic memories, often forgotten since childhood, offers the shape of a theory Freud was to name 'psychoanalysis' three years later. Freud's account is often seen as a radical break from Victorian physiological theories of mind. This is far from the case; discussions which centre solely on Freud also tend to forget that his theory was competing with a host of others in the 1890s. Investigations of the 'stream of consciousness' by William James and of the 'subliminal consciousness' by Frederic Myers suggest very different models of mind. We end on a refreshing riposte to the hysterias and perversities normally held to run riot in the fin de siècle: Clifford Allbutt could only remark on the robustness of British youth in 1895, the year of Nordau's panic narrative of *Degeneration*.

Secondary reading: Crabtree; Ellenberger; Oppenheim, '*Shattered Nerves*'; Owen; Scull; Walkowitz, *City of Dreadful Delight*; Woodward and Ash.

1   from H. B. Donkin, 'Hysteria', *A Dictionary*
         of Psychological Medicine (1892)

Hysteria—There is a fairly general consensus as to the kind of affections, which
are to be labelled as *hysteria*. This term, though etymologically indefensible,
must be retained from long prescription.[1] The symptoms are so numerous and
diverse that a useful definition of hysteria must necessarily have reference to causation, and can be arrived at only by a careful study of these symptoms, the subjects they affect, and the conditions in which they arise. It will then be seen (1) that
hysterical disorder claims the whole of the nervous system as its domain, both in
its physical aspect and psychical relationships; (2) that, search as we may, no
demonstrable disease can be found to explain it, however often its phenomena
may be specially occasioned by peripheral disturbances arising from the body
itself or from the outside world; (3) that varying combinations of abnormal nervous instability and relatively excessive stress of internal and external conditions
must take place for its display; and (4) that some degree of mental disorder,
mainly in the sphere of feeling, is a nexus between all its phenomena, predominantly physical in expression though they may be in many instances. The clinical
study of hysteria, on the one hand, excludes definitions implying an origin from
any system or organ other than the higher cerebral regions, and on the other indicates at every stage aberrations from what we know as nervous and psychological
order. [. . .]

For the normal working of the human organism there must be a given amount
of systemic nervous control or stability, and a certain sum of environmental conditions. Inherent defect of the one, or default or excess of the other, or both, leads
to abnormal reactions, some of which are by consent termed 'hysterical.' From
this point of view it may be said that all persons are potentially hysterical, and it
may be objected that this explanation is too wide to be of use; but the limits of the
normal are great in respect of both of these factors, and there is a sufficiently well-
marked set of nervous and mental peculiarities, and a sufficient similarity of
conditions in which they are displayed to justify the potential classification of
hysteria as a distinct malady. A wide definition of this disorder is necessitated by
the scope of its phenomena, some of which are closely allied to insanity, and
others with difficulty distinguishable from demonstrable local disease. Although
in many instances the bodily symptoms are predominant, and may simulate,
apart even from voluntary imposture which not seldom co-exists with genuine
symptoms, almost any organic nervous disorder, and many other actions as well,

---

[1] 'Hysteria' derives from the Greek *husterikos*, meaning 'of the womb', some disorders being
attributed to a moving womb.

yet a certain degree of mental aberration obtains in all hysterics. To recognise the element of psychical disorder is of the first importance, for it involves the whole question of accurate diagnosis and appropriate treatment, and there is much less risk of error in roughly classing hysteria as a species of insanity than in taking one of its physical expressions, the hysterical fit, for instance, or sexual disorder, as its central fact, and grouping the rest of its phenomena round these as secondary. [. . .]

The subjects of hysteria are, in a very large proportion, of the female sex, the symptoms most often appearing at or soon after puberty. Children, however, even when quite young, may suffer from it, the sexual distribution being much less unequal in the earlier years; and marked cases occur not infrequently in men. The typical subject of hysteria, however, is the young woman; in her organism and her social conditions the potential factors of hysteria are present in a notable degree. Apart from whatever fundamental difference of nerve-stability there may be between the sexes, and this is probably very great, the girl usually meets with far more obstacles to uniform development and consequent nervous control than the youth. The stress of puberty, marked in both sexes by a great increase in the complexity and activity of the organism, is more sudden and intense in the female, the sexual organs which undergo these great changes are of relatively greater importance in her physical economy, and consequently invoke a larger area of central innervation than in the male. The nervous balance is thus in especially unstable equilibrium. With this greater internal stress on the nervous organism there are in the surroundings and general training of most girls many hindrances to the retention or restoration of a due stability and but few channels of outlet for her new activities. It is not only in the educational repression and ignorance as regards sexual matters of which she is the subject that this difference is manifest, but all kinds of other barriers to the free play of her powers are set up by ordinary social and ethical customs. 'Thou shall not' meets a girl at almost every turn. The exceptions to this rule are found in those instances where girls and women of all conditions, owing to the influence of good education or necessity, or both, have regular work and definite pursuits. The comparative freedom and the various and necessary occupations of the youth offer many safety valves for his comparatively minor nervous tension. In proportion as the energies are in some way satisfied, the nervous control is retained. Amongst the activities thus artificially repressed in girls, it must be recognised that the sexual play an important part and, indeed, the frequent evidence of dammed-up sexual emotions by both the special act of masturbation and numerous extraordinary vagaries of conduct have led many to regard unsatisfied sexual desire as one of the leading causes of hysteria. It may be briefly said in this context that this is but one cause, or rather occasion, for hysterical display. The most severe form of this affection may be seen in both men, women, and children, where there is no disorder, inability, or repression as regards the sexual organs or function; but enforced abstinence from the gratification of any of the inherent and primitive desires, in the absence of other outlets for the activities of the natural organism, must have untoward results, and in certain cases, when this special desire is in excess, may, even when other conditions are favourable, be in itself an adequate exciting cause of morbid display. There are clearly other stresses which render women especially liable to hysteria. The periodical disturbance of menstruation, the times of pregnancy and parturition and the numerous and multiform anxieties of home life, have their influence in contributing to the number of sufferers. There are, perhaps, as many or more instances of neurotic women commencing hysterics after marriage, as there are of hysterical girls showing greater nervous stability with the same change of condition.

Mental characteristics of hysterics.—The cardinal fact in the psychopathy of hysteria is an exaggerated self-consciousness dependent on undue prominence of feelings uncontrolled by intellect—that is to say, on the physical side, an undue preponderance of general widely diffused, undirected nervous discharges and an undue lack of determination of such discharges into definite channels. Thus the hysteria is pre-eminently an individualist, an unsocial unit, and fails in adaptation to organic surroundings. This predominant disorder in the sphere of feeling is generally accompanied by more or less evidence of intellectual disturbance, as shown in the multiform vagaries of conduct which are so prominent among hysterical symptoms; but in the majority of cases intellectual disorder is not conspicuous, and mental abnormality is mainly evidenced by exaggerated impressionability or tumultuous emotion on apparently slight provocation. It is difficult or impossible in some cases to draw a hard-and-fast line between insanity and hysteria and we may find all grades of temporarily disordered thought; but as a rule the hysteric recognises the impropriety or outrageousness of those actions which spring from this cause and shows that, if she has lost control of 'will power' she at least admits the want of it. Hysterics are deficient in energy, or in appropriate direction of energy, some become inert, others actively mischievous. Her abnormal action or inaction is the result of the passion for sympathy or notoriety, and instances of this range from mere giving way to or exaggeration of suffering to wilful imposture, simulation of all kinds of diseases and even to actual crimes. The steps from the lowest to the highest grade of hysteria are imperceptible, and the intermixture of imposture is often hard to recognise or duly appreciate. [. . .]

Motor disturbances in hysteria are legion, many of them pointing again to a lower level of nervous disorder than obtains in the more especially mental forms of the malady, though some are connected with the latter class in a marked degree. [. . .] Vomiting, a very frequent hysterical symptom, may be due to spasm of the stomach. It may be urgent and repeated, and cause considerable wasting in some instances, though by no means generally, food being often taken and retained in secret—and the symptom is apt to suddenly disappear under many of the various environmental stimuli which are appropriate to the treatment of hysterical disorders. [. . .] The commonest and most fundamental example of hysterical spasm are laughter and weeping with comparatively inadequate cause, symptoms which obviously connect hysteria, by invisible links with the normal neurosis underlying all human emotion.

Lastly, we have numerous examples of spasm of limbs and the voluntary muscles generally, transient or of long duration, often simulating the organic forms of spastic paraplegia and other diseases in various degrees. The most chronic instances of this affection are known as contractures; sudden recovery may occur in any case, but some become permanent with visible nerve-changes. The most familiar example of spasm is the hysterical fit, which constitutes the essence of what is vulgarly known as hysteria, and attacks a very large number of hysterics, but need not be dwelt upon at any length for the present purpose. [. . .]

Paralysis or any degree of lessened motor power may take place in all grades of hysteria, affecting any part of the nervous system, visceral or voluntary, and arising, like other symptoms, from both general and local exciting causes. [. . .] Rigidity, common with these paralyses, never endures continuously from the outset in the organic form. Aphonia may be the only prominent motor symptom in some cases, without marked mental peculiarities; and is common in young girls and boys, as well as adults. It is due to temporary adductor paralysis, as evidenced laryngoscopically, and can almost always be made to disappear, often permanently, by even one application of the faradic current. It is only necessary that the application be painful; but for the sake of exciting the due mental impression and voluntary effort to speak it is far better to apply the poles to the larynx itself externally; for success largely depends on the effect of the first experiment. [. . .] It must be remembered that both these and other hysterical symptoms are often grafted on to organic disease, both nervous and otherwise. [. . .]

Exciting causes of hysterical disorder.—The essential element of hysteria has been seen to be a neurosis marked by certain mental and physical symptoms. Heredity plays an all important part in its production. The limits of resistance to any given nervous stress vary widely in different individuals, and the disturbance which makes one person hysterical is not felt by another. The excessively frequent circumstance of hysterical women having obviously hysterical offspring is partly to be put down to example, and is an instance of untoward conditions as well as of heredity, but there is ample evidence of the close connection of other recognised neuroses in the families of hysterical subjects. Insanity, chorea, epilepsy, migraine and various forms of neurasthenia figure very largely in this context, as also do some of the recognised organic instances of nervous disease. Such hereditary relationships are especially prominent in those cases of hysterical disorder which are at once least amenable to treatment and least referable to demonstrable stress. On the vulnerable nervous material of the hysterical subject many exciting agents work to produce disorder. Prominent among these are great and sudden emotions, such as fear in all its forms—a notable element in the hysteria of childhood; disappointment; forcibly repressed desires, especially sexual; enforced mental overwork; nervous shock, as, *e.g.*, the result of railway accidents, earthquakes &c.; traumatism of all kinds, including surgical operations; general exhausting conditions, such as haemorrhages, anaemia, the menstrual periods, pregnancy, parturition, poisoning by alcohol, chloroform, mercury, &c.; diseases such as enteric and other fevers, pneumonia, malaria, syphilis; organic nervous diseases as tumour of the brain, disseminated sclerosis, tabes dorsalis, and especially paralysis agitans; and local affections of the generative and other organs, though it is to be observed here that marked disease of the uterus, such as cancer, is not a frequent exciting agent in hysterical display. [. . .]

Treatment.—The rational and successful treatment of hysteria depends on bearing in mind the nature of the predisposing neurosis and the various causes which excite its display. The sooner the hereditary neurosis is recognised, the more readily can its encouragement and development by exciting agents be prevented. Almost all treatment must be directed to counteracting those influences which disturb the impressionable organism; it is generally unnecessary and often harmful to treat a local manifestation. [. . .] In most cases of hysteria, of whatever nature, when the physician's aid is required, it is best, and sometimes imperative, to remove the patient from home influence and the conditions in which the disorder has developed, and to place her among strangers. This alone will cure many. Judicious hospital treatment, consisting mainly of observant neglect, proves this in what to some seems a surprising degree. When once the diagnosis of hysteria has been deliberately made, and the patient separated as far as possible from ascertainable exciting conditions, the doctor's visits should be few or should cease, and no one should by word or manner show any doubt as to the mode or success of the treatment proposed. In the class of cases known as hysterical anorexia and allied conditions the method of treatment known by the name of Weir Mitchell numbers its most important successes.[2] It may be fully conceded that the rubbing (*massage*), which in the popular mind is the main

---

[2] Silas Weir Mitchell (1829–1914) was a poet, novelist, and doctor, whose treatments described in texts like *Wear and Tear, or Hints for the Overworked* (1871) proved influential in the treatment of nervous diseases in America and Europe. Everything recommended by Donkin in this paragraph is owed to Mitchell.

point, and the concomitant *forced feeding* contribute in many cases to a more rapid success than when these means are dispensed with, but it is equally true that even with most advanced cases the third element of *isolation* alone will work wonders, a consoling fact to those who are unable to afford the great expense, both for doctors and nurses, which usually attaches to the complete treatment now in vogue. It must also be borne in mind that many cases which improve rapidly under the triple method relapse as quickly when the ceremonial ceases; and it is evidenced all over the field of hysteria that the simpler the method of cure, and the more it evokes self-reliance, the more enduring are its results. The patient's belief in the means used, however, is in many cases a great help towards success, and hysterical patients of many kinds may lose the symptoms, at least for a while, under almost any treatment which happens to be in fashion or to 'impress their minds.' Thus, a well-nourished person with good appetite and digestion is obviously not in physiological need of the artificial metabolism induced by the Weir Mitchell treatment, may be cured of an 'irritable spine' in a few days by 'massage' conducted with due gravity; and a subject of true hysterical anorexia of long standing, or hysterical vomiting, may make a rapid recovery after a few applications of faradism, made with an air of confidence, to the apigastrium.[3] The habit of many hysterical symptoms, such as anaesthesia, pain, paralysis, or spasm, of shifting their position, either spontaneously or from external suggestion or appliances, as pointedly shown by the transference phenomena in hemi-anaesthesia, indicates many modes of treatment to the reflecting physician, and at the same time reminds him of the necessarily evanescent nature of many of his successes. There is no doubt, however, that firmness and other qualities of mind and manner in those who are conducting the cases play an important part in the number and permanence of the cures.

When any physical disorder, general or local, co-exists with, or has excited, hysteria, it is generally imperative to treat it when possible, or to ignore it. [. . .] In all cases the rules of treatment laid down should be definite and strictly enforced. The best results will be obtained by exciting the will, which is most often in abeyance, by presenting the patients with sufficient objects for effort, and by acting on the faculties of imagination and belief. It is by these methods that modern miracle workers and priests and ministers of all colours succeed in curing many disorders when physicians ignorant of psychology are left resourceless.

---

[3] The last clause might be loosely rendered as: a few electrical shocks applied to the stomach.

2   from Josef Breuer and Sigmund Freud, 'On the
Psychical Mechanism of Hysterical Phenomena:
Preliminary Communication' (1893)

1

A chance observation has led us, over a number of years, to investigate a great variety of different forms and symptoms of hysteria, with a view to discovering their precipitating cause—the event which provoked the first occurrence, often many years earlier, of the phenomenon in question. In the great majority of cases it is not possible to establish the point of origin by a simple interrogation of the patient, however thoroughly it may be carried out. This is in part because what is in question is often some experience which the patient dislikes discussing; but principally because he is genuinely unable to recollect it and often has no suspicion of the causal connection between the precipitating event and the pathological phenomenon. As a rule it is necessary to hypnotize the patient and to arouse his memories under hypnosis of the time at which the symptom made its first appearance; when this has been done, it becomes possible to demonstrate the connection in the clearest and most convincing fashion.

This method of examination has in a large number of cases produced results which seem to be of value alike from a theoretical and a practical point of view.

They are valuable theoretically because they have taught us that external events determine the pathology of hysteria to an extent far greater than is known and recognized. It is of course obvious that in cases of 'traumatic' hysteria what provokes the symptoms is the accident. The causal connection is equally evident in hysterical attacks when it is possible to gather from the patient's utterances that in each attack he is hallucinating the same event which provoked the first one. The situation is more obscure in the case of other phenomena.

Our experiences have shown us, however, that the most various symptoms, which are ostensibly spontaneous and, as one might say, idiopathic products of hysteria, are just as strictly related to the precipitating trauma as the phenomena to which we have just alluded and which exhibit the connection quite clearly. The symptoms which we have been able to trace back to precipitating factors of this sort include neuralgias and anaesthesias of very various kinds, many of which had persisted for years, contractures and paralyses, hysterical attacks and epileptoid convulsions, which every observer regarded as true epilepsy, *petit mal*[4] and

---

[4] *Petit mal* refers to early stages of hysteria in the taxonomy of hysterical states theorized by Jean-Martin Charcot. Charcot (1825–93) gave intellectual respectability to the study of hysteria; his 'Tuesday lectures' at the Salpêtrière hospital in Paris, at which hysterics 'performed' for the audience, were visited by medics and non-medics alike.

disorders in the nature of *tic*, chronic vomiting and anorexia, carried to the pitch of rejection of all nourishment, various forms of disturbance of vision, constantly recurrent visual hallucinations, etc. The disproportion between the many years' duration of the hysterical symptom and the single occurrence which provoked it is what we are accustomed invariably to find in traumatic neuroses. Quite frequently it is some event in childhood that sets up a more or less severe symptom which persists during the years that follow.

The connection is often so clear that it is quite evident how it was that the precipitating event produced this particular phenomenon rather than any other. In that case the symptom has quite obviously been determined by the precipitating cause. We may take as a very commonplace instance a painful emotion arising during a meal but suppressed at the time, and then producing nausea and vomiting which persists for months in the form of hysterical vomiting. A girl, watching beside a sick-bed in a torment of anxiety, fell into a twilight state and had a terrifying hallucination, while her right arm, which was hanging over the back of her chair, went to sleep; from this there developed a paresis of the same arm accompanied by contracture and anaesthesia. She tried to pray but could find no words; at length she succeeded in repeating a children's prayer in English. When subsequently a severe and highly complicated hysteria developed, she could only speak, write and understand English, while her native language remained unintelligible to her for eighteen months.[5] [. . .]

In other cases the connection is not so simple. It consists only in what might be called a 'symbolic' relation between the precipitating cause and the pathological phenomenon—a relation such as healthy people form in dreams. For instance, a neuralgia may follow upon mental pain or vomiting upon a feeling of moral disgust. We have studied patients who used to make the most copious use of this sort of symbolization. In still other cases it is not possible to understand at first sight how they can be determined in the manner we have suggested. It is precisely the typical hysterical symptoms which fall into this class, such as hemi-anaesthesia, contraction of the field of vision, epileptiform convulsions, and so on. An explanation of our views on this group must be reserved for a fuller discussion of the subject.

Observations such as these seem to us to establish an analogy between the pathogenesis of common hysteria and that of traumatic neuroses, and to justify an extension of the concept of traumatic hysteria. In traumatic neuroses the operative cause of the illness is not the trifling physical injury but the affect of fright—the psychical trauma. In an analogous manner, our investigations reveal, for many, if

---

[5] This refers to one of the most famous and most discussed patients of psychoanalysis—'Anna O' (Bertha Pappenheim), who coined the term 'talking cure' for Breuer's method of encouraging her to recall and cathartically talk through her traumatic memories. Her case history is the first in *Studies in Hysteria*.

not for most, hysterical symptoms, precipitating causes which can only be described as psychical traumas. Any experience which calls up distressing affects—such as those of fright, anxiety, shame or physical pain—may operate as a trauma of this kind; and whether it in fact does so depends naturally enough on the susceptibility of the person affected (as well as on another condition which will be mentioned later). In the case of common hysteria it not infrequently happens that, instead of a single, major trauma, we find a number of partial traumas forming a group of provoking causes. These have only been able to exercise a traumatic effect by summation and they belong together in so far as they are in part components of a single story of suffering. There are other cases in which an apparently trivial circumstance combines with the actually operative event or occurs at a time of peculiar susceptibility to stimulation and in this way attains the dignity of a trauma which it would not otherwise have possessed but which thenceforward persists.

But the causal relation between the determining psychical trauma and the hysterical phenomenon is not of a kind implying that the trauma merely acts like an *agent provocateur* in releasing the Symptom, which thereafter leads an independent existence. We must presume rather that the psychical trauma—or more precisely the memory of the trauma—acts like a foreign body which long after its entry must continue to be regarded as an agent that is still at work; and we find the evidence for this in a highly remarkable phenomenon which at the same time lends an important *practical* interest to our findings.

For we found, to our great surprise at first, that *each individual hysterical symptom immediately and permanently disappeared when we had succeeded in bringing clearly to light the memory of the event by which it was provoked and in arousing its accompanying affect, and when the patient had described that event in the greatest possible detail and had put the affect into words.* Recollection without affect almost invariably produces no result. The psychical process which originally took place must be repeated as vividly as possible; it must be brought back to its *status nascendi* and then given verbal utterance. Where what we are dealing with are phenomena involving stimuli (spasms, neuralgias and hallucinations) these re-appear once again with the fullest intensity and then vanish for ever. Failures of function, such as paralyses and anaesthesias, vanish in the same way, though, of course, without the temporary intensification being discernible. [. . .]

We may reverse the dictum '*cessante causa cessat effectus*'[6] and conclude from these observations that the determining process continues to operate in some way or other for years—not indirectly, through a chain of intermediate causal links, but as a directly releasing cause—just as a psychical pain that is

[6] 'When the cause ceases the effect ceases'.

remembered in waking consciousness still provokes a lachrymal secretion long after the event. *Hysterics suffer mainly from reminiscences.*

2

At first sight it seems extraordinary that events experienced so long ago should continue to operate so intensely—that their recollection should not be liable to the wearing away process to which, after all, we see all our memories succumb. The following considerations may perhaps make this a little more intelligible.

The fading of a memory or the losing of its affect depends on various factors. The most important of these is *whether there has been an energetic reaction to the event that provokes an affect.* By 'reaction' we here understand the whole class of voluntary and involuntary reflexes—from tears to acts of revenge—in which, as experience shows us, the affects are discharged. If this reaction takes place to a sufficient amount a large part of the affect disappears as a result. Linguistic usage bears witness to this fact of daily observation by such phrases as 'to cry oneself out', and to 'blow off steam'. If the reaction is suppressed, the affect remains attached to the memory [. . .]

'Abreaction' however, is not the only method of dealing with the situation that is open to a normal person who has experienced a psychical trauma. A memory of such a trauma, even if it has not been abreacted, enters the great complex of associations, it comes alongside other experiences, which may contradict it, and is subjected to rectification by other ideas. After an accident, for instance, the memory of the danger and the (mitigated) repetition of the fright becomes associated with the memory of what happened afterwards—rescue and the consciousness of present safety. Again, a person's memory of a humiliation is corrected by his putting the facts right, by considering his own worth, etc. In this way a normal person is able to bring about the disappearance of the accompanying affect through the process of association.

To this we must add the general effacement of impressions, the fading of memories which we name 'forgetting' and which wears away those ideas in particular that are no longer affectively operative.

Our observations have shown, on the other hand, that the memories which have become the determinants of hysterical phenomena persist for a long time with astonishing freshness and with the whole of their affective colouring. We must, however, mention another remarkable fact, which we shall later be able to turn to account, namely, that these memories, unlike other memories of their past lives, are not at the patients' disposal. On the contrary, *these experiences are completely absent from the patients' memory when they are in a normal psychical state, or are only present in a highly summary form.* Not until they have been questioned under hypnosis do these memories emerge with the undiminished vividness of a recent event.[7]

Thus, for six whole months, one of our patients reproduced under hypnosis with hallucinatory vividness everything that had excited her on the same day of the previous year (during an attack of acute hysteria). A diary kept by her mother without her knowledge proved the completeness of the reproduction. Another patient, partly under hypnosis and partly during spontaneous attacks, re-lived with hallucinatory clarity all the events of a hysterical psychosis which she had passed through ten years earlier and which she had for the most part forgotten till the moment at which it re-emerged. Moreover, certain memories of aetiological importance which dated back from fifteen to twenty-five years were found to be astonishingly intact and to possess remarkable sensory force, and when they returned they acted with all the affective strength of new experiences.

This can only be explained on the view that these memories constitute an exception in their relation to all the wearing-away processes which we have discussed above. It appears, that is to say, that these memories correspond to traumas that have not been sufficiently abreacted; and if we enter more closely into the reasons which have prevented this we find at least two sets of conditions under which the reaction to the trauma fails to occur.

In the first group are those cases in which the patients have not reacted to a psychical trauma because the nature of the trauma excluded a reaction, as in the case of the apparently irreparable loss of a loved person or because social circumstances made a reaction impossible or because it was a question of things which the patient wished to forget, and therefore intentionally repressed from his conscious thought and inhibited and suppressed. It is precisely distressing things of this kind that, under hypnosis, we find are the basis of hysterical phenomena (e.g. hysterical deliria in saints and nuns, continent women and well-brought-up children).

The second group of conditions are determined, not by the content of the memories but by the psychical states in which the patient received the experiences in question. For we find, under hypnosis, among the causes of hysterical symptoms ideas which are not in themselves significant, but whose persistence is due to the fact that they originated during the prevalence of severely paralysing affects, such as fright, or during positively abnormal psychical states, such as the semi-hypnotic twilight state of day-dreaming, auto-hypnoses, and so on. In such cases it is the nature of the states which makes a reaction to the event impossible. [. . .]

---

[7] Freud soon ceased to hypnotize his patients, marking a further distinguishing feature of the psycho-analytic method as it developed in the 1890s.

It may therefore be said that the ideas which have become pathological have per-sisted with such freshness and affective strength because they have been denied the normal wearing-away processes by means of abreaction and reproduction in states of uninhibited association. [. . .]

5

It will now be understood how it is that the psychotherapeutic procedure which we have described in these pages has a curative effect. It brings to an end the operating force of the idea which was not abreacted in the first instance, by allowing its strangulated affect to find a way out through speech; and it subjects it to associative correction by introducing it into normal consciousness (under light hypnosis) or by removing it through the physician's suggestions, as is done in somnambulism accompanied by amnesia.

In our opinion the therapeutic advantages of this procedure are considerable. It is of course true that we do not cure hysteria in so far as it is a matter of disposition. We can do nothing against the recurrence of hypnoid states. Moreover, during the productive stage of an acute hysteria our procedure cannot prevent the phenomena which have been so laboriously removed from being at once replaced by fresh ones. But once this acute stage is past, any residues which may be left in the form of chronic symptoms or attacks are often removed, and permanently so, by our method, because it is a radical one; in this respect it seems to us far superior in its efficacy to removal through direct suggestion as it is practised today by psychotherapists.

———

3.   from William James, 'The Stream of Thought',
              Principles of Psychology (1890)

[. . .] *Within each personal consciousness, thought is sensibly continuous.*

I can only define 'continuous' as that which is without breach, crack, or division. I have already said that the breach from one mind to another is perhaps the greatest breach in nature. The only breaches that can well be conceived to occur within the limits of a single mind would either be interruptions, time-gaps during which the consciousness went out altogether to come into existence again at a later moment; or they would be breaks in the quality, or content, of the thought, so abrupt that the segment that followed had no connection whatever with the one that went before. The proposition that within each personal consciousness thought feels continuous, means two things:

1. That even where there is a time-gap the consciousness after it feels as if it belonged together with the consciousness before it, as another part of the same self.

2. That the changes from one moment to another in the quality of the consciousness are never absolutely abrupt.

The case of the time-gaps, as the simplest, shall be taken first. [. . .] On waking from sleep, we usually know that we have been unconscious, and we often have an accurate judgment of how long. The judgment here is certainly an inference from sensible signs, and its ease is due to long practice in the particular field. The result of it, however, is that the consciousness is, *for itself*, not what it was in the former case, but interrupted and continuous, in the mere time-sense of the words. But in the other sense of continuity, the sense of the parts being inwardly connected and belonging together because they are parts of a common whole, the consciousness remains sensibly continuous and one. What now is the common whole? The natural name for it is *myself, I*, or *me*.

When Paul and Peter wake up in the same bed, and recognize that they have been asleep, each one of them mentally reaches back and makes connection with but one of the two streams of thought which were broken by the sleeping hours. As the current of an electrode buried in the ground unerringly finds its way to its own similarly buried mate, across no matter how much intervening earth, so Peter's present instantly finds out Peter's past, and never by mistake knits itself on to that of Paul. Paul's thought in turn is as little liable to go astray. The past thought of Peter is appropriated by the present Peter alone. He may have a *knowledge*, and a correct one too, of what Paul's last drowsy states of mind were as he sank into sleep, but it is an entirely different sort of knowledge from that which he has of his own last states. He *remembers* his own states, whilst he only *conceives* Paul's. Remembrance is like direct feeling; its object is suffused with a warmth and intimacy to which no object of mere conception ever attains. This quality of warmth and intimacy and immediacy is what Peter's *present* thought also possesses for itself. So sure as this present is me, is mine, it says, so sure is anything else that comes with the same warmth and intimacy and immediacy, me and mine. What the dualities called warmth and intimacy may in themselves be will have to be matter for future consideration. But whatever past feelings appear with those qualities must be admitted to receive the greeting of the present mental state, to be owned by it, and accepted as belonging together with it in a common self. This community of self is what the time-gap cannot break in twain, and is why a present thought, although not ignorant of the time-gap, can still regard itself as continuous with certain chosen portions of the past.

Consciousness, then, does not appear to itself chopped up in bits. Such words as 'chain' or 'train' do not describe it fitly as it presents itself in the first instance. It is nothing jointed; it flows. A 'river' or a 'stream' are the metaphors by which it is most naturally described. *In talking of it hereafter, let us call it the stream of thought, of consciousness, or of subjective life.*

But now there appears, even within the limits of the same self, and between thoughts all of which alike have this same sense of belonging together, a kind of jointing and separateness among the parts, of which this statement seems to take no account. I refer to the breaks that are produced by sudden *contrasts in the quality* of the successive segments of the stream of thought. If the words 'chain' and 'train' had no natural fitness in them, how came such words to be used at all? Does not a loud explosion rend the consciousness upon which it abruptly breaks, in twain? Does not every sudden shock, appearance of a new object, or change in a sensation, create a real interruption, sensibly felt as such, which cuts the conscious stream across at the moment at which it appears? Do not such interruptions smite us every hour of our lives, and have we the right, in their presence, still to call our consciousness a continuous stream?

This objection is based partly on a confusion and partly on a superficial introspective view.

The confusion is between the thoughts themselves, taken as subjective facts, and the things of which they are aware. It is natural to make this confusion, but easy to avoid it when once put on one's guard. The things are discrete and discontinuous; they do pass before us in a train or chain, making often explosive appearances and rending each other in twain. But their comings and goings and contrasts no more break the flow of the thought that thinks them than they break the time and the space in which they lie. A silence may be broken by a thunderclap, and we may be so stunned and confused for a moment by the shock as to give no instant account to ourselves of what has happened. But that very confusion is a mental state, and a state that passes us straight over from the silence to the sound. The transition between the thought of one object and the thought of another is no more a break in the thought than a joint in a bamboo is a break in the wood. It is a part of the *consciousness* as much as the joint is a part of the *bamboo*. [. . .]

As we take, in fact, a general view of the wonderful stream of our consciousness, what strikes us first is this different pace of its parts. Like a bird's life, it seems to be made of an alternation of flights and perchings. The rhythm of language expresses this, where every thought is expressed in a sentence, and every sentence closed by a period. The resting-places are usually occupied by sensorial imaginations of some sort, whose peculiarity is that they can be held before the mind for an indefinite time, and contemplated without changing; the places of flight are filled with thoughts of relations, static or dynamic, that for the most part obtain between the matters contemplated in the periods of comparative rest.

Let us call the resting-places the 'substantive parts,' and the places of flight the 'transitive parts,' of the stream of thought. It then appears that the main end of our thinking is at all times the attainment of some other substantive part than the one from which we have just been dislodged. And we may say that the main use of the transitive parts is to lead us from one substantive conclusion to another.

Now it is very difficult, introspectively, to see the transitive parts for what they really are. If they are but flights to a conclusion, stopping them to look at them before the conclusion is reached is really annihilating them. Whilst if we wait till the conclusion be reached, it so exceeds them in vigor and stability that it quite eclipses and swallows them up in its glare. Let anyone try to cut a thought across in the middle and get a look at its section, and he will see how difficult the intro-spective observation of the transitive tracts is. The rush of the thought is so head-long that it almost always brings us up at the conclusion before we can arrest it. Or if our purpose is nimble enough and we do arrest it, it ceases forthwith to be itself. As a snowflake crystal caught in the warm hand is no longer a crystal but a drop, so, instead of catching the feeling of relation moving to its term, we find we have caught some substantive thing, usually the last word we were pronouncing, stati-cally taken, and with its function, tendency, and particular meaning in the sen-tence quite evaporated. The attempt at introspective analysis in these cases is in fact like seizing a spinning top to catch its motion, or trying to turn up the gas quickly enough to see how the darkness looks. And the challenge to produce these psychoses, which is sure to be thrown by doubting psychologists at anyone who contends for their existence, is as unfair as Zeno's treatment of the advocates of motion, when, asking them to point out in what place an arrow is when it moves, he argues the falsity of their thesis from their inability to make to so preposterous a question an immediate reply.

---

4   from F. W. H. Myers, 'The Subliminal Consciousness' (1891)

[. . .] I suggest, then, that the stream of consciousness in which we habitually live is not the only consciousness which exists in connection with our organism. Our habitual or empirical consciousness may consist of a mere selection from a multi-tude of thoughts and sensations, of which some at least are equally conscious with those that we empirically know. I accord no primacy to my ordinary waking self, except that among my potential selves this one has shown itself the fittest to meet the needs of common life. I hold that it has established no further claim, and that it is perfectly possible that other thoughts, feelings, and memories, either isolated or in continuous connection, may now be actively conscious, as we say, 'within me,'—in some kind of co-ordination with my organism, and forming some part of my total individuality. I conceive it possible that at some future time, and under changed conditions, I may recollect all; I may assume these various personalities under one single consciousness in which ultimate and complete consciousness the empirical consciousness which at this moment directs my hand may be only one element of many.

Before we draw out the implications of such a statement, let us pause to consider the obvious reasons which a man may give for considering his empirical consciousness as identical with his total self.

The first remark of the ordinary reader will probably be that if there were in fact any other consciousness within him, he would certainly be aware of it.

This, however, is simply to beg the question. We must reply that the dicta of consciousness have already been shown to need correction in so many ways which the ordinary observer could never have anticipated,—the world of realities (so far as we can get at any intelligible notion of it) is so utterly unlike what our empirical consciousness suggest to us,—that we have no right to trust our consciousness, so to say, a step further than we can feel it;—to hold that anything whatever—even a separate consciousness in our own organism—can be proved *not* to exist by the mere fact that we (as we know ourselves) are not aware of it.

But dropping this first untenable demurrer, a man may still give two reasons, which look valid enough, for supposing that there can be comparatively little psychical action going on within him of which he cannot give an account. He may say, in the first place: 'the deeds which I have done in life—the movements which my body has made—have been executed in obedience to the will of my conscious self. There has been no room for the operation of any imaginary will in the background.' And, in the second place, he may add: 'besides the sensations and movements originating in my own frame, there have been sensations and movements impressed upon me from without. But all this, though I could not *control* it, I can nevertheless *remember*. I can feel sure that nothing of importance has happened to me which I cannot recall by voluntary act of recollection. Here again, therefore there is no room for the operation of an imaginary memory beneath the threshold. In short, to put the matter in a nutshell, I receive my letters at my front door, and I give my orders in my library. Why should I suppose that my house is governed by an imaginary conspiracy in the kitchen?'

Now I need not examine how far contentions like these would be valid if we kept to the realm of pure physical speculation. For we happen to be able to prove, by actual and easy experiment, that they are entirely inconclusive.

In the first place, it is now well known that very often if a man in the hypnotic trance be ordered to perform a certain act after he has been awakened—to execute, as it is called, a post-hypnotic suggestion—he will execute that suggestion, in complete unconsciousness of having received a command, and in the full belief that he is acting from his own choice, and with complete freedom of will. [. . .]

Again. The chain of memory of which our superficial self is master, and which in common parlance is spoken of as extending over the whole past life, is seen on closer inspection to be imperfect and interrupted in a high degree. For all men it omits the periods of infancy and of sleep; for many men there are further gaps representing delirium, hypnotic trance, and various disturbances of consciousness. [. . .]

What, then, is the practical conclusion to be drawn as regards the mode of conducting our present inquiry? It is simply this: that we must regard this ordinary stream of waking consciousness—in which I write these words and my readers read them—with just the same impartial, objective scrutiny which we apply to the consciousness, say, of a person in spontaneous somnambulism or in hypnotic trance. [. . .]

But this—although it is pretty nearly all that has been hitherto attempted in this direction—stands to a complete experimental psychology in something the same relation that the digging a pit in my garden stands to a knowledge of the earth's crust. I can easily discover that after digging (say) through a stratum of gravel I come to clay, and I can describe the clay as damper and less healthy than the gravel. As a householder I may accept this stratum of gravel above the clay as an ultimate and satisfactory feat. As a geologist I am bound to ask what it all means. Why is the gravel on the top? Why is there clay below it? What is there below the clay? Do the strata always occur in the same order, or must the gravel at any rate always be on the top? I can no longer say, 'My house is built on gravel,' as though that were all I need know. It is built upon an unknown number of strata, of which, for an unknown reason, the gravel is uppermost at this particular point.

Now I maintain that the prevalent French mode of treating these subjacent psychological states—although they have proved in more than one case capable of beneficially supplanting the superficial state—as though they were, nevertheless, mere morbid variations or splittings-up of the superficial states, resembles the reasoning of a man who should say that the clay, or chalk, or granite which he found beneath the gravel was a kind of degenerate gravel—an agglomeration of particular elements in the gravel, but nothing really new.

I think that the time has come for a rather deeper investigation. I think that we have now observed enough out-croppings of subjacent strata to enable us at least to seek—I do not say as yet to find—some sort of provisional law of stratification which does not assume as a primary truth that because gravel is that stratum on which we have chosen to build our houses, gravel is therefore the normal type which ought always to be uppermost, and of which all other minerals

are a degenerate modification. Not so; phenomena of so far-reaching a significance as these demand a wider purview than the mere pathologist's in those who
would explain them. They open questions as to man's psychical being which
have always been deemed to lie *inter apices philosophiae*.[8] [. . .]

For such is my hypothesis. I suggest that each of us is in reality an abiding
psychical entity far more extensive than he knows—an individuality which can
never express itself completely through any corporeal manifestation. The Self
manifests through the organism; but there is always some part of the Self un-
manifested; and always, as it seems, some power of organic expression in abeyance
or in reserve. Neither can the player express all his thought upon the instrument,
nor is the instrument so arranged that all its keys can be sounded at once. One
melody after another may be played upon it; nay,—as with the messages of duplex
or multiplex telegraphy,—simultaneously or with imperceptible intermissions,[9]
several melodies can be played together; but there are still unexhausted reserves of
instrumental capacity, as well as unexpressed treasures of informing thought.

All this psychical action, I hold, is conscious; all is included in an actual or
potential memory below the threshold of our habitual consciousness. For all
which lies below that threshold subliminal seems the fittest world. 'Unconscious,' or even 'subconscious,' would be directly misleading; and to speak (as is
sometimes convenient) of the secondary self may give the impression either that
there cannot be more selves than two, or that the supraliminal self, the self above
the threshold, the self of common experience—is in some way superior to other
possible selves.

I hold (to continue) that this subliminal consciousness and subliminal
memory may embrace a far wider range both of physiological and of psychical
activity than is open to our supraliminal consciousness, to our supraliminal
memory. The spectrum of consciousness, if I may so call it, is in the subliminal
self indefinitely extended at both ends.

At the inferior, or physiological end, in the first place, it included much that is
too archaic, too rudimentary, to be retained in the supraliminal memory of an
organism so advanced as man's. For the supraliminal memory of any organism is
inevitably limited by the need of concentration upon recollections useful in the
struggle for existence. The recollection of processes now performed automati-
cally, and needing no supervision, drops out from the supraliminal memory, but
may be in my view retained in the subliminal. To this point we shall again recur.

[8] Literally, 'between the summits of philosophy'—Myers suggesting that psychic phenomena have
been 'improper' objects of knowledge.
[9] Duplex telegraphy—the ability to send messages in opposite directions simultaneously down the
same wire—had only been in commercial use since the mid-1870s. Myers had coined the term 'multiplex
personality' in 1885 to discuss cases of what is now called multiple personality. One of Myers's co-
workers in the Society for Psychical Research, Oliver Lodge, was active in early 'wireless telegraphy'
experiments in the 1880s and 1890s.

In the second place, and at the superior or psychical end, the subliminal memory includes an unknown category of impression which the supraliminal consciousness is incapable of receiving in any direct fashion, and which it must cognise, if at all, in the shape of messages from the subliminal consciousness.

---

5.   from T. Clifford Allbutt, 'Nervous Diseases and Modern Life' (1895)

The outcry of the modern neurotic has made itself heard rather unduly of late. It is said that we are drooping with the century, a century of stress and of unsatisfied desires; that the struggle for life has revealed itself in naked and brutish forms which shock the happier children of our time, and dishearten and crush the less fortunate; that religious beliefs, which kindled an inner joy in those whose outer lives were hard and bare, and divine charity in those to whom fortune has been kind have crumbled away, that even those colder consolations which were drawn from a rational acquiescence in the order of a majestic and beautiful world are now denied to philosophers who have lost faith in the progress of man, who see but a vulgar material triumph in the arts of our generation, the elements of decay in the most vigorous national life, and the encroachment of peoples of lower standards and lower ethical capacities upon the seats of nations whose genius has made a great history and created a glorious tradition. [. . .]

But, before falling back upon such a theory of life as this, let us first inquire into the truth of the allegation that the nervous energy of our race is being exhausted, that worries and cares are killing us, and that, after all, as we are in a stage of decadence, it does not much matter.

Among the gravest apprehensions of the moment is that the alleged increase of insanity may be true, and that, if true, it is due to a turbulent or carking mode of life which overthrows the reason or corrodes the tissues which are its instruments. Now, in respect of an alleged increase, we find that experts are not agreed; or, if agreed, they believe that the apparent is not a real increase.

In the Census we have some approximate estimates of the number of insane persons living in our country at certain dates of enumeration. As the population of Great Britain increases the number of such insane persons increases also: this we should naturally expect and the regret we feel concerning such an absolute increase is that the conditions which favour the occurrence of insanity continue in force but it is asserted that there is an increase of insanity beyond this proportion—that the rate of increase of insanity has multiplied beyond that of the population. Now the only evidence of such a disproportionate increase is that the number of *known* lunatics increases at a greater rate than the population. The number of known lunatics (that is, the number of persons formally recorded as insane) and the number of existing lunatics are measures of different things. The number of known lunatics may be increased even without any multiplication of persons, as for instance, by a prolongation of the mean duration of life in the class: if the mean of life be lengthened more persons will survive to be recounted in successive years. We have no large figures to prove that the mean duration of life in the insane has been lengthened, but we see probabilities of it which are scarcely less convincing. When I was a boy, the village 'naturals' were the slaves of the men if their services were useful, of the lads and lasses if they were feckless. In the former case, they were driven and beaten, in the latter case harried and tormented.

Even if fagged or bullied, there was no sympathetic care to interpret their needs or to supply their inability to care for themselves. Nearly all such daft creatures are now gathered in asylums where they are properly fed, properly clad, properly protected from the weather, and their lives, on the whole, no doubt, greatly prolonged.

Again, within the walls of asylums, persons who are suicidal or afflicted with epilepsy and other acute or chronic diseases of the brain, are nursed, watched and regulated at the present day with a skill and vigilance which must prolong the mean duration of life in them; and evidence supporting this probability may be found in the records of these institutions. [. . .]

Yet, it may be said, when you come to probabilities, does it not stand to reason that the conditions of modern life must increase and intensify insanity? [. . .] Every age has its own dangers, but history does not seem to indicate that the most civilised States are the maddest. The evidence on the face of it lies rather the other way. In spite of the more direct and brutal elimination of the unfit among savages, we seem to see obscurely in the gloom of the past, or of the remoter parts of the earth, that possession by devils, attacks of fury, hallucinations, phrensies, phantasies and epidemic manias have been at least as common in ruder peoples than our own. [. . .]

Meanwhile, I see no evidence that there is an increase of insanity due to the conditions of modern civilisation; if, indeed, it be true, on the one hand, that insane persons are set more at liberty to produce offspring, it seems to me, on the other hand, that healthier conditions of life are tending to reinvigorate or crowd out weakly stocks. To turn now from insanity ordinarily so called, to other nervous maladies—to nervous debility, to hysteria, to neurasthenia, to the fretfulness, the melancholy, the unrest due to living at a high pressure, to the whirl of the railway, the pelting of telegrams, the strife of business, the hunger for riches, the lust of vulgar minds for coarse and instant pleasures, the decay of those controlling ethics handed down from statelier and more steadfast generations— surely, at any rate, these maladies and these causes of maladies are more rife than

they were in the days of our fathers? To this question let us anxiously set ourselves, and see what answer must be given. There is, I know, but one opinion on
the subject in society, in the newspapers, in the books of philosophers, and even
in the journals and treatises of the medical profession. [. . .]

Not only do we hear, but daily we see neurotics, neurasthenics, hysterics, and
the like: is not every large city filled with nerve-specialists, and their chambers
with patients; are not hospitals, baths, electric-machines and massages multiplying daily for their use; nerve-tonics sold behind every counter, and health-resorts
advertised for their solace and restoration?

Well, rich and idle people are increasing in number, no doubt, and they run, as
they always did, after the fashionable fad of the day; what was 'liver' fifty years ago
has become 'nerves' to-day. Moreover, we must remember that nervous diseases
are long diseases and as a rule do not tend to death; so that one patient may
be a lucrative visitor to twenty physicians, may occupy successive beds in many
hospitals, or may wander in the saloons of half the cure-houses in Europe. We
must remember too that one of the features of nervous disease is restlessness,
quackishness and craving for empathy; and that the intellectual acuteness of
many of these sufferings, the swift transmission of news by the press, and the
facilities of modern locomotion all favour the neurotic traffic. [. . .]

There is some ground, I believe for the assertion that dwelling exclusively in
large cities is tending to dwindle and impoverish the bodily health of the wage-
earners, or permanently resident, class, but it is not in this class that the effects of
'brain pressure' of ambitious projects, of business competition, of pampered aestheticism are to be sought. Will any serious person, looking round at our foot-
balling young men, our tennis-playing and bicycling young women, our maturer
alpinists and golfers of both sexes, our 'Ancient Mariners' and sporting matrons
declare that the standard of physical health in our upper and middle classes is
falling? To me, at any rate, their trials and pains seem to agree with them mightily.
As I have no longer youth, I must be content with memory and experience, and
I do not hesitate to say that when I look back upon the young men and women
of forty and thirty years ago, I am amazed rather at the physical splendour and
divine energy of our young friends of to-day. The world seems to have filled with
Apollos and Dianas; cheap food and clothing, improved sanitation, athletics
which bring temperance with them, frequent changes of air and scene, and a more
scientific regulation of all habits, seem since my adolescence to have transformed middle-class youth; and the change is rapidly spreading downwards.

Women especially seem to be changed for the better. Freedom to live their own
lives, and the enfranchisement of their faculties in a liberal education, which,
physically put, means the development of their brains and nerves, far from
making women more whimsical or languorous, seem not only to have given them
new charms and fresher and wider interests in life, but also to have promoted in

them a more rapid and continuous flow of nervous spirits, and to have armed and animated them with a new vitality both of body and mind. [. . .]

All this talk of decadence is a wild absurdity, the Wertherism of the young West,[10] this West which has grown out of the dogmas of its childhood and the splendid barbarities of its teens; the intellectual life of our secular manhood, having a few gleams on the way, is but now beginning to know the light. It is our new self-consciousness disturbs us; we have not fully learned how to use our new dominion over the ministries of Nature to the worthiest ends.

Have we then no reason for fear? Are all things for the best in the best possible of nervous systems? By no means: in my judgement things are getting no worse; on the contrary, the conditions of our nervous functions are bettering year by year; but to say that there is not much to be done, that there are not obvious evils to be removed, and means of good to be organised, would be an absurd optimism. I have said that we are on the threshold of manhood, not in the chamber of senility, nor even in the fulfilment of maturity. [. . .]

There is no more pretentious nonsense than the cry that our nerves are too sensitive, too excitable. It is of no use to be angry with an individual fool, but one is tempted to be angry with the man or woman who bewails his nervous excitability. May I ask what is the virtue of nerves but to be excitable?—the more excitable the more efficient; as the racehorse differs from an ass, so is man civilised by virtue of this very excitability of his nerves. What does sword-play mean, or political debate, the fine line of the painter, the rare intonation of the violinist—what mean these but the most exquisite excitability of the nerves? Nervous tension, like muscular tension or any other such function, may no doubt be heedlessly pushed to extreme fatigue, especially if the impressions be too uniform; but the risk of error is small when I repeat that the quickening of the nerves, like that of any other organ, tends not to weakening, but to strength. Great artists have found that fatigue is averted not by breaking up their works, but by changes of mode in their calls upon our attention.

It were, I think, no paradox to say that by virtue of its more and more complete adaptation to the varying degrees and kinds of social pressure—that is to say, of its very complexity—the nervous tissue, delicate as it is, exquisite as it is, shows a tenacity and persistence beyond most others. Old age rarely enters by the paths of the nerves, or finds its first seat in the cerebral centres: if the circulation be maintained, and the excretions do not fail, the brain of old persons retains a marvellous efficiency. [. . .]

No rate of activity, which we can foresee, will be dangerous to human and social

---

[10] 'Wertherism' was coined in the wake of Johann Goethe's *Sorrows of Young Werther* (1774), a novel about an artist so sensitive in his unfulfilled love that he commits suicide. Young men throughout Europe emulated the hero, and Wertherism came to define an adolescent melancholy. For the 1890s, it connected to notions of dandyism and morbid psychology.

life if society provide that it do not suffer as a whole by collisions and injuries in its parts; this it must secure, not on the whole by slackening its rates of speed, but by economising and combining its constituent forces for larger and larger ends. There is no more brutal and hopeless counsel than to apply crude Darwinism to men and women, and to compare individual lives in human societies with the several rivalries of the beasts: that weak lives were not trampled down in the onward march of the people is a hideous regret; and it is no less an error to hold that a mature society can flourish upon such an advantage. Every fainting man or child is a loose link; in society, and, happily, our general practice is better than the precepts of some of us. By the great work of public health we are bringing it about that no child shall begin life with preventible disease, and our weakly children are as often crippled as killed by preventible disease; bad rearing and the microbe maim as often as they 'eliminate': by educational reforms, which as yet are rather in sight than in action, we shall not attempt to repress but to intensify the nervous faculties of our young men and women; and this we shall attain, not by quickening only the nervous apparatus which lies near the surface by casual and transient stimulants, but we shall endeavour to broaden and enrich their minds by those more systematic and penetrating exercises which call forth vibrations from the inward nervous structures and harmonise the elements of action in wider and wider orders of perception and response.

EDITORS' NOTES

1. Horatio Bryan Donkin (1845–1929). Educated in Classics at Oxford, before training in medicine, qualifying in 1873. He worked in the East London Children's Hospital, before specializing in women's health. He was a member of Karl Pearson's freethinking Men and Women's Club in the 1880s (hence becoming doctor to the feminist Olive Schreiner); he was later a member of important Edwardian government committees on mental illness and the social problem of the 'Feeble Minded', for which work he was knighted in 1911.

2. Josef Breuer (1842–1925). Viennese Jewish doctor, qualifying in 1867 and combining neurological research with a highly successful private practice to the wealthy families of Vienna. It was whilst treating a man in 1880 that he observed the severe psychological disturbance of the daughter, who became the case history 'Anna O'. His treatment involved the use of hypnosis (only just gaining a small measure of medical respectability at the time), and a cathartic recall of traumatic memories. He discussed the case with the young Sigmund Freud, who first used the treatment method in 1888. Their joint research was published in 1893, with *Studies in Hysteria* published in 1895. In the following year, Breuer stopped all collaboration with Freud, and never spoke to him again. The reasons for the split were likely to be related to

Freud's developing theory that most hysterical phenomena derived from sexual trauma.

Sigmund Freud (1856–1939). Eldest son of a middle-class Jewish family in Vienna. He trained in anatomy and neurology from 1873, before beginning medical training in 1881. In 1885 he visited Charcot's hospital in Paris for three months, a visit which led him to change his focus of study to hysteria and neurosis. He developed the theory of the origin and treatment of hysteria with Breuer, a method he termed 'psychoanalysis' in 1896. Despite his many publications, Freud remained a marginal figure in Viennese medicine for another ten years. In 1910, however, he was invited to America to lecture at Clark University. With a small but growing group of dispersed European adherents, he fostered the institutions that would assist in the amazing permeation of psycho-analytic ideas through the twentieth-century Western world. Fleeing anti-Semitic persecution after Hitler invaded Austria in 1938, he moved to London, where he died in September 1939.

3. Frederic William Henry Myers (1843–1901). The son of a clergyman, he studied Classics at Cambridge, and lectured in Classics at Trinity College until 1870, whilst gaining a small reputation as a poet and essayist. He moved through a sequence of enthusiasms—the Greek ideal, Christian evangelism—before arriving at the séance table in 1874. With his mentor Henry Sidgwick he founded the Society for Psychical Research in 1882. He spent the rest of his life theorizing the psychical events he witnessed, and seeking definitive empirical proof of 'survival of bodily death'. He did this, however, by training himself as an expert in the leading developments in psychology—he was a friend of leading European experimental psychologists, who often referred to his work, and he was among the first to discuss Sigmund Freud's theories in England, in 1894. His contribution to the English language was to coin the term 'telepathy'. He died in 1901, William James at his bedside with a blank sheet of paper, anxiously awaiting the first message from beyond. In his obituary, James claimed that psychology would henceforth be concerned with what lies beneath the subliminal threshold: 'the Myers problem'.

4. William James (1842–1910). For a biographical note see Chapter 1. *Principles of Psychology* remains one of the most significant textbooks of psychology, marking a shift away from psycho-physiological paradigms towards a more 'dynamic' psychology, in which subjective mental states are not immediately tied to biology. This extract clearly evokes one of the defining Modernist narrative techniques—the 'stream of consciousness'—although William James objected to the intensely obscure subjective style of one of its first practitioners: his brother Henry.

5. Sir Clifford Allbutt (1836–1925). Had a Cambridge education in Natural Sciences before training in medicine in London. He worked in Leeds hospitals, developing new instruments (such as the portable clinical thermometer). After 1889 he became a Commissioner in Lunacy, touring the asylum system.

11

PSYCHICAL RESEARCH

Psychical research is, in many ways, the exemplary marginal science of the fin de siècle. On the one hand, its attempt to seek material proof of spiritual entities offers a remarkable instance of the authority that secular science exercised over cultural beliefs at the time, producing a fascinatingly scientized rhetoric for sometimes transparently religious yearnings. On the other hand, psychical researchers, being among the first to discuss seriously the implications of hypnosis and double consciousness for thinking about the psychology of selfhood, were an important vector for the advance of Continental psychology into England. Of the contributors to Chapter 10 above, Myers and William James both served as presidents of the Society for Psychical Research, and Freud was a corresponding member who contributed to its journal in 1912.

The Society for Psychical Research was established in 1882 partly at the prompting of the Professor of Physics in Dublin, William Barrett, but principally by an influential group of Cambridge dons centred around Henry Sidgwick and Frederic Myers. Unlike many spiritualists, both men were extraordinarily well connected: Sidgwick was brother-in-law to Arthur Balfour, future prime minister; Myers married Eveleen Tennant, a fashionable beauty and talented photographer. Sidgwick's wife, Eleanor Balfour, remained the sceptical intellectual centre of the Society until her death. If the 'Spookical Society' was often lampooned by contemporaries (Bernard Shaw considered it the most ridiculed society in London—after the Browning Society), it could rely on powerful sociological networks of support. Its much-contested contributions to fin-de-siècle culture were the investigation of instances of 'telepathy' and its enquiries into 'phantasms of the living' and 'phantasmogenetic centres' (ghosts and haunted houses, to the uninitiated). The Society survived the deaths of Sidgwick in August 1900 and Myers in January 1901, and continues to operate today.

Included below are articles from a range of sources. From the first part of the Society's voluminous *Proceedings*, the 'Objects of the Society' outlines claims to neutrality and a structure of research committees which operated only intermittently. This displays the very conscious attempts to formulate the Society on the model of other scientific societies in London. Sidgwick's first presidential address indicates the kind of rhetoric—the 'scandal' of ignored evidence—that officers of the Society commonly used. 'Thought-Reading' is included as the first utterance of the Society to a general readership: its passage from the opening parlour game to the heights of scientific, analogic speculation in the last paragraph is typical of early work. Readers can see here the origins of probabilities based on card-guessing that remain the foundation of 'ESP' experiments even today.

If objections could be raised to the Society, the nature of the objection suggested by the leader comment from the *Pall Mall Gazette* is notable for its reliance on fears that 'ghost-hunting' marks a degeneration to primitive beliefs. The polymathic W. T. Stead appears in this section in the form of his remarkable occult journal *Borderland*, which ran from 1893 to 1897. Its aim, as the opening statement reproduced here announces, was to popularize the somewhat abstruse formulations of psychical research for a mass readership. Stead had launched his ambitious *Review of Reviews* in 1890, and its precarious financial state had been aided by a special Christmas issue of *Real Ghost Stories* culled from readers 'trained' in the kinds of evidence wanted by the Society for Psychical Research. In 1891 he discovered an ability to engage in 'automatic writing'—entering a trance state in which his body would be occupied by living and dead friends, who would leave messages by dictation. When he began receiving lengthy messages from a recently dead American journalist, Julia Ames, the recipe for *Borderland* was in place. It lost money consistently, and Stead's influence further declined from the heights of his New Journalism in the 1880s. Andrew Lang's world-weary comments on the psychologization of the good old-fashioned ghost story belies his extensive contributions to the discourse of psychical research, a combination of his interests in folklore, old ghost stories, and 'primitive' superstition. His tone probably best catches the way in which some responded to the amazing *possibilities* hinted at by the Society's researches, whilst remaining sceptical.

Secondary reading: Barrow; Brandon; Crabtree; Gauld; Oppenheim; Shamdasani; Frank Turner, *Between Science and Religion*.

1   from 'Objects of the Society' (1882)

It has been widely felt that the present is an opportune time for making an organised and systematic attempt to investigate that large group of debatable phenomena designated by such terms as mesmeric, psychical, and Spiritualistic.

From the recorded testimony of many competent witnesses, past and present, including observations recently made by scientific men of eminence in various countries, there appears to be, amidst much illusion and deception, an important body of remarkable phenomena, which are *prima facie* inexplicable on any generally recognised hypothesis, and which, if incontestably established, would be of the highest possible value.

The task of examining such residual phenomena has often been undertaken by individual effort, but never hitherto by a scientific society organised on a sufficiently broad basis. As a preliminary step towards this end, a Conference, convened by Professor Barrett, was held in London, on January 6th, 1882, and a Society for Psychical Research was projected. The Society was definitely constituted on February 20th, 1882, and its Council, then appointed, have sketched out a programme of future work. The following subjects have been entrusted to special Committees: —

1. An examination of the nature and extent of any influence which may be exerted by one mind upon another, apart from any generally recognised mode of perception.

2. The study of hypnotism, and the forms of so-called mesmeric trance, with its alleged insensibility to pain; clairvoyance and other allied phenomena.

3. A critical revision of Reichenbach's researches[1] with certain organisations called 'sensitive', and an inquiry whether such organisations possess any power of perception beyond a highly exalted sensibility of the recognised sensory organs.

4. A careful investigation of any reports, resting on strong testimony, regarding apparitions at the moment of death, or otherwise, or regarding disturbances in houses reputed to be haunted.

5. An inquiry into the various physical phenomena commonly called Spiritualistic; with an attempt to discover their causes and general laws.

---

[1] Baron Carl von Reichenbach (1788–1869) was a chemist and neurologist, who theorized the existence of a unifying force in nature, which he called 'odic force' (after the Norse god Odin). He claimed that certain 'sensitive' people could see odic force—as an efflorescence from magnets, for instance. *Reichenbach's Letters on Od and Magnetism* was translated in 1852, at the same time that spiritualism arrived in England from America (see n. 2 below).

6. The collection and collation of existing materials bearing on the history of these subjects.

The aim of the Society will be to approach these various problems without prejudice or prepossession of any kind, and in the same spirit of exact and unimpassioned inquiry which has enabled Science to solve so many problems, once not less obscure nor less hotly debated. The founders of this Society fully recognise the exceptional difficulties which surround this branch of research; but they nevertheless hope that by patient and systematic effort some results of permanent value may be attained.

The Council desire to conduct their investigations as far as possible through private channels; and they invite communication from any person, whether intending to join the Society or not, who may be disposed to favour them with a record of experiences, or with suggestions for inquiry or experiment. Such communications will be treated, if desired, as private and confidential. [. . .]

The Society for Psychical Research is now in a position to invite the adhesion of Members. It is desirable to quote here a preliminary Note, which appears on the first page of the Society's Constitution.

'NOTE.—To prevent misconception it is here expressly stated that Membership of this Society does not imply the acceptance of any particular explanation of the phenomena investigated, nor any belief as to the operation, in the physical world, of forces other than those recognised by Physical Science.'

---

2   from Henry Sidgwick, 'Address by the
           President at the First General Meeting' (1882)

The first general meeting of the Society was held at Willis's Rooms, London, on July 17th 1882.

HENRY SIDGWICK, ESQ., PRESIDENT, IN THE CHAIR

Before we proceed to what has been marked out as the business of this meeting, as it is the first general meeting of our new Society since the time it was definitely constituted, it has been thought that I should make a few brief remarks on the aims and methods of the Society, which will form a kind of explanation in supplement to our prospectus defining those aims and methods,—which, I suppose, has been seen by all the members, and perhaps by some who are not as yet members. This prospectus has not been subjected to much instructive public criticism. It has been received, either with entire cordiality, or with guarded neutrality, or with uninstructive contempt. Still, several private criticisms on that prospectus and questions suggested by it have come to my notice; and it seems to me that I might perhaps employ the few minutes of your time that I wish to take up in no better way than in replying to these criticisms and objections.

The first question I have heard is, Why form a Society for Psychical Research at all at this time, including in its scope not merely the phenomena of thought-reading (to which your attention will be directed chiefly this afternoon), but also those of clairvoyance and mesmerism, and the mass of obscure phenomena commonly known as Spiritualistic? Well, in answering this, the first question, I shall be able to say something on which I hope we shall all agree; meaning by 'we', not merely we who are in this room, but we and the scientific world outside; and as, unfortunately, I have but few observations to make on which so much agreement can be hoped for, it may be as well to bring this into prominence, namely, that we are all agreed that the present state of things is a scandal to the enlightened age in which we live. That the dispute as to the reality of these marvellous phenomena,—of which it is quite impossible to exaggerate the scientific importance, if only a tenth part of what has been alleged by generally credible witnesses could be shewn to be true,—I say it is a scandal that the dispute as to the reality of these phenomena should still be going on, that so many competent witnesses should have declared their belief in them, that so many others should be profoundly interested in having the question determined, and yet that the educated world, as a body, should still be simply in the attitude of incredulity.

Now the primary aim of our Society, the thing which we all unite to promote, whether as believers or non-believers, is to make a sustained and systematic attempt to remove this scandal in one way or another. Some of those whom I address, feel, no doubt, that this attempt can only lead to the proof of most of the alleged phenomena; some, again, think it is probable that most, if not all, will be disproved; but regarded as a Society, we are quite unpledged, and as individuals, we are all agreed that any particular investigation that we may make should be carried on with a single-minded desire to ascertain the facts, and without any foregone conclusion as to their nature.

But then here comes the second question, which I have had put by many who are by no means unfriendly to our efforts,—that is, Why should this attempt succeed more than so many others that have been made during the last thirty years? To this question there are several answers. The first is, that the work has to go on. The matter is far too important to be left where it now is, and, indeed, considering the importance of the questions still in dispute, which we hope to try to solve, as compared with other scientific problems on which years of patient and unbroken investigation have been employed, we may say that no proportionate amount of labour has yet been devoted to our problems; so that even if we were to grant that previous efforts had completely failed, that would still be no adequate reason for not renewing them. But, again, I should say that previous efforts have not failed; it is only true that they have not completely succeeded. Important evidence has been accumulated, important experience has been gained, and important effects have been produced upon the public mind. [. . .]

If anyone asks me what I mean by, or how I define, sufficient scientific proof of thought-reading, clairvoyance, or the phenomena called Spiritualistic, I should ask to be allowed to evade the difficulties of determining in the abstract what constitutes adequate evidence. What I mean by *sufficient evidence* is evidence that will convince the scientific world, and for that we obviously require a good deal more than we have so far obtained. I do not mean that some effect in this direction has not been produced: if that were so we could not hope to do much. I think that something has been done; that the advocates of obstinate incredulity— I mean the incredulity that waives the whole affair aside as undeserving of any attention from rational beings—feel their case to be not *prima facie* so strong now as it was.

Thirty years ago it was thought that want of scientific culture was an adequate explanation of the vulgar belief in mesmerism and table-turning.[2] Then, as one man of scientific repute after another came forward with the results of individual investigation, there was a quite ludicrous ingenuity exercised in finding reasons for discrediting his scientific culture. He was said to be an amateur, not a professional; or a specialist without adequate generality of view and training; or a mere discoverer not acquainted with the strict methods of experimental research; or he was not a Fellow of the Royal Society, or if he was it was by an unfortunate accident. Or again, national distrust came in; it was chiefly in America that these things went on; or as I was told myself, in Germany, some years ago, it was only in England, or America, or France, or Italy, or Russia, or some half-educated country, but not in the land of *Geist*.[3] Well, these things are changed now, and though I do not think this kind of argument has quite gone out of use yet it has on the whole been found more difficult to work; and our obstinately incredulous friends, I think, are now generally content to regard the interest that men of undisputed scientific culture take in these phenomena as an unexplained mystery, like the phenomena themselves.

---

[2] The first wave of spiritualism arrived in England in 1852, having emerged in the isolated rural communities on the east coast of America. These spirits communicated by table raps, and sudden movements of the séance table. The eminent Royal Institution scientist Michael Faraday pronounced in 1852 that tables were moved by the 'unconscious cerebration' of the sitters. The 1840s also marked the height of influence of Mesmerism (belief in the curative powers of animal magnetism) in England. As Sidgwick was writing, a despised Mesmerism was coming into a degree of acceptance by professional medicine as hypnotism.

[3] The land of *Geist*, or Spirit, is Germany. Sidgwick is referring to Georg Hegel's (1770–1831) *Phenomenology of Spirit*.

For these various reasons I think we may say that on the whole matters are now more favourable for an impartial reception of the results of our investigation, so far as we can succeed in obtaining any positive results, than they were twenty years ago. [. . .] The great gain that I hope may accrue from the formation of this Society is that the occurrence of phenomena—*prima facie* inexplicable by any ordinary natural laws—may be more rapidly and more extensively communicated to us who desire to give our time to the investigation, so that in the first instance we may carefully sift the evidence, and guard against the danger of illusion or deception which even here may, of course, come in; and then, when the evidence has been sifted by accumulation of personal experiments, make it more available for the purpose of producing general conviction. [. . .]

Scientific incredulity has been so long in growing, and has so many so strong roots, that we shall only kill it, if we are able to kill it at all as regards any of those questions, by burying it alive under a heap of facts. We must keep 'pegging away' as Lincoln said; we must accumulate fact upon fact, and add experiment upon experiment, and, I should say, not wrangle too much with incredulous outsiders about the conclusiveness of any one, but trust to the mass of evidence for conviction. The highest degree of demonstrative force that we can obtain out of any single record of investigation is, of course, limited by the trustworthiness of the investigator. We have done all we can when the critic has nothing left to allege except that the investigator is in the trick. But when he has nothing else left to allege he will allege that. [. . .]

We must drive the objector into the position of being forced either to admit the phenomena as inexplicable, at least by him, or to accuse the investigators either of lying or cheating or of a blindness or forgetfulness incompatible with any intellectual condition except absolute idiocy.

I am glad to say that this result, in my opinion, has been satisfactorily attained in the investigation of thought-reading. Professor Barrett will now bring before you a report which I hope will be only the first of a long series of similar reports which may have reached the same point of conclusiveness.

---

3   from William Barrett, Edmund Gurney, and
         F. W. H. Myers, 'Thought-Reading' (1882)

Among the 'petits jeux innocents' of modern drawing-rooms, a form of pastime known as the *willing game* has enjoyed of late considerable popularity. The game admits of many variations, but is usually played somewhat as follows. One of the party, generally a lady, leaves the room, and the rest determine on something which she is to do on her return—as to take a flower from some specific vase, or to strike some specified note on the piano. She is then recalled, and one or more of the 'willers' place their hands lightly on her shoulders. Sometimes nothing happens; sometimes she strays vaguely about; sometimes she moves to the right part of the room and does the thing, or something like the thing, which she has been willed to do. Nothing on first sight could look less like a promising starting point for a new branch of scientific inquiry. It is pretty obvious that the *will* of the players is generally most efficacious when it expresses itself in a gentle *push*. And even when the utmost care is used to maintain the light contact without giving any impulse whatever, it is impossible to lay down the limits of any given subject's sensibility to slight muscular impressions. [. . .]

[I]s there even a *prima facie* case, in performances of the sort described, for any obscurer case than mere muscular susceptibility?[4] Scattered instances, pointing to an affirmative answer, will, we think, be encountered from time to time by those interested in the search. [. . .] By a fortunate accident, after long waiting, one of us heard of a family in which the attempt to obtain phenomena of the kind in question, regarded purely as an evening's amusement, had been attended with singular success.

Our informant was Mr. C—, a clergyman of unblemished character, and whose integrity indeed has, it so happens, been exceptionally tested. He has six children; five girls and one boy, ranging now between the ages of ten and seventeen, all thoroughly healthy, as free as possible from morbid or hysterical symptoms, and in manner perfectly simple and childlike. The father stated that any one of these children (except the youngest), as well as a young servant-girl who had lived with the family for two years, was frequently able to designate correctly, without contact or sign, a card or other object fixed on in the child's absence. During the year which has elapsed since we first heard of this family, seven visits, mostly of several days' duration, have been paid to the town where they live, by ourselves and by several scientific friends, and on these occasions daily experiments have been made. [. . .]

The outline of results during the present investigation, which extended over six days, stands as follows:—Altogether 382 trials were made [. . .] Cards were far most frequently employed, and the odds in their case may be taken as a fair medium sample; according to which, out of the whole series of 382 trials, the average number of successes at the first attempt by an ordinary guesser would be $7\frac{1}{3}$. Of our trials, 127 were successes on the first attempt, 56 on the second, 19 on the third, making 202 in all. [. . .] Our most striking piece of success, when the thing

---

[4] The 'willing game' was, at the start of the 1880s, a fashionable public entertainment. Two famous practitioners, Stuart Cumberland and Washington Irving Bishop, were famous 'thought-readers', although Cumberland claimed no special powers beyond on acute sensitivity to reading thought in the muscular reactions of the body, and Bishop was contemptuous of believers in the supernatural.

selected was divulged to none of the family, was five cards running named correctly on a first trial; the odds against this happening once in our series were considerably over a million to 1. [. . .]

The phenomena here described are so unlike any which have been brought within the sphere of recognised science, as to subject the mind to two opposite dangers. Wild hypotheses as to how they happen are confronted with equally wild assertions that they cannot happen at all. Of the two, the assumption of *a priori* impossibility is, perhaps, in the present state of our knowledge of Nature, the most to be deprecated; though it cannot be considered in any way surprising. We have referred to the legitimate grounds of suspicion, open to all who have only chanced to encounter the alleged phenomena in their vulgarest or most dubious aspects. Even apart from this, it is inevitable that, as the area of the known increases by perpetual additions to its recognised departments and by perpetual multiplication of their connections, a disinclination should arise to break loose from association, and to admit a quite new department on its own independent evidence. And it cannot be denied that the department of research towards which the foregoing experiments form a slight contribution presents as little apparent connection with any ascertained facts of mental as of material science. Psychological treatises may be searched in vain for any account of the transmission of mental images otherwise than by ordinary sensory channels. At the same time it may serve to disarm purely *a priori* criticism if we point out that the word 'thought-reading' is merely used as a popular and provisional description, and is in no way intended to exclude an explanation resting on a physical basis. It is quite open to surmise some sort of analogy to the familiar phenomena of the transmission and reception of vibratory energy. A swinging pendulum suspended from a solid support will throw into synchronous vibration another pendulum attached to the same support if the period of oscillation of the two be the same; the medium of transmission here being the solid material of the support. One tuning-fork or string in unison with another will communicate its impulses through the medium of the air. Glowing particles of a gas, acting through the medium of the luminiferous ether, can throw into sympathetic vibration cool molecules of the same substance at a distance. A permanent magnet brought into a room will throw any surrounding iron into a condition similar to its own; and here the medium of communication is unknown, though the fact is undisputed. Similarly, we may conceive, if we please, that the vibration of molecules of brain-stuff may be communicated to an intervening medium, and so pass under certain circumstances from one brain to another, with a corresponding simultaneity of impressions. No more than in the case of the magnetic phenomena is any investigator bound to determine the *medium* before inquiring into the *fact* of transit. On the other hand, the possibility must not be overlooked that further advances along the lines of research here indicated may necessitate a modification of that general view of the relation of mind to matter to which modern science has long been gravitating.

---

4   Leader Comment, 'Psychical Research',
         Pall Mall Gazette (21 October 1882)

Great is the power of words, as those two eminent poets, Homer and Mr. Matthew Arnold, have justly remarked; and when you call ghost stories 'psychical research', you certainly dignify them to all outward appearance with a sort of adventitious scientific importance. But it is a pity to see another good word go wrong; for if the researchers have own way to the top of their bent, the word 'psychical', which used to form a very apt antithesis to 'physical', will soon be practically spoiled for all serious philosophical purposes. Twenty years ago, when the mesmerists were in the full swing of their apparent success, that excellent term 'biology' was nearly ruined in the same fashion, being adopted as a short form of what the mesmerists, with their usual trick of jumping at the feeblest analogies, were pleased to call electro-biology. But there is a more serious danger attending this new form of psychical research than the mere degradation of a truthful word; and when one looks at the high intellectual status of many among the researchers, it seems hardly superfluous to point that danger out.

In themselves, ghost stories, like all other possible phenomena, are matter for some science or other; because, in fact, there is no product of general laws, however small, mean or absurd, which is not itself capable of leading back inductively to those laws, and which is not therefore, viewed abstractly, part of the universal domain of science. As treated by Mr. Tylor, Mr. Herbert Spencer, and other anthropologists, ghost stories do actually yield scientific material of a very valuable sort.[5] But as approached by the psychical researchers, no matter in how sceptical a spirit, they enclose a very real danger—a danger, perhaps, all the greater in proportion to the general mental powers of the would-be investigator. The fact is, the belief in ghosts, in witchcraft, in second-sight, and all the rest of it is a continuous inheritance of our race from a very remote and savage period. Even among the relics of the cave men, certainly among the relics of the later stone-age men, there are numerous objects which point back clearly to the existence of a ghost theory. Our ancestors have seen and known ghosts for countless generations; in many parts of the world people still know them as commonly and

---

[5]   See Ch. 13 below. The risk of degeneration in psychical states suggested by this paragraph is heavily informed by the developmental theories of Herbert Spencer, particularly his evolutionary conception of mental states in *Principles of Psychology* (1855).

familiarly as they know dogs or horses. It is impossible that a belief so ancient, so universal, and so constantly present should not have produced profound modifications in the brain and the whole psychical mechanism of the entire race. Though the idea of a ghost is not of course innate in the scholastic sense, it may perhaps be considered as innate in the evolutionary sense, with the vast majority of mankind; a sort of blank form answering to the concept of a ghost must most probably be potentially present in almost every human brain. Connections of fibres or dynamical paths must exist along which impressions favourable to a ghost theory are readily conveyed. The idea, once suggested by teaching, is quickly snapped up: the mechanism falls easily into the train of thought familiar to all its predecessors, and provided for in its own structure by the mechanism of heredity. Nay, even to some extent, it would seem, the idea tends to occur more or less spontaneously as a gratuitous or untaught explanation of sundry incidental phenomena; for certain deaf mutes, on being taught late to speak, have asserted that the notion was familiar to them in their untaught state; and our children, however carefully guarded, seem instinctively to acquire superstitious fears of the dark, which are probably due to these deeply ingrained ancestral notions.

Now, even the highest and most advanced European thinkers, though they may themselves have risen quite above lower childish superstitions, are yet separated from them at best by a very few recent generations. The Middle Ages stand but twelve or fifteen lives away from all of us; only eight or nine lives stand between ourselves and the revolting puerilities of the witchcraft mania. In some parts of Ireland, of Scotland, of rural England, equal puerilities are even now extensively believed. Slowly, and by painful degrees, a few of us here in Western Europe have risen above the most degrading views of supernaturalism, and have attained, more or less completely, to a reasonable scientific standpoint. But we have done so only by a very gradual hereditary and successive ascent, and by carefully keeping our faces set forward instead of backward, in the pursuit of naturalistic explanations. As yet, we must still retain in the very constitution of our nervous mechanism innumerable connections of fibres, answering potentially to connections of ideas, which make for older and more superstitious views. By steadily neglecting to develop these—nay, rather by intentionally suffering them to fall into disuse (for most of us have had more or less tincture of the floating superstitions in early childhood)—we have managed to throw overboard the whole load of interfering supernaturalism in everyday life. But we can none of us boast that we have entirely got rid of the old leaven; the thing is too deeply stamped into our very natures to be completely eradicated in a couple of generations or so. Though those who are not likely to relapse are not likely to meddle with psychical research, there are yet many who still cherish an evident hankering after the visibly supernatural (often as a safeguard to failing faith), and who cannot deal with such dubious material in any way. People of this sort are clearly playing with edged-tools. Once let the old current get the upper hand again, and, as the doings of the Spiritualists sufficiently show, the whole pent-up flood of supernaturalism comes down with a rush. No man has hands so clean that he can afford to touch pitch. As, in the moral department of our nature, ethical feelings are so newly developed that they are for the most part only kept up by want of familiarity with vice, so, in the intellectual department, the scientific attitude is so new and unfixed a possession that it can only be preserved by careful abstention from dangerous trains of thought. Even the ablest and most scientific observers, when they have taken the first step by 'inquiring,' may sink to the very bottom of the pond before they finish. If anybody doubts this, he need only read a remarkable publication by Mr. Crookes, detailing his own conversion: it begins with the most reasonable scientific precautions: it ends with an open-mouthed acceptance of the most barefaced impositions of professional mediums.[6]

---

5   from W. T. Stead, 'How We Intend to
              Study Borderland' (1893)

BORDERLAND? Of what?

Of 'the immense ocean of Truth' which Sir Isaac Newton saw lying unexplored before him.

In what spirit is it to be explored?

In the spirit of the principle laid down by Professor Huxley as the fundamental axiom of modern Science, 'to try all things, and to hold fast by what is good'.

It is the Method of the Agnostic applied vigorously to the phenomena of the region which has hitherto been relegated to Superstition. [. . .]

But if the method be the method of the Agnostic, the goal which we hope to attain is the goal of the Believer.

We seek the scientific verification of that Life and Immortality which were brought to light nineteen hundred years ago.

Life—for at present we are but half alive—that we may have life and that we may have it more abundantly, that we may understand something more of the marvellous capacities latent in ourselves, that we may secure for everyday use the almost inconceivable powers possessed by our subjective selves, of which we have stray hints in the phenomena of hypnotism and of dream—that is one object.

---

[6] William Crookes, chemist, journalist, and important member of the scientific community, announced in 1870 that he would investigate 'alleged Spiritual phenomena.' To the consternation of his fellow scientists and polite society, he confirmed the existence of what he called 'psychic force' in 1871, and became involved in rancorous disputes throughout the 1870s.

Immortality—or at least the persistence of the personality of man after the dissolution of this vesture of decay, that is the second object. It is indeed a corollary of the first. For if Life is manifested independently of the body, even while the body exists, it cannot be supposed to terminate merely because the organs of sense are no longer in use.

It would be as rational to suppose that a man ceases to exist when he rings off the telephone through which he has been speaking, as to suppose that Life, as we are now discovering it, terminates when it lays aside the bifurcated telephone which we call the body.

'If a man dies shall he not live again?' That is the question. We seek to solve it, believing that the true answer is that he no more dies when he lays aside his body than he dies when he puts off his topcoat.

But belief is one thing. Certitude is another. What we have to do is to prove what is the fact so clearly that, as Mr. Minot Savage says, 'to doubt it would be an impeachment of a man's intelligence'.[7]

It may be that we may fail in proving what we hope to be able to demonstrate. But the attempt may not be less fruitful on that account.

Columbus, in commemoration of whose discovery of the Western Hemisphere the World's Fair is now being held at Chicago, set out on his memorable journey across the Atlantic with no design of discovering America. What he dreamed of was merely a short cut to India. Yet his pursuit of that phantasy created for Civilisation a New World.

So it may be with us. The goal which we seek to reach may evade us. The great ideals which we pursue may ever recede and again recede, but in the quest we may attain to many results of which we have as little conception to-day as Columbus had of the United States of America when he set sail from the coast of Spain in his tiny caravels. [. . .]

'Europe's wise men in their snail shells curled', sneered at the Genoese dreamer. His friends deplored that he should waste his great natural talents over such a fool's quest. Had he acted on their advice he might have made a fortune in the carrying trade of the Levant, he would not have been brought home in chains to die in disgrace—but he would never have discovered America.

That is our answer to those kind friends who give BORDERLAND—our little caravel—a send-off in the shape of a chorus of sympathetic regrets, not unmingled with prognostications that our ultimate destination will be no New World, but that familiar institution of the old world which stands at Bedlam or Colney Hatch.[8]

---

[7] The Reverend Minot Savage (1841-1918) was an American Unitarian minister noted for his sermons, which attempted to seek a reconciliation between theology and modern science. He published extensively, and became involved in psychical research in the 1890s.

[8] These were both large mental institutions.

They may be right, but better face that risk than turn a deaf ear to the imperious summons that bids us venture boldly into the dim unknown.

But the enterprise is not so foolhardy as it may at first sight appear, nor is the hope that buoys us up so chimerical as most men think. [. . .]

If mankind has investigated steam and electricity in the haphazard, intermittent way that it has investigated the spiritual world, we should still be travelling in stage coaches, and the telegraph and the telephone would have been scouted by all our wise men as the fantastic imaginings of a disordered brain.

For centuries the application of the inquiring spirit to those hidden forces was summarily checked by the rough methods of the rack and the tar-barrel in this life and the grim menace of eternal perdition in the next.

Even in our day the student is overwhelmed with ridicule, and punished for his temerity by the pitying compassion of his friends and the contempt and ostracism of the multitude. [. . .]

If anything is to be done, nay, if anything is even to be attempted, we must change all that.

The publication of BORDERLAND is at least a practical illustration that some of us are determined to make the attempt.

We shall seek to do so by popularizing Psychical Research, and bringing to the study of these obscure phenomena the religious enthusiasm born of a great hope, wedded to the scientific spirit which accepts nothing on trust, which recognises no authority but that of truth, and which subjects every assertion to the searching interrogation of the methods of experimental research.

As for the interdict by which the orthodox superstition endeavours to forbid even an examination of the evidence as to the existence of the phenomena, we shall treat it with the pity born of profound compassion. The telescope was once under the taboo, but Galileo triumphed over the inquisition. [. . .]

Time and patience! Yes, these are the philosopher's stone of our modern alchemy. Without them we shall achieve nothing. How many years of patient labour Edison gave to the invention of the phonograph, and we do not imagine that we are going to penetrate the arcanum of nature where there are secrets compared to which the phonograph is but a toy of the nursery, with a hop, a step, and a jump.[9]

But even now we have reaped the first fruits of the coming harvest, and in the discovery of auto-telepathic writing I have stumbled upon a fact, the ultimate consequences of which it is impossible to foresee.

However incredible it may appear, I can, and do constantly, receive messages

[9] Thomas Alva Edison (1847–1931), the American inventor who patented the phonograph recording device in 1876.

from my assistant editor, Miss X.,[10] as accurately and as constantly as I receive telegrams from those with whom I do business, without the employment of any wires or any instrument. Whenever I wish to know where she is, whether she can keep an appointment, or how she is progressing with her work, I simply ask the question, and receive her answer. Distance does not affect the messages, they are received equally when she is asleep or awake. Nor is this faculty of using my hand as a writing telephone without wires confined to Miss X. I can communicate with many of my friends in the same way. But with Miss X. I constantly communicate every day on matters of business in this way.

This I know of my own certain knowledge, and as the result of daily experience, to be a fact. How it is done I do not pretend to know. That it is done is certain. It is no longer an experiment, it is a practical every-day addition to the conveniences of human intercourse.

Knowing this, and having my feet firmly planted upon this indisputable fact, is it any wonder that I feel encouraged to press on? To draw back now would be as criminal as it would have been for Columbus after he had seen the lights flickering on the horizon of the New World, to have put his ship about and returned to Spain.

We shall not sail back to Spain. Forward is our watchword! Forward! Ever forward, let what will betide!

---

6   from W. T. Stead, 'Telepathy: A Passing Note Reporting Progress in Telepathic Automatism' (1894)

A CASE OF AUTO-TELEPATHY

When Miss X., my assistant editor on BORDERLAND, returned from her recent interesting expedition in search of the gifted seers of the Highlands, she wrote telepathically with my hand a long report covering three closely written quarto pages, describing the result of her visits, her plans and intentions in the future, reporting upon the condition of the office and its work, and discussing questions of practical business. All this was written out with my hand at Wimbledon, while Miss X. was in town. I had not seen her for nearly six weeks, during which time I had not once written to her. When I met her I read over to her the telepathic

[10] Miss X was eventually revealed as Ada Goodrich-Freer, traveller and peculiarly reluctant psychic and psychical researcher. She co-edited *Borderland*, which contained transcripts of her séances with Lady Isabel Burton and the bad-tempered ghost of Sir Richard Burton; her true identity was exposed during a very public dispute over her attempts to investigate a haunted house in the Scottish Highlands in 1898. Her *Essays in Psychical Research* was published in 1899; she died in 1931.

message. When I had finished, she said, 'You have made one mistake. You say "So-and-so is very painstaking but very stupid." That is not my opinion. So-and-so is very painstaking, but only occasionally stupid.' And that was the only error in three closely-written quarto pages.

LONG-DISTANCE TELEPATHY

It may be said that it was not more than ten miles from Wimbledon. But when I was at Grindelwald, I found no more difficulty in telepathic correspondence with London than when I was at Wimbledon. Of this I may perhaps be permitted to give an instance, where telepathic communication anticipated a telegram by three hours, in a case in which I was personally very deeply interested. Although the incident was comparatively slight, the evidence is so clear and so well attested, and, moreover, the telepathic communication followed immediately upon a message purporting to come from a disembodied spirit, and was in turn followed by a confirmatory letter and telegram, that it may be worth while simply reproducing them here.

When I was in Grindelwald in July, I was grieved to receive bad news as to the health of one of my nearest and dearest friends. Three days in succession I received letters from London, each more gloomy in its tidings, and when the third arrived I decided to return at once. I went to Dr. Lunn's office, and asked him when I could get a reply from a London suburb to a telegram. It was then four. He said he did not think I could expect a reply before eight o'clock. I discussed the question of leaving that night, or of waiting till the morning. Ultimately I decided that I would adopt the latter course, and, going across to the telegraph office, I sent off a despatch, saying, 'Grieved to hear of——'s illness. Will return tomorrow. Telegraph doctor's latest report.' Returning to the hotel to make all preparations for departure, I found a friend in my room to whom I told my bad news.

A TELEGRAM ANTICIPATED

Sitting down at the table, I determined to try whether or not I could, by the aid of my automatic hand, obtain any news from London. I first asked the ever-faithful friend who some three years ago passed from our sight whether she could tell me how the patient was. My hand wrote without a moment's hesitation: —

Your friend is better. You need not return. The proof of this is that about seven o'clock you will receive a telegram to this effect, when you will see I am correct.

I then asked mentally if I should ask my friend's son to use my hand telepathically to give me the latest news. The answer came at once as follows: —

No, you had better ask her daughter; she is at home, and can give you the latest news.

I then asked the daughter to use my hand, and tell me how her mother was. My hand then, as always, unconscious of the least difference in the control of the embodied or disembodied, wrote as follows: —

Mother had a better sleep last night. There is no need for you to return earlier. We have taken a house at the seaside at (name unintelligible). Mother thinks she will be all right after her visit.

I feared to believe the good news. I read the messages to my friend, who signed them as confirmation, and remarked that if this turned out right it would be a great score for the spooks, but that I feared my own strong desire for better news had vitiated the accuracy of the despatch. I then left the hotel, and went down to Dr. Lunn's chalet, where I told Dr. Lunn, Mr. Clayden, Dr. Lindsay, and other friends that I must return to London next day.

CONFIRMATION COMPLETE

At seven o'clock dinner is served at the Bar. I saw the head waiter, told him I was expecting an important telegram, and asked him to bring it me at table. This he promised to do. Dinner passed. Eight o'clock approached. 'I am afraid,' I said to my friend, 'the spooks are no go this time,' and set off for the church. I had not got half-way there when my boy Jack ran after me, shouting, 'Father, here's your telegram; it was delivered by mistake in Uncle Herbie's room.' I opened it, and found that it had arrived at 7.10. It ran as follows: —

— better. Don't come back

.

Two days later I received a postcard from the daughter, partly written before my telegram arrived. Here it is: —

Mother is rather better. We have taken a house at W——. Later: Your telegram has just come. There is no need for you to come back. [I quote from memory the contents of the letters and telegrams. I put them all together into an envelope for the Psychical Research Society, and I cannot lay hands upon them at the moment of writing. I can swear, however, to the substantial accuracy of the above narrative.]

There was only one point left unconfirmed. Did the patient think she would be quite set up by a stay at the seaside? When I returned to London I put the question to her daughter. She replied, 'I never heard my mother say anything about that. But the doctor said so when he called that day.'

THE BODY AS A TELEPHONE

Now if I am asked to explain how my automatic hand got that message, I cannot explain it, excepting on the hypothesis that the mind, whether for the time being in or out of a body of flesh and blood, has the capacity of communicating directly with other minds without being in the least degree hampered by the limitations of space, or by the accident of its embodiment or disembodiment. The more I experiment with telepathy the more is the conviction driven in upon me that the mind uses the body as a temporary two-legged telephone for purposes of communication at short range with other minds, but that it no more ceases to exist when the body dies than we cease to exist when we ring off the telephone.

---

7   from Andrew Lang, 'Ghosts up to Date' (1894)

The most frivolous pastimes have now a habit of degenerating into scientific exercises. Croquet was ruined, as a form of lounging, by the precision attained by some players; lawn-tennis is a serious affair; and even ghost stories, the delight of Christmas Eve, have been ravaged and annexed by psychology. True, there are some who aver that the science of the Psychical Society does not hold water; but, in any case, it is as difficult as if it were some orthodox research dear to Mr. Herbert Spencer. To prove this fact, I had marked for quotation some remarks, by eminent ghost-hunters, on the provinces and parts of the brain, on the subjective and the objective, the conscious, the reflex, the automatic,—*tout le tremblement*,[11] as we may well say,—which would frighten off the most intrepid amateurs. 'The oldest aunt' would forget 'the saddest tale', if plied with remarks on the 'dextro-cerebral hemisphere' of the brain. If we must understand that kind of thing before we can enjoy a ghost story, we who are middle aged may despair. But I hope to give the gist of what a psychological science (if it is a science) has to say about the existence of a bogie, and to do so without overtaxing intellects above the average. Science has tackled this theme before. By aid of about two cases of hallucination, Nicolai's and 'Mrs A.'s' (whoever Mrs A. may have been), Ferrier and Hibbert decided that ghosts were merely 'hallucinations', 'revived impressions'.[12] Very good; but hallucinations caused by what? and wherefore so frequently coincident with the death of the person who seems to be seen? I ventured to ask these questions long ago. [. . .] Materials were scanty then, mere tales of one's grandmother, and legends in old books concerned with what was called 'the Supernatural'. In the interval hypnotism has been accepted as a fact by science, the Psychical Society has been founded, a great collection of some six hundred stories of 'phantasms of the living' has been printed; phantasms of the dead are

---

[11] 'all atremble'.
[12] David Ferrier (1843–1928) was a neurologist and founder of the journal *Brain* in 1878. Hibbert's essay on hallucinations was first published in 1825, and remained influential throughout the 19th century.

also brought forward in considerable numbers; committees have reported on haunted houses in a friendly sense; and Mrs Besant has acquired a creditable number of beliefs.[13] [. . .]

What are we to answer now when people ask, 'Do you believe in ghosts?' No reply can be made (except by a downright sceptic) till we have defined the term 'ghost'. Even popular usage has made one step towards a definition by employing the word 'wraith' to note the phantasm of a living person, while 'ghost' means the phantasm of a dead person. But the difficulty begins when we inquire what is the phantasm in either case?

'Gin a body meet a body,'[14]

who is actually not there, but elsewhere, and in life, what is the thing met? The old idea was that the thing is a spiritual double of its living owner, a separable self, or, as the Esoteric Buddhists do vainly talk, an 'astral body'. That body, or double, is an actual entity, filling space, and, as it seems, is really material, and capable of exercising an influence on matter. The phantasm of a dead person, the ghost, again, was regarded as the surviving soul, made visible, and was really material, as far as being ponderable and able to affect matter—for example, to draw the bed-curtains—involves materiality. We may argue about matter and spirit as we please, but wraiths, and ghosts, and souls, on the old theory, are obviously matter, though matter of a refined sort: the soul, for example, was capable of material pains and pleasures, could touch a harp, or rejoice in the society of houris, or burn in mate-rial fire, or freeze in material ice.

Now there are many educated persons, who, if asked, 'Do you believe in ghosts?' would answer, 'We believe in apparitions; but we do not believe that the apparition is the separable or surviving soul of a living or a dead man. We believe that it is a hallucination, projected by the brain of the percipient, which, again, in some instances, is influenced so as to project that hallucination, by some agency not at present understood'. To this experience of the percipient, who is sensible, by emotion, by sight, hearing, or touch, or by all of these at once, of the presence of the absent, or of the dead, the name *telepathy* (feeling produced at a distance) is given. Any one may believe, and many do believe, in telepathy, yet not believe in the old-fashioned ghost. [. . .]

The human race, then, at present, may be divided into certain categories of sceptics and believers. The sceptics, probably the large majority in civilised

[13] Annie Besant (1847–1933): an early career as a radical freethinker, campaigning for birth control and for trade union rights, led to an association with W. T. Stead. They published a newspaper together during the docker's strikes of 1889. In the 1890s, like Stead, she became interested in mysticism, particu-larly the Theosophy movement, which synthesized various Eastern religious and philosophical beliefs for a largely Western audience. She became Theosophy's principal spokesperson after the death of its founder Mme Blavatsky.

[14] Line from Robert Burns's poem 'Comin' thro' the rye'.

countries, say, 'Mere stuff and nonsense!' According to them, all who report a phantasm as in their own experience, are liars, drunkards, or maniacs; or they mistook a dream for waking reality, or they are 'excitable' and 'imaginative', or they were placed under an illusion, and placed a false interpretation on some actual perception. [. . .]

To the sceptic à outrance,[15] believers of both kinds, believers in ghosts and believers in telepathy, must grant that many people who report abnormal experiences may fall under the uncomplimentary categories of mad, drunk, knave, fool, visionary, and so forth. But it is urged that there are hundreds of other cases in which men and women of good character, sober, sane, not in a condition of expectancy, not excited in any way, declare themselves to have had abnormal experiences. These, again, might be classed as empty hallucinations; but the experiences have coincided with some crisis, usually death, in the history of the person whose apparition was perceived. Further, these experiences, as a rule, have been *unique* in the case of the percipients. [. . .] If a man sees an absent acquaintance only once in his life, and if, at the moment, the acquaintance is dying; still more, if this unique experience, with the coincident death, be comparatively common,—then the theory of chance hallucination becomes untenable. The spokesmen of the Psychical Society have made statistical researches, not, of course, on the scale of a national census, and they have convinced themselves that the ratio of empty to veridical hallucinations, to apparitions coincident with death, does not justify the hypothesis of mere accident. They must be credited with very considerable assiduity in the collection and comparison of evidence, and, though I am not certain that they have been zealous enough in setting forth the particulars of the empty hallucinations of the sane, I must confess that the coincidence of events with apparitions does seem to me to exceed what the laws of chance allow.

EDITORS' NOTES

2. **Henry Sidgwick (1838-1900).** Leading philosopher and educational reformer at Cambridge University. His strongly ethical agnosticism led him to resign his Fellowship of Trinity College in 1869 because he could no longer uphold the religious beliefs required of Fellows. This action was an important influence on the abolition of the religious test at Cambridge, and marked a notable advance in secular reform. He went on to found, with his wife Eleanor Balfour, Newnham College for women scholars,

[15] 'To the out and out sceptic . . .'

and promoted women's education. His highly principled reputation made him an ideal figure to be the first president of the Society for Psychical Research.

3. **William Barrett (1844-1925).** Trained in physics, and was the assistant of John Tyndall at the Royal Institution between 1863 and 1866. He became Professor of Physics in Dublin in 1873. It was in Ireland that he first encountered instances of 'thought reading', and he delivered a highly controversial paper to the British Association for the Advancement of Science on the topic in 1876. He was the founder of the Society for Psychical Research, although he was rapidly marginalized. The analogies to 'sympathetic vibrations' in the last paragraph of this essay show the use of contemporary physics in psychical research. Other key figures in the Society, like Oliver Lodge and Lord Rayleigh, were also physicists.

Edmund Gurney (1847-1888) is an intriguing figure. He attended Trinity College, Cambridge (thus coming into contact with Henry Sidgwick), and became a Fellow in 1872. His first passion was music, and he trained intensively in piano from 1872 to 1875 before giving up in despair. He next attempted to train in medicine, but abandoned his studies due to an acute hypersensitivity to others' pain. He then attempted law before being appointed as the first full-time officer of the Society for Psychical Research. The extent of the researches and administration he undertook for the Society was phenomenal, principally writing the 1,400 pages of the Society's first book, *Phantasms of the Living* (1886). A charming and dashing figure (it was claimed by Leslie Stephen that he was the model for George Eliot's Daniel Deronda), his death in a Brighton hotel in 1888 was in suspicious circumstances. A passage in the diary of Alice James (sister of Henry and William) laments that his family had covered up his suicide.

F. W. H. Myers (1843-1901). For a biographical note see Chapter 10.

4. The editor of the *Pall Mall Gazette* at this time was the liberal rationalist and associate of the scientific naturalists John Morley, which explains to some extent the position of the leader on psychical research. Ironically, his assistant editor was W. T. Stead, who became the editor in 1883 and an enthusiastic psychical researcher himself by 1891.

5 and 6. **W. T. Stead (1849-1912).** For a biographical note see Chapter 2. Stead's enthusiasm for the occult is consistently mapped onto advances in new technology in both these selections: he called his own body a 'bifurcated telephone'. Stead went on to found 'Julia's Bureau' in 1909, a kind of telephone switchboard service which would put mourning relatives into contact with dead relatives via a bank of mediums. Stead's enthusiasm for new technologies was his downfall: he was the most famous man lost on the maiden voyage of the *Titanic* in 1912. Needless to say, his mediumistic daughter Estelle received early communications of his survival of bodily death.

7. **Andrew Lang (1844-1912).** Scottish historian, critic, anthropologist, classicist, novelist, and poet. For his impact on literary world at the fin de siècle, see Chapter 5 and the biographical note to that chapter. Lang wished most to be remembered for his contributions to anthropology. His interest in folklore and fairy-tale, combined with work

on primitive religious belief (*Myth, Ritual and Religion* (1887); *The Making of Religion* (1898)) meant that he was inevitably interested in the evidences of psychical research, which he viewed as a useful source of comparative material, as well as suggesting that 'savage' thought about the supernatural may have been based on actual occurrences of clairvoyance and telepathy. *Cock Lane and Common Sense* (1894) was an analysis of ghost stories in this light, and he became President of the Society for Psychical Research in 1911.

12

SEXOLOGY

One of the most influential developments in critical and historical approaches to the fin de siècle has been Michel Foucault's *History of Sexuality* (1976), which took aim at the view of the nineteenth century as prudishly secretive about matters sexual. Foucault suggested the reverse: that there was a positive injunction, an incitement to discourse endlessly about sex, discernible in policy debates on prostitution and contagious diseases, institutional histories of schools, prisons, and asylums, and in a vast literature of handbooks and tracts detailing the sins of the flesh. A crucial element in Foucault's theory is the emergence of a 'scientia sexualis', a new science of the acts and behaviours of those subject to a new disciplinary object: sexuality. This, he suggests, is 'implanted' initially in the bourgeois body, and is then progressively mapped onto larger populations. In English culture, the 1880s and 1890s can be seen as a moment of intensification of this sexual mapping. Foucault's work, with other analyses of sexological taxonomies by feminist, gay, and lesbian historians, has resituated the more familiar Freudian narrative of the sexual being in the context of an emergent discipline.

Sexology is a contradictory discourse. It knows itself to be marginal and disreputable, and so insistently tries to legitimate itself as useful to a tiny group of policy-makers in the criminal justice system—see Krafft-Ebing and Symonds below. On the other hand, the new beings in these accounts (nymphomaniac, masochist, invert) were incredibly influential as models well into the twentieth century, acting well beyond the tiny minority that might actually have been able to read these works. The accounts of 'perversity' they offer can be transparently normative and moralistic against any form of activity outside heterosexual, procreative marriage. Again though, these writers can be surprisingly 'liberal' in their views about other sexualities.

Beginning with a sample account of the nymphomaniac and a

sequence of perversities from Krafft-Ebing's important compendium of sexual proclivities, our selections concentrate on the emergence of theories of the 'sexually inverted man' in England. Edward Carpenter and John Addington Symonds—two very different men who were privately circulating documents promoting men's love of men—both came into contact with Havelock Ellis at the beginning of the 1890s. Ellis was a radical figure at the heart of the British progressive scene: he shared rooms with Arthur Symons, wrote for the *Savoy*, moved in Karl Pearson's circle, and had a brief liaison with Olive Schreiner. After 1891 he was to specialize in the 'psychology of sex'.

These documents display how they calculated that scientific discourse might legitimate 'unnatural' desires. The history of their publication also shows the disastrous impact on discussions of other sexualities of the arrest and imprisonment of Oscar Wilde in 1895. Carpenter had published three pamphlets on 'sex-love' in 1894; he was to collect these with his privately circulating essay 'Homogenic Love' into book form as *Love's Coming of Age* for Fisher Unwin. Wilde's trial intervened, and Unwin removed all of Carpenter's work from their lists. The book was eventually published in London in 1902; an expanded 1906 edition revised 'Homogenic Love' as 'The Intermediate Sex'. In his lifetime, Symonds only privately printed his long essays on same-sex love, despite being one of the most respected literary figures of the time. He began his collaboration with Havelock Ellis to write a joint work in 1891, but died soon after. This work, *Sexual Inversion*, suffered a complex fate. It initially appeared in Germany in 1896. After being rejected by several English publishers, the book appeared in April 1897 as *Sexual Inversion* by Havelock Ellis and J. A. Symonds, the preface stating 'It is owing to the late John Addington Symonds that this part of my work has developed to its present extent'. Symonds's surviving family bought up the entire run of this edition, effectively suppressing it. When a new edition appeared in October 1897, every single mention of Symonds had been erased. He survived only anonymously as 'Case XVIII', reprinted below. In May 1898 Ellis was to discover that 'The University Press, Watford' was a fraudster's scam; worse, the book became the means by which the police suppressed the anarchist Legitimation League (campaigning for liberal divorce and illegitimacy laws, and publishers of the free-love journal *The Adult*). An undercover detective pur-chased Ellis's book from George Bedborough's bookshop. Bedbor-ough was eventually brought to trial for selling 'a certain lewd, wicked, bawdy, scandalous libel' of a book. In October 1898 Ellis could only stand by as Bedborough pleaded guilty, whilst the judge declared the book 'a pretence and a sham'. Ellis only ever published with American presses after this trial, *Sexual Inversion* becoming a part of the multi-volume *Studies in the Psychology of Sex* published by Random House in New York.

These selections are replete with Latinate medical and sexological terms, which we have chosen not to gloss in detail. Such terminology was, of course, designed to exclude certain audiences, with medical experts constantly anxious that texts would fall into the 'wrong' hands. When Freud treated 'Dora' in 1899, one theory for the girl's precocious sexual knowledge was that it had derived from illicit readings of half-comprehended sexological encyclopedias.

Secondary reading: Bland and Doan; Bristow, *Sexuality*; Brome; Foucault, *An Introduction to the History of Sexuality*; Greig; Grosskurth; Mort; Weeks.

———

1   Gustave Bouchereau, 'Nymphomania', *A Dictionary of Psychological Medicine* (1892)

Definition—Under this term we understand a morbid condition peculiar to the female sex, the most prominent character of which consists in a irresistible impulse to satisfy the sexual appetite—the same pathological condition which in the male has received the name of satyriasis (q.v.). Some alienists have with Esquirol attempted to distinguish erotic insanity of purely cerebral origin from an irresistible impulse caused by morbid irritation of the reproductive organs.[1] This thesis may be maintained as a theory, and cases may be quoted to support it. It would, however, be rash to affirm that it is always so, and the proof is difficult to establish. Nobody disputes that morbid love may be entirely intellectual or platonic, and may have as its object a living or dead person, a souvenir, a statue, or a picture, but in addition to this, there exists a violent, irresistible sexual appetite which must be satisfied, regardless of age or any other consideration. Of the two kinds of phenomena, the former is the consequence of a disorder in which the brain predominates over the sexual organs; the latter is the result of a reverse action of the sexual organs upon the brain, but without a reciprocal re-action, without our being always able to determine, however, the starting-point with sufficient precision.

Nymphomania must not be considered as a morbid entity, but rather as a form or variety of mental derangement connected with affections, which may differ as

---

[1] Jean Esquirol (1722–1840) was an early psychologist, who signalled a move towards *treatment* of the mentally ill by unchaining them and attempting to ameliorate their condition.

regards their seat, nature, and development. We describe it as an impulse, even if the doctrine of pre-impulsive monomania has disappeared from mental pathology. Its aetiology is the most interesting part of its history. The appetite in question is not the same in all women. There is also a difference between the sexes, and there are racial differences also. In some women it appears early, and remains to a very advanced age; in others it develops slowly, is dormant, and becomes prematurely extinct, so that such women never reach their full sexual development. Longitude and latitude have but a limited effect on this function, but a high temperature, together with stimulating food, intensifies it. Thus, the negro in his tent under the burning rays of the sun, and the Esquimaux, during the long winter nights in his over-heated hut, equally give themselves up to repulsive excesses in the midst of orgies which constitute their festivals; the civilised man obeys the same instincts when his imagination, excited by sensuous representations, and his stomach filled with exciting aliment, have aroused his animal passions. Temperature, food, surroundings, and example increase, therefore the activity of this sense, and moderate excitement is too often followed by an irresistible morbid impulse. Education may diminish or augment the appetite, and hence impressions received in childhood, and especially at puberty, have a great influence on the development; the innate morbid germs or proclivities do not necessarily thrive, but may be easily fostered. On the one hand, a pathological predisposition, wisely restricted, may even be turned to the benefit and preservation of the species whilst on the other hand, if not moderated, it terminates in the premature extinction of the individual, or in the degeneration of the race. The final result often depends on accidental causes: the woman, as a child or an adult, very easily receives impressions from her environment; she unconsciously receives the motive of her actions from her reading, from pictures, statuary, plays or daily scenes. When the neuropathic condition affects and dominates her, all the impressions appeal to her morbidly impressionable state, and she often becomes the slave of her instincts.

Nymphomania frequently appears in the course of various mental disorders, differing in seat and lesion: idiocy and its varieties, mania, circular insanity, hypochondriasis, hysteria, epilepsy, general paralysis, hypochondriacal insanity, and brain degeneration. Exceptionally, it persists during the whole duration of the principal disorder, but generally it is only a transitory phenomenon. Nymphomania is frequent at the commencement of different forms of insanity, but its duration is short; it is frequently observed during the first two stages of general paralysis, and seems to be directly connected with lesions of the brain and spinal cord. After the nerve-cells and fibres have become atrophied, sexual impotency ensues, and we no longer observe erotic insanity or sexual excitement. Nymphomania is observed as a temporary phenomenon in old women whose intellect has become deranged, and who later on are affected with cerebral softening and encephalitis around a localised lesion. In religious insanity of mystic forms, erotic insanity amounting to an irresistible impulse is by no means rare; later it is succeeded by remorse which causes the patient most painful suffering. The affections of the spinal cord, myelitis, incipient softening, and locomotive ataxia, cause the same sexual disorders (reflexly), which we have described as resulting from cerebral disease.

Causes—Nymphomania may have as a cause disease of the genital apparatus: eruptions on the labia majora and minora, inflammation of the vagina, uterus, Fallopian tubes, and organic affections of the uterus and the commencement of the vagina. Women given to the use of opium, morphia, and haschish may, in the same way as men, exhibit sexual excitement bordering on nymphomania—a condition in which their imagination dwells in consequence, upon erotic ideas and images. Later on, when the intoxication has become chronic, the sexual appetite slowly diminishes and becomes extinct; the annihilation of the intellectual faculties, combined with general exhaustion, become complete. Nymphomania presents various degrees of symptoms. At first it shows itself by simple excitement of the reproductive organs, which is brief, and upon which the will still exercises control; subsequently there is irresistible erotic impulse. The patient's expression is bright, the face turgid, the respiration quickened, the sexual organs are congested, and the gestures amatory. The appetite demands satisfaction without regard to age or person; the desire may even lead to murder if resistance is offered to the patient's desires. The duration and termination of such a disorder depends upon the primary cause; most frequently temporary, it becomes a permanent and predominant phenomenon in certain idiots and chronic lunatics, and causes general weakening with disorders of the bodily functions; diseases and traumatisms of the genital organs are the consequence; very exceptionally death is the direct result; if it occurs, it is in consequence of some accidental affection, for the enfeebled organism is more disposed to contract any malady.

Various intoxicants are apt to produce nymphomania: poisoning by cantharides was formerly supposed to have this effect, but subsequently it was denied; irritation of the genito-urinary apparatus is noticed after the absorption of cantharides, but it does not cause eroticism. This subject requires fresh investigation, as the observations reported by former observers can be interpreted by various ways. It is well known that fatal poisoning by cantharides causes painful tumescence of the generative organs without any sexual impulse. From the moment we are able to prove that nymphomania is accompanied by a mental disorder or is its immediate consequence, a nymphomaniac must be declared to be irresponsible from a legal point of view, if under such circumstances she obeys an irresistible morbid impulse. As a general rule, the man solicits and the woman complies, but it may be that she is the one to solicit. It would be unjust to attribute all the actions of libertinism in women to morbid proclivities; perverted immorality often accomplishes actions which the most vivid imagination would scarcely be able to conceive, and such actions fall within the reach of the law, if not caused by mental derangement. But insanity must be suspected and looked for, if a woman after a long life of propriety and modesty gives herself suddenly to debauchery, thus bringing scandal and contempt upon her family and herself. This sudden change of conduct frequently finds its explanation in commencing organic lesions or in an insanity as yet doubtful, but which will soon become obvious. General paralysis in its commencement often produces in women a condition of sexual excitement liable to become nymphomania; such excitement strikes the observer for its exaggeration, whilst the insanity remains obscure or passes by altogether unrecognised. Nurses and servants, to whom the care of children is confided, should be kept under strict surveillance by the parents, because it is not uncommon that under the influence of hysteria or of a morbid disposition they subject the children to manipulations which affect their health and compromise their existence. Many cases have been divulged, but how many happen of which we hear nothing! A habit of our times, which is far spread and most dangerous for our children, is, not to keep the dogs, which are now in almost every house, in the yard of the stables, but to allow them to come into the house and even into the bed; their habit of introducing their tongues everywhere causes the child to contract habits against which it is unable to strive, whilst the parents are too much absorbed in their pursuits to notice what passes around them. For many years a whole literature of romance and plays has been occupied in the description of Lesbic love, to the great damage of young girls and neuropathic women; curiosity at first attracts and soon misleads them; the sensation experienced enslaves them and then aided by the use of morphia, ether and cocaine, nymphomania establishes itself. The word has spread from the unfortunates to the women of the theatres, and from thence has taken possession of unoccupied women of all classes of society with unsatisfied desires.

Hypnotism is stated to have been used for the purpose of committing crimes on women, and this may be done under hypnotism as well as any other anaesthetic. It is useful to keep here in mind that simulation may always be expected in hysterical women, and that it is well to remember the possibility of its existence. We cannot, however, discuss these questions here, and it must therefore suffice merely to indicate them. A hypnotiser, who, by repeated manoeuvres, has tried the disposition of his subject (a woman easy to hypnotise), might experience little resistance if he wished to excite her amativeness. His responsibility is exactly the same as that of an individual who abuses a weak, imbecile or idiotic person. Intercourse calms the natural want but does not cure the morbid excitement. Marriage only results in introducing unhappiness into two families, and, in addition to this a child resulting from the union will probably be a source of new pathological conditions. Hence abstention from marriage is the best advice to give both for the individual and for society.

The treatment must be directed to the principal disease which causes nymphomania. Anaphrodisiacs are useful, without, however, being very effective; bromide of camphor and of potassium, Sitz baths and sedative lavements, moderate exercise, regular work, life in the open air, and a good physical, moral and intellectual hygiene should be prescribed.

As regards surgical operations, clitoridectomy, nymphotomy, circumcision and oöphorectomy, are useless, and some of them are even to be condemned. It is evident that the cause of nymphomania is a lesion or disease of the cerebrospinal axis. To revive here an old subject of debate would serve no useful purpose. It has been demonstrated in important discussions in medical societies, the authority of which is indisputable. Observations made on different sides, seem to confirm their conclusions.

2   from Richard von Krafft-Ebing, *Psychopathia Sexualis, with Especial Reference to Antipathic Sexual Instinct: A Medico-Forensic Study* (1886)

PREFACE TO THE FIRST EDITION

Few people are conscious of the deep influence exerted by sexual life upon the sentiment, thought and action of man in his social relations with others. [. . .]

The object of this treatise is merely to record the various psychopathological manifestations of sexual life in man and to reduce them to their lawful conditions. This task is by no means an easy one, and the author is well aware of the fact that, despite his (varied) far-reaching experience in psychiatry and criminal medicine, he is yet unable to offer anything but an imperfected system.

The importance of the subject, however, demands scientific research on account of its forensic bearing and its deep influence upon the common weal. The medical barrister only then finds out how sad the lack of our knowledge is in the domain of sexuality when he is called upon to express an opinion as to the responsibility of the accused whose life, liberty and honour are at stake. He then begins to appreciate the efforts that have been made to bring light into darkness.

Certain it is that so far as sexual crimes are concerned erroneous ideas prevail, unjust decisions are given, and the law as well as public opinion are *prima facie* prejudiced against the offender.

The scientific study of the psychopathology of sexual life necessarily deals with the miseries of man and the dark sides of his existence, the shadow of which contorts the sublime image of the deity into horrid caricatures, and leads astray aestheticism and morality.

It is the sad privilege of medicine, and especially that of psychiatry to ever witness the weaknesses of human nature and the reverse side of life.

The physician finds, perhaps, a (satisfaction) solace in the fact that he may at times refer those manifestations which offend against our ethical or aesthetical principles to a diseased condition of the mind or the body. He can save the honour of humanity in the forum of morality, and the honour of the individual before the judge and his fellow-men. It is from the search of truth that the exalted duties and rights of medical science emanate. [. . .]

He appeals to men engaged in serious study in the domains of natural philosophy and medical jurisprudence.

A scientific title has been chosen, and technical terms are used throughout the book in order to exclude the lay reader. For the same reason certain portions are written in Latin. [. . .]

V. PATHOLOGICAL SEXUALITY IN ITS LEGAL ASPECTS

The laws of all civilised nations punish those who commit perverse sexual acts. Inasmuch as the preservation of chastity and morals is one of the most important reasons for the existence of the commonwealth, the state cannot be too careful, as a protector of morality, in the struggle against sensuality. Their contest is unequal; because only a certain number of the sexual crimes can be legally combated, and the infractions of the laws by so powerful a natural instinct can be but little influenced by punishment. It also lies in the nature of the sexual crimes that but a part of them ever reach the knowledge of the authorities. Public sentiment, in that it looks upon them as disgraceful, lends much aid.

Criminal statistics prove the sad fact that sexual crimes are progressively increasing in our modern civilisation. This is particularly the case with immoral acts with children under the age of fourteen.

The moralist sees in these sad facts nothing but the decay of general morality, and in some instances comes to the conclusion that the present mildness of the laws punishing sexual crimes, in comparison with their severity in past centuries, is in part responsible for this.

The medical investigator is driven to the conclusion that this manifestation of modern social life stands in relation to the predominating nervous condition of later generations, in that it begets defective individuals, excites the sexual instinct, leads to sexual abuse, and, with continuance of lasciviousness associated with diminished sexual power, induces perverse sexual acts.

It will be clearly seen from what follows how such an opinion is justified, especially with respect of the increasing number of sexual crimes committed on children.

It is at once evident, from what has gone before, that neuropathic, and even psychopathic, states are largely determinate for the commission of sexual crimes. Here nothing less than the responsibility of many of the men who commit such crimes is called in question.

Psychiatry cannot be denied the credit of having recognised and proved the psycho-pathological significance of numerous monstrous, paradoxical sexual acts.

Law and Jurisprudence have thus far given but little attention to the facts resulting from investigations in psycho-pathology. Law is, in this, opposed to Medicine, and is constantly in danger of passing judgment on individuals who, in the light of science, are not responsible for their acts. [. . .]

The *nature of the act* can never, in itself, determine a decision as to whether it lies within the limits of mental pathology, or within the bounds of mental physiology. *The perverse act does not indicate perversion of instinct.* At any rate, the most monstrous and most perverse sexual acts have been committed by persons of sound mind. *The perversion of feeling must be shown to be pathological.* This proof is to be obtained by learning the conditions attending its development, and by proving it to be part of an existing general neuropathic or psychopathic distinction. [. . .]

To obtain the facts necessary to allow a decision of the question whether immorality or abnormality occasioned the act, a medico-legal examination is required—an examination which is made according to the rules of science; which takes account of both the past history of the individual and the present condition,—the anthropological and clinical data.

The proof of the existence of an *original*, congenital anomaly of the sexual sphere is important, and points to the need of an examination in the direction of a condition of psychical degeneration. An *acquired* perversity, to be pathological, must be found to depend upon a neuropathic or psychopathic state. [. . .]

RAPE AND LUST-MURDER

Case 183. *Lust-murder; moral imbecility.* A man of middle age; born in Algeria; said to be of Arabic descent. Had served for several years in the colonial troops; had then shipped as a sailor between Algeria and Brazil, and later on, in the hope of finding lighter employment, had gone to North America. He was known among his acquaintances as being lazy, cowardly and brutal. Several times he had been sentenced for vagrancy; it was said that he was a thief of the lowest kind; that he knocked about with women of the lowest class, and made common cause with them. His perverse sexual relations and acts were also well known. On several occasions he had bitten and beaten women with whom he sexually conversed. According to the description given of him, the authorities thought they had secured a certain unknown party who had scared at night the women in the streets by embracing and kissing them, and had the nick-name of 'Jack the Kisser.'

He was a tall man (over six feet), slightly bent forward. Low forehead, very prominent cheek bones, massive jaw bones; small, narrow, inflamed eyes, piercing look; big feet, hands like birds' claws; shambling gait. His arms and hands were tattooed all over. Remarkable was the picture of a woman in colours, around which the name 'Fatima' was inscribed, because tattooing the female form upon the body is considered to be disgraceful among the Arabs of the Algerian army; and prostitutes generally have a cross tattooed in their skin. His general appearance gave the impression of a low grade of intelligence.

N. was convicted of the murder of an elderly female with whom he had spent the night. The corpse bore the various wounds, some remarkable for their length; the abdomen was ripped open, pieces of the intestines were cut out, so was one of the ovaries; other parts were strewn around the corpse. Several of the wounds were like crosses; one was in the shape of a crescent. The murderer had strangled his victim. He denied the deed, and every inclination to commit such an act. [. . .]

MASOCHISM AND SEXUAL BONDAGE

Masochism may under certain circumstances attain forensic importance [. . .] Psychologically speaking, the facts of *sexual bondage* are of greater criminal importance.

If sensuality is predominant, or in other words, if a man is held in fetich-thraldom and his moral power of resistance is weak, he may by an avaricious or vindictive woman into whose bondage his passion has led be goaded on to the very worst crimes. [. . .]

Case 190. *Sexual bondage in a lady.* Mrs. X., thirty-six years of age; mother of four children. Comes from a neuropathic and heavily-tainted mother. Father psychopathic. She began to masturbate at the age of five, had an attack of melancholia at the age of ten, during which period she was troubled with the delusion that she could not go to heaven on account of her sins. This made her nervous, excitable, emotional, neurasthenic. At the age of seventeen she fell in love with a man who was denied her by her parents. She now showed symptoms of hysteria. When twenty-one she married a man by many years her senior who had but little sexual appetite. Her conjugal relations with him never satisfied her; coitus produced severe *erethismus genitalis* which she could not satisfy with masturbation. She suffered tortures from this *libido insatiata*, yielded more and more to onanism, became heavily hystero-neurasthenic, capricious and quarrelsome, so that marital relations grew ever colder.

After nine years of mental and physical anguish, Mrs. X. succumbed to the blandishments of another man in whose arms she found that gratification for which she had so long languished.

But now she was tormented with the consciousness of having broken her marriage vow, often feared she would become insane, and only the love for her children prevented her from committing suicide.

She scarcely dared to appear before her husband whom she highly esteemed on account of his noble character, and felt dreadful qualms of conscience because she had to conceal the awful secret from him.

Although she found full gratification and immense sensual pleasure in the arms of the other man, she had repeatedly tried to give up this *liaison*. Her efforts were in vain. She got deeper and deeper into the bondage of this man, who recognising and abusing his power had merely to dissemble as if to leave her in order to possess her without restraint. He abused this bondage of the miserable woman only to gratify his sexual appetite, gradually even in a perverse manner. She was unable to refuse him any demand.

When Mrs. X in her despair came to me for professional advice she declared that she could no longer continue such a life of misery and anguish. An insuperable *libido*, disgusting to herself, drew her to this man, whom she could not love but as little do without, whilst on the other hand she was constantly tormented with the danger of discovery, and with self-reproach on account of her offence against the law of God and man.

The greatest mental pain was caused by the thought of losing her paramour, who often threatened to leave her if she did not yield to his wishes, and who controlled her so thoroughly that she would do anything and everything at his bidding. [. . .]

UNNATURAL ABUSE (SODOMY)

[. . .]

A) VIOLATION OF ANIMALS (BESTIALITY)

[. . .]

Case 202. Y., twenty years of age, intelligent, well educated; claims to be free from any taint by heredity; physically sound except evidences of neurasthenia and *hyperaesthesia urethrae*; says he never masturbated. Always fond of animals, especially dogs and horses. Since the age of puberty increased love for animals, but sexual ideas in connection with sport seem to have been absent.

One day when he mounted a mare for the first time he experienced a sensation of lust; two weeks later, on a similar occasion, the same sensation with erection.

During his first ride he had ejaculation. A month after the same thing happened. Patient feels disgusted at the occurrence, and is angry with himself. He gave up the saddle. But from now on pollutions almost daily.

When he sees men on horseback, or dogs, he has erections. Almost every night he has pollutions accompanied by dreams in which he rides on horseback or is training dogs. Patient comes for medical advice.

Treatment with sounds removed the *hyperaesthesia urethrae* and diminished pollutions. The patient followed reluctantly the advice of the physician to have coitus, partly on account of dislike for women, partly on account of diffidence in his virility.

He made abortive attempts at coitus, but could not even bring about an erection, which, however, took place at the moment he saw a man on horseback. This depressed him; he considered his condition abnormal beyond remedy.

Continued medical treatment. A further attempt at coitus was successful with the assistance of fancied images of riders and dogs, which stimulated erection.

Patient grew more virile; his love for animals waned; erections at the sight of riders and dogs disappeared, nocturnal pollutions with dreams of animals became less frequent; he dreamed now of girls. Erection, which at first did not support *ejaculatio praecox*, and pathological coitus grew normal under treatment with sounds. Patient now finds sexual gratification, and is freed from his abnormal sexual impulse. [. . .]

B) WITH PERSONS OF THE SAME SEX (PEDERASTY; SODOMY IN THE STRICT SENSE)

[. . .] The study of antipathetic sexual instinct has placed male love for males in a very different light. [. . .] The principles laid down previously must also here be adhered to. Not the deed, but only an anthropological and clinical judgment of the perpetrator can permit a decision as to whether we have to do with a perversity deserving punishment, or with an abnormal perversion of the mental and sexual life, which, under certain circumstances, excludes punishment.

The next legal question to settle is whether the antipathic sexual feeling is congenital or acquired; and, in the latter case, whether it is a pathological perversion or a moral perversity.

Congenital sexual inversion occurs only in predisposed (tainted) individuals, as a partial manifestation of a defect evidenced by anatomical or functional abnormalities, or by both. The case becomes clearer and the diagnosis more certain if the individual, in character and disposition, seems to correspond entirely with his sexual peculiarity; if the inclination toward persons of the opposite sex is entirely wanting, or horror of sexual intercourse with them is felt; and if the individual, in the impulses to satisfy the antipathic sexual instinct, shows other anomalies of the sexual sphere, such as more pronounced degeneration in the form of periodicity of the impulse and impulsive conduct, and is a neuropathic and psychopathic person. [. . .]

The sexual instinct is one of the most powerful organic needs. There is no law that looks upon its satisfaction outside of marriage as punishable in itself; if the urning feels perversely, it is not his fault, but the fault of an abnormal condition natural to him.[2] His sexual instinct may be aesthetically very repugnant, but, from his morbid standpoint, it is natural. And again, in the majority of these unfortunates, the perverse sexual instinct is abnormally intense, and their consciousness recognises it as nothing unnatural. Thus moral and aesthetic ideas fail to assist them in resisting the instinct. [. . .]

The majority of urnings are in a painful situation. On the one hand, there is an impulse toward persons of their own sex that is abnormally intense, the gratification of which has a good effect, and is natural to them; on the other hand, there is public sentiment, which stigmatises their acts, and the law which threatens them with disgraceful punishment. Before them lies mental despair,—even insanity and suicide,—at the very least, nervous disease; behind them, shame, loss of position, etc. It cannot be doubted that, under these circumstances, states of stress and compulsion may be created by an unfortunate natural disposition and constitution. Society and the law should understand and appreciate these facts. The former should pity, and not despise, these unfortunates; the latter must cease to punish them,—at least while they remain within the limits which are set for the activity of their sexual instinct.

---

3   from Edward Carpenter, 'The Intermediate Sex' (1894/1906)

In late years (and since the arrival of the New Woman amongst us) many things in the relation of men and women to each other have altered, or at any rate become clearer. The growing sense of equality in habits and customs—university studies, art, music, politics, the bicycle, etc.—all these things have brought about a *rapprochement* between the sexes. If the modern woman is a little more masculine in some ways than her predecessor, the modern man (it is to be hoped), while by no means effeminate, is a little more sensitive in temperament and artistic feeling than the original John Bull. It is beginning to be recognised that the sexes do not or should not normally form two groups hopelessly isolated in habit and feeling

---

[2] Edward Carpenter's definition of the 'urning' is in n. 4 below.

from each other, but that they rather represent the two poles of *one* group—which is the human race; so that while certainly the extreme specimens at either pole are vastly divergent, there are great numbers in the middle region who (though differing corporeally as men and women) are by emotion and temperament very near to each other. We all know women with a strong dash of the masculine temperament, and we all know men whose almost feminine sensibility and intuition seem to belie their bodily form. Nature, it might appear, in mixing the elements which go to compose each individual, does not always keep here two groups of ingredients—which represent the two sexes—properly apart, but often throws them crosswise in a somewhat baffling manner, now this way and now that; yet wisely, we must think—for if a severe distinction of elements were always maintained, the two sexes would soon drift into far latitudes and absolutely cease to understand each other. As it is, there are some remarkable and (we think) indispensable types of character, in whom there is such a union or balance of the feminine and masculine qualities that these people become to a great extent the interpreters of men and women to each other. [. . .]

More than thirty years ago [. . .] an Austrian writer, K. H. Ulrichs,[3] drew attention in a series of pamphlets [. . .] to the existence of a class of people who strongly illustrate the above remarks, and with whom specially this paper is concerned. He pointed out that there were people born in such a position—as it were on the dividing line between the sexes—that while belonging distinctly to one sex as far as their bodies are concerned they may be said to belong *mentally* and *emotionally* to the other; that there were men, for instance, who might be described as of feminine soul enclosed in a male body (*anima muliebris in corpore virili inclusa*), or in other cases, women whose definition would be just the reverse. And he maintained that this doubleness of nature was to a great extent proved by the special direction of their love-sentiment. For in such cases, as indeed might be expected, the (apparently) masculine person instead of forming a love-union with a female tended to contract romantic friendships with one of his own sex; while the apparently feminine would, instead of marrying in the usual way, devote herself to the love of another feminine.

People of this kind (i.e. having this special variation of the love-sentiment) he called Urnings;[4] and though we are not obliged to accept his theory about the crosswise connexion between 'soul' and 'body,' since at best these words are somewhat vague and indefinite; yet his work was important because it was one of the first attempts, in modern times, to recognise the existence of what might be called an Intermediate sex, and to give at any rate *some* explanation of it. [. . .]

---

[3] Karl Heinrich Ulrichs, a German lawyer who from the 1860s until his death in 1895, campaigned vigorously for recognition of same-sex desire in men.

[4] [Carpenter's note:] From *Uranos*, heaven; his idea being that the Urning-love was of a higher order than the ordinary attachment.

Contrary to the general impression, one of the first points that emerges from this study is that 'Urnings,' or Uranians, are by no means so very rare; but that they form, beneath the surface of society, a large class. It remains difficult, however, to get an exact statement of their numbers; and this for more than one reason: partly because, owing to want of any general understanding of their case, these folk tend to conceal their true feelings from all but their own kind, and indeed often deliberately act in such a manner as to lead the world astray— (whence it arises that a normal man living in a certain society will often refuse to believe that there is a single Urning in the circle of his acquaintance, while one of the latter, or one that understands the nature, living in the same society, can count perhaps a score or more)—and partly because it is indubitable that the numbers do vary very greatly, not only in different countries, but even in different classes in the same country. [. . .]

In the second place it emerges (also contrary to the general impression) that men and women of exclusive Uranian type are by no means necessarily morbid in any way—unless, indeed, their peculiar temperament be pronounced in itself morbid. Formerly it was assumed, as a matter of course, that the type was merely a result of disease and degeneration; but now with the examination of the actual facts it appears that, on the contrary, many are fine, healthy specimens of their sex, muscular and well-developed in body, of powerful brain, high standard of conduct, and with nothing abnormal or morbid of any kind observable in their physical structure or constitution. This is, of course, not true of all, and there still remain a number of cases of weakly type to support the neuropathic view. Yet it is very noticeable that this view is much less insisted on by the later writers than by the earlier. It is also worth noticing that it is now acknowledged that even in the most healthy cases the special affectional temperament of the 'Intermediate' is, as a rule, ineradicable; so much so that when (as in not a few instances) such men and women, from social or other considerations, have forced themselves to marry, and even have children, they have still not been able to overcome their own bias, or the leaning after all of their life-attachment to some friend of their own sex. [. . .]

To call people of such temperament 'morbid,' and so forth, is of no use. Such a term is, in fact, absurdly inapplicable to many, who are amongst the most active, the most amiable and accepted members of society; besides, it forms no solution of the problem in question, and only amounts to marking down for disparagement a fellow-creature who has already considerable difficulties to contend with. [. . .]

We have so far limited ourselves to some very general characteristics of the Intermediate race. It may help to clear and fix our ideas if we now describe more in detail, first what may be called the extreme and exaggerated types of the race, and then the more normal and perfect types. By doing so we shall get a more definite and concrete view of our subject.

In the first place, then, the extreme specimens—as in most cases of extremes—are not particularly attractive, sometimes quite the reverse. In the male of this kind we have a distinctly effeminate type, sentimental, lackadaisical, mincing in gait and manners, something of a chatterbox, skilful at the needle and in woman's work, sometimes taking pleasure in dressing in women's clothes; his figure not unfrequently betraying a tendency toward the feminine, large at the hips, supple, not muscular, the face wanting in hair, the voice inclining to be high pitched, etc.; while his dwelling-room is orderly in the extreme, even natty, and choice of decoration and perfume. His affection too is often feminine in character, clinging and dependent and jealous, as of one desiring to be loved almost more than to love.

On the other hand, as the extreme type of the homogenic female, we have a rather markedly aggressive person, of strong passions, masculine manners and movements, practical in the conduct of life, sensuous rather than sentimental in love, often untidy, and *outré* in attire; her figure muscular, her voice rather low in pitch; her dwelling-room decorated with sporting-scenes, pistols, etc., and not without a suspicion of the fragrant weed in the atmosphere; while her love (generally to rather soft and feminine specimens of her own sex) is often a sort of furor, similar to the ordinary masculine love, and at times almost uncontrollable.

These are types which, on account of their salience, everyone will recognise more or less. Naturally, when they occur, they excite a good deal of attention, and it is not an uncommon impression that most persons of the homogenic nature belong to either one or other of these classes. But in reality, of course, these extreme developments are rare, and for the most part the temperament in question is embodied in men and women of quite normal and unsensational exterior. [. . .]

If now we come to what may be called the more normal type of the Uranian man, we find a man who, while possessing thoroughly masculine powers of mind and body, combines with them the tenderer and more emotional soul-nature of the woman—and sometimes to a remarkable degree. Such men, as said, are often muscular and well-built, and not distinguishable in exterior structure and the carriage of body from others of their own sex; but emotionally they are extremely complex, tender, sensitive, pitiful and loving, 'full of storm and stress, of ferment and fluctuation' of the heart; the logical faculty may or may not, in their case, be well-developed, but intuition is always strong; like women they read characters at a glance, and know, without knowing how, what is passing in the minds of others; for nursing and waiting on the needs of others they have often a peculiar gift; at the bottom lies the artist-nature, with the artist's sensibility and perception. Such an one is often a dreamer, of brooding reserved habits, often a musician, or a man of culture, courted in society, which nevertheless does not understand him—though sometimes a child of the people, without any culture, but almost always with a peculiar inborn refinement. De Joux, who speaks on the whole favourably of Uranian men and women, says of the former: 'They are enthusiastic for poetry and music, are often eminently skilful in the fine arts, and are overcome with emotion and sympathy at the least sad occurrence . . .' And in another passage he indicates the artist-nature, when he says: 'The nerve-system of many an Urning is the finest and most complicated musical instrument in the service of the interior personality that can be imagined.' [. . .]

[U]nfamiliar though the subject is, it begins to appear that it is one which modern thought and science will have to face. Of the latter and more normal types it may be said that they exist, and have always existed, in considerable abundance, and from that circumstance alone there is a strong probability that they have their place and purpose. As pointed out there is no particular indication of morbidity about them, unless the special nature of their love-sentiment be itself accounted morbid; and in the alienation of the sexes from each other, of which complaint is so often made to-day, it must be admitted that they do much to fill the gap.

---

4   from John Addington Symonds, *A Problem in Modern Ethics, Being an Inquiry into the Phenomenon of Sexual Inversion, Addressed Especially to Medical Psychologists and Jurists* (1896)

INTRODUCTION

There is a passion, or a perversion of appetite, which, like all human passions, has played a considerable part in the world's history for good or evil; but which has hardly yet received the philosophical attention and the scientific investigation it deserves. The reason for this may be that in all Christian societies the passion under consideration has been condemned to pariahdom: consequently, philosophy and science have not deigned to make it the subject of special inquiry. Only one great race in past ages, the Greek race, to whom we owe the inheritance of our ideas, succeeded in raising it to the level of chivalrous enthusiasm. Nevertheless, we find it present everywhere and in all periods of history. We cannot take up the religious books, the legal codes, the annals, the descriptions of the manners of any nation, whether large or small, powerful or feeble, civilized or savage, without meeting with this person in one form or other. Sometimes it assumes the calm and dignified attitude of conscious merit, as in Sparta, Athens, Thebes. Sometimes it stalks in holes and corners, hiding an abashed head and shrinking from the light of day, as in the capitals of modern Europe. It confronts us on the steppes of Asia,

where hordes of nomads drink the milk of mares; in the bivouac of Keltish war-
riors, lying wrapped in wolves' skins round their camp-fires; upon the sands of
Arabia, where the Bedaween raise desert dust in flying squadrons. We discern it
among the palm-groves of the South Sea Islands, in the card-houses and temple
gardens of Japan, under Esquimaux snow-huts, beneath the sultry vegetation of
Peru, beside the streams of Shiraz and the waters of the Ganges, in the cold clear
air of Scandinavian winters. It throbs in our huge cities. The pulse of it can be felt
in London, Paris, Berlin, Vienna, no less than Constantinople, Naples, Teheran,
and Moscow. It finds a home in Alpine valleys, Albanian ravines, Californian
canyons, and gorges of Caucasian mountains. It once sat, clothed in Imperial
purple, on the throne of the Roman Caesars, crowned with the tiara on the chair
of St Peter. It has flaunted, emblazoned with the heraldries of France and England, in coronation ceremonies at Rheims and Westminster. The royal palaces of
Madrid and Aranjuez tell their tales of it. So do the ruined courtyards of Granada
and the castle-keep of Avignon. It shone with clear radiance in the gymnasium of
Hellas, and nerved the dying heroes of Greek freedom for their last folorn hope
upon the plains of Chaeronea. Endowed with inextinguishable life, in spite of all
that has been done to suppress it, this passion survives at large in modern states
and towns, penetrates society, makes itself felt in every quarter of the globe where
men are brought into communion with men.

Yet no one dares to speak of it; or if they do, they bate their breath, and preface
their remarks with maledictions.

Those who read these lines will hardly doubt what passion it is that I am hinting at. *Quod semper ubique et ab omnibus*[5]—surely it deserves a name. Yet I can
hardly find a name which will not seem to soil this paper. The accomplished languages of Europe in the nineteenth century supply no term for this persistent
feature of human psychology, without importing some implication of disgust,
disgrace, vituperation. Science, however, has recently—within the last twenty
years in fact—invented a convenient phrase, which does not prejudice the matter
under consideration. She speaks of the 'inverted sexual instinct'; and with this
neutral nomenclature the investigator has good reason to be satisfied.

Inverted sexuality, the sexual instinct diverted from the normal channel,
directed (in the case of males) to males, forms the topic of the following discourse.
The study will be confined to modern times, and to those nations which regard
the phenomenon with religious detestation. This renders the enquiry peculiarly
difficult, and exposes the enquirer, unless he be a professed expert in diseases of
the mind and nervous centres, to almost certain misconstruction. Still, there is no
valid reason why the task of statement and analysis should not be undertaken.
Indeed one might rather wonder why candid and curious observers of humanity

---

[5] Roughly translated, 'it is the same everywhere and for everyone'.

have not attempted to fathom a problem which faces them at every turn in their historical researches and in daily life. Doubtless their neglect is due to natural or acquired repugnance, to feelings of disgust and hatred, derived from immemorial tradition, and destructive to the sympathies which animate a really zealous pioneer. Nevertheless, what is human is alien to no human being. What the law punishes, but what, in spite of law, persists and energizes, ought to arrest attention. We are all of us responsible to some extent for the maintenance and enforcement of our laws. We are all of us, as evolutionary science surely teaches, interested in the facts of anthropology, however repellent some of these may be to our own feelings. We cannot evade the conditions of *atavism* and *heredity*. Every family runs the risk of producing a boy or a girl, whose life will be embittered by inverted sexuality, but who in all other respects will be no worse or better than the normal members of the home. Surely, then, it is our duty and our interest to learn what we can about its nature, and to arrive through comprehension at some rational method of dealing with it.

---

5   Havelock Ellis, 'Case XVIII' [John Addington Symonds], *Sexual Inversion* (1897)

A was the son of a physician. Father's family robust, vigorous, healthy and prolific. They had been Puritans since the middle of the 16th century. Mother's family tainted with both insanity and phthisis. A's maternal grandmother and one aunt died of phthisis. The two eldest children of A's parents were girls: one of these died of phthisis at the age of 42. Next came male twins, born dead. Next a boy, who died of hydrocephalic inflammation at the age of three to four. A was born in 1840, and had a sickly childhood, suffering from night-terrors, somnambulism, excessive shyness, religious disquietude. The last of the family was a girl, who has grown up into a healthy and intellectually robust woman.

A has communicated these facts concerning the development of his sexual instincts.

1. In early childhood, and up to the age of 13 he had frequent opportunities of closely inspecting the genital organs of both boys and girls, his playfellows. The smell of the female parts affected him disagreeably. The sight of the male organ did not arouse any particular sensation. He is, however, of the opinion that, living with sisters, he felt more curious about his own sex as being more remote from him. He showed no effeminacy in his preference for games or work.

2. About the age of 8, if not before, he became subject to singular half-waking dreams. He fancied himself seated on the floor among several adult and naked sailors, whose genitals and buttocks he contemplated and handled with relish. He called himself the 'dirty pig' of these men, and felt that they were in some way his masters, ordering him to do uncleanly services to their bodies. He cannot remember ever having seen a naked man at that time; and nothing in his memory explains why the men of his dreams were supposed to be sailors.

3. At the same period, his attention was directed to his own penis. His nurse, out walking one day, said to him, 'When little boys grow up, their p's fall off.' The nursery-maid sniggered. He felt that there must be something peculiar about the penis. He suffered from irritability of the prepuce; and the nurse powdered it before he went to sleep. There was no transition thence to onanism.

4. At the same period, he casually heard that a man used to come and expose his person before the window of a room where the maids sat. This troubled him vaguely.

5. Between the age of 8 and 22 he twice took the penis of a cousin into his mouth in the morning, after they had slept together; the feeling of the penis pleased him.

6. When sleeping with another cousin, they used to lie with hands outstretched to cover each other's *penes* or *nates*.[6] A preferred the *nates*, but his cousin the *penes*. Neither cousin, just mentioned, was homosexual; and there was no attempt at mutual masturbation.

7. He was in the habit of playing with five male cousins. One of these boys was unpopular with the others, and they invented a method of punishing him for supposed offences. They sat round the room on chairs together, each with his penis exposed. The boy went round on his knees and took each penis into his mouth in turn. This was supposed to humiliate him. It did not lead to masturbation.

8. He accidentally observed a boy who sat next to him in school, playing with his penis and caressing it. This gave him a powerful uneasy sensation. With regard to all these points, A observes that none of the other boys with whom he was connected at that period, and who were exposed to precisely the same influences, became homosexual. He also remarks that most boys thrown together will have the fact of the penis brought frequently before their notice.

9. One of the very first events in his life which he can recall is the following. A male cousin of about 22 was reclining on an armchair, with legs spread out. A

---

[6] 'penis or buttocks'.

jumped upon his lap, and felt his hand fall upon a soft yielding thing in the young man's trousers. A perceived that his cousin shrank together with pain, and wondered what this meant.

10. A was mentally precocious. When he began to read books, he felt particularly attracted to certain male characters: the Adonis of Shakespeare's poems (he wished he had been Venus), Anzoleto in George Sand's *Consuelo*, Hermes in Homer. He was very curious to know why the Emperors kept boys as well as girls in their seraglios, and what the male gods did with the youths they loved.

11. While at public school, he never practised onanism with other boys, though they often tempted him, and he frequently saw the act in process. It inspired him with a disagreeable sense of indecency. Still in his 15th year, puberty commenced with nocturnal pollutions and occasional masturbation. His thoughts were not directed to males while masturbating, nor to females. A spoke to his father about these signs of puberty; and on his father's recommendation, he entirely abandoned onanism. *Footnote*. He reckons that he may have practised self-abuse about once a week during a period of from six to seven months.

12. The nocturnal pollutions became very frequent and exhausting. They were medically treated by tonics—quinine and strychnine. A thinks this treatment exasperated his neurosis. All this while, no kind of sexual feeling for girls made itself felt. With the exception of a comradely liking for his younger sister and her Swiss governess, he was perfectly indifferent to them. He could not understand what his school fellows found in women, or the stories they told about wantonness and the delights of coitus.

13. His old dreams about sailors disappeared. But now he enjoyed visions of beautiful young men and exquisite Greek statues. Occasionally he saw in sleep the erect organs of powerful grooms or peasants. The gross visions offended his taste and hurt him; he took a strange poetic pleasure in the ideal forms. But the seminal losses which attended both kinds were a perpetual source of misery to him. There is no doubt that at this time, i.e. between the 15th and 17th years, a homosexual diathesis had become established in A.

14. It was in his 18th year that an event which A regards as decisive in his development occurred. He read the *Phaedrus* and *Symposium* of Plato. A new world opened, and he felt that his own nature had been revealed. Next year he formed a passionate but pure friendship with a boy of 15. Personal contact with the boy caused erections, extreme agitation, and aching pleasure: not ejaculation however. Through 4 years of intimacy A never saw him naked, or touched him pruriently. Only twice he kissed him. A says that those two kisses were the most perfect joys he ever felt.

15. A's father became seriously anxious both about his health and reputation. He warned him of the social and legal dangers attending his temperament. Yet he did not encourage A to try coitus with women. A's own sense of danger would, he thinks, have made this method successful: at least, the bait of intercourse with females would have lessened his neurosis and diverted his mind to some extent from homosexual thoughts.

16. Now opened a period of great pain and anxiety for A. It is true that at the University he made very brilliant studies, and won for himself a distinguished reputation. As poet and prose-writer he was already known in his 22nd year. Still his neurasthenia increased. He suffered from insomnia, obscure cerebral discomfort, stammering, chronic conjunctivitis, inability to concentrate attention, and dejection. It must be added that, when he was 25, a chronic disease of the lungs declared itself, which forced him to winter out of England.

17. Meanwhile A's homosexual emotions strengthened and assumed a more sensual aspect. Yet he abstained from indulging them, as also from onanism. Fear of infection prevented him from seeking relief in ordinary coitus. Having no passion for women, it was easy to avoid them. And yet they inspired him with no exact horror. He used to dream of finding an exit from his painful situation by cohabitation with some coarse, boyish girl of the people. But his dread of syphilis stood in the way.

18. A now felt that he must conquer himself by efforts of will and by persistent direction of his thoughts to heterosexual images. He sought the society of distinguished women. Once he coaxed up a romantic affection for a Bernese maiden. But this came to nothing, probably because the girl felt a want of absolute passion in A's wooing.

19. He was now strongly advised to marry by his father and other physicians. He did so when he was exactly 24 years and 1 month old. Then he found that he was potent. But to his disappointment he also found that he only cohabited with his wife *faute de mieux*.[7] He still dreamed of men, desired them, even began to desire soldiers. He begat in all four children, females. His wife, the member of a noble family, disliked sexual connection and hated pregnancy. This was a great misfortune for A. His wife's temperament led to long intervals of separation *a toro*.[8] During those months, this physical, mental and moral discomfort was acute. At last, unable to bear it any longer, he indulged his passion with a young man of 19. This took place when he was 30 years of age. Soon afterwards he wholly abandoned matrimonial connections. He did this with the full approval of his wife, to whom the step brought relief.

---

[7] 'for want of anything better'.   [8] 'marriage-bed'.

The reason assigned was that his pulmonary disease made slow but sure advances, rendering further procreation of children morally wrong.

20. When A had once begun to indulge his inborn sexual instincts, he rapidly recovered his health. The neurotic disturbances subsided; the phthisis— which had progressed as far as profuse hemorrhage and formation of cavity—was arrested. By the age of 50, that is during the next 20 years, he made himself one of the leaders of English literature.

21. A has not informed me what form of homosexual intercourse he practises. He is certainly not simply passive and shows no sign of *effeminatio*. He likes sound and vigorous young men of a lower rank from the age of 20 to 25. I gather from his conversation that the mode of pleasure is indifferent to his tastes.

22. A believes firmly that his homosexual appetite was inborn and developed exactly the same way and by the same exciting causes as the heterosexual appetite in normal persons. He is persuaded that, having in boyhood frequented the society of boys and girls alike, he leaned toward the suggestions of the male because there was in him a congenital bias of sex in that direction. He has no moral sense of doing wrong, and is quite certain that he suffers or benefits in health of mind and body according as he abstains from or indulges in moderate homosexual pleasure. He feels the intolerable injustice of his social position, and considers the criminal codes of modern nations, in so far as they touch his case, to be iniquitous. As an artist and a man of letters he regrets the fate which has forced him to conceal his true emotions, and thereby to lose the most genial channels of self-expression.

EDITORS' NOTES

2. Richard von Krafft-Ebing (1840–1902), was a prominent Viennese psychologist, who wrote widely on insanity, hypnotism and 'aberrant' sexualities. The *Psychopathia Sexualis* was first translated into English in 1893, and had reached its tenth edition by his death. The book was still being updated and used by psychiatrists into the 1960s, reflecting some fairly persistent conceptions of deviance.

3. Edward Carpenter (1844–1929). Educated at Cambridge, and Fellow of Trinity Hall, a position which he abandoned on reading Walt Whitman's poetry and essays. In 1883 he purchased a smallholding in Millthorpe outside Sheffield and lived self-sufficiently. From 1898 until his death he lived openly with his male partner, George Merrill, a brave move in the years immediately following the trial of Oscar Wilde. E. M. Forster's pilgrimage to Millthorpe in 1913 inspired him to write *Maurice*, the novel of

same-sex, cross-class love that was only published in 1970. Carpenter was a radical democrat and socialist thinker, an influential intellectual in the labour movement. His pamphlets on sexuality and 'homogenic love' circulated amongst the freethinking intellectual groupings of the 1890s.

4. John Addington Symonds (1840–93) was one of the most widely respected men of letters in the late Victorian period. Educated at Harrow and Oxford, he became a Fellow of Magdalen College in 1862, but resigned through ill health. He married in 1864, in an attempt to suppress his strong desires for other men. His interest in Greek and Renaissance culture (he wrote *The Renaissance in Italy* in seven volumes between 1875 and 1886) was, like that of his contemporary Walter Pater, suffused with homoeroticism. From 1877 until his death he resided in the Alpine health resort of Davos, in an attempt to find a suitable climate to ease the symptoms of his pulmonary disease. Davos became a fashionable resort with the English as a result, although another sufferer of lung disease, Robert Louis Stevenson, was horrified at the clinical frigidity of the mountains, and chose tropical heat instead. The *Dictionary of National Biography* hints that Symonds suffered 'morbid introspection' and 'spiritual maladies'—code words for homosexuality. At the time of his death, Symonds was becoming increasingly militant about the need for society to acknowledge same-sex desire, and this would have been well known in literary circles. Had he lived, Oscar Wilde's trial would have left him ambivalent given his jealousy of Wilde: he also adored Lord Alfred Douglas, Wilde's lover.

5. Havelock Ellis (1859–1939) was educated in London, and spent his formative years in Australia recovering from a prolonged illness. He trained in medicine from 1881 to 1889, but never fully qualified, becoming involved in the radical, freethinking circles of London instead. As editor, he began the 'Mermaid' series of drama texts, and was general editor of the Contemporary Science series, one of the most important and influential bodies of science education texts published at the fin de siècle. He became sexually involved with Olive Schreiner (see Chapter 6) during his association with the Men and Women's Club and the Fellowship of the New Life (which evolved into the Fabian Society). He married Edith Lees in 1891, who became one of his case histories, given her same-sex affairs. He wrote six volumes of *Studies in the Psychology of Sex* (1897–1910), which was published abroad following the prosecution of *Sexual Inversion* in 1897. Ellis was a point of contact for both J. A. Symonds and Edward Carpenter in the 1890s.

13

ANTHROPOLOGY AND RACIAL SCIENCE

Travel narratives from distant territories, often centring on exotic customs, had long been a popular genre, one intensified in the mid-Victorian period by the exploits of explorers like Richard Burton and David Livingstone. Racial difference and demarcations between different racial characteristics became a significant means of thinking about identity as the empire continued to expand. Anthropology, the scientific study of mankind, though, emerged as a discipline late in the century, and remained relatively marginal, with a mere handful of university teachers by 1900. Between 1870 and 1910, however, anthropology underwent a paradigm shift, moving from 'armchair' to 'field', or, in other words, from syntheses of evidence in the ethnologist's study in the metropolitan centre, to a commitment to living amid specific groups of people and learning their culture 'from within'. The shift from the undisputed authority of imperial centre to the uneasy cultural relativisms of living 'in the field' is a suggestive transition when considering the move from the Victorian to the Edwardian era.

Edward Tylor's role in making anthropology legitimate was critical: his *Primitive Culture* appeared in 1871 just as the Anthropological Institute emerged from the ruins that had split the liberal scientists of the Ethnological Society and the pro-slavery racists of the Anthropological Society in the 1860s. Tylor successfully campaigned for a separate section for anthropology at the British Association for the Advancement of Science; his aim was realized in 1884, the year in which he was made a Reader in Anthropology at Oxford University. Tylor's *Primitive Culture* was a classic statement of scientific naturalism, asserting uniformity of natural law and development along evolutionary lines. Of man, he suggested that races could be lined up along a developmental line from the most savage (Fuegians or Tasmanians) to the most civilized (northern Europeans). Spatial distribution of race was thus read as occupying different temporal stages of evolution, allowing cross-comparisons between peoples regarded as being at different stages of development. True to scientific naturalist aims, one of the purposes Tylor outlined for anthropology was the pinpointing of savage 'survivals' in contemporary culture—the superstitions and rituals that made, as he put it, 'scarce a hand's breadth of difference between an English ploughman and a negro of central Africa'.

Tylor's work may be 'racist', but, as the historian George Stocking suggests, it is necessary to go beyond the blanket term 'pseudo-scientific racism' and 'usefully distinguish different currents of racial assumption' at the time. *Primitive Culture* in fact resulted in two distinct strands of anthropological writings in the fin de siècle. One, like Herbert Spencer's famous synthetic statement of the inferiority of the savage, used the evolutionary hypothesis to assert a hierarchy of races and implicitly to justify the 'civilizing' imperial mission. The concern with ensuring the survival of the fittest British race was brought home by the new science of eugenics, a term coined by Francis Galton. The sources of an end-of-century anxiety about possible racial decline are transparently on display in the selections below: Pearson starts by evoking the traumatic losses inflicted on the British army by a ragged peasant army of Boers in 1899. The science of eugenics, in which anxiety about the overly reproducing working classes and the decadent middle and upper class was insistently raced, was principally an Edwardian phenomena. It had its origins, though, in the fin-de-siècle discourses of degeneration that have so often been evident in our selections.

The second strand of anthropology to emerge came into conflict with assertions of hierarchy or white superiority, however. Tylor always promoted the training of professional observers in the field, distrusting 'amateur' reports. This resulted in a body of professionals who began discovering the complex and sophisticated social organizations of apparently 'primitive' societies. One key transitional figure from travel writer to anthropologist was Mary Kingsley. In a brief but meteoric public career between 1895 and 1900, she travelled through West Africa studying native customs, and came to the conclusion that British imperial policy was failing because it disregarded tribal laws. Her assertion 'try Science and master the knowledge of the native and his country' was a radical one, demanding a conceptual revolution in relation to the native that the imperial administrators largely refused to take. Perhaps the most important event in developing 'fieldwork' was the Torres Straits expedition in 1898. A team of six professional scientists, led by Alfred Haddon, lived on Murray Island amidst the native population. It was here that William Rivers, ironically collecting data on families in accord with Galton's obsession about hereditary weakness, began annotating kin-

ship relations, and 'discovered' how complexly yet systematically organized native society was. Five large folio volumes of quantitative results
were published between 1901 and 1912, making this paradigmatic of a
new attempt to become saturated in native culture. Although evidences
of paternalistic attitudes to the Torres Straits islanders undoubtedly
remain in the selections below, we choose to end this reader with them,
suggestive as they are of early attempts to negotiate cultural difference
with a productive relativism, rather than through violence or hierarchy.
This, too, is a legacy from the fin de siècle.

Secondary reading: Bolt; Burdett; Clifford; Kuper; Langham; Lorimer; Stocking,
Victorian Anthropology and *Observers Observed*; Lynnette Turner; Young.

---

1   from Edward Tylor, 'The Science of Culture',
                    Primitive Culture (1871)

Culture or Civilization, taken in its wide ethnographic sense, is that complex
whole which includes knowledge, belief, art, morals, law, custom, and any other
capabilities and habits acquired by man as a member of society. The condition of
culture among the various societies of mankind, in so far as it is capable of being
investigated on general principles, is a subject apt for the study of laws of human
thought and action. On the one hand, the uniformity which so largely pervades
civilization may be ascribed, in great measure, to the uniform action of uniform
causes: while on the other hand its various grades may be regarded as stages of
development or evolution, each the outcome of previous history, and about to do
its proper part in shaping the history of the future. To the investigation of these
two great principles in several departments of ethnography, with especial consideration of the civilization of the lower tribes as related to the civilization of the
higher nations, the present volumes are devoted.

Our modern investigators in the sciences of inorganic nature are foremost to
recognize, both within and without their special fields of work, the unity of
nature, the fixity of its laws, the definite sequence of cause and effect through
which every fact depends on what has gone before it, and acts upon what is to
come after it. They grasp firmly the Pythagorean doctrine of pervading order in
the universal Kosmos. They affirm, with Aristotle, that nature is not full of incoherent episodes, like a bad tragedy. They agree with Leibnitz in what he calls 'my
axiom, that nature never acts by leaps (la nature n'agit jamais par saut),' as well as
in his 'great principle, commonly little employed, that nothing happens without

sufficient reason.'[1] Nor again, in studying the structure and habits of plants and animals, or in investigating the lower functions even of man, are these leading ideas unacknowledged. But when we come to talk of the higher processes of human feeling and action, of thought and language, knowledge and art, a change appears in the prevalent tone of opinion. The world at large is scarcely prepared to accept the general study of human life as a branch of natural science, and to carry out, in a large sense, the poet's injunction to 'Account for moral as for natural things.' To many educated minds there seems something presumptuous and repulsive in the view that the history of mankind is part and parcel of the history of nature, that our thoughts, wills, and actions accord with laws as definite as those which govern the motion of waves, the combination of acids and bases, and the growth of plants and animals. [. . .]

[O]bstacles to the investigation of laws of human nature arise from considerations of metaphysics and theology. [. . .] [K]eeping aside from considerations of extra-natural interference and causeless spontaneity, let us take this admitted existence of natural cause and effect as our standing-ground, and travel on it so far as it will bear us. It is on this same basis that physical science pursues, with ever-increasing success, its quest of laws and nature. Nor need this restriction hamper the scientific study of human life. [. . .]

The philosophy of history at large, explaining the past and predicting the future phenomena of man's life in the world by reference to general laws, is in fact a subject with which, in the present state of knowledge, even genius aided by wide research seems but hardly able to cope. Yet there are departments of it which, though difficult enough, seem comparatively accessible. If the field of enquiry be narrowed from History as a whole to that branch of it which is here called Culture, the history, not of tribes or nations, but of the condition of knowledge, religion, art, custom, and the like among them, the task of investigation proves to lie within far more moderate compass. [. . .] This may appear from a brief preliminary examination of the problem, how the phenomena of Culture may be classified and arranged, stage by stage, in a probable order of evolution.

Surveyed in a broad view, the character and habit of mankind at once display that similarity and consistency of phenomena which led the Italian proverb-maker to declare that 'all the world is one country,' 'tutto il mondo è paese.' To general likeness in human nature on the one hand, and to general likeness in the circumstances of life on the other, this similarity and consistency may no doubt be traced, and they may be studied with especial fitness in comparing races near the same grade of civilization. Little respect need be had in such comparisons for date in history or for place on the map; the ancient Swiss lake-dweller may be set aside the mediaeval Aztec, and the Ojibwa of North America beside the Zulu of South

---

[1] Gottfried Leibniz (1646–1716), German philosopher whose search for a rational basis for belief in the existence of God did not preclude a relatively 'naturalist' approach to phenomena.

Africa. As Dr. Johnson contemptuously said when he read about Patagonians and South Sea Islanders in Hawkesworth's Voyages, 'one set of savages is like another.'[2] How true a generalization this really is, any Ethnological Museum may show. Examine for instance the edged and pointed instruments in such a collection; the inventory includes hatchet, adze, chisel, knife, saw, scraper, awl, needle, spear and arrow-head, and of these most or all belong with only differences of detail to races the most various. So it is with savage occupations; the wood-chopping, fishing with net and line, shooting and spearing game, fire-making, cooking, twisting cord and plaiting baskets, repeat themselves with wonderful uniformity in the museum shelves which illustrate the life of the lower races from Kamchatka to Tierra del Fuego, and from Dahome to Hawaii. Even when it comes to comparing barbarous hordes with civilized nations, the consideration thrusts itself upon our minds, how far item after item of the life of the lower races passes into analogous proceedings of the higher, in forms not too far changed to be recognized, and sometimes hardly changed at all. Look at the modern European peasant using his hatchet and his hoe, see his food boiling or roasting over the log-fire, observe the exact place which beer holds in his calculation of happiness, hear his tale of the ghost in the nearest haunted house, and of the farmer's niece who was betwitched with knots in her inside till she fell into fits and died. If we choose out in this way things which have altered little in a long course of centuries, we may draw a picture where there shall be scarce a hand's breadth of difference between an English ploughman and a negro of Central Africa. These pages will be so crowded with evidence of such correspondence among mankind, that there is no need to dwell upon its details here, but it may be used at once to override a problem which would complicate the argument, namely, the question of race. For the present purpose it appears both possible and desirable to eliminate considerations of hereditary varieties or races of man, and to treat mankind as homogeneous in nature, though placed in different grades of civilization. The details of the inquiry will, I think, prove that stages of culture may be compared without taking into account how far tribes who use the same implement, follow the same custom, or believe the same myth, may differ in their bodily configuration and the colour of their skin and hair. [. . .]

It being shown that the details of Culture are capable of being classified in a great number of ethnographic groups of arts, beliefs, customs, and the rest, the consideration comes next how far the facts arranged in these groups are produced by evolution from one another. It need hardly be pointed out that the groups in question, though held together each by a common character, are by no means accurately defined. To take up again the natural history illustration, it may be said that they are species which tend to run widely into varieties. And when it

[2] A reference to John Hawkesworth's *An Account of the Voyages undertaken by the order of his present Majesty for making discoveries in the Southern Hemisphere* (1773), a typical travel narrative of the time.

comes to the question of what relations some of these groups bear to others, it is plain that the student of the habits of mankind has a great advantage over the student of the species of plants and animals. Among naturalists it is an open question whether a theory of development from species to species is a record of transitions which actually took place, or a mere ideal scheme serviceable in the classification of species whose origin was really independent. But among ethnographers there is no such question as to the possibility of species of implements or habits or beliefs being developed one out of another, for development in Culture is recognized by our most familiar knowledge. [. . .]

Among evidence aiding us to trace the course which the civilization of the world has actually followed, is that great class of facts to denote which I have found it convenient to introduce the term 'survivals.' These are processes, customs, opinions, and so forth, which have been carried on by force of habit into a new state of society different from that in which they had their original home, and they thus remain as proofs and examples of an older condition of culture out of which a newer has been evolved. Thus, I know an old Somersetshire woman whose hand-loom dates from the time before the introduction of the 'flying shuttle,' which new-fangled appliance she has never even learnt to use, and I have seen her throw her shuttle from hand to hand in true classic fashion; this old woman is not a century behind her times, but she is a case of survival. Such examples often lead us back to the habits of hundreds and even thousands of years ago. The ordeal of the Key and Bible, still in use, is a survival; the Midsummer bonfire is a survival; the Breton peasants' All Souls' supper for the spirits of the dead is a survival. [. . .] The study of the principles of survival has, indeed, no small practical importance, for most of what we call superstition is included within survival, and in this way lies open to the attack of its deadliest enemy, a reasonable explanation. Insignificant, moreover, as multitudes of the facts of survival are in themselves, their study is so effective for tracing the course of the historical development through which alone it is possible to understand their meaning, that it becomes a vital point of ethnographic research to gain the clearest possible insight into their nature. This importance must justify the detail here devoted to an examination of survival, on the evidence of such games, popular sayings, customs, superstitions, and the like, as may serve well to bring into view the manner of its operation. [. . .]

In carrying on the great task of rational ethnography, the investigation of the causes which have produced the phenomena of culture, and of the laws to which they are subordinate, it is desirable to work out as systematically as possible a scheme of evolution of this culture along its many lines. [. . .] By comparing the various stages of civilization among races known to history, with the aid of archaeological inference from the remains of prehistoric tribes, it seems possible to judge in a rough way of an early general condition of man, which from our point of view is to be regarded as a primitive condition, whatever yet earlier state may in reality have lain behind it. This hypothetical primitive condition corresponds in a considerable degree to that of modern savage tribes, who, in spite of their difference and distance, have in common certain elements of civilization, which seem remains of an early state of the human race at large. If this hypothesis be true, then, notwithstanding the continual interference of degeneration, the main tendency of culture from primaeval up to modern times has been from savagery towards civilization. On the problem of this relation of savage to civilized life, almost every one of the thousands of facts discussed in the succeeding chapters has its direct bearing. Survival in Culture, placing all along the course of advancing civilization way-marks full of meaning to those who can decipher their signs, even now sets up in our midst primaeval monuments of barbaric thought and life. Its investigation tells strongly in favour of the view that the European may find among the Greenlanders or Maoris many a trait for reconstructing the picture of his own primitive ancestors.

---

2   from Herbert Spencer, *The Principles of Sociology* (1876)

THE PRIMITIVE MAN—PHYSICAL

24. In the light of the fact that the uncivilized races include the Patagonians, ranging from six feet to seven feet in height, while in Africa there still exist remnants of the barbarous peoples referred to by Herodotus as pygmies, we cannot say that there is any direct relation between social state and stature. Among the North-American Indians there are hunting races decidedly tall; while, elsewhere, there are stunted hunting races, as the Bushmen. Of pastoral peoples, too, some are short, like the Kirghiz, and some are well-grown, like the Kaffirs. And there are kindred differences between races of agricultural habits.

Still, the evidence taken in the mass implies an average relation between barbarism and inferiority of size. [. . .]

How far is this an original trait of inferior races, and how far is it a trait superinduced by the unfavourable habitats into which superior races have driven them? Evidently the dwarfishness of Esquimaux and Laplanders may be due partly, if not wholly, to the great physiological cost of living entailed by the rigorous climate they have to bear; and it no more shows the dwarfishness of primitive men than does the small size of Shetland ponies show that primitive horses were small. Similarly in the case of the Bushmen, who are wanderers in a territory 'of so barren and arid a character, that by far the greater portion of it is not permanently habitable by any class of human beings,' it is supposable that chronic innutrition has produced a lower standard of growth. Manifestly, as the weaker were always thrust by the stronger into the worst localities, there must ever have been a tendency to make greater any original difference of stature and strength. Hence the smallness of these most degraded men, may have been original; or it may have been acquired; or it may have been partly original and partly acquired. [. . .]

25. [. . .] Men of inferior types appear to be generally characterized by relatively-defective development of the lower limbs. Sufficiently marked as this is to have attracted the attention of travellers among various unrelated races, we shall probably not be wrong in setting it down as a primitive character. [. . .]

That the balance of power between legs and arms, which was originally better adapted to climbing habits, is likely to have been changed in the course of progress, is manifest. During the struggles between races, ever invading one another's localities, an advantage must have been gained by those having the legs somewhat more developed at the expense of the body at large. I do not mean chiefly an advantage in swiftness or agility; I mean in the trials of strength at close quarters. In combat, the power exercised by arms and trunk is limited by the power of the legs to withstand the strain thrown on them. Hence, apart from the advantages in locomotion, the stronger-legged races have tended to become, other things equal, dominant races.

Among other structural traits of the primitive man which we have to note, the most marked is the larger size of jaws and teeth. This is shown not simply in that prognathous form characterizing various inferior races, and, to an extreme degree, the Akka, but it is shown also in the races otherwise characterized: even ancient British skulls have relatively massive jaws. That this trait is connected with the eating of coarse food, hard, tough, and often uncooked, and perhaps also with the greater use of the teeth in place of tools, as we see our own boys use them, is fairly inferable. Diminution of function has brought diminution of size, both of the jaws and the attached muscles. [. . .]

28. Among the physiological traits which distinguish man in his primitive state from man in his advanced state, we may certainly set down relative hardiness. [. . .]

Inevitably, survival of the fittest must ever have tended to produce and maintain a constitution capable of enduring the miseries, hardships, injuries, necessarily accompanying a life at the mercy of surrounding actions; since there must ever have been a destruction of constitutions not enduring enough. [. . .] [W]e need but recall the ability of Negro-races to live in pestilential regions, to see that elsewhere there has been similarly produced a constitutional power to withstand deleterious vapours. So, too, is it with the bearing of bodily injuries. The recuperative power of the Australians, and others of the lowest races, are notorious. Wounds which would be quickly fatal to Europeans they readily recover from.

Whether this gain entails loss in other directions, we have no direct evidence. [. . .] It seems highly probable that this physiological advantage is purchased by some physiological disadvantage—a disadvantage escaped by the higher races whose arts of life enable them to evade these deranging conditions. And if so, this fitness for primitive conditions entails some further impediment to the establishment of higher conditions.

29. A closely-related physiological trait must be added. Along with this greater ability to bear injurious actions, there is a comparative indifference to the disagreeable or painful sensations those actions cause; or rather, the sensations they cause are not so acute. [. . .]

Here we have a further characteristic which might have been inferred *a priori*. Pain of every kind, down even to the irritation produced by discomfort, entails a physiological waste of a detrimental kind. [. . .] Among primitive races it must continually have happened that individuals with the keenest sensations, worn more than others in bearing hardships and the pains of wounds, succumbed when others did not. The most callous must have had the advantage when irremediable evils had to be borne; and thus relative callousness must have been made, by survival of the fittest, constitutional. [. . .]

30. As preliminary to the summing up of these physical characters, I must name a most general one—early arrival at maturity. Other things equal, the less evolved types of organisms take shorter times to reach their complete forms than do the more evolved; and this contrast, conspicuous between men and most inferior creatures, is perceptible between varieties of men. There is reason for associating this difference with the difference in cerebral development. The greater costliness of the larger brain, which so long delays human maturity, as compared with mammalian maturity generally, delays also the maturity of the civilized as compared with that of the savage. Causation apart, however, the fact is that (climate and other conditions being equal) the inferior races reach puberty sooner than the superior races. Everywhere the remark is made that the women early bloom and early fade; and a corresponding trait of course holds in the men. This completion of growth and structure in a shorter period is of interest to us as implying less plasticity of nature: the rigidity and unchangeableness of adult life sooner make modification difficult.

THE PRIMITIVE MAN—EMOTIONAL

33. [. . .] Indirect evidence that early human nature differed from later human nature by having this extreme emotional variability, is yielded us by the contrast between the child and the adult among ourselves. For on the hypothesis of evolution, the civilized man, passing through phases representing phases passed through by the race, will, early in life, betray this impulsiveness which the early race had. The saying that the savage has the mind of a child with the passions of a man (or, as it would be more correctly put, has adult passions which act in a childish manner) thus possesses a deeper meaning than appears. There is a genetic relationship between the two natures such that, allowing for differences of kind and degree in the emotions, we may regard the co-ordination of them in the child as fairly representing the co-ordination in the primitive man. [. . .]

38. [. . .] Governed as he is by despotic emotions that successively depose one another, instead of by a council of the emotions in which they all take part, the primitive man has an explosive, chaotic, incalculable behaviour, which makes combined action very difficult. [. . .]

THE PRIMITIVE MAN—INTELLECTUAL

39. [. . .] Familiar only with the particular facts coming within the narrow range of his experiences, the primitive man has no conceptions of *general facts*. Being something common to many particular truths, a general truth implies a wider and more heterogeneous correspondence than do particular truths; it implies higher representativeness, since it necessarily colligates more numerous and varied ideas under the general ideas; and it is more remote from reflex action—will not, indeed, of itself, excite action at all.

Having only those indefinite measures of time yielded by the seasons, having no records, but only statements carelessly made and randomly repeated in language that is very imperfect, man, in his uncivilised state, cannot recognise long sequences. Successions in which antecedents and consequents are tolerably near, can be fully grasped; but no others. Hence *prevision of distant results*, such as is possible in a settled society having measures and written language, is impossible to him. That is to say, the correspondence in Time comes within narrow limits. The representations include few relations of phenomena, and these not comprehensive ones. And there is but a moderate departure from the reflex life in which stimulus and act stand in immediate connection.

The environment of the primitive man being such that his converse with things is relatively restricted in Space and Time, as well as in variety, it happens that the associations of ideas he forms are little liable to be changed. As experiences (multiplying in number, gathered from a wider area, added to by those which other men record) become more heterogeneous, the narrow notions first framed, fixed in the absence of conflicting experiences, are shaken and made more plastic— there comes greater *modifiability of belief*. In the relative rigidity of belief characterizing undeveloped intelligence, we see a smaller correspondence with an environment containing facts destructive of that belief; we see less of that representativeness which simultaneously grasps and averages much evidence; and we see a smaller divergence from those lowest mental actions in which impressions cause, irresistably, the appropriate motions.

While the experiences are few and but slightly varied, the concreteness of the corresponding ideas is but little qualified by the growth of *abstract ideas*. [. . .]

Until there have grown up general ideas and abstract ideas, and until the notion of uniformity has developed along with the sense of measures, thought cannot have much *definiteness*. Inequality and unlikeness being characteristic of primitive experiences, there is little to yield the idea of agreement; and so long as there are few experiences of exact equality between objects, or perfect conformity between statements and facts, or complete fulfilment of anticipations by results, the notion of *truth* cannot become clear. This is a highly-evolved notion, arising only after the antithesis between definite agreement and definite disagreement have been made familiar; and the experiences of the primitive man do not make it familiar. [. . .]

48. The intellectual traits of the uncivilized, thus made specially difficult to change, may now be recapitulated while observing that they are traits recurring in the children of the civilized.

Infancy and nursery-life, show us an absorption in sensations and perceptions, akin to that which characterizes the savage. In pulling to pieces its toys, in making mud-pies, in gazing at each new thing or person, the child exhibits a predominant perceptiveness with comparatively little reflectiveness.

There is, again, an obvious parallelism in the mimetic tendency. Children are ever dramatizing the lives of adults; and savages, along with their other mimicries, similarly dramatize the actions of their civilized visitors.

Want of power to discriminate between useful and useless facts, characterizes the juvenile mind, as it does the mind of the primitive man. Indeed, on observing how the facts learned by a child, either as lessons or by spontaneous observation, are learnt for their own sakes only, without thought of their values as materials from which to generalize, it becomes manifest that this inability to select nutritive facts, is a necessary accompaniment of low development; since until generalization has made some progress, and the habit of generalizing has become established, there cannot be reached the conception that a fact has a remote value apart from any immediate value it may have.

Again, we see in the young of our own race a parallel inability to concentrate the attention on anything complex or abstract. The mind of the child, like that of the savage, soon wanders from sheer exhaustion when generalities and involved propositions have to be dealt with.

Necessarily, along with the feebleness of the higher intellectual faculties, there goes, in both cases, an absence, or a paucity, of the ideas grasped by those faculties. The child, like the savage, has few words of even a low grade of abstractness, and none of a higher grade. [. . .]

And seeing this, we cannot fail to see that development of the higher intellectual faculties has gone on pari passu with social advance, alike as cause and consequence; that primitive man could not possibly evolve these higher intellectual faculties in the absence of a fit environment; and that in this, as in other respects, his progress was retarded by the absence of capacities which only progress could bring.

---

3   from Karl Pearson, *National Life from the Standpoint of Science* (1900)

In the fore-part of this year, when I was asked to give a lecture at Newcastle, the minds of men were not inclined to be interested in the fascinating problems of pure science. The spirits of one and all, whatever their political party or their opinions on the rights or wrongs of British action in South Africa might be, were depressed in a manner probably never experienced by those of our countrymen now living. We can, in the light of what has happened since, afford, perhaps, to admit the truth now. We had been defeated, I may venture even to say badly defeated, by a social organism far less highly developed and infinitely smaller than our own. We felt like the giant bewildered, not by the strength, but by the skill and ingenuity, of our opponent. We had lost the power of foreseeing, and our soldiers the power of adapting themselves to a change in environment. We had to learn from our foe the very armament suitable to the conditions; we had to learn that guns of great calibre could be taken into the field and, what is more, withdrawn from it; we had to learn the existence of something which was neither cavalry nor mounted infantry; we, a nation of horse-breeders and horse-riders, had to learn the right horse for a rough country and the right manner of handling him; nay, to some troops we even issued a new rifle, and let them practically gain their first experience of it in the field. We, no doubt, felt in those days of depression, that we should learn, all this, and perhaps more; we hoped, with a distinguished statesman, that we should 'muddle through somehow.' We refrained, if not completely, yet fairly successfully, from making scapegoats.

But those who saw beyond the immediate national danger were filled with a more abiding sense of risk. They recognised that the struggle for existence among nations will not necessarily be settled in favour of the biggest nation, nor in favour of the best-armed nation, nor in favour of the nation with the greatest material resources. I speak not only of war, but of the more silent, but none the less intense, struggle of peace. [. . .] I shall therefore endeavour to lay in broad outlines before you what I hold to be the scientific view of a nation, and of the relationship of nations to each other. [. . .]

I want you to look with me for awhile on mankind as a product of Nature, and subject to the natural influences which form its environment. I will, first, notice a point which bears upon man as upon all forms of animal life. The characters of both parents—their virtues, their vices, their capabilities, their tempers, their diseases—all devolve in due proportion upon their children. Some may say, 'Oh yes; but we know such things are inherited.' I fear that the greatest majority of the nation does not realize what inheritance means, or much that happens now would not be allowed to happen. Our knowledge of heredity has developed enormously in the last few years; it is no longer a vague factor of development, to be appealed to vaguely. [. . .]

Here is a great principle of life, something apparently controlling all life from its simplest to its most complex forms, and yet, although we too often see its relentless effects, we go on hoping that at any rate we and our offspring shall be the exceptions to its rules. For one of us as an individual this may be true, but for the *average* of us all, for the nation as a whole, it is an idle hope. You cannot change a leopard's spots, and you cannot change bad stock to good; you may dilute it, possibly spread it over a wider area, spoiling good stock, but until it ceases to multiply it will not cease to be. A physically and mentally well-ordered individual will arise as a variation in bad stock, or possibly may result from special nurture, but the old evils will in all probability reappear in a definite percentage of the offspring.

I know of the case of just such a good variation appearing in a certain bad stock as far back as 1680, and the offspring of which married in the early eighteenth century into a number of good stocks, several of which we can trace in the records of the religious community of which they were members for nearly 150 years. And what do we find? In each generation the same sort of proportion of cases of drunkenness, insanity, and physical breakdown arising to distress and perplex their kinsfolk.

Now, if we once realize that this law of inheritance is as inevitable as the law of gravity, we shall cease to struggle against it. This does not mean a fatal resignation to the presence of bad stock, but a conscious attempt to modify the percentage of it in our own community and in the world at large. [. . .] If you have once realized the force of heredity, you will see in natural selection—that choice of the physically and mentally fitter to be the parents of the next generation—a most munificent provision for the progress of all forms of life. Nurture and education may immensely aid the social machine, but they must be repeated generation by generation; they will not in themselves reduce the tendency to the production of bad stock. Conscious or unconscious selection alone can bring that about.

What I have said about bad stock seems to me to hold for the lower races of man. How many centuries, how many thousands of years, have the Kaffir and the Negro held large districts in Africa undisturbed by the white man? Yet their inter-tribal struggles have not yet produced a civilization in the least comparable with the Aryan. Educate and nurture them as you will, I do not believe that you will succeed in modifying the stock. History shows me one way, and one way only, in which a high state of civilization has been produced, namely, the struggle of race with race, and the survival of the physically and mentally fitter race. If you want to know whether the lower races of man can evolve a higher type, I fear the only course is to leave them to fight it out among themselves, and even then the struggle for existence between individual and individual, between tribe and tribe, may not be supported by that physical selection due to a particular climiate on which probably so much of the Aryan's success depended.

If you bring the white man into contact with the black, you too often suspend the very process of natural selection on which the evolution of a higher type depends. You get superior and inferior races living on the same soil, and that co-existence is demoralizing for both. They naturally sink into the position of master and servant, if not admittedly or covertly into that of slave-owner and slave. Frequently they intercross, and if the bad stock be raised the good is lowered. [. . .]

Mr. Francis Galton has suggested that we might progress far more rapidly than we at present do under this crude system of unconscious wastage if we turned our thoughts more consciously to the problem, if we emphasized the need of social action in this direction, and made men and women feel the importance of good parentage for the citizens of the future. But I fear our present economic and social conditions are hardly yet ripe for such a movement; the all-important question of parentage is still largely felt to be solely a matter of family, and not of national importance. Yet, how anti-social such a view may be can be easily realized. From the standpoint of the nation we want to inculcate a feeling of shame in the parents of a weakling, whether it be mentally or physically unfit. We want parents to grasp that they have given birth to a new *citizen*, and that this involves, on the one hand, a duty towards the community in respect of his breed and nurture, and a claim, on the other hand, of the parents on the State, that the latter shall make the conditions of life favourable to the rearing of healthy, mentally vigorous men and women. Bear in mind that one quarter only of the married people of this country—say, a sixth to an eighth of the adult population—produce 50 per cent. of the next generation. You will then see how essential it is for the maintenance of a physically and mentally fit race that this one-sixth to one-eigth of our population should be drawn from the best and not the worst stocks. A nation that begins to tamper with fertility may unconsciously have changed its national characteristics before two generations have passed.

---

4   Francis Galton, 'Eugenics: Its Definition,
            Scope and Aims' (1904)

Eugenics is the science which deals with all influences that improve the inborn qualities of a race; also with those that develop them to the utmost advantage. The improvement of the inborn qualities, or stock, of some one human population, will alone be discussed here.

What is meant by improvement? What by the syllable *Eu* in Eugenics, whose English equivalent is *good*? There is considerable difference between goodness in the several qualities and in that of the character as a whole. The character depends largely on the *proportion* between qualities whose balance may be much influenced by education. We must therefore leave morals as far as possible out of the discussion, not entangling ourselves with the almost hopeless difficulties they raise as to whether a character as a whole is good or bad. Moreover, the goodness or badness of character is not absolute, but relative to the current form of civilisation. A fable will best explain what is meant. Let the scene be the Zoological Gardens in the quiet hours of the night, and suppose that, as in old fables, the animals are able to converse, and that some very wise creature who had easy access to all the cages, say a philosophic sparrow or rat, was engaged in collecting the opinions of all sorts of animals with a view of elaborating a system of absolute morality. It is needless to enlarge on the contrariety of ideals between the beasts that prey and those they prey upon, between those of the animals that have to work hard for their food and the sedentary parasites that cling to their bodies and suck their blood, and so forth. A large number of suffrages in favour of maternal affection would be obtained, but most species of fish would repudiate it, while among the voices of the birds would be heard the musical protest of the cuckoo. Though no agreement could be reached as to absolute morality, the essentials of Eugenics may be easily defined. All creatures would agree that it was better to be healthy than sick, vigorous than weak, well fitted than ill-fitted for their part in life. In short that it was better to be good rather than bad specimens of their kind, whatever that kind might be. So with men. There are a vast number of conflicting ideals of alternative characters, of incompatible civilisations; but all are wanted to give fulness and interest to life. Society would be very dull if every man resembled the highly estimable Marcus Aurelius or Adam Bede. The aim of Eugenics is to represent each class or sect by its best specimens; that done, to leave them to work out their common civilisation in their own way.

A considerable list of qualities can be easily compiled that nearly every one except 'cranks' would take into account when picking out the best specimens of his class. It would include health, energy, ability, manliness and courteous disposition. Recollect that the natural differences between dogs are highly marked in all these respects, and that men are quite as variable by nature as other animals in their respective species. Special aptitudes would be assessed highly by those who possessed them, as the artistic faculties by artists, fearlessness of inquiry and veracity by scientists, religious absorption by mystics, and so on. There would be self-sacrificers, self-tormentors and other exceptional idealists, but the representatives of these would be better members of a community than the body of their electors. They would have more of those qualities that are needed in a State, more vigour, more ability, and more consistency of purpose. The community might be trusted to refuse representatives of criminals, and of others whom it rates as undesirable.

Let us for a moment suppose that the practice of Eugenics should hereafter raise the average quality of our nation to that of its better moiety at the present day and consider the gain. The general tone of domestic, social and political life would be higher. The race as a whole would be less foolish, less frivolous, less excitable and politically more provident than now. Its demagogues who 'played to the gallery' would play to a more sensible gallery than at present. We should be better fitted to fulfil our vast imperial opportunities. Lastly, men of an order of ability which is now very rare, would become more frequent, because the level out of which they rose would itself have risen.

The aim of Eugenics is to bring as many influences as can be reasonably employed, to cause the useful classes in the community to contribute *more* than their proportion to the next generation.

The course of procedure that lies within the functions of a learned and active Society such as the Sociological may become, would be somewhat as follows:—

1. Dissemination of a knowledge of the laws of heredity so far as they are surely known, and promotion of their farther study. Few seem to be aware how greatly the knowledge of what may be termed the *actuarial* side of heredity has advanced in recent years. The *average* closeness of kinship in each degree

now admits of exact definition and of being treated mathematically, like birth and death-rates, and the other topics with which actuaries are concerned.

2. Historical inquiry into the rates with which the various classes of society (classified according to civic usefulness) have contributed to the population at various times, in ancient and modern nations. There is strong reason for believing that national rise and decline is closely connected with this influence. It seems to be the tendency of high civilisation to check fertility in the upper classes, through numerous causes, some of which are well known, others are inferred, and others again are wholly obscure. The latter class are apparently analogous to those which bar the fertility of most species of wild animals in zoological gardens. Out of the hundreds and thousands of species that have been tamed, very few indeed are fertile when their liberty is restricted and their struggles for livelihood are abolished; those which are so and are otherwise useful to man becoming domesticated. There is perhaps some connection between this obscure action and the disappearance of most savage races when brought into contact with high civilisation, though there are other and well-known concomitant causes. But while most barbarous races disappear, some, like the negro, do not. It may therefore be expected that types of our race will be found to exist which can be highly civilised without losing fertility; nay, they may become more fertile under artificial conditions, as is the case with many domestic animals.

3. Systematic collection of facts showing the circumstances under which large and thriving families have most frequently originated; in other words, the *conditions* of Eugenics. The names of the thriving families in England have yet to be learnt, and the conditions under which they have arisen. We cannot hope to make much advance in the science of Eugenics without a careful study of the facts that are now accessible with difficulty, if at all. The definition of a thriving family, such as will pass muster for the moment at least is one in which the children have gained distinctly superior positions to those who were their classmates in early life. Families may be considered 'large' that contain not less than three adult male children. It would be no great burden to a Society including many members who had Eugenics at heart, to initiate and to preserve, a large collection of such records for the use of statistical students. The committee charged with the task would have to consider very carefully the form of their circular and the persons entrusted to distribute it. The circular should be simple, and as brief as possible, consistent with asking all questions that are likely to be answered truly, and which would be important to the inquiry. They should ask, at least in the first instance, only for as much information as could be easily, and would be readily supplied by any member of the family appealed to. The point to be ascertained is the *status* of the two parents at the time of

their marriage, whence its more or less eugenic character might have been predicted, if the larger knowledge that we now hope to obtain had then existed. Some account would, of course, be wanted of their race, profession, and residence; also of their own respective parentages, and of their brothers and sisters. Finally, the reasons would be required why the children deserved to be entitled a 'thriving' family, to distinguish worthy from unworthy success. This manuscript collection might hereafter develop into a 'golden book' of thriving families. The Chinese, whose customs have often much sound sense, make their honours retrospective. We might learn from them to show that respect to the parents of noteworthy children, which the contributors of such valuable assets to the national wealth richly deserve. The act of systematically collecting records of thriving families would have the further advantage of familiarising the public with the fact that Eugenics had at length become a subject of serious scientific study by an energetic Society.

4. Influences affecting Marriage. The remarks of Lord Bacon in his essay on Death may appropriately be quoted here. He says with the view of minimising its terrors:

> There is no passion in the mind of men so weak but it mates and masters the fear of death. Revenge triumphs over death; love slights it; honour aspireth to it; grief flyeth to it; fear pre-occupieth it.[3]

Exactly the same kind of considerations apply to marriage. The passion of love seems so overpowering that it may be thought folly to try to direct its course. But plain facts do not confirm this view. Social influences of all kinds have immense power in the end, and they are very various. If unsuitable marriages from the Eugenic point of view were banned socially, or even regarded with the unreasonable disfavour which some attach to cousin-marriages, very few would be made. The multitude of marriage restrictions that have proved prohibitive among uncivilised people would require a volume to describe.

5. Persistence in setting forth the national importance of Eugenics. There are three stages to be passed through. *Firstly* it must be made familiar as an academic question, until its exact importance has been understood and accepted as a fact; *Secondly* it must be recognised as a subject whose practical development deserves serious consideration; and *Thirdly* it must be introduced into the national conscience, like a new religion. It has, indeed, strong claims to become an orthodox religious tenet of the future, for Eugenics co-operates with the workings of Nature by securing that humanity shall be represented by the fittest races. What Nature does blindly, slowly, and ruthlessly, man may do

---

[3] Francis Bacon, 'Of Death', in *The Essays or Counsels, Civil and Moral* (1625).

providently, quickly, and kindly. As it lies within his power, so it becomes his duty to work in that direction; just as it is his duty to succour neighbours who suffer misfortune. The improvement of our stock seems to me one of the highest objects that we can reasonably attempt. We are ignorant of the ultimate destinies of humanity, but feel perfectly sure that it is as noble a work to raise its level in the sense already explained, as it would be disgraceful to abase it. I see no impossibility in Eugenics becoming a religious dogma among mankind, but its details must first be worked out sedulously in the study. Over-zeal leading to hasty action would do harm, by holding out expectations of a near golden age, which will certainly be falsified and cause the science to be discredited. The first and main point is to secure the general intellectual acceptance of Eugenics as a hopeful and most important study. Then let its principles work into the heart of the nation, who will gradually give practical effect to them in ways that we may not wholly foresee.

5   from Mary Kingsley, 'The Clash of Cultures',
               West African Studies (1899)

'[. . .] What we are really attempting, however, is nothing less than to crush into twenty years the revolution in facts and in ideas, which, even in energetic Europe, six long centuries have been needed to accomplish. No one will, of course, be found to dispute that the strides made in our knowledge of the art of government since the thirteenth century are prodigious and vast, nor that the general condition of the people of Europe has been immensely improved since that day; but nevertheless one cannot but sympathise with the Malays who are suddenly and violently translated from the point to which they have attained in the natural development of the race, and are required to live up to the standard of people who are six centuries in advance of them in national progress. [. . .]'[4]

Now, the above represents the state of affairs caused by the clash of different culture levels in the true Negro States, as well as it does in the Malay. These two sets of men, widely different in breed, have, from the many points of agreement in their State-form, evidently both arrived in our thirteenth century. The African peoples in the Central East, and East, and South, except where they are true Negroes, have not arrived in the thirteenth century, or, to put it in other words, the True Negro stem in Africa has arrived at a political state akin to that of our own

---

[4] This first paragraph is a citation from H. Clifford, *East Coast Etchings* (1896). Kingsley's argument follows from the notion of primitives being 'six centuries' behind Europe—like Tylor, reading spatial distribution of races along a temporal axis.

thirteenth century, whereas the Bantu stem has not; this point, however, I need not enter into here.

There are, of course, local differences between the Malay Peninsula and West Africa, but the main characteristics as regard State-form among the natives are singularly alike. They are both what Mr. Clifford aptly likens to our own European State-form in the thirteenth century; and the effect of the white culture on the morals of the natives is also alike. The main difference between them results from the Malay Peninsula being but a narrow strip of land and thinly peopled, compared to the densely populated section of a continent we call West Africa. Therefore, although the Malay in his native state is a superior individual warrior to the West African, yet there are not so many of him; and as he is less guarded from whites by a pestilential climate, his resistance to the white culture of the nineteenth century is inferior to the resistance which the West African can give.

The destruction of what is good in the thirteenth century culture level, and the fact that when the nineteenth century has had its way the main result is seedy demoralised natives, is the thing that must make all thinking men wonder if, after all, such work is from a high moral point of view worth the nineteenth century doing. I so often think when I hear the progress of civilisation, our duty towards the lower races, &c., talked of, as if those words were in themselves Ju Ju, of that improving fable of the kind-hearted she-elephant, who, while out walking one day, inadvertently trod upon a partridge and killed it, and observing close at hand the bird's nest full of callow fledglings, dropped a tear, and saying 'I have the feelings of a mother myself,' sat down upon the brood. This is precisely what England representing the nineteenth century is doing in thirteenth century West Africa. She destroys the guardian institution, drops a tear and sits upon the brood with motherly intentions; and pesky warm sitting she finds it, what with the nature of the brood and the surrounding climate, let alone the expense of it. And what profit she is going to get out of such proceedings there, I own I don't know. 'Ah!' you say, 'yes, it is sad, but it is inevitable.' I do not think it is inevitable, unless you have no intellectual constructive Statecraft, and are merely in that line an automaton. If you will try Science, all the evils of the clash between the two culture periods could be avoided, and you could assist these West Africans in their thirteenth century state to rise into their nineteenth century state without their having the hard fight for it that you yourself had. This would be a grand humanitarian bit of work; by doing it you would raise a monument before God to the honour of England such as no nation has ever yet raised to him on earth.

There is absolutely no perceivable sound reason why you should not do it if you will try Science and master the knowledge of the nature of the native and his country. The knowledge of native laws, religion, institutions, and state-form would give you the knowledge of what is good in these things, so that you might develop and encourage them; and the West African, having reached a thirteenth century state, has institutions and laws which with a strengthening from the European hand would, by their operation now, stamp out the evil that exists under the native state. What you are doing now, however, is the direct contrary to this: you are destroying the good portion and thereby allowing the evil, or imperfect, in it as in all things human, to flourish under your protection far more rankly than under the purely native thirteenth century state-form, with Fetish as a state religion, it could possibly do.

I know, however, there is one great objection to your taking up a different line towards the native races to that which you are at present following. It is one of those strange things that are in men's minds almost without their knowing they are there, yet which, nevertheless, rule them. This is the idea that those Africans are, as one party would say, steeped in sin, or, as another party would say, a lower or degraded race. While you think these things, you must act as you are acting. They really are the same idea in different clothes. They both presuppose all mankind to have sprung from a single pair of human beings, and the condition of a race today therefore to be to its own credit or blame. [. . .]

The story which you will often be told to account for the blackness and whiteness of men by Africans who have not been in direct touch with European, but who have been in touch with Mohammedan, tradition—which in the main has the same Semitic source—is that when Cain killed Abel, he was horrified at himself, and terrified of God; and so he carried the body away from beside the altar where it lay, and carried it about for years trying to hide it, but not knowing how, growing white the while with the horror and the fear; until one day he saw a crow scratching a hole in the desert sand, and it struck him that if he made a hole in the sand and put the body in, he could hide it from God, so he did; but all his children were white, and from Cain came the white races, while Abel's children are black, as all men were before the first murder. The present way of contemplating different races, though expressed in finer language, is practically identical with these; not only the religious view, but the view of the suburban agnostic. The religious European cannot avoid regarding the races in a different and inferior culture state to his own as more deeply steeped in sin than himself, and the suburban agnostic regards them as 'degraded' or 'retarded' either by environment, or microbes, or both. [. . .]

The desire to develop our West African possessions is a worthy one in its way, but better leave it totally alone than attempt it with your present machinery; which the moment it is called upon to deal with the administration of the mass of the native inhabitants gives such a trouble. And remember it is not the only trouble your Crown Colony system can give;[5] it has a few glorious opportunities left of further supporting everything I have said about it, and more. But I will say

[5] The argument of Kingsley's *West African Studies* is insistent that the British policy of turning the Royal Niger Company (run by George Goldie) into an annexed dependent 'Crown Colony' of the empire will be bad for business interests and the natives of the country.

no more. You have got a grand rich region there, populated by an uncommon fine sort of human being. You have been trying your present set of ideas on it for over 400 years; they have failed in a heart-breaking drizzling sort of way to perform any single solitary one of the things you say you want done there. West Africa today is just a quarry of paving-stones for Hell, and those stones were cemented in place with men's blood mixed with wasted gold.

Prove it! you say. Prove it yourself by going there—I don't mean to blazes—but to West Africa.

---

6   from *Reports of the Cambridge Anthropological Expedition to Torres Straits*, volume ii (1901)

VOLUME II: PHYSIOLOGY AND PSYCHOLOGY

PREFACE (A. C. HADDON)

During the years 1888–9 I spent some eight months in Torres Straits investigating the marine zoology of that district, and having become interested in the natives I devoted my spare time to recording many of their present and past customs and beliefs. Some of the results of these studies have already been published. Later I proposed to publish a Memoir on the Ethnography of the Islands of Torres Straits, but on going over my material I found it was too deficient to make into a satisfactory monograph. I then determined to go once more to Torres Straits in order to collect more data, with a view to making, with the aid of colleagues, as complete a study of the people as was practicable.

I had long realised that no investigation of a people was complete that did not embrace a study of their psychology, and being aware of the paucity of our knowledge of the comparative physiology and psychology of primitive peoples, I determined that this branch should be well represented. I was able to secure Dr W. H. R. Rivers as a colleague, and I gladly left all the arrangements of this important section of our work to him. We obtained the cooperation of Messrs. C. S. Myers and W. McDougall, who undertook special branches of experimental psychology. Some assistance in this department was also given by Mr C. G. Seligman.[6]

Perhaps a few words are necessary to explain why we visited a district appar-

---

[6] Charles Myers (1873–1946) and William McDougall (1871–1938) were students of A. C. Haddon at the time of the Torres Straits expedition. Both went on to significant careers in psychology, McDougall writing the influential textbook *Social Psychology*, and Myers at the forefront of treatments of shell-shock in the First World War. Charles Seligman (1873–1940) later wrote on anthropological topics.

ently so insignificant as Torres Straits. As explained above, I had a good deal of unpublished material on the ethnography of the people and it would naturally take less time to gain a good insight into the life of a people about whom a fair amount was known than to begin afresh on a new people. From what I knew of my old friends and acquaintances I was sure that we could at once get to work instead of having to lose more or less time while entering into friendly relations with a people who, after all, might prove to be suspicious and refractory. Our experience fully justified the good impression I had formed of the willingness of the Torres Straits islanders to impart information and to render personal assistance.

For the special work we had to do it was necessary to visit a people who were amenable and with whom communication was easy; but, on the other hand, who were not far removed from their primitive past. This peculiar combination was found in these people.

This region has some ethnological importance as it is on the frontier between two large land areas inhabited respectively by the Papuans and Australians, and it was a matter of some interest to determine whether any mixture had taken place there and also to endeavour to find out if any traces could be found in the islands or on the adjacent coast of New Guinea of a migration of the Australian stock from North to South. The islanders are as a matter of fact distinctly Papuan.

The Murray Islands were selected for the most prolonged and detailed study on account of the difficulty in getting there. They lie out of the track of what little commerce there is, neither are they frequented by pearl-shellers nor bêche-de-mer fishermen, consequently the natives have not mixed so much with Europeans and other alien races as has been the case at Erub (Darnely Island) and the western group of islands. On the other hand, the islands have been subject for a quarter of a century to missionary influence and teaching, with the result that most of the natives are professed Christians, and for about ten years English has been taught to the children. The foreign cult and civilization have undoubtedly had some effect, but experience proved that they were not detrimental for many of the purposes of the expedition. Perhaps it would not be easy to find a more favourable spot for the study of a simple and primitive people.

The reports of the expedition will consist of several volumes, each of which will contain memoirs on related subjects. It is proposed to publish the various reports as they are completed.

INTRODUCTION (W. H. R. RIVERS)

The work to be described in this volume of the Reports of the Cambridge Anthropological Expedition is the result of an attempt to study the mental characteristics of the natives of Torres Straits and the Fly River district of British New Guinea by the methods of experimental psychology.

This attempt was due to the initiation of Dr Haddon, and I should like to take the opportunity of saying how much those engaged in this work owe his guidance and assistance. [. . .]

The chief part of our work was done on Murray Island by Messrs McDougall, Myers and myself. We lived on this island, which is about five miles in circumference, with a population of about 450, for four months. During the greater part of this time the other members of the expedition were travelling on the mainland of New Guinea. We had taken out with us the equipment of a small psychological laboratory, and the disused missionary house in which we lived was fortunately large enough to enable us to fit up the more complicated apparatus, especially that for reaction-times, in one room, while other parts of the house and verandah were used for different purposes. After four months' work, Messrs McDougall and Myers went on to Borneo. The remaining members of the expedition stayed for about a week in Kiwai and for about a month in Mabuiag, in which islands the psychological work was done by myself with assistance from Mr Seligman. [. . .]

Murray Island had great advantages for our work. With so small a population we were able to become more or less acquainted with nearly all the inhabitants, certainly all the males, of the island, and were able to form a fairly accurate estimate as to how far the natives examined were representative of the whole community. [. . .]

We had little difficulty in getting the natives to make the observations we required. Owing to their previous acquaintance and friendship with Dr Haddon, we found ourselves on arrival already on the most friendly terms, and were able to commence work at once. There was no evidence that the people were afraid that our instruments would do them any harm, a difficulty which has been encountered among other races in such matters as testing eyesight. We met with a certain amount of reluctance in many cases, and a few natives in Murray Island avoided us altogether, but we had good reason to know that this was due to other causes. The natives were told that some people had said that the black man could see and hear etc., better than the white man, and that we had come to find out how clever they were, and that their performances would all be described in a big book so that everyone would read about them. This appealed to the vanity of the people and put them on their mettle, and in nearly all their observations there was no doubt that they were doing their best; in fact, I am doubtful whether, when collecting comparative data in some more or less primitive European community, it will be possible to excite the same amount of interest and to be certain that the observations are being made with zest and conscientiousness equal to that of the Torres Straits Islanders. Some of our investigations were distinctly laborious and made a considerable demand on the attention, and in some cases there is no doubt that the natives were careless and did not try to do their best, but in most cases they exhibited a degree of application which was surprising in face of the widespread belief in the difficulty of keeping the attention of the savage concentrated on any one thing for any length of time. [. . .]

Our work in Murray Island differs from [other] such investigations in that we examined most of the male members of a small community among whom we lived and with many of whom we became very intimate. We had, in consequence, many opportunities of general, as well as of experimental, observation. Secondly, our investigation was carried over several months, so that a certain number of individuals were examined many times and in different subjects of investigation on different days, so that the fatigue induced by one set of observations did not influence other measurements, as must be the case when a number of observations are taken rapidly one after the other.

EDITORS' NOTES

1. Sir Edward Burnett Tylor (1832–1917). From a working-class Quaker family, he was apprenticed in brass foundry but ill health led him to travel to seek a restorative climate. He met the ethnologist Henry Christy in Havana in 1856, and joined an expedition to Mexico. He published *Researches into the Early History of Mankind* in 1865, and the defining Darwinian anthropological text, *Primitive Culture*, in 1871. He was made keeper of the Oxford museum in 1883 after the traveller Pitt-Rivers left his huge collection of native objects to the university. He was made Reader in Anthropology in 1884, and given the first professorial Chair in 1896. He was knighted in 1912. Tylor was an ideological ally of Huxley and Darwin, although he remained peripheral to their group.

2. Herbert Spencer (1820–1903). An associate and leading ideologue of the scientific naturalists, he was briefly romantically involved with George Eliot in 1851, although most women could not stand his egotism. In 1852 he published 'The Developmental Hypothesis', and then dedicated his life to pursuing its implications in all areas of human knowledge in his multi-volume *System of Synthetic Philosophy* written between 1860 and 1896. He synthesized a vast amount of data, although he was famously cavalier with facts and sources. The hypothesis was broadly evolutionary— that there was a development from simple forms to the increasingly complex—and this was traced through biological forms (single-cell amoebae to humans), psychological ideas (concrete to abstract thought), and races (simple, childlike aboriginals to complex, mature Aryans). It was Spencer who coined the phrase 'survival of the fittest'; historians of science, though, are careful to distinguish Spencer's theory of development from Darwin's theory of evolution. Spencer's influence reached its height in the 1880s and 1890s, then rapidly collapsed as genetics reoriented biological science.

3. Karl Pearson (1857–1936). For a biographical note see Chapter 9. Pearson institutionalized Galton's ideas on race improvement, setting up the Galton Eugenics Laboratory at University College, founding the journal *Biometrika* in 1901, and having a stormy relationship with the Eugenics Education Society, founded in 1907. *National Life from the Standpoint of Science*, a lecture from November 1900, given some time before eugenics gained an institutional locus, continued the appeal, seen in *The Grammar of Science*, for the ideological coupling of science education and responsible citizenship. Race improvement elements are clearly involved in Pearson's assertions, however. His first paragraph was written after the initial heavy losses of the Boer War had been reversed, and the Boer 'Free' States had been captured.

4. Francis Galton (1822–1911). A polymath who might have appeared in any number of sections of this reader: as explorer of 'darkest' Africa (noted for his travels through South-West Africa, 1850–2) and leading light of the Royal Geographical Society; as leading ideologue of the scientific naturalists, theorizing the particular 'genius' of English scientists in *English Men of Science: Their Nature and Nurture* (1874); as innovative statistician and quantitative analyst of data in scientific experiment; as psychologist interested in hallucinations and visions, who also attended the early experiments in telepathy by the Society for Psychical Research in 1882; and as a Darwinian fascinated by the problem of heredity. It is only for the last of these ideas—improvement of the race by measures to ensure the fittest reproduced and the weakest did not—that Galton is now remembered. These were first articulated in *Hereditary Genius* (1869) and informed all of his subsequent work. Although both Darwin and Huxley disfavoured this 'utopian' scheme, Galton's eminence drew into eugenics leading intellectuals of the day: members of the Eugenics Society included George Bernard Shaw, H. G. Wells, the sexologist Havelock Ellis, the Fabian socialists Sydney and Beatrice Webb, and the Tory leader Arthur Balfour.

5. Mary Kingsley (1862–1900). Niece of novelist Charles Kingsley, daughter of the dissolute George Kingsley. Both her parents died in 1892, and she immediately embarked on travelling, ostensibly to complete her father's ethnographic work. She made two lengthy trips into West African territory, writing *Travels in West Africa* (1897) and *West African Studies* (1899). These works, and her lectures and articles that appeared from 1895, were controversial in that they opposed the interference of missionaries in Africa, but also argued that West African interests were better served by private business interests like Sir George Goldie's Royal Niger Company than by the area becoming a British colony. The ethnographic work, tracing the religious and legal institutions of tribes in West Africa, demonstrated, for instance, that war in Sierra Leone had been the result of a failure to understand laws of ownership in the tribal system. Her criticism of the Colonial Secretary, Joseph Chamberlain, did not exclude her being an ardent imperialist and member of the Council of the British Empire League. The failure of one of her other campaigns, for a colonial nursing service to prevent needless deaths in tropical territories, led to her own death treating wounded and fevered Boer prisoners in the South African war in June 1900.

6. Alfred Cort Haddon (1855–1940). Came from an impoverished background, but gained a first-class degree from Cambridge in 1878. He was made curator of the Zoo-

logical Museum, then, in 1880, Professor of Zoology at Dublin. He made a botanical and zoological field trip to Torres Straits in 1888; with no prior interest in ethnography, he began to record details of the tribal system. He lectured in physical anthropology at Cambridge from 1894 to 1898, building the team of six that would travel on the Torres Straits expedition. On his return, he was made Fellow of the Royal Society, and was President of the Anthropological Section of the British Association in 1902 and 1905. He was intensely concerned with saving 'vanishing' data of tribes prior to colonial contact.

William Halse Rivers Rivers (1864–1922). An interdisciplinary scientist, who trained as a doctor, and initially worked at the National Hospital for the Paralysed and Epileptic from 1891. He met neurologists Hughlings Jackson and Henry Head; with the latter, he investigated nerve regeneration. Recruited by Haddon for the Torres Straits expedition for his expertise in quantitative experiments in psychology, and in the midst of his stay on Murray Island, he began to pursue a rigorous study of structures of kinship. Kinship as social structuration became the principal means of analysing 'primitive' society, and he contributed to a move from the evolutionary anthropology of Tylor's generation to the modern functionalism of British social anthropology— that is, exploring the functional purpose of relations and objects in social structures. His later work as a psychologist with shell-shocked patients at Craiglockhart mental hospital, in particular his treatment of Siegfied Sassoon, was the subject of the contemporary trilogy of novels by Pat Barker, *Regeneration*, *The Eye in the Door*, and (concerning Rivers's anthropological investigations of funerary rites), *The Ghost Road*.

Sources of Material

1. DEGENERATION

1. Edwin Ray Lankester, *Degeneration: A Chapter in Darwinism* (London: Macmillan, 1880). Citations pp. 28–30, 32–3, 57, 58–62.
2. H. G. Wells, 'Zoological Retrogression', *Gentleman's Magazine*, 271 (1891), 246–53. Full text cited.
3. Max Nordau, *Degeneration* [*Entartung*, 1892] (New York: Appleton, 1895), translated from the second German edition. Citations pp. 5–7, 15–17, 18, 19, 19–20, 22.
4. [Egmont Hake], *Regeneration: A Reply to Max Nordau* (Westminster: Archibald Constable, 1895). Citations pp. 9, 20–2, 312–15.
5. William James, review of *Degeneration* by Max Nordau, *Psychological Review*, 2 (May 1895), 289–90. Citation pp. 289–90. Signed 'WJ' and attributed to William James in *The Works of William James: Essays, Comments and Reviews* (Cambridge, Mass.: Harvard University Press, 1987).
6. George Bernard Shaw, *The Sanity of Art: An Exposure of the Current Nonsense about Artists Being Degenerate* (London: New Age Press, 1908). Revised edition of article originally composed in 1895, for the anarchist newspaper *Liberty*. Citations pp. 63–7, 89–92, 103–4.

2. OUTCAST LONDON

1. Andrew Mearns and others, *The Bitter Cry of Outcast London: An Inquiry into the Condition of the Abject Poor* (1883), published anonymously as a penny pamphlet. Citations pp. 1–7, 10, 12, 14–15, 18–19, 24.
2. W. T. Stead, 'The Maiden Tribute of Modern Babylon', *Pall Mall Gazette* (6–10 July 1885). Citation 6 July, pp. 1–5.
3. Charles Booth, *Life and Labour of the People of London* [1889] (London: Macmillan, 1892). Citations pp. 32–3, 37–9, 41–6, 48–51, 53, 60–1.
4. William Booth, *In Darkest England and the Way Out* (London: International Headquarters of the Salvation Army, 1890). Citation pp. 9–16.

3. THE METROPOLIS

1. Gustave Le Bon, 'The Mind of Crowds', in *The Crowd: A Study of the Popular Mind* (London: T. Fisher Unwin, 1896). Citation Ch. 1, 'The Mind of Crowds', full text cited.

2. Georg Simmel, 'The Metropolis and Mental Life' [1903], repr. in *The Sociology of Georg Simmel*, trans. and ed. Kurt H. Wolff (New York: Free Press, 1950), 409–24. Citations pp. 409–11, 413–15, 420–1, 423–4.

3. Arthur Symons, 'At the Alhambra: Impressions and Sensations', *Savoy* (Sept. 1896), 75–83. Citation pp. 75–8.

4. Mrs Ormiston Chant, *Why We Attacked the Empire* (London: Horace Marshall & Son, 1895). Sixteen-page pamphlet; citation pp. 2–6.

4. THE NEW WOMAN

1. Mona Caird, 'Marriage', *Westminster Review* 130/2 (1888), 186–201. Citations pp. 186, 190–1, 194–5, 197–201.

2. 'Character Note: The New Woman', *Cornhill Magazine*, 23 (1894), 365–8. Full text cited.

3. Ella Hepworth Dixon, 'Why Women are Ceasing to Marry', *Humanitarian*, 14 (1899), 391–6. Full text cited.

4. Sarah Grand, 'The New Aspect of the Woman Question', *North American Review*, 158 (1894), 270–6. Citations pp. 270–3, 275–6.

5. M. Eastwood, 'The New Woman in Fiction and in Fact', *Humanitarian*, 5 (1894), 375–9. Citation pp. 375–9.

6. Mrs Humphry Ward *et al.*, 'An Appeal Against Female Suffrage', *Nineteenth Century* (June 1889), 781–8. Citation pp. 781–5.

7. Millicent Garrett Fawcett, 'The Appeal Against Female Suffrage: A Reply', *Nineteenth Century* (July 1889), 86–105. Citations pp. 87–9, 95–6.

5. LITERARY DEBATES

1. Andrew Lang, 'Realism and Romance', *Contemporary Review* (1886), 683–93. Citations pp. 683–90, 692–3.

2. Arthur Symons, 'The Decadent Movement in Literature', *Harper's New Monthly Magazine*, 87 (1893), 858–67. Citations pp. 858–62, 864–7.

3. Walter Besant, Eliza Lynn Linton, and Thomas Hardy, 'Candour in English Fiction', *New Review*, 2/8 (1890), 6–21. Citation pp. 6–21.

4. Hugh E. M. Stutfield, 'Tommyrotics', *Blackwood's Edinburgh Magazine*, 157 (1895), 833–45. Citations pp. 833–40, 844–5.

5. Editorial Comment, *Daily Telegraph* (14 Mar. 1891), 5. Full text.

6. Arthur Symons, 'Henrik Ibsen', *Universal Review*, 3 (1889), 567–74. Citations pp. 567–70, 572–4.

6. THE NEW IMPERIALISM

1. Sir John Seeley, *The Expansion of England: Two Courses of Lectures* (London: Macmillan, 1883). Citations pp. 7–11, 13–14, 16.

2. Joseph Chamberlain, 'The True Conception of Empire', *Foreign and Colonial Speeches* (London: Routledge, 1897), 241–8. Full text cited.

3. Cecil Rhodes, Drill Hall speech in 'Vindex', *Cecil Rhodes: Political Life and Speeches: 1881–1900* (London: Chapman Hall, 1900). Citation pp. 639–47.

4. 'General Gordon', *The Illustrated London News* (14 Feb. 1885). Citations pp. 169, 172.

5. Major F. R. Wingate, *Ten Years' Captivity in the Mahdi's Camp 1882–92, from the original manuscripts of Father Joseph Ohrwalder, late priest of the Austrian Mission Station at Delen, in Kordofan*, 10th, revised and abridged, edn. (London: Sampson Low, Marston & Co., 1893). Citations pp. 154–7 and 183–4.

6. G. W. Steevens, 'The Battle of Omdurman', *With Kitchener to Khartum* (London: Blackwood, 1898). Citations pp. 260–4, 266–9, 272–5.

7. 'Relief of Mafeking' and 'London's Roar of Jubilation', *Daily Mail* (19 May 1900). Citations p. 5, columns 1–2 and 4–5.

8. 'Affairs on the Upper Congo', *The Times* (14 May 1897). Full citation, p. 10, column 6.

9. R. B. Cunninghame Graham, ' "Bloody Niggers" ', *The Social Democrat: A Monthly Socialist Review*, 1 (Apr. 1897), 104–9. Citations pp. 104, 106, 107–9.

10. Olive Schreiner, *An English-South African's View of the Situation: Words in Season* (London: Hodder & Stoughton, 1899). Citations pp. 52–7, 84–5, 89–90.

11. J. A. Hobson, *Imperialism: A Study* (London: James Nisbet & Co., 1902). Citations pp. 51–4, 55–7, 60–2, 66–8.

12. E. D. Morel, 'The Story of the Congo Free State', in *The Black Man's Burden: The White Man in Africa from the 15th Century to World War One* [1920] (repr. New York: Monthly Review Press, 1969). Citation pp. 115–19.

7. SOCIALISM

1. William Morris, 'How We Live and How We Might Live', *Commonweal* 4 June–2 July 1887, 177–8, 186–7, 194–5, 203–4, 210–11. Citations pp. 177–8, 186, 204, 210–11.

2. George Bernard Shaw, 'The Economic Basis of Socialism' (1889). Reprinted in *Essays in Fabian Socialism* in *The Works of George Bernard Shaw*, vol. 30 (London: Constable, 1932), 3–30. Citations pp. 20–4, 26–30.

3. Oscar Wilde, 'The Soul of Man Under Socialism', *Fortnightly Review* (1891), 292–319. Citations pp. 292–6, 301–5, 313–14, 317, 319.

4. Isabella O. Ford, *Women and Socialism* (London: Independent Labour Party, 1907). Sixteen-page pamphlet; citations pp. 2–3, 7–14.

8. ANARCHISM

1. Peter Kropotkin, *Paroles d'un révolté* [1885], trans. George Woodcock as *Words of a Rebel* (Montreal and New York: Black Rose Books, 1992). Citation pp. 90–4.

2. Johann [John] Most, 'Die Anarchie', *Internationale Bibliothek* [1888], trans. Frederic Trautmann in *The Voice of Terror: A Biography of Johann Most* (Westport, Conn.: Greenwich Press, 1980). Citations pp. 101–4.

3. William Morris, letter to *Commonweal* (18 May 1889), 157. Full text cited.

4. 'Anarchist', letter to *Commonweal* (22 June 1889), 197. Full text cited.

5. 'The Explosion in Greenwich Park' and 'Bourdin's Antecedents', *The Times* (17 Feb. 1894), 5. Full texts cited.

6. Emma Goldman, 'Anarchism: What it Really Stands For', in *Anarchism and Other Essays* [1911] (New York: Dover Publications, 1969), pp. 47–67. Citations pp. 47–50, 52–6, 59–60, 62, 67.

9. SCIENTIFIC NATURALISM

1. T. H. Huxley, 'On the Physical Basis of Life', *The Fortnightly Review* (Feb. 1869), 129–45. Citation pp. 142–5.

2. W. K. Clifford, 'On the Aims and Instruments of Scientific Thought', in *Lectures and Essays*, 2 vols., ed. Leslie Stephen and Frederick Pollock (London: Macmillan, 1879), i. 124–57. Citations pp. 128–9, 131–2, 155–7.

3. John Tyndall, 'Inaugural Address of Prof. John Tyndall, D.C.L., LL.D., F.R.S., President', [The Belfast Address] *Nature* (20 Aug. 1874), 309–19. Citations pp. 309, 316, 317, 318–19.

4. Karl Pearson, *A Grammar of Science* (London: Walter Scott, 1892). Citations pp. 2–3, 3–4, 6–7, 7–10.

5. T. H. Huxley, *Evolution and Ethics* (London: Macmillan, 1894). Citation pp. 137–44.

10. PSYCHOLOGY

1. H. B. Donkin, 'Hysteria', in *A Dictionary of Psychological Medicine*, ed. D. Hack Tuke, vol. ii (London: J. & A. Churchill, 1892), 618–27. Citations pp. 618–19, 619, 619–20, 622, 622–3, 625, 626–7, 627.

2. Josef Breuer and Sigmund Freud, 'On the Psychical Mechanism of Hysterical Phenomena: Preliminary Communication' [1893], trans. James and Alix Strachey. Reprinted from *Studies in Hysteria: Pelican Freud Library*, vol. iii, ed. Angela Richards (Harmondsworth: Penguin, 1974), 53–69. Citations pp. 53–5, 55–7, 58–9, 59–61, 62, 68–9.

3. William James, 'The Stream of Thought', in *The Principles of Psychology*, vol. i [1890] (repr. New York: Dover Publications, 1950), Chapter 9. Citations pp. 237, 238, 238–40, 243–4.

4. F. W. H. Myers, 'The Subliminal Consciousness: Chapter 1—General Characteristics of Subliminal Messages', *Proceedings of the Society for Psychical Research*, vol. vii, pts. 18–20 (1891–2), 298–327. Citations pp. 301–2, 303, 303–4, 305–6.

5. T. Clifford Allbutt, 'Nervous Diseases and Modern Life', *Contemporary Review* (1895), 210–31. Citations pp. 210, 211–12, 212, 214, 214–15, 217, 219, 221–2, 222, 228.

11. PSYCHICAL RESEARCH

1. 'Objects of the Society', *Proceedings of the Society for Psychical Research*, 1/1 (1882–3), 3–6. Citations pp. 3–4, 5.
2. Henry Sidgwick, 'Address by the President at the First General Meeting', *Proceedings of the Society for Psychical Research*, 1/1 (1882–3), 7–12. Citations pp. 7–8, 9–10, 12.
3. William Barrett, Edmund Gurney, and F. W. H. Myers, 'Thought Reading', *Nineteenth Century* (June 1882), 890–901. Citations pp. 890, 891, 893, 895, 899–900.
4. 'Psychical Research', *Pall Mall Gazette* (21 Oct. 1882). Full text cited.
5. W. T. Stead, 'How We Intend to Study Borderland', *Borderland: A Quarterly Review and Index*, 1/1 (July 1893), 3–6. Citations pp. 3, 4, 5, 6.
6. W. T. Stead, 'Telepathy: A Passing Note Reporting Progress in Telepathic Automatism,' *Borderland: A Quarterly Review and Index* 1/6 (Oct. 1894), 506–8. Citation pp. 507–8.
7. Andrew Lang, 'Ghosts up to Date', *Blackwood's Magazine* (Jan. 1894), 47–58. Citations pp. 47, 47–8, 48, 49.

12. SEXOLOGY

1. Gustave Bouchereau, 'Nymphomania', in *A Dictionary of Psychological Medicine*, ed. D. Hack Tuke, vol. ii (London: J. & A. Churchill, 1892), 863–6. Full text cited.
2. Richard von Krafft-Ebing, *Psychopathia Sexualis, with Especial Reference to Antipathic Sexual Instinct: A Medico-Forensic Study* [1886]. Translation of 10th German edition by F. J. Rebman (London: Rebman Ltd., 1901). Citations pp. v, vi–vii, 472–3, 474, 474–5, 506–7, 514–16, 536–7, 540, 540–1, 541, 541–2, 542.
3. Edward Carpenter, 'The Intermediate Sex', in *Love's Coming-of-Age* (London: Methuen, 1914). Citations pp. 114–15, 116–18, 118–19, 126–8, 129–30, 133.
4. John Addington Symonds, *A Problem in Modern Ethics, Being an Inquiry into the Phenomenon of Sexual Inversion, Addressed Especially to Medical Psychologists and Jurists* (London: privately printed, 1896). Citation pp. 1–4.
5. Havelock Ellis, 'Case XVIII' [John Addington Symonds]. First published in Ellis and Symonds, *Sexual Inversion* (1897); reprinted as Appendix 1 of *The Memoirs of John Addington Symonds*, ed. and introd. Phyllis Grosskurth (New York: Random House, 1984), 284–8. Full text cited.

13. ANTHROPOLOGY AND RACIAL SCIENCE

1. Edward Tylor, 'The Science of Culture', in *Primitive Culture: Researches into the Development of Mythology, Philosophy, Religion, Art, and Custom*, 2 vols. [1871], 6th edn. (London: John Murray, 1920). Citations pp. 1–3, 5–7, 14–15, 16–17, 20–1.
2. Herbert Spencer, *The Principles of Sociology*, vol. i (London: Williams & Norgate, 1876). Citations pp. 44, 45–6, 47, 48–9, 49, 51–2, 53, 54–5, 55–6, 65, 79, 83–4, 85–6, 102, 104.

3. Karl Pearson, *National Life from the Standpoint of Science. An address Delivered at Newcastle, November 1900* (London: Adam & Charles Black, 1901). Citations pp. 9–11, 14–20, 26–7.

4. Francis Galton, 'Eugenics: Its Definition, Scope and Aims', lecture read before the Sociological Society, 16 May 1904, in *Essays in Eugenics* (London: Eugenics Education Society, 1909), 35–43. Full text cited.

5. Mary Kingsley, 'The Clash of Cultures', *West African Studies* [1899], 2nd edn. (London: Macmillan, 1901). Citations pp. 325–9, 333–4.

6. *Reports of the Cambridge Anthropological Expedition to Torres Straits*, vol. ii: *Physiology and Psychology* (Cambridge: Cambridge University Press, 1901). Citations pp. v–vi, 1–6.

Secondary Reading

ALEXANDER, SALLY. *Becoming a Woman and Other Essays in Nineteenth and Twentieth Century Feminist History* (London: Virago, 1994).

ARATA, STEPHEN. 'The Occidental Tourist: *Dracula* and the Anxiety of Reverse Colonisation', *Victorian Studies*, 33/4 (1990), 621–45.

ARDIS, ANN. *New Women, New Novels: Feminism and Early Modernism* (Brunswick, NJ: Rutgers University Press, 1990).

ASCHERSON, NEAL. *The King Incorporated: Leopold the Second and the Congo* [1963] (London: Granta, 1999).

BARROW, LOGIE. *Independent Spirits: Spiritualism and English Plebeians 1850–1919* (London: Routledge, 1986).

BARTON, RUTH. ' "An Influential Set of Chaps": The X-Club and Royal Society Politics 1864–85', *British Journal of the History of Science*, 23 (1990), 53–81.

—— 'John Tyndall, Pantheist: A Re-reading of the Belfast Address', *Osiris*, 3 (1987), 111–34.

BAUMAN, ZYGMUNT. *Modernity and Ambivalence* (Cambridge: Polity Press, 1991).

BECKSON, KARL. *Arthur Symons: A Life* (Oxford: Clarendon Press, 1987).

—— *London in the 1890s* (New York: Norton, 1992).

BENJAMIN, WALTER. *Charles Baudelaire: A Lyric Poet in the Era of High Capitalism*, trans. Harry Zohn (London: Verso, 1992).

BLAND, LUCY. *Banishing the Beast: English Feminism and Sexual Morality 1885–1914* (Harmondsworth: Penguin, 1995).

—— and DOAN, LAURA (eds.). *Sexology Uncensored: The Documents of Sexual Science* (Cambridge: Polity Press, 1998).

BOLT, CHRISTINE. *Victorian Attitudes to Race* (London: RKP, 1971).

BRANDON, RUTH. *The Spiritualists: The Passion for the Occult in the Nineteenth and Twentieth Centuries* (London: Weidenfeld, 1983).

BRANTLINGER, PATRICK. *In Crusoe's Footsteps: Cultural Studies in Britain and America* (London: Routledge, 1990).

—— *Rule of Darkness: British Literature and Imperialism, 1830–1914* (Ithaca: Cornell University Press, 1988).

BRISTOW, JOSEPH. *Empire Boys: Adventures in a Man's World* (London: Harper Collins, 1991).

—— *Sexuality* (London: Routledge, 1997).

—— ' "Sterile Ecstasies": The Perversity of the Decadent Movement', in *Essays and Studies* 1995 (Cambridge: D. S. Brewer, 1995), 65–88.

BROME, VINCENT. *Havelock Ellis, Philosopher of Sex: A Biography* (London: Routledge, 1979).

BURDETT, CAROLYN. 'The Hidden Romance of Sexual Science: Eugenics, the Nation and the Making of Modern Feminism', in Lucy Bland and Laura Doan (eds.) *Sexology in Culture: Labelling Bodies and Desires* (Cambridge: Polity Press, 1998), 44–59.

CARDWELL, D. S. L. *The Organisation of Science in England*, rev. edn. (London: Heineman, 1972).

CHAMBERLAIN, J. EDWARD, and GILMAN, SANDER (eds.). *Degeneration: The Dark Side of Progress* (New York: Columbia University Press, 1985).

CLIFFORD, JAMES. *The Predicament of Culture* (Boston, Mass.: Harvard University Press, 1988).

COHEN, ED. *Talk on the Wilde Side* (London: Routledge, 1993).

CRABTREE, ADAM. *From Mesmer to Freud* (New Haven: Yale University Press, 1993).

CRICK, M. *The History of the Social Democratic Federation* (Keele: Keele University Press, 1994).

DESMOND, ADRIAN. *Huxley*, vol. i: *Evolution's High Priest*; vol. ii. *The Devil's Disciple* (London: Michael Joseph, 1994 and 1997).

DIJKSTRA, BRAM. *Idols of Perversity: Fantasies of Feminine Evil in Fin-de-Siècle Culture* (Oxford: Oxford University Press, 1986).

DOLLIMORE, JONATHAN. *Sexual Dissidence: From Augustine to Wilde, Freud to Foucault* (Oxford: Oxford University Press, 1991).

DOWLING, LINDA. *Language and Decadence in the Victorian Fin de Siècle* (Princeton, NJ: Princeton University Press, 1986).

DYOS, H. J. and WOLFF, MICHAEL (eds.). *The Victorian City: Images and Realities* (London: RKP, 1973).

ELLENBERGER, HENRI. *The Discovery of the Unconscious: The History and Evolution of Dynamic Psychiatry* [1970] (London: Fontana, 1994).

FELDMAN, DAVID, and JONES, GARETH STEDMAN (eds.). *Metropolis London: Histories and Representations Since 1800* (London: Routledge, 1989).

FELSKI, RITA. *The Gender of Modernity* (Cambridge, Mass.: Harvard University Press, 1995).

FOUCAULT, MICHEL. *An Archaeology of Knowledge*, trans. Alan Sheridan (London: Tavistock Press, 1972).

—— *An Introduction to the History of Sexuality*, trans. Robert Hurley (Harmondsworth: Penguin, 1981).

GAGNIER, REGENIA. *Idylls of the Marketplace: Oscar Wilde and the Victorian Public* (Aldershot: Scolar Press, 1987).

GAULD, ALAN. *The Founders of Psychical Research* (London: Routledge, 1968).

GILMAN, SANDER. *Difference and Pathology: Stereotypes of Sexuality, Race and Madness* (Ithaca, NY: Cornell University Press, 1985).

GLOVER, DAVID. *Vampires, Mummies and Liberals: Bram Stoker and the Politics of Popular Fiction* (Durham, NC: Duke University Press, 1996).

GREENSLADE, WILLIAM. *Degeneration, Culture and the Novel 1880–1940* (Cambridge: Cambridge University Press, 1994).

GREIG, NOËL. 'Introduction', *Edward Carpenter: Selected Writings*, vol. i: *Sex* (London: Gay Men's Press, 1984), 9–77.

GROSSKURTH, PHYLLIS (ed.). *The Memoirs of John Addington Symonds* (London: Hutchinson, 1984).

HACKING, IAN. *Rewriting the Soul: Multiple Personality and the Sciences of Memory* (Princeton, NJ: Princeton University Press, 1995).

HARLOW, BARBARA and CARTER, MIA. *Imperialism and Orientalism: A Documentary Sourcebook* (Oxford: Blackwell, 1999).

HILL, TRACEY (ed.). *Decadence and Danger: Writing, History and the Fin de Siècle* (Bath: Sulis Press, 1997).

HOBSBAWM, ERIC. *The Age of Empire 1875–1914* (London: Weidenfeld & Nicolson, 1987).

—— *Industry and Empire* (Harmondsworth: Penguin, 1969).

HURLEY, KELLY. *The Gothic Body: Sexuality, Materialism and Degeneration at the Fin de Siècle* (Cambridge: Cambridge University Press, 1996).

HUYSSEN, ANDREAS. 'Mass Culture as Woman: Modernism's Other', in *After the Great Divide: Modernism, Mass Culture, Postmodernism* (Basingstoke: Macmillan, 1988), 44–62.

HYAM, RONALD. *Britain's Imperial Century 1815–1914* (New York: Barnes & Noble, 1993).

JACKSON, HOLBROOK. *The Eighteen Nineties: A Review of Art and Ideas at the Close of the Nineteenth Century* (London: Grant Richards, 1913).

JACKSON, TABITHA. *The Boer War* (London: Channel 4/Macmillan, 1999).

JONES, GARETH STEDMAN. *Outcast London* (Harmondsworth: Penguin, 1971).

JONES, GRETA. *Social Darwinism in English Thought* (Brighton: Harvester, 1980).

KEATING, PETER. *The Haunted Study: A Social History of the English Novel 1875–1914* (London: Fontana, 1991).

—— (ed.). *Into Unknown England, 1866–1913: Selections from the Social Explorers* (Manchester: Manchester University Press, 1976).

KUPER, ADAM. *The Invention of Primitive Society: Transformations of an Illusion* (London: Routledge, 1988).

LANGHAM, IAN. *The Building of British Social Anthropology: W. H. R. Rivers and his Cambridge Disciples in the Development of Kinship Studies, 1898–1931* (London: Reidel, 1981).

LAYBOURN, KEITH. *The Rise of Socialism in Britain, c.1881–1951* (Stroud: Sutton Publishing, 1997).

LEDGER, SALLY. 'In Darkest England: The Terror of Degeneration in Fin-de-Siècle Britain', *Literature and History*, 4/2 (1995), 71–86.

—— *The New Woman: Fiction and Feminism at the Fin de Siècle* (Manchester: Manchester University Press, 1997).

—— *Henrik Ibsen* (Plymouth, UK: Northcote House, 1999).

—— and McCRACKEN, SCOTT (eds.). *Cultural Politics at the Fin de Siècle* (Cambridge: Cambridge University Press, 1995).

LIGHTMAN, BERNARD. *The Origins of Agnosticism: Victorian Unbelief and the Limits of Knowledge* (Baltimore: Johns Hopkins University Press, 1987).

LIGHTMAN, BERNARD (ed.). *Victorian Science in Context* (Chicago: Chicago University Press, 1997).

LORIMER, DOUGLAS. 'Theoretical Racism in Late-Victorian Anthropology', *Victorian Studies*, 31/3 (1988), 405–30.

McCLINTOCK, ANNE. *Imperial Leather: Race, Gender and Sexuality in the Colonial Context* (London: Routledge, 1995).

MACDONALD, ROBERT H. *The Language of Empire: Myths and Metaphors of Popular Imperialism 1880–1918* (Manchester: Manchester University Press, 1994).

MACKENZIE, JOHN (ed.). *Imperialism and Popular Culture* (Manchester: Manchester University Press, 1986).

MACKENZIE, NORMAN, and MACKENZIE, JEANNE. *The First Fabians* (London and New York: Quartet Books, 1979).

MARSH, MARGARET S. *Anarchist Women 1870–1920* (Philadelphia: Temple University Press, 1981).

MILLER, JANE ELDRIDGE. *Rebellious Women: Feminism, Modernism and the Edwardian Novel* (London: Virago, 1994).

MORRIS, JAMES. *Heaven's Command: An Imperial Progress* (Harmondsworth: Penguin, 1973).

MORT, FRANK. *Dangerous Sexualities: Medico-Moral Politics in England since 1830* (London: Routledge, 1987).

MOSSE, GEORGE L. Introduction to Max Nordau, *Degeneration* (Durham, NC: University of Nebraska Press, 1993), pp. xiii–xxxvi.

NELSON, CAROLYN C. *British Women Fiction Writers of the 1890s* (New York: Twayne Publishers, 1996).

NETTLAU, MAX. *A Short History of Anarchism* [1934] (London: Freedom Press, 1996).

NORD, DEBORAH EPSTEIN. *Walking the Victorian Streets: Women, Interpretation, and the City* (Ithaca, NY: Cornell University Press, 1995).

NYE, MARY JO. *Before Big Science: The Pursuit of Modern Chemisty and Physics, 1800–1940* (Cambridge, Mass.: Harvard University Press, 1996).

OLIVER, HERMIA. *The International Anarchist Movement in Late-Victorian London* (London: Croom Helm, 1983).

OPPENHEIM, JANET. *The Other World: Spiritualism and Psychical Research in England 1850–1914* (Cambridge: Cambridge University Press, 1985).

—— *'Shattered Nerves': Doctors, Patients and Depression in Victorian England* (Oxford: Oxford University Press, 1991).

OWEN, ALEX. *The Darkened Room: Women, Power and Spiritualism in Late Victorian England* (London: Virago, 1989).

PAKENHAM, THOMAS. *The Boer War* (London: Wiedenfeld & Nicolson, 1979).

—— *The Scramble for Africa 1876–1912* (London: Abacus, 1992).

PARADIS, JAMES. 'Evolution and Ethics in its Victorian Contexts', in James Pardis (ed.), *T. H. Huxley's Evolution and Ethics with New Victorian Essays on its Victorian and Sociobiological Context* (Princeton: Princeton University Press, 1989), 3–55.

PICK, DANIEL. *Faces of Degeneration: Anatomy of a European Disorder c.1848–1918* (Cambridge: Cambridge University Press, 1989).

PORTER, BERNARD. *Critics of Empire: British Radical Attitudes to Colonialism in Africa 1895–1914* (London: Macmillan, 1968).

PORTER, ROY. *London: A Social History* (Harmondsworth: Penguin, 1994).

POSTLETHWAITE, DIANA. *Making it Whole: A Victorian Circle and the Shape of their World* (Columbus: Ohio State University Press, 1984).

PYKETT, LYN. *Engendering Fictions: The English Novel in the Early Twentieth Century* (London and New York: Edward Arnold, 1995).

—— *The Improper Feminine: The Women's Sensation Novel and the New Woman Writing* (London: Routledge, 1992).

—— (ed.). *Reading Fin-de-Siècle Fictions* (London: Longman, 1996).

ROBINSON, RONALD, and GALLAGHER, JOHN, with DENNY, ALICE. *Africa and the Victorians: The Official Mind of Imperialism*, 2nd edn. (London: Macmillan, 1981).

SAID, EDWARD. *Orientalism: Western Conceptions of the Orient* (1978; repr. Harmondsworth: Penguin, 1985).

SAVILLE, JOHN. *The Labour Movement in Britain* (London: Faber & Faber, 1988).

SCHNEER, JONATHAN. *London 1900: The Imperial Metropolis* (New Haven: Yale University Press, 1999).

SCULL, ANDREW (ed.). *Madhouses, Mad-Doctors and Madmen: The Social History of Psychology in the Victorian Era* (London: Athlone Press, 1981).

SHAMDASANI, SONU. 'Encountering Hélène', Introduction to Theodore Flournoy's *From India To Planet Mars* 1899 (Princeton, NJ: Princeton University Press, 1994), pp. xi–li.

SHOWALTER, ELAINE. *A Literature of their Own: British Women Novelists from Brontë to Lessing* (1977; repr. London: Virago, 1982).

—— *Sexual Anarchy: Gender and Culture at the Fin de Siècle* (London: Bloomsbury, 1991).

SHUTTLEWORTH, SALLY, and TAYLOR, JENNY (eds.). *Embodied Selves: An Anthology of Psychological Texts 1830–90* (Oxford: Oxford University Press, 1997).

SINFIELD, ALAN. *The Wilde Century: Effeminacy, Oscar Wilde and the Queer Moment* (London: Cassell, 1994).

STOCKING, GEORGE W. *Victorian Anthropology* (London: Free Press, 1987).

—— (ed.). *Observers Observed: Essays on Ethnographic Fieldwork* (Madison, Wis.: University of Wisconsin Press, 1983).

STOKES, JOHN. *In the Nineties* (Hemel Hempstead: Harvester Wheatsheaf, 1989).

—— *Oscar Wilde* (London: Macmillan, 1996).

—— (ed.). *Fin de Siècle/Fin du Globe: Fears and Fantasies of the Fin de Siècle* (Basingstoke: Macmillan, 1992).

STURGIS, MATTHEW. *Aubrey Beardsley: A Biography* (London: HarperCollins, 1998).

THOMPSON, E. P. *William Morris: Romantic to Revolutionary* (London: Merlin Press, 1977).

THORNTON, R. K. R. '"Decadence" in Later Nineteenth-Century England', in Ian Fletcher (ed.), *Decadence and the 1890s*. Stratford-upon-Avon Studies 17 (London: Edward Arnold, 1979), 15–30.

TRAUTMANN, FREDERIC. *The Voice of Terror: A Biography of Johann Most* (Westport, Conn., and London: Greenwood Press, 1980).

TROTTER, DAVID. *The English Novel in History, 1895–1920* (London: Routledge, 1993).

TURNER, FRANK. *Between Science and Religion: The Reaction to Scientific Naturalism in Late Victorian Britain* (Cambridge: Cambridge University Press, 1993).

—— *Contesting Cultural Authority: Essays in Victorian Intellectual Life* (Cambridge: Cambridge University Press, 1993).

TURNER, LYNNETTE. 'Feminism, Femininity and Ethnographic Authority', *Women: A Cultural Review*, 2/3 (1991), 238–54.

WALKOWITZ, JUDITH. *City of Dreadful Delight: Narratives of Sexual Danger in Late-Victorian London* (London: Virago, 1992).

—— *Prostitution and Victorian Society: Women, Class, and the State* (Cambridge: Cambridge University Press, 1980).

WEEKS, JEFFREY. *Coming Out: Homosexual Politics in Britain, from the Nineteenth Century to the Present* (London: Quartet, 1977).

WHITE, ALLON. *The Uses of Obscurity: The Fiction of Early Modernism* (London: Routledge, 1981).

WILLIAMS, RAYMOND. 'Social Darwinism', in *Problems in Materialism and Culture* (London: Verso, 1980), 86–102.

WOODWARD, WILLIAM, and ASH, MITCHELL (eds.). *The Problematic Science: Psychology in Nineteenth Century Thought* (New York: Praeger, 1982).

WORMELL, DEBORAH. *Sir John Seeley and the Uses of History* (Cambridge: Cambridge University Press, 1980).

YOUNG, ROBERT J. C. *Colonial Desire: Hybridity in Theory, Culture, and Race* (London: Routledge, 1994).

Index